MACKENZIE'S ROUTE TO THE ARCTIC

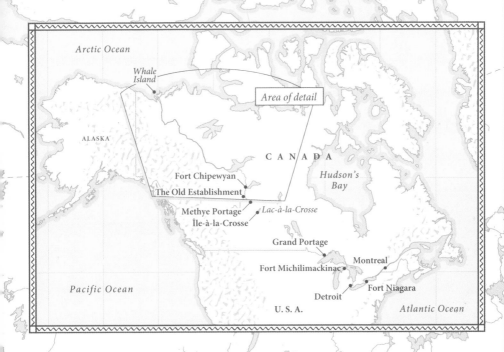

Arctic Ocean

Whale Island

Area of detail

ALASKA

CANADA

Fort Chipewyan

Hudson's Bay

The Old Establishment

Methye Portage

Lac-à-la-Crosse

Île-à-la-Crosse

Grand Portage

Montreal

Fort Michilimackinac

Fort Niagara

Pacific Ocean

Detroit

U. S. A.

Atlantic Ocean

(Yellowknife)

(Great) Slave Lake

(Fort Providence)

(Hay River)

(Fort Smith)

(Lake Athabasca) Lake of the Hills

(ALBERTA)

(SASKATCHAWAN)

Fort Chipewyan

Old Establishment

© 2018 Jeffrey L. Ward

DISAPPOINTMENT
RIVER

ALSO BY BRIAN CASTNER

All the Ways We Kill and Die
The Long Walk

DISAPPOINTMENT
RIVER

FINDING AND LOSING
THE NORTHWEST PASSAGE

BRIAN CASTNER

McCLELLAND & STEWART

Published simultaneously in the United States of America by Doubleday, an imprint of Penguin Random House LLC, New York.

Portions of this work first appeared, in different form, in the following publications:

The Atlantic: "A Disappearing Home in a Warming World" (10/12/16)

Motherboard: "The Best Place in the World to Set a Forest Fire" (9/14/16); "I Canoed to the Arctic Ocean, and What Did I Find? A Balmy Beach" (9/16/16); "The People Making Solar Power Where the Sun Doesn't Set" (9/15/16); "Silt Built This Town—And Melting Ice Will Eventually Destroy It" (9/13/16); "Why I Canoed 1,200 Miles to the Arctic Circle to Report on Climate Change" (9/12/16); and "The $20 Billion Arctic Pipeline That Will Haunt Forever" (10/9/16).

Supplemental travel support provided by the Pulitzer Center on Crisis Reporting.

Library and Archives Canada Cataloguing in Publication
Castner, Brian, author
Disappointment River / Brian Castner.

Issued in print and electronic formats.
ISBN 978-0-7710-2395-8 (hardcover).--ISBN 978-0-7710-2396-5 (EPUB)
1. Castner, Brian--Travel--Northwest Territories--Mackenzie River.
2. Mackenzie, Alexander, Sir, 1764-1820--Travel--Northwest Territories--
Mackenzie River. 3. Canoes and canoeing--Northwest Territories--
MacKenzie River. 4. Mackenzie River (N.W.T.)--Description and travel.
5. Northwest Passage. I. Title.

FC4194.4.C37 2018   917.19'3044   C2017-904775-2
                                                        C2017-904776-0

Endpaper map by Jeffrey L. Ward
Jacket image: © James P. Blair / National Geographic / Getty Images
Printed and bound in the United States of America

McClelland & Stewart,
a division of Penguin Random House Canada Limited,
a Penguin Random House Company
www.penguinrandomhouse.ca

1 2 3 4 5   22 21 20 19 18

Penguin
Random House
McCLELLAND & STEWART

For David, Jeremy, Landon, and Senny

I went to Alaska once, you know. I toured the Alaska-Canada road they built there during the war. Fantastic. Not the road, the landscape. The mighty road was just this insignificant little scratch across that landscape. You've never seen a world like that. It belongs to the God who was God before the Bible . . . God before he woke up and saw himself . . . God who was his own nightmare. There is no forgiveness there. You make one tiny mistake and that landscape grinds you into a bloody smudge, and I do mean right now, sir.

—Denis Johnson, *Tree of Smoke*

Contents

~~~~~~

Author's Note

〰〰〰〰

A significant portion of this book concerns the actions of people indigenous to lands now known as North America. The proper names for these people—not to mention their lands and the rivers that run through them—are still a matter of controversy. Preferred titles and spellings have changed over time, generally toward greater cultural sensitivity, but in the written historical record precision is complicated by the paucity of primary indigenous voices; white men almost exclusively do the speaking and use a variety of names and terms now considered offensive.

Today, in the United States, the original inhabitants of the continent are collectively known as Native Americans or American Indians. In Canada, they are the First Nations. The only name consistently used for hundreds of years, and even (perhaps surprisingly) throughout current academic literature today, is still the simple "Indian." In my travels, I found that term used quite often, especially by Indians themselves. So in this book, I will also use "Indian" when quoting or speaking of the history generally. When writing about the modern day, however, I'll use the term "indigenous" when a generic word is called for, because it has grown in popular acceptance over the last few decades, "aboriginal" and "native" now trending out of favor.

As often as possible, however, I will use the specific name of the indigenous group, using the historical name when appropriate for the setting. Today we know them as the Inuit and Dene, but when speaking of the eighteenth century, as Alexander Mackenzie knew them, I will write "Esquimaux," "Dogrib," "Slavey," "Hare," depending on the nation.

In this balance of accuracy and courtesy, any errors are mine alone.

DISAPPOINTMENT
RIVER

〰〰〰〰

The river was liquid glass, a cloud mirror that rolled beneath my canoe and made me dizzy, as if I might stumble and fall down into the heavens, and in the horizon the silvery sky and water fused as one.

We had been paddling for two days, and the river was so wide that the far bank appeared to be little more than a slight film of green. Reeds filled our shore, black ducks and seagulls and a steady succession of bald eagles feeding on both. Behind us, tumbling lake storms, and ahead, just a rumor of current.

This river. The many nations of Dene, the indigenous peoples in the upper and middle basin, know it as the Deh Cho. The Gwichya Gwich'in, of the lower interior bush, as the Nagwichoonjik. The Inuvialuit, the western Inuit at the river's end in the Arctic, as the Kuukpak. All the names are a variation on the same theme—the Big River—and for good reason. It is the second longest in North America. The island that plugs the river's upper mouth is larger than five Manhattans. Everything about the Deh Cho is enormous.

And yet I intended to canoe every drop of it, all eleven hundred miles. I am a fairly serious river guide, but never before had I undertaken a self-supported trip of this magnitude, and the scale of the journey weighed heavily. We paddled an eighteen-and-a-half-foot Sea Clipper canoe, wide and steady as the days, designed to track through whitecaps and swallow hundreds of pounds of gear. I had spent half a year researching, purchasing, testing, sorting, packing, and repacking that gear: an Everest-rated tent, solar panels and satellite link, a handcrafted curved splitting ax from Maine, ninety freeze-dried dinners from Quebec, plus apples, mandarins, bagels, peanut butter, chocolate, oatmeal, tea, chunk honey, and fifteen pounds of pemmican. All that and more, stuffed in waterproof barrels or lashed to the boat so a rogue wave couldn't end our trip.

That morning, as we broke our first camp on the sandy shore of Great Slave Lake, I felt smothered. By the scale of the job ahead of us, the labor required, the intense summer heat, the size of the river. It had taken two days of travel just to reach the starting line, weeks and weeks yet to go to find the end.

All day, the shore ground by reluctantly. Grueling progress in the hazy shimmer. But then, unexpectedly and with great relief, a breeze stirred behind us—how did a breeze come out of the east?—and the watery mirror shattered as wavelets formed about us.

I unfolded the small sail we had brought for just such an unlikely development, clipped it to a metal bar at the nose of the boat, and when a gust caught us I felt it tug hard against my line and we surged forward, surfing on and over the rising waves, making real headway for the first time.

We paddled with ease, and the wind filled our sail, and the current increased as the river coalesced, and so, by the end of that day, I felt it, for the first time. The optimism, the promise, felt by the men and women who attempted the first recorded descent of this river. In whose path, in fact, I was following.

For centuries, Europeans had been searching for a water route through North America. This mystical passage was known by many names: the Strait of Anián, the River Ouregan, the Mer de l'Ouest. Anyone who found it, mapped it, returned alive to tell the world, would solve the greatest geographic mystery of the day and secure the riches and fame commensurate with such an achievement.

Thousands of sailors and soldiers had tried and failed over the years. But none had explored the Deh Cho, not until a party of fur traders and their indigenous partners launched an expedition in 1789. This river—its channel so wide and flat, the size of a hundred Champs-Élysées—was the last best hope of finding a shipping lane through the continent.

Midnight approached, and the sun was just starting to curve toward the orange horizon. My face flushed in its glow. The wind drove us on, the river pulled us ever west, and I understood then, in that moment, why those explorers really did believe that in the Deh Cho they had finally found a route to China. The fabled Northwest Passage.

THE NORTH WEST COMPANY, 1788

〜〜〜〜〜

The previous winter had fallen early and hard, deep cold that clapped rivers icy tight, and so the men greeted the summer *rendezvous* of 1788 with more than the usual share of anticipation and excitement. Like sailors putting into port or whalers tying up ships in a gam, voyageurs thirsted for the *rendezvous* with a pent-up intensity bordering on lust: part reunion, part respite, part drunken revelry, the highlight of the year.

They descended upon the annual conclave from every direction. Great Lakes traders from Fort Michilimackinac and the Mississippi basin. *Mangeurs de lard*, the lowliest pork eaters, from the east, carrying in their massive birch-bark canoes a season's worth of gunpowder and casked rum. And of greatest esteem, the vaunted *hommes du nord*, the men who had survived the far interior and lived to tell about it. Half-starved, frost-bitten, weary; to reach the *rendezvous*, some had paddled for two or three months, over a thousand miles, from the Slave River, Île-à-la-Crosse, the Old Establishment, through the Rapids of the Drowned and the Rivière Maligne.

These men were human draft horses, known for their bravery, their drinking, their song, their whoring, their cheer, but most of all for their work ethic. For the fur-trading empire of Montreal was powered by the labor of illiterate farm boys from Quebec. At the *rendezvous*, the *hommes du nord* exchanged tens of thousands of beaver skins for the *mangeurs du lard*'s iron trade goods from London, a swap permitted by the bitter snow-driven land only once a year.

Voyageurs tended to be short—there was almost nowhere to put one's feet in a canoe packed to the gunnel with supplies—but powerful, to work all day and carry heavy *pièces* on dangerous portages. "If he shall stop growing at about five feet four inches, and be gifted with a good voice, and lungs that never tire, he is considered having been born under a good star," said one fur trader of the time.

A good voice, for they sang all day. They sang to synchronize their strokes. They sang to pass the time between smoked pipes. They sang to stay awake. The songs were filthy, bawdy versions of old religious hymns and children's rhymes with popular melodies. Songs of beautiful women, and dances, and work, and crows picking at the flesh of corpses butchered in an Iroquois raid.

> *Ce sont les voyageurs*
> *Qui sont de bons enfants;*
> *Ah! qui ne mangent guère,*
> *Mais qui boivent souvent!*
> . . .
> *Si les maringouins t'piq' la tête,*
> *D'leur aiguillon*
> *Et t'étourdissent les oreilles,*
> *De leurs chansons,*
> *Endure-les, et prends patience*
> *Afin d'apprendre*
> *Qu'ainsi le diable te tourmente,*
> *Pour avoir ta pauvre âme!*

> *We are voyageurs*
> *and good fellows. We seldom eat*
> *but we often drink!*
> *If the mosquitoes*
> *sting your head and deafen your ears with their buzzing,*
> *endure them patiently,*
> *for they will show you how*
> *the Devil will torment you*
> *in order to get your poor soul.*

The *rendezvous* was held at a place called Grand Portage, along a small bay on the western lip of Lake Superior, under the gaze of slumbering mounds of rock. For one month each summer, Grand Portage hosted both the headquarters of an international commercial empire and the rowdiest party in a thousand miles. Each was the reflection of the other, could not exist without the other. The facilities at Grand Portage were all related to commerce: warehouses, stables, forges, canoe depots. In truth, the fort constituted only a quasi-town. A communal garden but no church, a watchtower but no government's soldiers, a factory for a single industry, the hub of every spoke, the gangway to the north.

Via paddle and portage trail, the *rendezvous* appeared in the distant wilderness like a tiny gnat on a horse's rump. A palisade fence, shingled roofs, fields of white tents, hundreds of canoes at the fort. All the terms of trade were martial: Groups of canoes were a brigade, and they marched across the water. The Indians were kept on the outside of the picket, in teepees layered with bark. "Fence builders," the Ojibwa called the whites. They meant it as a pejorative.

The night before they reached Grand Portage, the voyageurs shaved, washed their hair, changed into clean white shirts saved for the occasion. All year, when laboring in the stacked boreal forest, wading through sucking muskeg, dodging Sioux war parties, curled for warmth with their Cree wives, they might dress in rags, filthy and emaciated. But when they arrived at the *rendezvous*, they intended to make an entrance, deep in song.

And waiting for them, upon disembarkation, a regale, a feast: a four-pound loaf of bread fresh out of the hot brick oven, half a pound of butter, and a bottle of rum; molasses-soaked Brazilian twist tobacco too, and roasts of freshly slaughtered hogs. For those few weeks, the north-men had nothing to do but talk and drink and screw and fight. While sober, they exchanged family news—who died, who was born, who was now married, all back in Quebec—and found clerks to read them long out-of-date newspapers. Then they hit the rum, and in service of their festivities some spent a year's worth of wages or went into debt, and not a few signed back on for another winter—or two, or three—based upon the depths of those debts. And then, a fortnight later, they headed back north.

The employer of all these voyageurs was a new business venture known as the North West Company. More a cartel than a proper corporation with a sole executive, the partnership was designed as a loose confederation of semiautonomous fur traders who pooled their resources for mutual benefit while always reserving the right to resume competition in the future. Borrowing the voyageurs' French, the shareholders called themselves *bourgeois*.

The ratio of voyageurs to invested partners was a hundred to one, and only a few dozen *bourgeois* gathered in the main lodge each day. While the men caroused, their masters feasted in the style of the European gentlemen they aspired to be. All the partners and clerks and trusted interpreters gathered together for a lavish midday meal: bread, pork, beef, hams, venison, butter, peas, corn, potatoes, tea, spirits, wine, and plenty of milk from cows quartered at the fort. The growing season was so short they ate root vegetables from the year prior, but no one seemed to mind. All of the gentlemen's pants were equipped with gussets so they could be cinched up in winter but, equally important, let out in summer.

But they did more than eat. Only at the *rendezvous* did so many *bourgeois* meet in one place. The northern agents and Montreal investors had business to discuss, and it was for that reason that Alexander and Roderic Mackenzie had traveled so far that summer.

Alexander and Roderic were cousins, Scottish refugees virtually alone in the world but for each other. Both were in their late twenties and up-and-comers, finding their way in the fiercely competitive trade. Their similarities were limited to age and acumen alone, though. Alexander was the more ambitious, energetic, direct. His partners thought him "blond, strong and well built." Where Alexander was fair and square-jawed, Roderic was moon-faced, fleshy, with flat dark hair. The only family feature they shared was a knowing smile.

Alexander had been in the trade several years longer than Roderic and by hard work and good timing had already been named a partner of the North West Company, the most junior member of that exclusive fraternity. Meanwhile, Roderic was still laboring as a clerk, a bookkeeping apprentice, and was wondering if his chance would ever come. But Alexander needed Roderic, if he was going to seize the opportunity that lay before him that summer.

The fur trade was a global business, and multicultural, reliant on London countinghouses, led by Scots and Americans, utilizing French labor, trading with Indians in a vast wilderness, and shipping around the world. Which caused the *bourgeois* of the North West Company endless problems.

The mechanics of their trade were slow. Ships and canoes moved only a hundred miles a day. Payment from Europe could take years, and so their capital was perpetually at risk; one bad season would drown them in their debt. The most valuable beaver furs lay ever more to the north and west, so their clerks and voyageurs pushed farther inland every year. And to top it all off, recent reports said that sea otters—and, more important, Indians willing to trade their pelts—were crawling all over the Pacific coast, a place to which they had no access.

For all those reasons and more, at that *rendezvous* in the summer of 1788, the Northwest Passage was on the agenda. Alexander Mackenzie was the one who put it there, because with his cousin's help he intended to persuade his partners to send him in search of it, a voyage that would make his fortune.

From the moment Christopher Columbus realized that he had stumbled upon a new continent, rather than China, there was always a tension, among European explorers, between exploiting the riches of the New World and finding a route around it.

Yes, this new land was full of tobacco and furs and gold. But it was also in the way. European markets clamored for tea, spices, blue-and-white porcelain dinner settings, silk stockings. For every businessman who sought to strip the New World of resources, another just wanted to get on to the real market in China; in 1497, even as Spain colonized the West Indies, John Cabot, an Italian sailing under an English charter, tried to find a northwest passage around America. The continent had only been known to Europeans for five years, and they were already trying to bypass it. Cabot failed, bumping into Newfoundland instead.

In this golden age of discovery, nothing was actually discovered. White humans stepped no place in North America that other human feet had not already trodden. But these Europeans did leave a mark, because they did two things that no one else had. They mapped the lands, and they told the rest of the world about them.

To the south, few rivers promised passage through the continent. John Smith, after founding Jamestown in 1607, tried to find the Pacific by sailing up the Chickahominy and the Potomac, but these rivers quickly dried up at the Endless Mountains of the Appalachians. In 1609, Henry Hudson's river option petered out, so he went to the north and gave his name to the frozen bay where he died in 1611, set adrift in a dingy by his mutinous and starving crew. Between Labrador and Greenland lie many gulfs, bays, and straits that tease passage to the Pacific, and all are now named for the naval officers—Frobisher, Davis, Baffin—who tried and failed to transit them in the sixteenth and seventeenth centuries. All were turned aside by pack ice. For practical purposes, the matter appeared to be settled. These most northerly reaches were perpetually encrusted in ice, and ever would be, so there could be no northwest passage above the Arctic Circle.

Therefore, between Florida and the northern cold, only one option remained: the St. Lawrence River. It was an obvious choice. The mouth of the waterway serves as a giant funnel, drawing in all ships over a four-hundred-mile swath; even in its relative narrows, the river forms a grand natural gateway, sheer cliffs on either side, a portal through which you could march all the world's armies. Only the St. Lawrence breached the Endless Mountains, ran free from ice most of the year, and accessed the heart of the continent. Many leading cartographers believed it would prove to be one end of an interior northwest passage.

That such a northwest passage should exist at all was a conclusion of inescapable logic. Since Aristotle, geographers subscribed to a philosophy of a balanced earth, in both weight and function. That the same amount of land must appear in the northern hemisphere as the southern, that features present in one area would be mirrored in all others, was axiomatic. This theory had already produced results; the long-sought *terra australis*, a large continent in the south required to balance Europe and Asia in the north, was found by Dutch sailors in the South Pacific in the seventeenth century. So too, if a southern passage existed around South America at Tierra del Fuego, a corresponding waterway must exist in the north.

And the North West Company intended to find it, because in the fur trade the competing goals of continental exploitation and bisection were finally united in one inescapable business imperative.

———

The North West Company wanted to ship furs directly to China, shortening a supply chain that crisscrossed the earth, first to London and then back around the southern tip of Cape Horn. And so *bourgeois* had long searched for a river that pierced the heart of the continent, the equivalent of a new Danube, Indus, or Volga. Claiming such a northwest passage would be a geographic coup and a profit bonanza.

And at the *rendezvous* of 1788, the North West Company partners heard, for the first time, that they were close to finding this river. The news originated with Peter Pond, an American from Connecticut and one of their most experienced traders and explorers. For a decade, Pond had worked farther north than any of them, made alliances with the Cree and Chipewyan to push into new territories, and always collected and cataloged geographic details everywhere he paddled. At Slave Lake, on the far edge of the North West Company trading empire, Red Knife Indians had reported to Pond the existence of a river of enormous size. It was larger than any river he knew, they said, and bore ever on into the setting sun.

The North West Company agents considered this news. And then they made a remarkable decision. They did not send Peter Pond to explore the river. They chose Alexander Mackenzie instead.

Mackenzie was only twenty-six years old. He was the youngest partner of the North West Company, and not by a small margin; most of the gentlemen were more than a dozen years his senior. Only four years before, Mackenzie had been overjoyed to simply be given "a small adventure of goods" to try his hand trading in Detroit. Now he was asking for the top assignment: to lead an expedition through the continent, a feat that had resisted the best attempts of famous explorers like Henry Hudson and Captain Cook. Both men were legend, vastly more educated, experienced, and respected than the unknown Mackenzie, and both died— Hudson abandoned, Cook in an attack by native Hawaiians—on their final voyages in search of the Northwest Passage.

This river that Mackenzie intended to follow cleaved lands unknown and largely unclaimed by Europeans, and official borders were not yet enforced in any meaningful way. The Treaty of Paris, ending the war between Great Britain and its thirteen colonies, had been signed only a few years before, but the British still held all the relevant inland garrisons. The Indian nations had been decimated by disease and displaced from their traditional homelands; like so many sitters on a long bench, each shoved west one space when the Europeans claimed the Atlantic coast. French-speaking Canadiens and their Indian mixed-blood families, as they were known, had settled broadly but were stateless. The Spanish owned Louisiana, the mostly uncharted territory that stretched hundreds of miles to the west of the *rendezvous,* but were nearly absent and let the place fend for itself. The few maps of the time showed a spidery network of rivers and lakes, interconnected and unbroken and framing vast tracts of nothingness, from New Orleans to Hudson's Bay.

Which is to say, the North West Company operated in a land of opportunity, not nationality or borders or law. Mackenzie himself called it a place of nothing but "drinking, carousing, and quarrelling." And these were just the sporadic inhabited areas; who knew what lay beyond?

But Mackenzie was undeterred by these obstacles. When he "contemplated the practicability of penetrating across the continent of America," he was "confident" in his "qualifications." He had resources: the reports from Pond, plus, back in the Barren Lands of the north, a trusted guide and business partner in the trading chief of the Chipewyan, whom he would ask to accompany him. Never mind that the journey would transit *terra nova* for them all, the Chipewyan chief included.

Under the terms Alexander proposed, he would follow the "water communications reported to lead from Slave Lake," while his cousin would run his trading post. "Roderic Mackenzie, if he will undertake it, will from his experience and local knowledge be in my opinion the fittest person you can find," he told the North West Company *bourgeois.*

The instructions from his partners returned just as Alexander had hoped. As he wrote in his journal, with flair, he was to go "by Order of the N.W Company, in a Bark Canoe in search of a Passage by Water through the N. W. Continent of America." His goal: "the Pacific Ocean in Summer 1789."

It was a time of great flux. In the former thirteen colonies, the Constitution was still being ratified. George Washington had been proposed as king. And at the annual *rendezvous,* young Alexander Mackenzie was chosen to lead an expedition through the continent's crown, the largest blank space left on the map of North America.

Into the North, 2016

~~~~~~

Alexander Mackenzie intended to find the Northwest Passage, and I would follow him.

Simple curiosity drove me forward. About the man himself, about this great river he descended. The Dene know it as the Deh Cho, but it's now officially named the Mackenzie River. How could such a mammoth body of water, over a thousand miles long, be hiding in plain sight?

Every American knows Lewis and Clark, their Corps of Discovery and search for the Pacific. So why not their forerunners? In 1789, when Mackenzie and his voyageurs and indigenous guides launched with the intent to cross the continent via the Northwest Passage, Meriwether Lewis was still a fourteen-year-old schoolboy in Virginia, and Sacajawea might not have yet been born.

I asked myself, if I had devoured the histories of Arctic explorers like Amundsen and Franklin and Shackleton, how had I never read of this man Mackenzie? And if I could trace the Missouri and Colorado Rivers, if I knew how the Hudson and Lake Champlain got their names, how could I not do the same for this waterway, greater than them all? I had never even heard of it; *Wikipedia* had to clue me in.

In Mackenzie and this river, my natural writerly inquisitiveness combined with a paddler's desire to explore new waters. To enter my own *terra nova*, one of the last places on earth unmapped by Google Street View, a place you have to see in person if you want to see it at all.

Mackenzie traversed those waters via canoe, and so I planned the same. My choice involved more than historic homage; it is the perfect slow vehicle to see the country. No noise, no pollution, no trace left of your passage, yet still able to travel far enough a day to give the sense one is making progress.

I had spent my share of time in flat-water canoes and kayaks, but my boating confidence was primarily drawn from my years guiding on the rivers of upstate and western New York: the Salmon, the Letchworth gorge, and the Cattaraugus, or Bad Smelling Banks in Seneca, named for the natural gas seeping out of the shale. Whitewater rafting had made me comfortable reading hydraulic cues, making quick decisions in rapidly moving water, and swimming to safety when required.

So I flattered myself as an experienced journeyman. New York State had certified me as a guide; I had to pass a test and everything. I told family that while I had never undertaken a trip of this size, I knew what I was getting into. That it differed from my experience only in degree, not in kind.

In reality, though, all I had done was convince myself that because I knew how to jog around the block, I could, given enough time, run a marathon. Or two months' worth of marathons, back to back to back. My wife was not so easily fooled and told me, from the moment I broached the idea to canoe the Mackenzie, that I would not be doing it alone. In fact, I must take someone who, far better than I, knew what he was doing.

I admit, the idea of going so far up the map made me a little nervous, in a giddy fear-of-heights sort of way. As if I would be climbing up to the top of a very tall ladder, and I'd need to maintain my balance "up" there or I'd fall somehow. That I'd get caught, and some authority was going to tell me that I wasn't allowed to go so high and for my own safety I had to get back down.

This latitude was new to me, north of 60 degrees, a chilly two-thirds of the way up from the equator. I had never been higher than Anchorage in Alaska, which hardly counted, I said to myself, because I flew there in a plane. In Europe, I had come close to that latitude, in Copenhagen, Edinburgh, and Göteborg, cities that feel more like extensions of continental culture than any northern frontier. And now I wanted to *start* at 60 degrees and travel from there, via canoe, another thousand miles north?

I laughed at myself; there were real and rational safety issues, I didn't need to invent any. In traditional American mythology, we associate the West with opportunity, but the North is known for hardship. Their conjunction—in the Northwest Passage, North West Company, Northwest Territories—speaks to both ideas. You go north and west to test yourself, but in pursuit of an objective. The suffering is made up for by hard-won furs, diamonds, Yukon gold. Something tangible that makes the trip worth it.

The motto of the *hommes du nord* was "Fortitude in Distress." But it could easily have been "Fortune from Distress."

I had advantages Mackenzie did not, paper topological charts and GPS, but I was impressed how little the land revealed of itself during such cartographic reconnaissance. On a map, it looks as if all the freshwater in the world were up there, though geologists say it is actually only one-fifth of the planet's supply. The satellite image is of a mirror shattered, a cup of water then poured over the surface, streams and pools in every crack. This is the effect of the indestructible Canadian Shield, the mound of ancient granite that stretches from Minnesota to New York's Adirondacks, Newfoundland to Greenland, across much of Canada's Arctic coast. Ponds and creeks stud the shield itself, and along its outer rim lie the largest lakes on earth: Huron, Michigan, Superior, Winnipeg, Athabasca, Great Slave, Great Bear, all in an arc. Their northern shores rock, their southern shores mud, like puddles on the edge of a parking lot where the asphalt meets the dirt.

Mackenzie was of an era when scientific knowledge could still be expanded through brute physical means, by exposing oneself to the rigors of travel and danger. He wanted to find a route to sell furs to the Orient. I wanted, well, something more existential. Pure urge, from the groin and gut and other anxious parts of the body. A need to flee, before death or quiet desperation or both. To light out for the territories with Huck. It's glandular. "Comes over one an absolute necessity to move," wrote D. H. Lawrence. He went to Sardinia; I would go north.

———

One muddy spring day, as I first began to plan my journey, I drove through the western Pennsylvania mountains to the home of Wick Walker, an unlikely friend. Wick lives on a horse farm outside Pittsburgh, in a nineteenth-century house with an adjoining ancient barn. Not much has changed in either structure since they were built, a little electricity here and there, very modest indoor plumbing. We all make choices of how much modern technology to accept into our lives; Wick, by choice, dials the clock back more than most. He cooks on a wood-fired stove and fed me eggs and English muffins off the griddle.

Wick is an expert on rivers and expeditions. He canoed at Dartmouth and placed eleventh in the men's C-1 slalom at the 1972 Olympics in Munich. His good friend Jamie McEwan took bronze. Over the next few decades, Wick, Jamie, and Jamie's brother Tom pioneered the use of modern plastic kayaks in whitewater. Together, they boast the first descent of many rivers and waterfalls around the world, culminating in their 1998 attempt of Tibet's Tsangpo gorge, at sixteen thousand feet the deepest canyon in the world.

I met Wick at a writing workshop; in a modestly embarrassing inversion, he the student and I the teacher. We stayed in touch, via our mutual interest in whitewater and the writing life. At my wife's instruction to find someone competent and experienced, I thought of Wick first and had already asked him to come with me, because he had somehow never done the Mackenzie River. But Wick politely declined, citing his aching knees. Instead, he offered to let me pick his brain, gather advice for the trip.

That evening, we sat in his upstairs library and drank three-finger whiskeys until late at night. His house is full of books and papers, organized by geography and conflict, the shelves set against every vertical surface, including the stairwell. Wick is a member of the famed Explorers Club—other members include Edmund Hillary and Neil Armstrong— and thus many of the books are first-person narratives written by friends.

Wick is seventy now, speaks slowly in a gravel voice, and closes his eyes when making an important point. I asked for advice in planning my trip, and in answer he handed me the binder he used for his Tsangpo expedition. Everything was orderly and slipped into plastic document protectors: his budget, his grant applications with National Geographic, permits and correspondence with the Chinese government, photographs of his team.

"What about your paddle?" Wick asked.

"I was just going to rent one, I guess," I said. "I hadn't given it much thought."

Wick gave me a disapproving look. "You'll swing it twelve hours a day, every day. It has to be right. Call Jim Snyder, a friend of mine in West Virginia. Tell him I sent you, and pay him whatever he asks."

I would contact Jim. He was so meticulous in his measurements, sizing the paddle to my needs and frame, that he had me draw an outline of each hand on a sheet of paper and mail it to him so he could tailor the T-grip to my fingers. The bespoke result was a work of art—curly maple shaft, blade an inlaid mix of black willow, red oak, and sassafras—that weighed less than a box of cereal.

After admonishing me about my paddle, Wick went on. "The other issue right now is your team. Who are you going with?"

I told him I wasn't sure yet. That I was having trouble finding a partner; who in their right mind signs up for such a journey?

Wick frowned and closed his eyes again.

"I think we've found the weak part of your plan," he said, and drank his whiskey.

The next morning, before I left, I searched Wick's shelves for books on Alexander Mackenzie. I didn't find any, confirming his obscurity even in an expedition scholar's library. And no wonder. His journals languish out of print, and in the historical record the earliest hints of Mackenzie lie mostly forgotten in a London archive, the story of his first long voyage at age twelve, when he fled Scotland.

SCOTLAND, 1774

〰〰

If you caught the view from the point at the right moment, when the skies were finally clear and the fog was down, the sunrise over the Minch would silhouette the Scottish Highlands on the far side of the water. The Minch was still twenty-five miles wide there, no narrow strait, but the irregular and ragged ridgeline on the far shore surged thousands of feet into the air, high enough to deceive. The mountains never stood in back-lit relief for long, though. Once the perpetual cloud banks re-formed, the Isle of Lewis, Alexander Mackenzie's boyhood home, might as well be adrift on the ocean.

He was born in Stornoway, the only village of any size on that grassy island, but he spent most of his childhood on a farm a few miles outside town. That homestead was known as Melbost, a tiny isthmus of land connecting the village to the wider point that dangled into the Minch like an apple off its stem. Looking from Alexander's family farm, to the north, one saw the sea. To the south, the sea. To the west, past Stornoway, the lochs and hinterlands of the empty Isle of Lewis. To the east, the point and the sea. The Minch.

Those were dangerous waters, as the blue men of the Minch caused trouble for sailors. They raised storms. Called lightning down with their long gray arms. Swam like fishes but spoke like men, challenging ship captains with verses of rhyme. Fail to complete the couplet, they'd cut your ship in two and drag you to the bottom. But on quiet mornings, when the blue men sleep just below the surface of the water, the skies are crisp, and, oh, those Highlands at sunrise.

Alexander Mackenzie left Stornoway at the age of twelve, after his mother died. He crossed the whole ocean, not just the Minch, sailing hard west for the New World. He had to escape. Scotland was dying too.

It's not exactly that the Mackenzies were poor. It was that all of Scotland was poor, the outer islands only more so. Capitalism, via a tenant culture that turned chieftains into mere landlords, had achieved in a few decades what centuries of medieval English kings never could: the clans were broken, the Scots a shade of their former selves.

Alexander grew up better than most. He went to school, for one, and was born, in 1762, in a sturdy slate-roofed two-story cottage with windows. His father was Kenneth, known as Corc, and in the Mackenzie clan he was a tacksman, the owner and leaser of land, the binding tissue between laird and peasant. Corc's chief, the last Earl of Seaforth, spent far more time in London with the Royal Society than tending to his Highland holdings, and in those days Corc Mackenzie was reduced to being the rent collector of Melbost. In times past, though, the tacksman was a military man, a traditional leader in battle. During the 1745 uprising of Bonnie Prince Charles, the Catholic pretender to the throne, Corc had been made an ensign and, in the name of the king, fortified the village of Stornoway against attack from the sea. It never came.

Corc lived as a gentleman farmer upon the land, peasant clansmen doing the hard labor of tilling the thin stony soil. He dwelled in a house, not a concave leaky hut, and during the long dark rainy winters he heated his home with peat, cut from the bog in heavy wedges. Alexander had one older brother, Murdoch, and two sisters, Sybilla and Margaret. Alexander was sturdy and towheaded. He and Murdoch grew up with as much privilege and culture as was possible in that outpost on the sea. They attended school, were literate in English and French, and read the classics in Latin and Greek. They kept a lively correspondence with their cousins, Alexander especially with Roderic, the son of his mother's brother. Roderic lived just on the other side of the Minch, in Achiltibuie, as one of the Highland Mackenzies, and the clan stayed as close as letters and the occasional fosterage allowed. Roderic was only one year older than Alexander, and the two grew together in affection.

When Alexander was still a boy, Murdoch left home and used his schooling to become a surgeon on a ship. But family lore says that ship was lost, pulled to the bottom by the blue men off "the coast of Halifax." His mother died soon after.

———

In 1773, the year before Alexander left home, the famous Samuel Johnson, towering man of letters, toured the Highlands, accompanied as always by his young protégé and biographer James Boswell. Johnson published his travelogue as *Journey to the Western Islands of Scotland*, and of the lands generally he wrote, "It must be confessed, that they have not many allurements, but to the mere lover of naked nature. The inhabitants are thin, provisions are scarce, and desolation and penury give little pleasure."

Johnson found the terrain either mountain or fen, the forests "denuded," the fields fallow, the streams devoid of fish, the churches "unroofed and useless," the houses mean and, like the roads, made entirely of loose stones. By nature, as mountaineers, the Highlanders, he expected, would be warlike and thievish. Instead, they were "represt," stripped of their natural personal courage, no longer wearing their tartans or even taking their weapons to Sunday services.

"An old gentleman, delighting himself with the recollection of better days, related, that forty years ago, a Chieftain walked out attended by ten or twelve followers, with their arms rattling," Johnson wrote. Now such men as Corc were gelded, and many average Scots whom Johnson encountered considered tacksmen "a useless burden."

Johnson blamed it on the introduction of commerce; until recently, both the concept and the reality of money were almost unknown. "Since the islanders, no longer content to live, have learned the desire of growing rich, an ancient dependent is in danger of giving way to a higher bidder, at the expense of domestick dignity and hereditary power."

Johnson traveled among the Scots as would an anthropologist sending back to civilization dispatches from a backward land. "The traditions of an ignorant and savage people have been for ages negligently heard, and unskilfully related," he wrote. He reported that the men had whiskey for breakfast every morning but were never drunk. That the women drove the cattle and harvested the corn. That the native language was coarse and vulgar and only meant for the grossest of thoughts. Johnson made a special point of investigating the Second Sight—"our desire of information was keen, and our inquiry frequent"—because he had heard Scots put great faith in these predictions of good or ill, visions of distant places. He found the belief near universal among those of the Western

Isles; only the ministers demurred. Most often the practitioners said they saw Death, which Johnson found appropriate for the clime.

"The dark months are here a time of great distress," he wrote, "because the summer can do little more than feed itself, and winter comes with its cold and its scarcity upon families very slenderly provided."

———

Of greatest distress to Johnson, though, was the "epidemick desire of wandering," especially after 1760. America was an immense land primed for settlement, all potential, rich in speculative "futures" of every kind. Tens of thousands of Scots made the journey in those years, and Alexander's home was hit particularly hard. Only a few thousand lived on the Isle of Lewis at its peak, but in the twelve months before Alexander's family fled, one in five inhabitants immigrated to the New World.

In those years, Stornoway's major export was disillusioned Scots; on a single day in June 1773, over eight hundred sailed away. Every spring and fall, the ships would come and siphon more of the destitute and adventurous and desperate. Many left to become indentured servants. In March 1774, after recruiting fifty adults for the domestic work, the captain of the *Friendship*, of Philadelphia, started picking teenage boys and girls off the beach, without the consent of their parents. Over a hundred ended up on board. Parliament was outraged, but a later investigation would show that the poverty-stricken children were volunteers, not victims of kidnapping.

Some of the affliction was local. The Earl of Seaforth sharply increased rents, leading to a face-to-face confrontation with tenants. But Johnson saw similar stories throughout the Western Isles. It was a contagion that must be stopped; "an island once depopulated will remain a desert," he predicted.

As tacksman, Corc Mackenzie held out longer than most, the tail end of the trend. Johnson saw that it was the tacksman's job to "impart knowledge" and "impress civility." But on whom, when whole districts were depopulated, leaving only want and disarray and shame? In its October 1774 issue, *Scots Magazine* said that Scotland was turning into a grass park, home to nothing but "owls and dragons."

The island was a broken shell with the yolk removed. Alexander's father was a warrior without a war. His mother and brother were dead.

Like thousands before them, Alexander, his father, and two aunts made for America.

They left just in time. In reaction to the crisis, Parliament banned emigration from Scotland less than a year later.

————

In November 1774, the Mackenzies booked passage on the *Peace & Plenty*. A representative of the Crown dutifully annotated each emigrant before he or she boarded. Young Alexander told the customs inspector that he was twelve years old and a schoolboy, the only child so identified on the ship.

The *Peace & Plenty* was a well-known merchant vessel, two masts and square sails and a four-hundred-ton burden, retrofitted to carry humans in bulk. Like a massive soup ladle, twice a year the ship dipped into the thin broth of Scotland and Ireland and poured its contents over New York, Philadelphia, Virginia, and the Carolinas. Profitably managing the business of the *Peace & Plenty* was a two-man job: one to entice the emigrants on the boat, the other to ship them out.

The captain of the *Peace & Plenty* was Charles McKenzie, no relation to Alexander. His partner was John Wyllie, a native of Stornoway who spent half his time in Belfast, hopping back and forth between Scotland and Ireland to enlist desperate refugees. As a team, they were very adept at recruiting passengers. Wyllie advertised on posters around Belfast: anyone who desired passage to America should meet at a certain place at a certain time. Everyone knew, the placard went on, that the *Peace & Plenty* was one of the finest in the kingdom, well suited to the "comfortable accommodation" of passengers due to the height of its decks. Plus, passengers would not starve: "As Captain McKenzie's Character is already so well established, it is sufficient to say, that Care will be taken to send Plenty of the best Provisions and Water."

The posters worked. In May 1774, McKenzie dropped a load of Belfast natives in New York and then sailed immediately for the Isle of Lewis, where Wyllie had recruited another ship full. That summer, Alexander watched four hundred of his neighbors load up on the *Peace & Plenty*.

It was a bonanza. Wyllie told McKenzie that so many Scots wanted to flee Stornoway he bet they could fill another ship. In October, the two made an official wager, five hundred pounds that Wyllie could find another three hundred emigrants within fifteen days. Alexander and his father and aunts booked passage, but the cupboards were bare otherwise, and Wyllie's recruitment efforts stalled. McKenzie waited the fifteen days for the promised passengers, and then another week besides, but only one-quarter of the expected three hundred ever showed. Captain McKenzie was finally so irritated at the delay that on November 8, 1774, he fired his gun into the air, signaling his intention to leave, and then suddenly pulled anchor before everyone was on board. Thirty wishful emigrants, all paying customers who had already loaded their worldly possessions in the hold, were stranded onshore. They boarded rowboats and tried to reach the ship, but Captain McKenzie put up his whole sail and left them behind.

Alexander and his family were fortunate that they were already on board and, with only fifty-eight fellow passengers, saved some of the worst depredations of sea travel. Like other merchant ships, the *Peace & Plenty* had three decks—the top, tween, and hold—and steerage-rate passengers were crammed into the center. Despite Captain McKenzie's advertisements to the contrary, emigrants spent the bulk of the voyage hunched over, scuttling about the five feet of space between the hold and the upper deck. Bulkheads sectioned off cargo areas for hogsheads of stores, leaving the dormitories airless cells: six feet by twenty inches the standard planning factor for adults, less for children. Families piled three or four to a bed. Buckets of salt water were available for washing, but only in first class. Decks were cleaned with vinegar when the weather allowed, but normally the hatches were fastened to keep out the spray and storms of a wintry north sea. If the hold were to fill with water, Alexander would join his brother among the blue men.

The trip across the Atlantic could take up to three months. Weekly rations consisted of a few pounds of oatmeal, the same for bread or biscuit, a pound of molasses, a pound of peas, less of beef or pork or cheese, a little brackish water. Most passengers spent the first week seasick in the dark, candles and lanterns being at a premium.

But Alexander's family, having a little bit of money, could at least afford a cabin where they were able to stand up straight.

Sailors said you could smell America before you saw it, a foreign lushness of forest and soil wafting on the breeze from over the horizon. Mackenzie landed at New York City, at a crowded dock on the East River, and was greeted by other smells. The fishmonger. The oxcart. The collected floating sewage of twenty-five thousand souls. But also gunpowder, and burning tar.

It was the spring of 1775, and when Alexander Mackenzie arrived in New York, he discovered that he had escaped the rural poverty of Scotland for a war.

NEW YORK, 1775

~~~~~~

Up and down the thirteen colonies, New York was known as a cosmopolitan city of whores and merchants and immigrants. Eighteen languages were commonly spoken on the street, five hundred ladies of pleasure welcomed sailors and businessmen alike, and seventeen churches of competing denominations stood intermixed with the coffeehouses, flophouses, and banking houses that made the city hum. "Our chiefest unhappiness here is too great a mixture," said one resident of the time. One-fifth of the city consisted of African slaves, and another one in ten New Yorkers was a Scottish immigrant who had just arrived in the last two years. The stories of their ocean crossings were great fodder for the many daily newspapers; the most genteel of New York's citizens—who lived in large fenced-off homes staffed with African footmen, coachmen, butlers, and maids—read with great appetite the sensational accounts of starving passengers, disease, quarantines, and freezing cold.

The *Peace & Plenty,* bearing the Mackenzie family under just such conditions, sailed through the narrows, between the wooded islands that enclose New York Bay, and approached the cluster of church spires and crumbling fortifications on the southern tip of hilly Manhattan. Fort George was built by the Dutch in 1626 and, even in its decrepitude, remained the seat of the royal governor, a hundred ancient naval guns in the grand battery guarding one of the world's finest harbors. Up the slope from the sea, the 175-foot steeple of Trinity Episcopal pinnacled the skyline. And beyond the farthest homes of Chambers Street lay open farms, the heights at Harlem, and then dense forest.

The piers on the Hudson side of Manhattan often iced up over the winter, so the *Peace & Plenty* and other passenger ships, often two a day, docked on the busy eastern wharf. Local customs officials were overwhelmed and only recorded immigrants sporadically. The Mackenzies exited the ship unnoticed and entered a city unlike Stornoway in almost every way.

Press gangs prowled along the East River piers. On the Hudson side, churches and brothels served their respective congregations. Common greens and middle-class homes filled the higher center slope. Incredibly dense, the city was only a mile long and half a mile wide; young Alexander's walk to school from Melbost to Stornoway was longer than the full length of Broadway. This was intentional, as the whole city focused on trade, and distances were measured in the time it took a horse to move a cartload of goods down the cobblestoned streets.

Mercantilists held all the highest positions in fashionable New York society. They loved French champagne, Canton china, and local oysters. All finished goods, anything of discernment or quality, came from Britain, four or five months between order placement and arrival. April and October were the prime time for British ship viewing, six months the average for a round-trip to London. The incoming holds were filled with perfume, mustard, tea, snuff, gloves, handkerchiefs, ribbons, lace, umbrellas. And on the return voyage, Alexander saw the ships carried white pine lumber and iron bars and furs. Especially furs, floated down the Hudson from the trading post at Albany. A Scottish visitor called America "the best country in the world for people of small fortunes; or in other words, the best poor man's country." All that was required to make one's way up in the world was "courage and resolution in the adventurer."

———

Until the war came. In the spring of 1775, soon after the Mackenzies arrived, letters began to trickle in from abroad. The British army was on its way, by sea, eleven regiments of foot and a seventy-four-gun man-of-war with them.

New York was too polyglot and multifarious to fit neatly into either side's camp. It was too full of immigrants to be trusted, too full of Loyalists for full-throated support of liberty and insurrection, too full of patriots for the British leadership to rest at ease. John Adams complained that New York was one-third loyal to the king, one-third revolutionary, and one-third undecided; George Washington was convinced the city was full of British spies. After the state legislators voted to refuse to send delegates to the Continental Congress, they sang a chorus of "God Save the King." When Washington and the British royal governor William Tryon rode through the city during separate parades, equal crowds lined the streets to cheer them, many of the same people attending both events.

It took four days for the news of the April skirmishes at Lexington and Concord to arrive in the city, but when it did, all patriots were summoned to an emergency meeting at the Liberty Pole on the Common. The crowd whipped itself into a frenzy, and a general insurrection broke out, men storming the arsenal at city hall and stealing six hundred muskets, bayonets, and cartridge boxes. The Continental Association deputized local committees to root out conspiracies and extract patriotic loyalty oaths from their fellow citizens, and British ships were turned away from port before they could unload cargo. A crowd attacked the home of the president of King's College; based on a tip from Alexander Hamilton, who hated rule by mob and Crown equally, the chancellor escaped in the middle of the night, half-dressed, over a fence. Later, the offices of the Loyalist *Gazetteer,* the leading newspaper of the time with a circulation of over thirty-five hundred, was sacked by patriots, who smashed the presses and stole all of the movable type.

By May 1775, the Crown representatives in New York were complaining of near anarchy, and anyone with the means was fleeing the city. But then the HMS *Asia* arrived and anchored in the harbor, defiantly flaunting the flimsy armaments that guarded the approaches. That August, when patriots snuck into the Battery to steal the British cannon, the *Asia* retaliated by firing into the city, first grapeshot, and then a full thirty-two-gun broadside. It was the first British shelling of New York, and all remaining citizens either turned against their king or fled. Lower Manhattan became a fortress, breastworks across every path leading down to the water, cobblestoned streets torn up to build walls. Average citizens, all males of a certain age, were put to work. "The city looks in some streets as if the plague had been in it, so many houses being shut up," wrote one resident.

Corc Mackenzie had just arrived, and decades of loyal service to his king outweighed months of kinship to his new home. This made him a Tory. "Pray, what is a Tory?" went the joke. "A Tory is a thing whose head is in England and its body in America and its neck ought to be stretched." The New York Provincial Congress ordered the death penalty for anyone providing aid or comfort to the British. Loyalists were pulled from their homes, stripped, covered in hot tar and then doused in feathers, tossed on a rail to be driven about town, where they could be pelted with sticks and stones by the mob. The American Revolution was a civil war as well.

The city was no place to raise a child; press gangs, on both sides, were nabbing boys as young as fifteen. When the Mackenzies had debarked the *Peace & Plenty* months before, all of the talk among new immigrants on the eastern wharf was the land available near Albany. Swindlers and speculators accosted every family with any visible sign of means, pitching them a sliver of farm up north for their very own. The Mackenzies had a little money and could land on their feet.

Every civilian with a dollar to his name was fleeing New York. Alexander and his family went north, up the Hudson to join his uncle, his mother's brother, John Maciver, called "Ready Money John" because of his access to cash. Alexander Mackenzie crossed the Endless Mountains of the Appalachians, his first step into the vast interior of the continent, to make a new home among the Mohawk and Mohican.

————

Sir William Johnson was the lord of the winding valley of the Mohawk and presided over all of the commerce and conflict that passed through it. Johnson was a Scots-Irish immigrant, arriving in North America in 1738, and became a trusted agent of King George, pushing out the few German and Dutch settlers from his valley and replacing them with kin. In this way, he created a fur-trading enterprise unlike any other in the New World, a fiefdom ruled by him in partnership with the Six Nations of the Iroquois.

The Iroquois were also known as the Haudenosaunee, the People of the Longhouse. In their original compact, predating European settlement of North America, the nations organized themselves using the idea of the longhouse as a unifying symbol. The Mohawk, near the Hudson River valley, were the Keepers of the Eastern Door. The Seneca, hard against the Niagara Frontier, the Keepers of the Western Door. The Onondaga, as the central nation, the Keepers of the Flame. The fur-trading post of Albany sat at the Eastern Door, and with the Mohawk, Sir William Johnson found his fortune.

Johnson settled on the north bank of the river, used his modest familial wealth to buy a farm and build a store and sawmill, and then, year by year, sought to monopolize the trading of all furs bound for New York City. To do this, he made peace with the Mohawk, forged an alliance, and was named a sachem of the tribe. In 1739, he married a young German indentured servant, and produced a white family, and at the same time wedded a Mohawk woman, and made a family they called mixed bloods. And his partner in all things was Hendrick, the Mohawk chief. Together they grew rich trading beaver fur, and Johnson clothed Hendrick in a great red cloak and had his portrait painted, bearing both hatchet and tricorn hat, as an Indian and a gentleman and a wealthy and powerful man.

With the consent of the Crown and the confederacy, Johnson and Hendrick raised an army to punish their enemies, the French and the Huron and the Mohican. Hendrick recruited hundreds of warriors to raid border settlements, and Johnson paid for each scalp the men returned. But these were mere skirmishes compared with the war that was to come in 1754.

In Great Britain and France, it came to be known as the Seven Years' War. On the Indian subcontinent, it was the Third Carnatic War. In Prussia, the Third Silesian War. In South America, the Fantastic War. In North America, in the colonies where Johnson fought, it was called the French and Indian War. The whole world was at war, it seemed, all of Western Christendom, wherever Protestants and Catholics ground against one another. On the New England frontier, this meant the British and Iroquois fighting the French, Huron, Ottawa, Ojibwa, and Algonquin.

In 1755, Johnson was formally appointed a major general, and he and Hendrick went to battle together, meeting their enemies near Crown Point, at the northern tip of Lake George. It was a costly victory; Hendrick was mortally wounded, and Johnson took a ball in the hip that gave him a permanent limp. He returned home with a remnant of his army and, with Hendrick gone, resigned his commission.

But four years later, after a sequence of failed raids and false starts, Britain found itself on the verge of victory. Johnson took command once more and fielded an army of colonial militia, British regulars, and one thousand Iroquois warriors, the entire military strength of the Six Nations. Johnson painted his face as an Iroquois war chief and led the combined force west to lay siege to the French castle at Fort Niagara.

Johnson assaulted the keep and blocked the French relief column, and, in the aftermath, the French forts and trading posts were burned, and the British would occupy the garrisons along the Niagara River and Great Lakes for two generations. The next year, 1760, Johnson rode north to Montreal and, with Lord Amherst, accepted the final surrender of New France.

Thick with victory, Johnson returned to his river valley and multiplied his kingdom several times over in the midst of the Mohawk people. He cleared a section of forest and constructed a new compound, Johnson Hall, and filled it with family and Mohawk allies, who bequeathed him vast tracts of land throughout northern New York. In the name of the Crown, Johnson made peace and traded furs with twenty-four Indian nations, the remaining Iroquois and Huron and Algonquin out to Lake Superior, and their good faith was enshrined in belts of beads. Johnson was already known as Warraghiyagey, One Who Does Much, and the assembled sachem presented him, and him alone, with the sacred Two Row Wampum Belt, a 160-year-old physical embodiment of peace and friendship. When Johnson died in 1774, the six chiefs of the Six Nations buried him as an Iroquois.

Johnstown was still in mourning when Alexander Mackenzie and his family arrived in 1775. By then the village was also known as Scotch Bush, a sign of the number of their fellow immigrants. The oldest son of Johnson's white union, John, inherited his father's estates and titles. He was known as a land dealer who could set up a family like the Mackenzies with a small farm. John Johnson continued the partnership with the Mohawk and carried on with the lucrative fur trade, and Alexander Mackenzie saw the generational wealth and power possible when white man and Indian aligned.

But Johnson also made close ties with the new center of British power, the governor-general in Montreal. When the American Revolution broke out in the colonies, there was no question that Baronet John Johnson and his pledged landowners would remain loyal to the Crown. In January 1776, the younger Johnson vowed to raise an army like his father and promised the king a battalion of loyal Scots and five hundred Iroquois warriors.

When the patriot army came for Johnson's guns, he led his retainers and Iroquois allies to Montreal. It was the last march of the united Iroquois people. By the end of the revolution, some nations would choose the side of the colonists, and some, like the Mohawk, would stay loyal to their British allies, and the house so divided against itself crumbled, the six-hundred-year confederacy of the Iroquois in crisis.

In Montreal, Johnson sought provisioning and counsel with the British military command. Corc Mackenzie accompanied him. As a new landowner, he served as one of Johnson's retainers and was named a lieutenant. Young Alexander stayed behind with his aunts. The old man had finally found his war. Alexander never saw his father again.

The British strategy in northern New York was two-pronged. The main force pushed south from Montreal, through the traditional invasion route used by European armies for two hundred years: Lake Champlain to Fort Ticonderoga on Lake George, down the Hudson to New York City. Johnson, on the other hand, as part of a second, smaller force, would sail up the St. Lawrence River to Lake Ontario, turn south, and then attack from the west along the Mohawk River, through his own lands at Johnson Hall. Resistance was expected to be light; Benedict Arnold and the American colonial army had already been turned aside at Quebec City in the winter of 1775, and thus the British still nominally controlled all of New York outside Manhattan. The two armies expected to face no more than ragged militia.

The war did not proceed as planned. John Johnson led Corc and the rest of the King's Royal Regiment of New York—also known as the Royal Yorkers, also known as the Royal Greens—on the large left hook as planned. But Johnson was stopped short by the colonial garrison at Fort Stanwix, upriver of his holdings. The Mohawk valley proved itself as politically divided as New York City. Most newly immigrated Scots, like the Mackenzies, stayed loyal to the Crown, but their long-settled German, Dutch, and English neighbors became patriots. With Johnson and his army delayed, there was no one to stop patriots from holding demonstrations and reprisals in the streets. The rebel colonists fell on Johnson Hall, burned nearby farms, and held Lady Johnson hostage.

The main force, moving directly south from Montreal, encountered even greater trouble. Defeated at the Battle of Saratoga in 1777, the British surrendered over sixty-five hundred prisoners. It was the decisive loss of the revolution. France would enter the war. The British would lose. America would be free, and the Loyalists would pay.

With Corc gone to war and unable to protect his family, Alexander Mackenzie and his aunts were forced to flee again, joining tens of thousands of refugees. Some Scots made for the Niagara Peninsula, for a hard farm life in places like Hamilton and St. Catharines. But thousands more went north, to Montreal and Quebec, the last remaining holdouts of urban British power on the continent. Sir John Johnson had many connections with the gentry in Montreal, and the sons of his retainers were the beneficiaries. In 1778, Alexander, aged sixteen, moved again, to take up a position afforded to privileged boys. He soon became a clerk in a countinghouse, apprenticed to the firm of Finlay & Gregory. His job was to tally beaver furs, and he could not know at the time that the direction of his life was set.

MONTREAL, 1778

wwwww

Montreal was an old French city with new British rulers and flooded with so many refugees that in only a decade it had doubled in size, to become nearly as large as New York City. Montreal attracted Loyalists on the losing end of the American Revolution, merchants who preferred profits to politics, poor Scots and former redcoat soldiers, failed English businessmen fleeing their debts.

The city was a place of stone and mud and cold. Montreal was surrounded by fresh new walls—twenty feet high and almost as thick—built by the French to keep out the English and Americans. Inside, the town hosted uniform row houses with high pitched roofs, the better to shed snow, and a skyline of smoking chimneys. Few of the streets were cobblestoned, leaving the majority an open sewer of slush or muck, depending on the season.

Along rue St.-François-Xavier, near the corner of rue St.-Paul and the old Market Gate, Alexander Mackenzie found work and lodging in a countinghouse, as a clerk for Mr. John Gregory, an up-and-coming English gentleman of twenty-eight years. Gregory was new to North America, but he had forged a partnership with a well-established trader, a Scot named Mr. James Finlay, who had first worked far to the west, in Detroit and Fort Michilimackinac, under the auspices of Sir William Johnson. Mackenzie heard that in 1768 Mr. Finlay had even traveled to a distant northern place called the Saskatchwine and survived the winter there, along a frozen river.

The two men used Finlay's experience, Gregory's energy, and their combined capital to grow the risky new business. They required educated boys who could write, to keep the ledgers of goods coming in and furs going out. "Most of the clerks were young men of good families, from the Highlands of Scotland," wrote the American chronicler Washington Irving. "A candidate had to enter, as it were, 'before the mast,' to undergo a long probation, and to rise slowly by the merits of his services. He began, at an early age, as a clerk, and served an apprenticeship of seven years."

Alexander was only sixteen, but many of his fellow clerks were years younger. Unmoored though he was, Alexander felt at home in the trade, with so many clannish Scots around, accepting the hardscrabble opportunities overlooked by most of their English wig-wearing cousins. Everyone knew, as Washington Irving wrote, that Scots were "characterized by the perseverance, thrift, and fidelity of their country, and fitted by their native hardihood to encounter the rigorous climate of the north." The standard joke held that Scots went to Canada to get warm.

But in Montreal, Alexander saw that despite those hardships, if he worked hard and made it, he could be a gentleman like Mr. Finlay, a *bourgeois*, the rich fur traders of the interior.

———

Montreal was in the heart of New France, a colony that often seemed to bore its host country and attracted only occasional Parisian interest. Each European power sought something different from its American holdings. The Spanish were hungry for plunder. The English grew prosperous with their farms and plantations. But the French never invested in New France and accidentally followed a policy of benign neglect.

First to colonize the New World was Spain, a country still very much in the grip of the Inquisition. In the Caribbean, Mexico, and South America, Spain found a rich bounty: Indian souls to speed along to a Catholic Christ, and gold to pay for wars at home. The armada ruled the seas, the conquistadors bled the land from Peru to Florida, and for the Spanish might and right were inseparable.

The English were delayed in their settlement of North America, but once they founded Jamestown in the early seventeenth century, a far different attitude prevailed. The first colonists of Massachusetts and Virginia were Calvinists, fleeing a state religion rather than spreading one. And in their portion of the continent, the riches lay in arable land, not gold. Stories of Pilgrims and the first Thanksgiving notwithstanding, the English colonists mostly ignored the local Indian tribes. Calvinism preaches predestination. Cotton Mather and the other Massachusetts Bay Colony immigrants were fated for heaven, the Indians for hell. What was there to talk about? Each tribe was forced off its land to secure plantations where the English then wished nothing more but to be left alone. Acre by acre, they migrated, inward from the coast, tilling as they went.

The French took a third tack. After crossing the upper Atlantic, they found forests and rivers and snow of seemingly endless depth. Few French settlers were enticed by the rocky farms. No more than a couple hundred Troupes de la Marine were regularly garrisoned in New France at any one time. The handful of missionaries preferred cohabitation to war with the Indians. "We rove about with them and hunt with them and live among them without arms and without fear," wrote one Jesuit in 1611. The French did not wish to conquer or displace these tribes; they wanted partners. The native Huron and Algonquin possessed vastly superior technology—canoes instead of rowboats, snowshoes and toboggans instead of boots and wagons—to gain access to the north.

Jacques Cartier explored the mouth of the St. Lawrence in the early 1530s as the Spanish conquered empires much farther south. But after mapping the river—sailing as far inland as the rapids at Hochelaga, a fortified village of several thousand Iroquois—Cartier returned home. The country was too hard, too cold, too grim; Cartier called it "frightful and ill-shaped . . . the land God gave to Cain." His colony failed, the French were distracted, and they ignored the land for the rest of the century.

Samuel de Champlain returned seventy years later. In 1608, at the narrows of the St. Lawrence—a place known to the Algonquin as Kebec—his men felled two trees, lashed their trunks together into a cross, and set it in the ground to reclaim the land for Catholicism and France. Champlain traveled extensively upriver and discovered the village of Hochelaga abandoned. There, in 1611, before the founding of New Amsterdam or the landing of the Pilgrims, he established a trading post that would become Montreal.

The French grew close to the Huron and Algonquin. In 1610, Champlain and the Huron traded wards, each sending a young man to live with the other. When Étienne Brûlé, the French youth, returned two years later, he dressed like a Huron and spoke like one too. The tribes asked for French help in their battles against the Iroquois to the south. Champlain said yes, and so began nearly a hundred years of continuous warfare.

Champlain, and the governors after him, made local alliances out of necessity. King Louis XIV, the Sun King, was more interested in building Versailles than in conquering America. The French footprint remained small, and New France proved stubbornly difficult to monetize. In 1542, Cartier was mocked for bringing "diamonds" back to France that were nothing but quartz. A century later, Voltaire dismissed the whole area as "several acres of snow." All that impenetrable icy forest eventually proved good for only one thing: not gold or land, but beaver fur.

Europe was crazed by beaver fur, an epidemic on the order of the Dutch obsession with tulips, though far more practical and useful. Fibrous beaver hair was scraped from pelts and, after a soak in mercury, molded into felt hats. All manner of hats, women's and men's, top hats and military caps, fashionable stovepipes and the tricornered "continental" made famous by American revolutionaries. Once European and Russian stocks were all but exterminated, beaver furs became the most sought-after commodity extracted from North America.

Montreal was the commercial hub, but the Huron and Algonquin delivered furs only sporadically. A venture to Montreal was risky, directly on the Iroquois warpath, though worth the trip, because iron pots and arrowheads were so superior to wood and bone. "In truth, my brother, the Beaver does everything to perfection. He makes us kettles, axes, swords, knives, and gives us drink and food without the trouble of cultivating the ground," said one Indian in 1637, according to his French stenographer.

But in their ongoing intertribal wars, the Iroquois were proving victorious. The Huron, the traditional traders along the Great Lakes, were nearly wiped out by 1650, and the Algonquin were forced to the north and west. Eventually, the French decided it was safer, and more effective, for white men to haul the furs and the Indians to stay in their lands to hunt. Some traders were officially licensed by the Crown, and some, including many forgotten French soldiers left to make their own way, were free agents and called themselves *coureurs de bois,* runners of the woods. All spent years at a time in the *pays d'en haut,* the upper country above Montreal, trading brandy and sewing awls for pelts. The mutually beneficial commerce was formalized in 1701, in the Great Peace. Montreal briefly doubled in size that summer, the leaders of so many Indian nations made the journey. To codify the pact, the French gave belts of wampum, and on a sheet of paper the chiefs drew pictures of sacred animals to sign their names, so that each nation honored the tradition of the other in a mutual display of respect.

Always in search of furs, the French used the rivers to move west. "In the canoes of the savages one can go without restraint, and quickly, everywhere," wrote Champlain in 1603. In this way, Montreal served as the launch point for expeditions that explored much of North America. But like their fellow Europeans, they were also caught up in a search for the Orient. In 1634, Jean Nicolet pushed inland as far as Lake Huron and took along a Chinese silk damask so he would be properly dressed for the royal court in Canton. Fifty years later, in 1682, the compulsive wanderer Robert de La Salle was sure he had found the river of the west, but instead he paddled the Mississippi to the Gulf of Mexico. Even the rapids just south of Montreal—"The water here is so swift that it could not be more so ... it is impossible to imagine one being able to go by boats through these falls," Champlain wrote in 1603—were named Lachine, for China. Whether earnestly or tongue in cheek, many thought the path to the Orient lay just around the next curve of the river.

The Jesuits and the *coureurs de bois* took the virtues and vices of European civilization into the far wilderness long before American colonists rebelled: across the Great Lakes, up to Lake Winnipeg, down the Ohio and Mississippi Rivers, up the Missouri, across the prairie, and to the Rocky Mountains. Hemmed in by the Appalachians, the Americans became sedentary farmers and turned their creative energies to protest. New France, in contrast, was full of highways. The St. Lawrence River was a mighty tree trunk, and its tributary rivers pushed like roots into the depth of the continent.

By the mid-eighteenth century, only 50,000 white *habitants* called Quebec home, while the thirteen colonies hosted over 1.5 million citizens. Left largely to make their own way, the *habitants* married the locals and crafted their own culture, blending so completely that to New Englanders the French and Indians had become nearly synonymous. The French stayed Catholic but added Indian ways in deference to the hard land. When the British invaded in 1759, closing out the French and Indian War, Major General James Wolfe, the British commander, wrote a letter to his mother to say that the French soldiers were the least of his troubles. "People must be of the profession to understand the disadvantages and difficulties we labour under arising from the uncommon natural strength of the country." To seize Quebec City, and thus New France, Wolfe's army ultimately crossed the St. Lawrence River in small boats and scaled the cliffs below the city. As he predicted, the terrain proved more challenging to overcome than the French marines; the ensuing battle lasted only fifteen minutes, though Wolfe was mortally wounded. In Benjamin West's famous 1770 painting, *The Death of General Wolfe*, the eponymous leader falls Christlike, attended by a retinue of officers. All are stationary and bowed in grief except two. Sir William Johnson—Warraghiyagey, One Who Does Much—sprints into the frame, a shock of industrious energy, dressed in the coat of an Englishman and the beaded breeches and moccasins of an Indian. Next to him, an Iroquois warrior looks on quizzically and wonders what is to come.

Montreal was seized the next year, a formality. The British officially claimed the whole territory via treaty in 1763. When Quebec fell, the *habitants* shrugged. Paris had never treated them particularly well anyway. Similarly, the new British rulers found their new French citizens, often called Canadiens, easier to work with than their own colonists to the south.

The long war had been bad for commerce, but slowly the fur trade resumed. English and Scottish and American merchants stepped into the shoes of the French *bourgeois* businessmen. They reopened the old routes, rediscovered the old posts rotting away in the *pays d'en haut*. There was money to be made, with only a few accommodations to the new reality required. British West Indian rum replaced French brandy, but otherwise the trade was back.

———

Alexander Mackenzie clerked for John Gregory for six years. Sitting at a tall wooden desk, keeping the books of the countinghouse, Mackenzie grew from a teenager into a confident man, tall and fit, a shock of wavy hair, cleft chin, bright eyes. "A constitution and frame of body equal to the most arduous undertakings," he wrote in his journal, treating the matter as fact, not boast.

Those years observing the fur trade left an overwhelming impression on Mackenzie. His interests now lay completely in "commercial views," "mercantile pursuits," and "perilous enterprise." Fortunately, he thought himself "endowed by Nature with an inquisitive mind and enterprising spirit."

As a clerk, it was Mackenzie's job to order "coarse woollen cloths of different kinds; milled blankets of different sizes; arms and ammunition; twist and carrot tobacco; Manchester goods; lines, and coarse sheetings; thread, lines, and twine; common hardware; cutlery and ironmongery of several descriptions; kettles of brass and copper, and sheet-iron; silk and cotton handkerchiefs; hats, shoes and hose; calicoes and printed cottons, etc etc etc." All of these goods came from British manufacturers, and in exchange Mackenzie's house shipped the furs of lynx, bear, wolverine, fox, fisher, raccoon, otter, wolf, muskrat, elk, marten, deer, mink, buffalo, and beaver. As many beaver as they could, more beaver skins than all the rest combined.

The business was one of credit; to make any money, one had to be wealthy already and willing to risk the loss. A cartel was required, partnerships between interior traders and principals in Montreal. Mackenzie's boss, Mr. Gregory, required a counterpart at the northern forts to handle the retail end of the trade, while he managed transfer of the pelts to London.

The cycle of the fur business went like this: In October, Mackenzie ordered trade goods from England, twenty months before they were scheduled to be shipped inland from Montreal. Packed into their ninety-pound *pièces*, taken upriver two summers following, they were exchanged at the *rendezvous* in Grand Portage for furs that had been skinned the previous winter. Those furs arrived in Montreal in the fall and were then shipped to London, with payment returning the next spring. The whole process was interminably slow. Mackenzie calculated that Montreal merchants did not receive their profits until "forty-two months after the goods were ordered in Canada." When he did the books for 1780, Mackenzie noted that the blankets and awls sold by the *bourgeois* had to be ordered in 1778, but Mr. Gregory would not receive final payment from London until 1782.

Even more frustrating, many of those furs were actually bound for China. Mackenzie saw that if there were a way to send the furs directly from the interior to those Asian markets, skipping London entirely, they could cut payment time nearly in half.

But no one had yet found such a northwest passage.

Besides tallies of manufactured goods and furs, Mackenzie kept the pay records for the men who paddled the canoes to the *rendezvous*. "The Goers and Comers," he called them, who made the circuit from Montreal to Grand Portage and back each summer. Most voyageurs were veterans of the French system who easily transitioned to new British masters. Their boats were known as *canots de maître*, or master canoes, and they were enormous. Thirty-six feet long, six foot at the beam, but weighing only six hundred pounds, a cedar skeleton sheeted with white birch bark. Fore and aft, the ends of the canoe curled up in large fiddleheads, to cut waves on the water and, when tipped upside down onshore, provide supports to create shelter at night. It was an Algonquin design, invented thousands of years before Mesopotamians discovered the wheel, gradually perfected since antiquity. Not only were canoes faster than European longboats with sailors at the oars, but the paddlers could see where they were going. On the best days, each canoe carried eight thousand pounds of goods over a hundred miles.

In his accountant's ledger, Mackenzie marked each voyageur's home parish and pay based upon his position in the canoe: as a *devant*, the guide in the nose, a *gouvernail*, the steersman in the back, or *milieux*, the middlemen, who powered the boat through ceaseless toil. Each man was provided with one blanket, one white shirt, one pair of trousers, and a journey's worth of pipe tobacco, plus a quart of beans and one pound of grease a day.

Death by drowning or fall or strangulated hernia was common, and back wages or debts had to be settled with the widowed families. All of this was tallied as well.

———

In 1779, Mackenzie witnessed an unprecedented shipment of furs arrive from the *rendezvous* in Grand Portage. They had come via the American named Peter Pond and were like nothing anyone had ever seen. Enormous furs, and thick, luxurious, as could be produced only by beaver facing the harshest cold. *Castor gras*, the French called them: the furs of beaver at winter's height. Pond had so many furs, the rumors went, that he couldn't even ship them all. "Twice as many furs as his canoes could carry," Mackenzie had heard. Pond had to stash some up north, to save for the next year's run, so great was the bounty.

Pond had secured the furs from a far-off place called Athabasca, "a country hitherto unknown but from Indian report," wrote Mackenzie. Pond had led a brigade of canoes up the English River the summer before and, following the direction of his Cree partners, made the arduous portage into a new northern watershed. He and his voyageurs were the first white men to ever carry the route.

Pond himself did not travel to Montreal with the furs, turning around at the *rendezvous* to return quickly to the north instead. But his partners were the talk of the town, as if conquering heroes. "You would be amazed," Washington Irving wrote, quoting a Montreal resident of the time, "if you saw how lewd these peddlers are when they return; how they feast and game, and how prodigal they are, not only in their clothes, but upon their sweethearts. Such of them as are married have the wisdom to retire to their own houses; but the bachelors act just as an East Indiaman and pirates are wont to do; for they lavish, eat, drink, and play all away as long as the goods hold out."

Alexander Mackenzie learned that the farther north one went, the farther west, the greater the trials, the greater the furs, the greater the legend upon returning home.

In 1783, to capitalize on Pond's discoveries, several Montreal traders formed a new partnership to fund the construction of new forts in this far northern region. They called it the North West Company, and the main organizers were two English brothers, Benjamin and Joseph Frobisher, and Simon McTavish, the richest man in Montreal. But John Gregory, Mackenzie's patron, was left out of the new venture, and his partner, James Finlay, decided to retire the same year. Suddenly on his own, Gregory formed a new house with a Mr. Normand MacLeod and named it, predictably, Gregory, MacLeod & Company.

MacLeod was from the island of Skye, just south of Mackenzie's birthplace of Stornoway. He had been an officer in the garrison at Fort Niagara following the French and Indian War, learned to trade furs under Sir William Johnson, and bought land near Detroit in 1774. Over the next decade, he traded furs there and at Fort Michilimackinac, on the upper Great Lakes. While the North West Company risked its investment in the north, Gregory, MacLeod & Company decided to exploit these well-established routes to the south.

The American rebellion was concluding. Optimism abounded, and Gregory had an offer for Mackenzie, fully apprenticed and ready to strike out on his own. The firm would supply Mackenzie with "a small adventure of goods," allowing him "to seek my fortune in Detroit."

Mackenzie did not need to be asked twice, and the decision was made easier by his orphanhood. After their losses in the Mohawk valley, John Johnson's Royal Yorkers had retreated to Carleton Island, a flat slab of rock at the place where Lake Ontario meets the St. Lawrence. There they constructed a new garrison, Fort Haldimand, built ships in the natural harbor, and launched a few small raids against patriot villages, but to little effect. Corc Mackenzie, the tacksman, died not in battle but of scurvy in his sickbed. He was forty-nine years old.

Before Alexander left for Detroit, he wrote to his childhood playmate, his cousin Roderic, to ask him to join him in the New World. After the death of his father and brother, Roderic was not only his closest male kin but also his confidant and confessor. Alexander suggested a clerkship for Roderic at Gregory, MacLeod & Company. The two young men could make their fortunes together.

And so that summer of 1784, Roderic took a ship from Scotland to Montreal, and Alexander did the same to Detroit. Martial law still held on Lakes Erie and Ontario, the English having closed the waters to commercial traffic, so Alexander boarded one of His Majesty's military vessels and sailed inland.

Detroit, 1784

wwwww

Alexander Mackenzie, a twenty-two-year-old fur-buying agent carrying a small cache of trade goods on his first independent venture, held no illusions about the hinterlands of North America.

"This trade was carried on in a very distant country," he wrote of the endeavor, "out of the reach of legal restraint, and where there was a free scope given to any ways or means of gaining advantage."

Ships bound for Detroit sailed from Montreal up the St. Lawrence River and into Lake Ontario. At that watery junction lie thousands of granite islands, including the one that housed the grave of Mackenzie's father. Lake Ontario was Alexander's first introduction to the freshwater seas of the continent, deep and gray. At the far western end they turned south for the Niagara River and the crumbling French castle that guarded its mouth.

When Mackenzie passed Fort Niagara, the château still bore the scars from Sir William Johnson's decisive seizure in 1759 and was ill-manned by a crew of British redcoat holdouts. As his ship plied upriver, the water turned a shocking emerald green, aerated by the falls ahead. Their destination was the Lower Landing, the start of the path around the great cataract of the Niagara.

The portage was a mile and a half long, up and across a two-hundred-foot embankment to avoid the swirling water of the gorge. War or not, the portage somehow kept operating. For a time, it was run by a mixed-blood man named Chabert Joncaire, who owned a trading post and paid two hundred Seneca twenty cents each to carry *pièces* up the escarpment. But that French and Seneca system fell to Johnson's Mohawk and was replaced by windlasses and farm labor, then a wide road cut by the English at the direction of Johnson. Oxcarts and horses, monopolized by the Stedman brothers, dragged the goods by the time Mackenzie arrived. At the Upper Landing, above the waterfall, were the wreckage of burned French ships, and two more small forts on the opposing banks of the river. The whole Niagara Frontier was still militarized from almost thirty years of war.

Upstream, Mackenzie passed the Isle de Grande and then entered the mouth of Lake Erie, where he boarded a new brig of war. The shallowest of the Great Lakes, Erie was known as a ship graveyard, a place of sudden violent squalls, so it would be with great relief that Mackenzie arrived at Detroit a few days later. Against the current and the west wind, the entire trip, from Montreal to Detroit, could take several weeks.

At this fortified outpost flying the British flag, Mackenzie was greeted by fifteen-foot-tall cedar and oak pickets. An array of six-pound guns guarded each gate, and two more batteries overlooked the river. The surrounding lands were thick with orchards and farms and encampments of Indians, each segregated by their tribe, but Detroit itself stood alone as a muddy armed camp.

The British ruled, but like Montreal, Detroit was a French town, and distinctly so, though only a sliver of the former. In every measure of importance, it proved lacking: population, wealth, growth, communication to the outside world. Montreal was the grand stone commercial capital of England's North American enterprise, while Detroit was a timber backwater full of miscreants and rebellious Indians.

The commander of the fort was Major William Ancrum, a petty man known for tyrannizing the French settlers. One day, walking near the river, Ancrum purposely kicked over a bucket of water carried by a lowly *habitant*. When the major overheard the man say that if it wasn't for his "red coat, he'd give him a flogging," Ancrum, a boxer, took off his jacket and then beat the man with his bare fists.

———

On July 24, 1701, while commanding a flotilla of twenty-five canoes, Antoine de la Mothe, Sieur de Cadillac, a busybody French aristocrat and veteran of the inland fur trade, was moved by the scene he observed on the riverbank: a hardwood forest canopy draped in grapevines, abounding with "timid deer and faun," "apples and plums," turkey, partridge, woodcock, "golden pheasant," and "wooly buffaloes, of magnificent size and proportion." It all formed "a charming perspective, which sweetens the sad lonesomeness of the solitude."

Cadillac was not in search of an idyll, though; he traveled for reasons of military necessity, not sport. He led fifty French soldiers, clad in blue uniforms, and fifty farmers and voyageurs, and they had come to build a settlement on the northern bank of that river, at the place that "opens and closes the door of passage" to the great inland seas of Huron, Michigan, and Superior. At the site Cadillac chose, the river narrowed into a strait. *De troit*. The name stuck.

The French spent the summer erecting a palisade of sharpened oak trunks, a sturdy inner fort, and a church dedicated to Saint Anne, who would grant them all protection. Huron refugees, long granted sanctuary by the Jesuits, settled to the west of the village. "They are an exceedingly industrious nation. They hardly dance at all," read a contemporary report. Cadillac invited more nations, and by the second winter he was joined by thousands of other Indians, whom he meant to pacify through marriage and alcohol. "All the villages of our savages are only Taverns, as regards drunkenness; and Sodoms, as regards immorality," one priest complained of Cadillac's policy.

Immoral or not, Cadillac thought communion would bring peace. He was wrong. The fort was attacked constantly; the church burned down only two years later.

Disgruntled Ottawa Indians, who the French believed were allies, struck first, setting fire to half the fort, including the homes of the Recollet priests and Cadillac himself. Then, in 1706, the dog of a French officer bit an Ottawa man. Retaliations followed: the Indian beat the dog, the French officer killed the Ottawa, the tribe ambushed six Miami—partners of the French—and took a Recollet priest hostage. They released the priest, but in the confusion that followed, the French opened fire on the Ottawa tribe, killing thirty, and the priest as well, as he struggled back to the fort's gate.

In August 1707, Cadillac hosted a council of chiefs, to soothe relations and persuade them to leave Detroit in peace. It didn't work. The Fox and Moscoutin, raiding Detroit from lands to the west, laid siege in 1712. The garrison was almost empty, and the townsfolk burned their own church this time, to keep it from being desecrated. But a relief force arrived, an extraordinary alliance of Ottawa, Huron, Potawatomi, Illinois, Missouri, and Osage. "Casting my eyes toward the woods, I saw the army of the nations of the south issuing from it," the French commandant wrote later. "Detroit never saw such a collection of people." Every male member of the Fox and Moscoutin party was killed, and a thousand women and children were taken into slavery.

Detroit was a strategic larder, providing corn and wheat to fuel the *pays d'en haut* fur trade, but also a place of disease, and the town's overall population stayed stubbornly small. Smallpox swept through in 1734 and 1752, and famine soon after, when crops either failed or were diverted to government soldiers. In November 1760, the end of the French and Indian War, a British force of a few dozen rangers easily captured Detroit. They were dressed like Mohican, armed with hatchets and snowshoes, and they relied on stealth for victory. The rangers were led by Major Robert Rogers, and through his Rules for Ranging he had taught them to walk single file in snow but abreast through the swamps, to avoid river fords, to never sleep past dawn, to ambush with surprise. The British settled into occupation, and many French settlers left for St. Louis, leaving behind a mix of soldiers, voyageurs and *coureurs de bois,* African and Indian chattel slaves, and Huron huddled in wigwams outside the stockade walls.

Rogers considered the Northwest Passage a "moral certainty" and believed that he was standing in the nexus of Aristotle's balanced earth. From the Great Lakes, massive rivers flowed in three cardinal directions: the Mississippi to the Gulf of Mexico in the south, the St. Lawrence to the Atlantic in the east, and the Nelson, which Rogers called the "Christino," to Hudson's Bay and the Arctic in the north. It would only make sense that a great river also flowed west to the Pacific. He called it the River Ouregan, and he ordered several of his rangers to find it. They had barely passed over the Grand Portage, at the western edge of Lake Superior, before they returned home in defeat. For organizing the journey without the consent of the Crown, Rogers was charged with treason, and though acquitted of that charge, he was later arrested a second time for trying to secure an officer's commission from both the British and the patriot Continental Army during the American Revolution.

As the rulers of Detroit, the British could be cruel. "We will soon see that half of the inhabitants deserve the gallows," wrote the new garrison commander. They considered the *habitants* "a lazy, idle people" who had lost all civilized decorum. "It is not uncommon to see a Frenchman with Indian shoes and stockings, without breeches, wearing a strip of woolen cloth to cover what decency requires him to conceal," noted one Englishman. Ignorant of protocol and dismissive of custom, the British stopped providing gifts—some ceremonial, like pipes, and some new-found staples, like gunpowder and wool—to the local tribes. In response, the Seneca and Huron plotted to massacre the entire garrison in 1761 but were foiled by a force led by Sir William Johnson. When the Ottawa chief, Pontiac, raised a full rebellion in 1763, Rogers led ranger volunteers to break the siege.

Detroit remained a primitive, boorish outpost. In a letter dated 1776, the town's British lieutenant governor and superintendent of Indian affairs, Henry Hamilton, described his farmers as "careless and very igno-rant." During the American rebellion, Hamilton could spare few trained soldiers to guard his out-of-the-way fort, so he relied on new Indian allies instead. Hamilton was known as the "Hair-Buyer General," for purchasing scalps from Shawnee war parties that raided Ohio, Kentucky, and Penn-sylvania. After one such raid, in 1778, the frontier fighter Daniel Boone was brought before Hamilton as a prisoner of war. Hamilton already held hundreds of American prisoners—so many that they boarded with local families and were allowed to walk the streets freely—so he returned Boone to his Shawnee captors, to avoid the hassle the already-famous man's presence would cause.

The British were defeated, but they didn't leave. In 1783, the new American secretary of war dispatched a man named Ephraim Doug-lass to Detroit, to give wampum to the local tribes to make peace and to deliver the news to the British of the American victory. Once he arrived at the fort, he handed over his letter to the governor, but it had no effect.

"Though he knew from the King's Proclamation that the war with America was at an end," Douglass wrote in a letter, "he had had no offi-cial information to justify his supposing the States extended to this place, and therefore could not consent to the Indians being told so." The British commander sent Douglass back home.

Alexander Mackenzie arrived the next year. Detroit had barely grown in eighty years—within the walls were little more than five acres—and was still a violent, unpacified place. The British were quick with the noose; once, rival fur traders were hanged for stabbing each other. Other men were hanged for selling liquor to the Indians or *not* selling liquor to the Indians, depending on the whims of the governor, the sole law of the land.

Fear of the Indian drove much of daily Detroit life. The gates opened at sunrise and closed at nine o'clock, and within the walls no Indian was allowed to carry a knife or tomahawk, or gather in large groups, or remain after dark. Outside the fortified town, farms hugged the riverbank, each only a few hundred feet wide, thin like a ribbon with one end dipped in the river. In this way, every *habitant* had access to water but could also quickly reach the safety of the walls in case of attack.

And yet Mackenzie's mission was to meet and trade with these tribes. In its way, Detroit was as much a great mixture of diverse peoples as New York. There were Seneca, Miami, Potawatomi, Huron, Ottawa, Chippewa, Shawnee, and Taway, as well as Moravian missionaries to tend to them. The traders were Scots, British, Irish, French, Spanish, and American Yankees, and almost one man in ten was an African slave. The Catholic church stood next to a Masonic hall, and down the narrow street was the Council House for official meetings with the tribes.

Mackenzie had been entrusted with only a few trade goods, mostly consumables, because the market for durable items had passed: alcohol, gunpowder, and highly regarded Brazilian twist tobacco, a braided rope sold in sections that were the size, shape, color, and smell of dog turds. Mackenzie proved himself adept at navigating the trade, alone against rivals, and despite a lousy market. One of his competitors, the experienced American trader Alexander Henry, reported that year that "the Detroit trade has been very bad." The area was trapped out, the shipping still unreliable due to wartime restrictions.

But Mackenzie successfully gained his boss's confidence and soon got important news, Normand MacLeod himself traveling to Detroit to deliver it. The firm was shifting its focus away from Detroit and the Mississippi valley of America, following the lead of the North West Company. Gregory, MacLeod & Company would go north, where the fortunes were greater and the territory effectively unclaimed; there was no British or American presence to dodge above the Great Lakes.

What's more, as part of the move, MacLeod was offering something else. "That I should be admitted a partner in this business," Mackenzie wrote, "on condition that I would proceed to the Indian country in the following spring, 1785." Plans called for his cousin Roderic, the new apprentice clerk in the firm, to be dispatched to the north as well. The two best friends could reunite at the great *rendezvous* at Grand Portage. Upon being offered such an opportunity, Mackenzie, with the proper reserve of a gentleman, "readily assented to it."

Alexander left Detroit in the spring, sailing north through Lake Huron before turning west for Fort Michilimackinac and the St. Marys River. At the same time, Roderic left Montreal on a canoe brigade via the Ottawa River, the traditional route to the *pays d'en haut*, used by *coureurs de bois* and voyageurs for nearly three hundred years, and the Huron and Algonquin for thousands of years before that.

Roderic would note each and every step of this freshwater staircase. The Scot had never seen anything like it, and for good reason. Such an inland passage is unknown anywhere else in the world.

———

It was early June 1785, and the rivers above Montreal, finally free from ice, were in full flood. The canoe brigades embarked from Lachine, the boats and goods dragged by horses to avoid the rapids on the St. Lawrence that formed a barricade to the south.

That spring, Gregory, MacLeod & Company sent a total of eight canoes with ninety men into the interior: 750 gallons of rum, 64 gallons of wine, 99 rifles, and 3,300 pounds of gunpowder, all wrapped in white cloth, squared into *pièces* for easy transport. Roderic saw that the birch-bark *canots de maître* were still only two-thirds full after such lading, leaving room for "six hundred weight of biscuit, two hundred weight of pork, three bushels of pease, for the men's provision; two oil cloths to cover the goods, a sail, an axe, a towing-line, a kettle, and a sponge to bail out the water."

When they launched, the men onshore fired rifles into the air as a departing salute, and the voyageurs responded with the whoops of the Iroquois and Algonquin. In a dozen miles, at the southern tip of the Île de Montréal, Roderic and the men turned northwest, toward the Lake of Two Mountains, and, unloading the boats, floated the empty canoes through the light rapids. There sat a small stone chapel, dedicated to Anne, the mother of the Virgin and their patron saint. The men put a penny in the offering box, and Roderic thought he ought to as well. They received a final blessing, attending their final Mass prostrate on the ground, and then, loading the boats and paddling to camp at the far end of the lake, finished that day's journey by drinking their final cask of rum.

Up the Ottawa River. The channel narrowed, the land rose, farmers' fields were left behind, and then came the Long Sault, twelve miles of rapids and cascades, in three sets—the first and second Portage de Chaudière, then the Portage de Chats. The first waterfall was a twenty-five-foot tumble "over cragged, excavated rocks, in a most wild, romantic manner," Roderic wrote. Another fell nearby, as a curtain. All the men doffed their toques in respect to Adam Dollard des Ormeaux and his sixteen volunteers, who died on that spot in 1660. They had fought the Iroquois there for a week, to stop them from reaching their families in Montreal. Eight of the men were killed in battle, and the remaining nine were captured, tortured, and eaten.

The Long Sault required the first portage of the journey. To carry the *pièces* on their backs, the voyageurs used tumplines—broad straps across their foreheads—as the Algonquin had taught them. Two ninety-pound *pièces* to a man, sometimes three. And they didn't walk; they trotted. A dog's canter. When the portage was long, they dropped their loads at intermediate *pauses* and leapfrogged the baggage. Because each *milieu* was responsible for six *pièces*, he ran the portage a total of five times.

Roderic counted every step of the first Portage de Chaudière. Six hundred and forty-three paces. He counted every other portage as well. Seven hundred paces, then 740 paces, then 274 paces. The rock was black, the rapids thatched with dead tree limbs. Above one waterfall, the tight tree canopy hung over the water, along the shore, and the voyageurs pulled themselves in the canoes branch to branch, hand over hand.

The *devant* in the nose of the canoe was always on the lookout for *le fil d'eau*, the easiest water to face. Against the current they paddled. Against riffles they poled. Against rapids they executed a *décharge*, unloading the goods but pulling the canoe through with a strong line. Against falls they finally relented and portaged. Anything to keep the boat in the water; even fully loaded, a *canot de maître* could make four miles an hour against the current, but only a net rate of half a mile an hour over land, when carried by four men. Roderic counted sixteen *décharges* and portages on the four-hundred-mile Ottawa River; the longest, Grand Calumet, was 2,035 paces.

The voyageurs woke before the sun and paddled until dark. On a full moon, they worked through the night. They ate a mash of peas, suet, lard, and cornmeal, boiled to remove the husk. Also *galette*, bread made from pouring water into salt and flour, kneaded into pancakes and fried in a pan. Their paddles were short and colorful like them, long blades and stubby shafts. When in full song, they could swing those paddles once a second, every second, all day.

"*Quand un chrétien se détermine / A voyager / Faut bien penser qu'il se destine / A des dangers,*" one song began. "When a Christian decides to voyage, he must think of the dangers that will beset him. A thousand times Death will approach him, a thousand times he will curse his lot during the trip."

Then the song turned, to address each man personally. "Friend, do you plan to travel on the water, amid the winds, and where the waves and tempest menace?"

At Rivière Creuse, where the riverbed dropped to unimaginable depths and around them the rock rose to corresponding heights, a sandy point stuck out from the western shore, and the canoes pulled over for a special ceremony. When the Indians passed the place, they shot arrows with twists of tobacco at the cliffs and water as a sacrifice. The voyageurs, though, had named the place Pointe au Baptême. They told Roderic that because it was his virgin run, he needed to be dunked in the water and blessed with pine boughs, and then each man demanded a *regale* of rum before he would move on.

Leaving the Ottawa, the brigades turned up a small branch, the Petite Rivière, where eleven more portages and *décharges* awaited. The worst carry was Mauvais de Musique, where, lifting the boat between boulders, the men often slipped and were mangled by falling canoes. The way was narrow now, the forest crushed tight to the river, and near one shin-breaking waterfall lay the Porte de l'Enfer, a cave in the rock wall rimmed with dried blood. The voyageurs told Roderic that within that gate lay hell and a creature that feasted on men lost in the rapids.

But relief came at the end of that small river. The view opened, for they had attained the height of land, as they pressed through swampy headwaters. On the horizon were hills of rock that Roderic thought had "the appearance of having been over-run by fire." Like his Scottish Highlands home, but stripped of the heather. They gained long Lake Nipissing, speckled with islands at its western exit, and then Rivière des

Français, where they could toss aside their setting poles with relish. For the first time they were heading downstream.

"There is hardly a foot of soil to be seen from one end of the French river to the other," Roderic wrote. Nothing but pink granite and stunted trees; seventy miles with the current, they ran it in one day. Even the river mouth looked petrified, the water leaking through tiny rock channels before finally spilling into Georgian Bay. A gale came on, and Lalonde, the guide of Roderic's brigade, ordered every canoe to shore. "In less than half an hour, our tents were down about our ears and our baggage in a moment deluged with rain," Roderic said.

It was here, at this bay—in the "dreary wilderness," wrote Roderic—where the French River and Lake Huron meet, that the cousins' paths finally overlapped. Roderic in a canoe, Alexander on his ship, but each making for the summer *rendezvous* of 1785 at the Grand Portage.

Into the Pays d'en Haut, Spring 2016

〰〰〰

I went searching for Alexander Mackenzie—in the great cities he had walked in their infancies, in museums and historical sites, on the water route of his earliest travels—and I did not find him until the French River. Fitting, that kinship should start on the edge of the rocky Canadian Shield, where the north begins and Alexander Mackenzie joined up with the upper country's main voyageur trunk line for the first time.

In New York City, I walked the twisting alleys of old lower Manhattan on an early spring day, the kind of day on which the Mackenzies landed on the *Peace & Plenty*. It was raining—drizzle as a minimum, followed by the occasional downpour—and unlike most locals I had failed to remember to bring an umbrella. New York has largely shed its brick colonial past in favor of glass banking towers. The Liberty Pole at the Common has been replaced by City Hall, the gun batteries by Battery Park, the fortifications by ticket booths selling Statue of Liberty cruises. The lone remaining icons are loomed over by the titan Wall Street firms; how does any sun even reach the grass of Bowling Green, whose fence once provided lead for patriot bullets? The curry-yellow Fraunces Tavern, target of an HMS *Asia* cannonball in 1775, was locked up tight, so in the rain I quickly pressed uptown along Broadway, which is exactly that. In Mackenzie's day, it was the major route to the farms that fed the town. Now the Canyon of Heroes leads to Nolita and SoHo, and plates pressed in the sidewalks name the celebrities who have been feted there, presidents and kings and the '62 Yankees and the Apollo astronauts. Old colonial Broadway ends at St. Paul's, at Fulton Street. I ducked inside, to get out of the weather, and found myself in the middle of a choir's a cappella concert. The church was half-full; we were all taking refuge from the storm. Along the walls of the plain square chapel were historical displays: mementos left by the firefighters who responded to the World Trade Center on 9/11; the pew where George Washington knelt in prayer before his inauguration in 1789. Mackenzie was in the far, far north by then.

Nor did I find Mackenzie at Fort Niagara. That French castle is full of wood smoke and costumed actors, but despite the promises of the brochures I find the history at such places to be less alive than reanimated, cobbled together and zombielike. There is too much "re-" in reenactor. People tend to save wedding dresses, not jeans, so everyone dressed in "authentic" clothing looks like they are bound for a ball. And no matter how many times the kindly gentleman behind the restored wooden counter declared himself the *bourgeois* of the trading post, that didn't make him so.

Similarly, south of the fort, along the trade corridor of the Niagara River, few hints remain. There's a popular ice cream stand at the lower end of the old portage path around Niagara Falls, and at the upper end the intakes for the largest hydroelectric plant in the northeastern United States. Continue upstream, you reach my home. I live on an island in the Niagara River: Grand Island, only fancied Isle de Grande in online advertisements. One warm spring day, my father and I took his canoe out to faux-play voyageur reenactors ourselves. We launched a mile from my house, paddled the old route down along the western side of the island. The view was pretty in the sparkling light, but the Canadian and American shores are coated with McMansions, and invasive species besides. Farther upstream, the river narrows at present-day Buffalo, the French's Beau Fleuve. But at the city's red-tiled water intake, one finds the strength of industry, not wooden ships or supple canoes. There is a tremendous converging current here, so strong that Erie Canal barges found the Niagara River impossible to use; a separate adjacent channel had to be dug instead. The Peace Bridge spans the area now, tall enough to allow cargo ships to pass underneath. At the base of each support pillar is a massive ironclad wedge that splits the waters into tumbling white boils, like the prow of a ship sailing ever on against the current.

In these long-settled places, I was not surprised to find nothing of Mackenzie; I had visited these, and his other haunts, many times before. The St. Lawrence Seaway is managed for container ships bearing iron ore and grain. Detroit long ago paved over its colonial footprint. South of Montreal, there is still a church at St. Anne, but it is a new one, and the old portage path is covered by a train trestle and highway and a strip of fashionable restaurants; one bar, bearing Corona beer signs, is named Annie's.

No, when I pecked along Mackenzie's route, looking for a telltale sign, I did not find him until the French River, north of Toronto, north of Detroit, off the industrialized footprint. The granite of the Canadian Shield bursts from the ground, and in response the trees shrank like toy props in a train set. I drove north and—as the river approached—backward in time. Our cities naturally absorb and repurpose and build on top of. The view from the French, though, is nearly unchanged.

The tannin-stained water still flows. Spruce and cedar and birch line its shores. The voyageur paths are still open. I searched the riverbanks and identified all the runes of the *pays d'en haut:* lobstick and lichen and cairn.

The rock is the same. The genuine article, not a reenactment.

———

The woman who rented me the canoe to paddle the French River said I had to avoid Recollet Falls.

"Don't go up to it. A man drowned there, two summers ago," she said. "A boy was with him, his son, I think. Really sad."

An hour later, as I crouched in the illicit spray of the Recollet, I thought of that drowned man, and the dozens of voyageurs who must have preceded him. Recollet Falls is named for the order of French missionaries that helped Cadillac settle Detroit. They probably lost a priest here too. Maybe the first white casualty, thus the name.

By the time Roderic Mackenzie came through, it had been known as Recollet Falls for over a hundred years. "Recolet, forty-five paces" is all Roderic says about it. But why not count each step, I thought. He and Alexander spent the best years of their lives on little carrying trails like these.

"In several parts there are guts or channels, where the water flows with great velocity, which are not more than twice the breadth of a canoe," Roderic wrote of the river generally. Recollet Falls is one of those places, extending the width of the French River. Rocky outcrops squeeze the water into a few tumbling cataracts that drop ten or fifteen feet. It doesn't look like much on the map, but up close you can see the water churns back on itself in a frightening way. The river digs and digs, creating holes on the river bottom. Holes that keep whatever is placed within them, like the bodies of French priests and summer tourists.

Early that day, I had set up camp at one of the few destinations for those tourists, a small RV park at the end of a dirt road. It fronted the water and was a place for fishing and drinking, often at the same time, the locals using tiny skiffs with buzzy outboard motors. It was late spring, early in the season, and I was the only customer who wished to rent a canoe. The manager gave me an aluminum tub, the generic kind one would see prominently featured in a movie about summer camp. It was far too long, unwieldy to paddle alone, and when I sat in the back the nose lifted out of the water. Still, I wanted so much to get on the river, see the view the right way.

Henry David Thoreau understood. "Everyone must believe in something," he said. "I believe I'll go canoeing."

So I paid the woman ten dollars, pulled on my life vest, promised not to go to Recollet Falls, and then made it my primary destination; I was always the kid who had to touch the stove after being warned it was hot.

The French is a creature of the Canadian Shield, the ancient core of the continent exposed by relentless and patient geologic force. The river drains a segment of that mound of four-billion-year-old granite, and on a map the waterway looks fractured, as if the bowl holding Lake Nipissing cracked and is leaking down a seam in the rock.

The view from the canoe is different, though. The water is dark, like iced tea, the result of rain slowly steeping through dried leaves and pine needles. And the channel itself is a broad thoroughfare, a straight-as-an-arrow boulevard lined with high stone walls. It was like a modern limited-access highway but nature-made for canoe travel. The analogy is apt. The voyageurs formed a people-powered expressway, moving products in U-Haul-sized increments.

Alone in the canoe, using a double-bladed kayak paddle to keep the boat headed generally in the right direction, I carefully eased the nose out of the eddy into the current, shifting my weight. Everything was still. No waves, no wind, no birdcalls, no drifting clouds.

Soon I reached a small rapid, a crease across the river, swift and jumbled just enough to force me to the bank. The voyageurs would have cruised through without noticing, but alone, with no other human in sight, I got out and carefully walked, the moving water up to my knees. Using the old voyageur trick, I used a rope to line the boat through the treacherous rock garden. The danger here was not that I would be swept away but that my canoe would be, and then I would . . . what? Swim back to the campground? With the sheer rock walls, there was no shore to walk.

Once past the worst of the current, I hopped back in my canoe, paddling even as I sat down, to avoid drifting into the rapid. Soon, I could hear the Recollet, though I still couldn't see it. Such places usually bark worse than they bite, and when I arrived at the base of the falls, I found plenty of space to maneuver my boat toward the north side, a boulder field leading to a small slick ridge of rock at the rapid's base.

I sat alone with the water. The roar was calming in a hydropower-white-noise-machine sort of way. I wondered if I sat on the same silicon, potassium, iron, magnesium atoms that the voyageurs did. I wondered if they found the cataract calming as well; no way to know for sure, not a single letter survives from those illiterate men.

The Mackenzies were always practical, though, so then I tried to find the portage route. Forty-five paces, Roderic said. No way to lift the canoe up the sheer rock bank in the north. Did they go through the center, across one of the knobs of granite that formed islands between the rapids? And then beach their canoes on the same boulder field as I? These little wilderness paths reminded me of the escalator in the JFK Airport, between the main concourse and the AirTrain. When the world comes to New York City, they do not pass through any broad welcoming avenue. Rather, they negotiate a series of dingy choke points, subway turnstiles, and walkways. So too were these narrow portages, along the highway of their day.

Solo with a heavy aluminum canoe, I decided against experimenting with possible upstream portage routes myself. I turned around and returned to camp, lining again around the swift wrinkled water. Ten years ago, when I was still in my twenties, I would have run the small rapid, alone or not. Since then, I've learned a little discretion.

When I got back to the campground, someone had cranked up "Your Cheatin' Heart," put the stereo speakers out on the porch of the single-wide so everyone could hear. The original Hank Williams version, 1953, full reverb.

Compared with New York City, music is the most ephemeral of human footprints. And yet, where I intended to go, to follow Alexander Mackenzie to his unfortunate end, I'd leave even that behind too.

TO GRAND PORTAGE AND THE
ENGLISH RIVER, 1785

~~~~~~

The granite of Georgian Bay is a rosy gray, the barrier islands mounded like the backs of breaching whales. In the early summer heat, the black biting flies set up in clouds, and schools of their larva squirm in shallow pools in the rocky sand. When a person walks through the flies, the clouds attach themselves and follow until he submerses himself in the lake and swims away. "If I had not kept my face wrapped in cloth, I am almost sure they would have blinded me, so pestiferous and poisonous are the bites of these little demons," wrote one French traveler. "They make one look like a leper, hideous to behold. I confess this is the worst martyrdom I suffered in this country: hunger, thirst, weariness and fever are nothing to it. These little beasts not only persecute you all day but at night they get into your eyes and mouth, crawl under your clothes, or stick their long stings through them, and make such a noise that it distracts your attention, and prevents you from saying your prayers."

The voyageur route skirted the upper rim of the lake, hopping from island to island. Before sailing to the *rendezvous,* though, most ships and many canoes made the "Detour" to "the Westernmost military position which we have in this country," as Alexander Mackenzie wrote. Lakes Michigan, Huron, and Superior come together in a confusing jumble of straits, archipelagoes, rapids, and peninsulas. There is no Gibraltar, one strategic mass that controls all passes, and so the French and British built an iteration of forts and posts on various islands and shores. All bore variations on the same name, an attempt to latinize the Ojibwa name for the great turtle that slept in the bay: Michilimackinac, Mackinac, Mackinaw.

In 1675, the Jesuit missionary Jacques Marquette left Fort Michilimackinac, paddling west and south. He was searching for a route to the

Pacific, a northwest passage. Marquette paddled into a bay along Lake Michigan's western shore, followed a small stream up a series of rapids and portages, and then discovered a great river flowing south. He was in the land of the Illinois; French explorers later called it the "most beautiful that is known between the mouth of the Saint Lawrence and that of the Mississippi." The primary virtues cited for the majesty of this idyllic place? Good soil, and plenty to eat.

Marquette followed the river into the humid deciduous lowlands, and when it finally became clear he was going in the wrong direction, fear of attack—by the Spanish or Indian tribes or both—forced him back. But he never made it home. Marquette died on the eastern shore of Lake Michigan and was abandoned there until the Illinois gathered his bones and returned them to Mackinac, where they were buried at the mission along the shore.

By the time Alexander Mackenzie arrived, Marquette had been dead for over a century, his mission long since burned, his grave lost. These abandoned Jesuit outposts, when the voyageurs could find them, were treated with reverence, but Alexander himself had little use for the missionaries. They "should have been contented to improve the morals of their own countrymen," he wrote.

Fort Michilimackinac was a place of mixed loyalties: like Detroit, a British fort on newly American soil, surrounded by Indian encampments trading furs and seeking gifts. Mackenzie thought that the British behaved nobly, but not the Americans, who paid the Indians "very little attention, and tell them that they keep possession of their country by right of conquest." The Americans promised only that they will be "friends with them while they deserve it."

But it was a good place for a logistics post. White birch and cedar, the essentials of canoe construction, grew everywhere. The brigades took on additional provisions, some for the remainder of their journey on Lake Superior, some to deliver to Grand Portage. They traded their peas and pork lard for fish and maple sugar, a welcome, though temporary, dietary change. Roderic's brigade was in a hurry and skipped Fort Michilimackinac, but Alexander's ship couldn't sail up the rapids at Sault Sainte Marie, so he stopped to transfer to a canoe. Up and around the peninsula, Alexander passed a village on the south side of the *sault*, a mix of Algonquin and white *habitants*, that appeared to him to spend "one half of the year starving, and the other half intoxicated." It had dwindled with the region's failing fur trade, and like Detroit, these lands were all trapped out.

Alexander found that Lake Superior "justifies the name that has been given to it." He thought it "the largest and most magnificent body of fresh water in the world" and the "grand reservoir of the River St. Laurence." He marveled at the great varieties of berries and bear and moose and fish, and measured the distance from St. Marys to Grand Portage as 160 leagues along the coast.

They followed the lake's northern edge, often through fog, along cliffs taller than any they had yet seen—"a continued mountainous embankment of rock," Alexander called it—nearly a thousand feet above the water. The granite was black and deep purple in the peaks, pale gray near the waterline, and there the Ojibwa painted the story of their people's migration from the east. The stone canvas depicted tiny vermilion men in canoes, fleeing Mishipeshu, the master of the waters, half lynx and half serpent, clawed and horned, scaled and spiked tailed, with the call of a churning cataract. Mishipeshu lived in the deepest part of the deepest lake and raised storms, and only specific ceremonies would placate the beast. Failure to sacrifice generous offerings ensured a canoe-wrecking tempest.

As they approached the western end of the lake, the land in the distance bore the profile of a giant asleep. Bulbous, lumpy mountains speckled the coast. The voyageurs cleaned up, shaved, donned new shirts. They were nearing the end.

At the end of the last bay—the forest pushed back to form an "amphitheater," Alexander thought—at the foot of the Grand Portage, a temporary city the size of Detroit. The *rendezvous*.

———

After more than a decade apart, Alexander and Roderic were finally reunited. They had not seen each other since they were children in Scotland, and now they were up-and-coming businessmen, agents of the same fur company, making their way in the wilderness. Alexander was eager for the opportunity, Roderic less so, complaining that there were so few bunkhouses, "I often made the *comptoir* [the counter] my pillow."

It was Alexander's first experience with the "licentiousness of manners" of the voyageurs when in full drunken revelry. He thought that they indulged themselves "in extravagance and dissipation during the short space of one month in twelve or fifteen," and in so doing "generally contrived to squander away all their gains," as if in those brief *rendezvous* moments they could balance out what they had been deprived of the rest of the year.

In 1785, only two dozen or so total *bourgeois* traded in the north, and the *rendezvous* was young Alexander's chance to meet and interact with the businessmen he had only heard about. All except Peter Pond, the American who had famously shipped the first Athabascan furs in 1778. Pond skipped that year's meeting, traveling all the way back to Montreal, an odd and unexplained choice.

But Alexander did meet the veteran *bourgeois* John Ross and Peter Pangman, the partners whom Gregory and MacLeod took on to manage the northern venture. The two men had worked together for years and owned their own storehouse at the *rendezvous*. Pangman was from New Jersey, forty-one years old, and their most experienced trader. He started at Fort Michilimackinac in 1767, then spent a decade in the country of the Saskatchwine. In 1778, Pangman was one of the traders who helped fund Pond's journey to Athabasca. Two years later, Pangman partnered with John Ross, who had worked similar low river country, and together they took a share of the fledgling North West Company. But both men knew that fur traders set up temporary partnerships of convenience, and a man on the ins could soon find himself on the outs, and when the North West Company reorganized several years later, they were the latter.

Gregory, MacLeod, Pangman, Ross, and Mackenzie called themselves the New Concern, and in their competitor, the North West Company, they were facing down a relative giant. That year, under the direction of the Frobisher brothers and using the wealth of Simon McTavish, Montreal's top investor, their rivals had sent dozens of traders with twenty-five canoes and eight flat-bottomed bateaux boats' worth of goods to Grand Portage and Detroit. In contrast, the New Concern had only three wintering partners selling from eight canoes.

Still, they made a plan. Pangman would return to Fort des Prairies, on the Saskatchwine, where he had spent so much time. Ross, as the second most experienced man, would take the toughest assignment, to go all the way to Athabasca and compete directly with Peter Pond. Mackenzie would start geographically between the two, at the Île-à-la-Crosse on the English River.

Sending Alexander alone was risky. Benjamin and Joseph Frobisher themselves were robbed by the Indians on their first trip north in 1769. But though far from their homeland, the Scots still exhibited a clan loyalty, and MacLeod trusted Mackenzie.

The members of the New Concern went their separate ways. The primary investing partners, John Gregory and Normand MacLeod, would travel back with the *mangeurs du lard* and arrive home in Montreal by September. New to the firm, and with little experience as a clerk, Roderic would stay behind at Grand Portage to keep the books as part of the skeleton crew. And Alexander would travel hundreds of miles north, to enter the ranks of the *hommes du nord*.

———

The Grand Portage was just that, an infamous nine-mile climb of backbreaking root steps and slick rock. Every six hours, the voyageurs could lug two *pièces* of trade goods over the portage and two more *pièces* of furs back. For this eighteen-mile trip, Alexander Mackenzie paid each man a Spanish silver dollar.

Waiting for them, on the northern end of the portage, were their canoes. Much smaller than the grand craft the pork eaters had paddled from Montreal, they were *canots du nord,* crewed by half the men, able to carry two-thirds of the freight. But they fitted the tight rivers of the north, and only two men were required to portage the boat, the rest tumplining the wrapped goods. And on the few stretches of open water they would encounter, they could still make six miles an hour, admirable time.

But not yet. Grand Portage was just the first obstacle; the carrying work had barely begun. Long portages, thousands of paces long, from lake to lake, awaited them, always to the north and west, in search of the height of land separating the watersheds of Lake Superior and Hudson's Bay. The carries were all named: Partridge Portage, Carreboeuf Portage, Outard Portage, Elk Portage, Portage de Cerise. On this last, Mackenzie said he marched "in the face of a considerable hill." The lakes were full of rocks or sucking mud, and only a few miles long in any case; by the time they reloaded the canoes, they were back out of them, carrying again. Twenty-nine total portages had to be traversed before they reached a high rocky ledge, almost a thousand feet above the waters of Lake Superior; to their relief, the rivers then slowly began to run with them again.

Here the voyageurs pulled Mackenzie aside. As at Pointe au Baptême, they dipped a pine bough in the water and blessed him with it. They made him promise to baptize every other man who went that same way and to never kiss another voyageur's wife while she waited for her husband to return. Mackenzie agreed, and then the men cheered and shot a barrage of rifles into the air and demanded a glass of rum each as their reward.

The whole country before them was broken, rocky, mosquito infested, and so thickly forested that the party could see no farther than the end of the next channel. The route was neither lake nor river but rather a combination of the two, rapids in pond narrows and short portages around falls. The *devant* in the nose of the canoe found each rock with a push of a paddle, steered them aside with one stroke, nodded to the *gouvernail* in the back to track left or right. It was slow, grueling work, and lonely. One large cliff bore a mash of arrows, fired by the Sioux as a warning, proving the breadth of their war party's advance. But mostly the land was empty, the Algonquin having been ravaged by disease. On either side of their tiny scratch of water, the wilderness pushed endlessly in all directions.

Several weeks of toil later, Mackenzie's brigade reached Rainy Lake, where Mackenzie wrote that "there had been an extensive picketed fort and building possessed by the French; the site of it is at present a beautiful meadow, surrounded by groves of oaks." Everywhere Mackenzie went, only the slightest physical traces of the French missionaries and fur traders remained. Rotted away, as if they had never been, reclaimed by the forest.

Finally, though, after Rainy Lake, they were in real current in the one-hundred-mile Lac à la Pluie River. The Algonquin still lived in this area, harvesting wild rice and setting out fishing nets. The canoes cut through the maze of the Lac des Bois, the Lake of the Woods, with so many islands and peninsulas pushing into its surface that the lake somehow seemed more land than water. Hemming them in were thick forests of ironwood and poplar and white birch, used to make the Algonquin boats. Appropriate, Mackenzie thought, because "the country is so broken by lakes and rivers, that people may find their way in canoes in any direction they please."

They followed the Rat Portage to the Winnipeg River, which was full of rapids, twenty-six carries required in all; at one point, the portages were so tightly packed together that seven could be seen ahead at one time. The water tumbled in fierce torrents, and at each the voyageurs took off their hats and made the sign of the cross. Along the shore were thick stands of wooden crosses, set by the men to mark their brethren lost in those waters. At each portage site, the Algonquin had laid wreaths of flowers and set out piles of stones of memory, and the voyageurs recited their rosaries and prayed fervently to the Virgin, for they knew that she and the apostles had appeared to so many men like themselves, on paths such as these, to drive away the Iroquois, or lead them to safety across dark water, or even pull them from the grip of a cataract.

One waterfall came after another, until the Winnipeg River discharged into a lake of the same name. For the first time since Lake Superior, the view expanded as the last basswood and maple trees fell away. Instead, prairie hugged the shores. Mackenzie marveled at herds of buffalo and saw so many animals, birds, and fish that he declared, "There is not, perhaps, a finer country in the world for the residence of uncivilized man." Nevertheless, he also found evidence of the pox and noted that among the Algonquin clans "the widows were more numerous than the men."

According to Mackenzie's map, canoe brigades could travel from Lake Winnipeg in many directions. To Hudson's Bay along the Nelson River, to the Mississippi via the Red. But Mackenzie wanted to go north, the length of the shallow lake. So shallow, only ten or twenty feet deep in many places, that the constant wind formed huge waves, steep chop that tossed canoes. Mackenzie's voyageurs would put out a sail briefly and then, for fear of capsizing, quickly drop it in storms rolling off the plains. The lake was full of sunken boats and lost *pièces*. They hugged the coast and prayed for calm, especially when they made the five-mile *grande traverse* to the western shore.

Mackenzie noticed that "this lake, in common with those of this country, is bounded on the North with banks of black and grey rock, and on the South by a low, level country." Lake of the Woods had been the same. There was a rhythm to these portages, Mackenzie saw. As they worked their way north and west out of the Great Lakes, a simple pattern pervaded. Fight a river up the granite, carry over the height of land, follow the rapids down to a mud lake, cross and follow the next stream upriver, until you find the granite again. A water ladder, climbing up and down, to traverse the continent.

At the north end of the lake they entered the Saskatchwine River. Up that valley Mackenzie's new partner Peter Pangman would spend the winter at Fort des Prairies, at the same point his former master, James Finlay, had wintered two decades before. Back in Montreal, when Mackenzie was a clerk, the place seemed so impossibly distant. But now he was there, and heading even farther north.

The Saskatchwine was a muddy river, and over a mile wide, the largest they had encountered since the Great Lakes. A three-mile-long rapid formed its mouth, and flocks of pelicans hung nearby, seeking sturgeon tossed on the rocks by the rushing water. Soon they hit Cedar Lake and Mud Lake, separated by vast quantities of earth and silt discharged by the Saskatchwine, the whole area marshy and full of willows and swamp ash, islands and channels that appeared recently dry. Mackenzie found more fragments of the earlier French settlements, the furrowed rows and wheel ruts from farming implements and carriages, but he also thought that "this river will, in the course of time, convert the whole of the Cedar Lake into a forest."

A break in the wilderness was at hand. Along the Saskatchwine, just past Mud Lake, sat an outpost of Europe on a mounded slough of silt. It was Cumberland House, the lone inland outpost of the Hudson's Bay Company, the largest landholding private enterprise the world had ever seen.

In the eighteenth century, two centers of power competed for the fur trade: the French, British, Scottish, and American merchants in Montreal, and the monopoly known as the Hudson's Bay Company. Counterintuitively, the British HBC was founded in 1670 by two French *coureurs de bois*, Pierre-Esprit Radisson and Médard des Groseilliers. They wished to trade in the far north and, after being rebuffed by French authorities, found a rich patron in Prince Rupert, the cousin of the English king. He granted them a royal charter to conduct business in all the lands in that Arctic watershed, and they named the venture the Company of Adventurers of England Trading into Hudson's Bay.

Sometimes, the rivalry between Montreal and the HBC mirrored the French and English conflict. In 1686, seventy *coureurs de bois* led thirty regular French musketeers up the Ottawa River and through the deep forests to attack forts along the bay. The English were so surprised that they offered almost no resistance, and the French only retreated for lack of men to suitably garrison the three seized HBC posts. Most often, though, the competition was simply for profit. The HBC made the Indians come to them, to cross the "starving country" of the barrens, to trade at the bay's shore. Moving goods via ship, rather than canoe, was so much cheaper, and the business therefore so much more profitable, that for most of its history the HBC could lose half the trade to Montreal without worry.

Cumberland House was only a decade old, the Hudson's Bay Company's first acknowledgment that it needed to adopt Montreal methods and move to where the Indians lived and hunted. "Why they did not do it before is best known to themselves," Mackenzie wrote.

The HBC fort hoisted a white flag with the red crest of the company. Relations were not cordial between traders, proper Englishmen versus Scottish and American castoffs. Mackenzie's brigade moved on.

The Saskatchwine was the last wide muddy river. After Cumberland, the rivers tightened, the water cleared to crystal in the tumult. The Sturgeon-Weir River was so fraught with cataracts that the solid northmen called it the Rivière Maligne. Mackenzie thought it "an almost continual rapid," voyageurs climbing granite the color of rust and storm clouds. At the top of that rickety staircase they hit a bizarre waterway, more a series of fragmented lakes than any proper channel. And more strangely, the route was marked with the stretched skin of a frog.

The frog was a warning to other tribes that they were now entering the land of the Cree, who controlled this country and would hunt beaver on it for sale to the white men in Montreal and Hudson's Bay. Mackenzie knew the Cree by their French name, the Knisteneaux, and that they were powerful from having acquired rifles from white men long before their rivals. Whatever tribe had previously occupied this land had fled west, ahead of the guns.

This jagged river, the Cree called it the Missinipi, the Big Waters, but the Montreal traders knew it as the English River. Joseph Frobisher, of the rival North West Company, had penetrated this far in 1774. But a decade later, much progress had been made, and Mackenzie was still almost three hundred miles from his winter post.

Now that they were laboring in the far interior, the voyageurs' appetites had expanded commensurate with the work. They could eat eight pounds of meat a day, fish and geese and ducks, four birds a day sometimes, or pemmican when time did not permit a hunt. It was the Cree who first gave the voyageurs the food they named pemmican: the meat of the woolly bison, smashed and ground, and mixed with equal parts fat and, unintentionally, dirt, shit, hair, and gravel. Sometimes they added cranberries for flavor. The voyageurs turned pemmican into a substance called rubbaboo, by boiling it in a pot of water and adding a little flour to thicken it, and then a bit of sugar and a glass of rum to force it down. Mackenzie thought "a little time reconciles it to the palate."

The land of the Cree was fractured, an assembly of oddly segmented lakes divided by rapids. Portage des Ecors, Portage du Galet, Portage des Morts, "covered with human bones, the relics of the small pox." Every waterway was full of the Mamaygwessey, tiny spirit creatures with six fingers that snatched the voyageurs' paddles and untied their lines and tipped their canoes in rapids. Whitewater like Mackenzie had never seen, including a "silent whirlpool" named *rapid qui ne parle point,* the rapid that never speaks. They passed a rock in the shape of a bear, its head and snout painted red. A river of grass. A lake named for the serpent. And always, more portages.

These carrying paths were ancient, as much a natural part of the landscape as any tree or stone. The voyageurs did not make the paths; they were shown them by their Indian guides. But the Algonquin and Cree knew that they had not made the paths either. They were made in the distant past, when the endless winter broke, the ice retreated, and the moose and bear and fallow deer first walked the rivers. The guides knew their people had simply found the carrying paths, a gift thousands of years old.

Mackenzie and his men had crossed a hundred rapids since the muddy banks of Cumberland House and twice that many portages since the grand one after the *rendezvous.* But finally, at Île-à-la-Crosse, on the bank of the Deep River, Mackenzie spotted a fort on "a low isthmus," he wrote, "in latitude 55.25 North, and longitude 107.48 West."

It was the North West Company post, built by the Frobishers a decade before, now manned by the experienced *bourgeois* Patrick Small and his clerk Toussaint Lesieur. Mackenzie was in over his head, a fledgling competing with experienced *bourgeois*. Still, next to that pioneering outpost, he would construct his own sturdy cabin, as much a home as he would have for the next seven months of winter.

———

Île-à-la-Crosse was farther from Grand Portage than Grand Portage was from Montreal; civilization, already tenuous along the Great Lakes, was a memory. The lake took its name not from its shape but from "the game of the cross, which forms a principal amusement among the natives," Mackenzie said, a contest that involved sticks, nets, and much slashing and bloodletting.

Upon arrival, the voyageurs had no time for sport, though. They immediately got to work felling trees, clearing the land, and raising a wall. The post consisted of only a few connected buildings, the trading area up front, storehouse in back. The voyageur billeting and *bourgeois* accommodations were co-located in a squat log house fitted together with squared logs, requiring few iron nails, which were hard to come by. They made space for a small garden to grow root vegetables in the spring. The men had paddled for months, but there was no rest; the voyageur life, as one *bourgeois* said, was to "live hard, lie hard, sleep hard, eat dogs."

Once the post opened, Mackenzie's job was to make the Cree dependent on European goods—metal shot, gunpowder, tools, kettles, food, cloth—to ensure they had to keep returning to his post as often as possible, taking on more and more credit, so that they owed many furs by the time spring came. But he was always on guard to intercept the Cree before they visited Patrick Small or journeyed to Hudson's Bay for cheaper goods.

Mackenzie spent the winter handing out sewing needles and liquor, and the Cree spent the year killing. Beaver were the choicest prize, and in the warm months the hunters could use deadfalls, nets, and dogs to corner the animals. In the winter, though, when the beaver coats were thickest, the animals hid in their burrows, to eat the branches they'd stored away. So then the Cree hunters dug into their dams, pulled the slumbering beavers out of their homes with hooked poles, and then clubbed them to death one by one.

These were the *castor gras*, the furs Mackenzie wanted. And even better, most valuable of all, were those same furs a year later, after they had been worn for a season in the robes of the Indians. The traders called those furs greasy beaver. After so much use, the unwanted guard hairs were worn off and the remaining pelt softened from human oils.

Trade was challenging, the two cultures so unlike each other, always grating on the other's nerves. "They seem to be entirely unacquainted even with the name of gratitude," said one frustrated English trader. When the Cree visited the trading posts, "there is not a one of them who has not a thousand wants." Meanwhile, the Indians grumbled about the white men's lack of etiquette, scaring away game, lacking survival skills, breaking taboos of which animals to hunt and eat at each time of year. In European culture, it was polite to offer food to guests but not ask for it, which would be considered begging; Indian culture considered the exact inverse rude. The *mangeurs de lard* had very little interaction with the Indians, but the *hommes du nord* spent their working lives on their land, and still conflict often arose.

Mackenzie bemoaned the use of alcohol and noted that there had been "a very excellent tendency, but is now unfortunately discontinued, of not selling any spirituous liquor to the natives." Those days were gone, and he found alcohol essential to woo hunters and secure deals, though he had heard how dangerous it could be. In 1780, after a night of hard drinking and fighting, one trader had given an Indian "a dose of laudanum in a glass of grog, which effectually prevented him from giving further trouble to any one, by setting him asleep for ever," Mackenzie wrote. In the ensuing fight, the *bourgeois* and several voyageurs were killed, and the rest abandoned the fort.

The solution to bond the Cree to the white foreigners was marriage. Mackenzie was expected to marry the daughter of the local chief so that the two men would do business not as buyer and seller but as father and son-in-law. The voyageurs gratefully married *à la façon du pays,* in the custom of the country, growing large families at the posts they returned to year after year. On the night of the wedding, the tribe and white men would all gather to smoke the calumet pipe, while the women scraped the skin of the bride, removing all grease and hair, so they could dress her as a European in a gown.

The decorum could devolve at any time, especially when stressed by war, or starvation, or disease. Mackenzie thought that "it requires much less time for a civilized people to deviate into the manner and customs of savage life, than for savages to rise into a state of civilization." He found the lands of the English River depopulated, writing that the small pox was a "destructive and desolating power, as the fire consumes the dry grass of the fields." Mackenzie saw the pox eliminate entire nations with its "pestilential breath," and in the emptied villages "the putrid carcasses, which the wolves, with a furious voracity, dragged forth from the huts, or which were mangled within them by the dogs, whose hunger was satisfied with the disfigured remains of their masters." Mackenzie had heard that fathers would kill every member of their own family to escape that fate.

——————

The winter was horrific. Unbreakable cold, drifts of snow above the rooflines, the new unseasoned timbers of the fort walls shrinking to let in the wind. And yet the Indian elders told Mackenzie that when the world was new, the weather was somehow even colder, trees and earth cracking from the ice. Back then, their people lived in comfort, the elders said, without any of the manufactured European goods that they so readily purchased at Mackenzie's post.

There was nothing to do besides chop wood, fish the lake, shiver, lie in bed with one's wife, and wait for the Cree to bring furs for trade. They ate trout and pike and whitefish all winter, pulled from beneath the ice, four per man per day, when they could catch it. Dried provisions, like wild rice and grease, were saved for lean times, or New Year's Day, when Mackenzie let the men feast on rum and cake made of flour and water. But when they ran out of food, the *hommes du nord* ate "tallow and dried cherries," or blueberries pulled out of bear shit.

To pass the time, the voyageurs whipped their dogs, or drove them ahead of toboggans yelling "*mouche,*" or shot guns in the air to scare Mackenzie into believing the Cree were attacking, or played other tricks they learned from their *à la façon du pays* wives, who knew how the spirit of raven undid men's plans. Mackenzie was isolated as the only native English speaker. He was conversant a bit in French and could have attempted a winter of talk with his voyageurs, but about what? As one of his fellow *bourgeois* said, "What conversation would an illiterate ignorant Canadian be able to keep up? All of their chat is about Horses, Dogs, Canoes and Women, and strong men who can fight a good battle." If they were lucky, a man knew how to play the fiddle or beat an Indian drum.

That year, 1786, winter gripped the land long into April, hard-blown snowstorms that kept the warm southern winds at bay until late in the month, and so it was not until May that John Ross, Mackenzie's partner in the New Concern, arrived at Île-à-la-Crosse to deliver the bad news.

All winter, Ross and his North West Company rival, Peter Pond, had been competing for the affections of the Chipewyan, a northern tribe that traveled great distances delivering furs. Ross knew that he was outmatched—fewer clerks, fewer voyageurs, fewer goods—so he made the risky choice to leave the post and travel north on his own, to seek out the leader of these Chipewyan. He planned to lie to them, to say that he was from the Hudson's Bay Company, and that if they traded with him, he would give the best prices and they could avoid the long journey to the bay.

With a few individual hunters, this strategy worked, and they believed him. But in all his searches out on the land, Ross never found the true Chipewyan leader, because at that very moment, as Ross sought him in the wilderness, that Chipewyan trading chief was back at the post that Ross had left, delivering a year's worth of furs to the North West Company.

All the company's fortunes could be made or lost from this one Chipewyan man, and when he arrived at the post, at the head of a long party of forty hunters, Peter Pond clothed him in a great red coat, as befitted his prominence and stature.

To the Cree, this chief was known as Mistapoose. Alexander Mackenzie, for reasons he never explained, would come to call him Nestabeck. Among his own Chipewyan people, he was called Awgeenah. But to decades of European fur traders, from Hudson's Bay to Montreal, across the barren tundra and boreal and Great Lakes, he was known, with deference, as the English Chief, the most powerful Indian in the northwest.

Matonabbee and Awgeenah

〰〰〰

Awgeenah was the trading chief of the Chipewyan, the People of the Barrens, a position he assumed upon the death of one greater, the leader Matonabbee. In his youth, Awgeenah was a follower of Matonabbee's and traveled with him across the land, even in a war party against the Esquimaux, when Matonabbee led a white man to the Far Off Metal River.

Matonabbee's mother was a Chipewyan woman, enslaved by the Cree and taken to Prince of Wales Fort during their annual trading migration to Hudson's Bay. She was detained at the post by the British and given to a Chipewyan man who married her and filled her belly and then died soon after. Thus Matonabbee was adopted by the governor of the fort.

The Hudson's Bay Company kept a Home Guard, to defend its factories and hunt its food and provide wives to comfort the lonely Englishmen stationed in that inhospitable place. As a child and member of the guard, Matonabbee learned to speak English and Cree, in service to the business of the trade. As he grew older, he was taken in by his father's family, and roamed the land, learning to speak Chipewyan and gather furs to sell at the bay. For a hundred years, the members of the HBC felt no need to venture farther inland than to fish a stream for their dinner. Why should they, when the Chipewyan would do the grueling and dangerous work for them? The English called Matonabbee and his people "the great travelers of the known world."

In time, Matonabbee grew into a striking figure: six feet tall, copper skin, dark hair, beardless, clear cheeks untouched by his nation's traditional tattoos. He enjoyed Spanish wines but not brandy or rum, and never to excess. He heard enough of the Christian faith to reject it and all other "belief in any future state." To the governors of Prince of Wales Fort, he became a trusted guide and mediator between Cree and

Chipewyan, negotiating trading deals and the release of prisoners, even with the Copper Indians on far-off Slave Lake. Once, to rescue a stranded Copper Indian and his furs, Matonabbee paddled a canoe alone into a storm-tossed river, stripping naked in case he was thrown out and forced to swim. He had earned the esteem and trust of the HBC men, who said that he possessed "the vivacity of a Frenchman, . . . the sincerity of an Englishman, . . . the gravity and nobleness of a Turk."

When Matonabbee was a very young man, Moses Norton, the governor of the fort, sent him and another Chipewyan, Idotlyazee, to the north, to report on what they saw and bring back a map of the rivers and lakes and other resources. The two men walked the far north, along the coast of the northern ocean, and surveyed the rim of Slave Lake and all the adjoining drainages of Hudson's Bay. Their journey lasted five complete turns of the seasons, but when Matonabbee and Idotlyazee returned, they brought with them a map made of deerskin and drawn with charcoal.

The map showed Slave Lake as the heart of the land, over a dozen rivers reaching out in all directions toward the coasts. The widest river on the map, on the far edge of their trading empire, "which flows from a large lake in ye Athapeskan Country into ye Western Ocan," Norton ignored. Instead, he focused on a river with "3 Copper mines wch are marked with 3 Red Spots." Matonabbee had brought back a small chunk of the metal as proof of discovery.

Norton had heard rumors of such a land—"far to ye Northward where ye sun dont set," he wrote—passed down over the years, from reports and map fragments. They all stemmed from the curiosity of a previous governor, James Knight, who had become enraptured with a Chipewyan woman named Thanadelthur.

In 1713, Thanadelthur escaped her Cree captors and fled to York Factory on Hudson's Bay. Knight was impressed by her beauty and her sharp tongue, and though she was not yet twenty years old, he sent her back west to negotiate trade deals with her people. Though nominally only the interpreter, in reality she led the delegation, and saved her party of HBC men from starvation through force of will.

Upon returning, Thanadelthur told Knight many tales of her homeland. That there were white giants with beards who guarded bags of gold and mountains of copper. That beyond these hills lay a strait that shifted with the tide and a great sea full of strange ships. She promised Knight her affection, that she would show him these lands, but then she took a fever and died soon after.

Knight was undeterred. In 1719, he procured two vessels, filled them with sailors and stores, and set out to the upper lip of Hudson's Bay to find these lands. No one saw him or his men alive ever again.

Moses Norton would not follow Knight's fate. But he did want Thanadelthur's copper, and Matonabbee had found it.

————

One winter day, several seasons after delivering the map, Matonabbee was out on the land, accompanied by his wives and a band of Chipewyan hunters, when he came upon a white man leading a party of several Cree. The young Englishman was freezing and half-starved, slogging through the deep snows with no *raquettes* or toboggan. He said his name was Samuel Hearne and he had spent the last year fruitlessly searching the barrens for "the great Leader" Matonabbee, who could guide him to the Far Off Metal River.

Hearne was a Hudson's Bay Company trader but, unlike his companions, full of a restless spirit. Norton had sent him in search of the river of copper, and twice he had struck out north from Prince of Wales Fort, only to be turned back by the hardship of such travel. Hearne's quadrant was broken, so he could take no navigational readings, and he was dangerously short on supplies. Before finding Matonabbee, over the course of seven days he ate only "a few cranberries, water, scraps of old leather, and burnt bones." He watched his helpless Cree hunters pick over their clothing to "consider what part could best be spared," so they could eat a "half rotten deer skin" to alleviate the feelings of extreme hunger.

Matonabbee took pity on Hearne. He dressed the Englishman in a coat of otter skins, and then showed him a river where small trees grew, so the party could fashion snowshoes and sleds. Hearne was out of rifle ammunition and, desperate to take down game, cut an iron ice chisel into square chunks to create a poor substitute for bullets. But Matonabbee's hunters easily fed them as they completed the journey back to Prince of Wales Fort.

As they walked, Matonabbee asked, "Will you attempt another journey for the discovery of the Coppermines?" Hearne said yes, and Matonabbee volunteered to be his guide, on a few conditions. First, that a certain price be met by the governor of the fort. And second, that Matonabbee's wives accompany them. This was the most important point. It was the lack of women on the expedition that had doomed Hearne, Matonabbee said.

"For when all the men are heavily laden," the Chipewyan said, "they can neither hunt nor travel to any considerable distance; and in case they meet with success in hunting, who is to carry the produce of their labor? Women are made for labor. One of them can carry, or haul, as much as two men can do."

Hearne readily agreed to Matonabbee's conditions. It took them another two months of walking to reach the fort.

———

Upon arrival, Hearne immediately secured the Chipewyan chief's official appointment to the expedition. Moses Norton instructed Matonabbee to escort Hearne north, back to the copper mines, taking "a few of his best men," including Awgeenah. He also assured Hearne that Matonabbee was well supplied for the journey and "has promised to take great care of you." Their party left Prince of Wales Fort only days later. The white man marked the day as December 7, 1770.

They struggled north. The snow was deep and game scarce. On Christmas Day, Hearne found himself longing for Europe and the "great variety of delicacies which were then expending in every part of Christendom." But Matonabbee told him to keep his spirits up, and deer would soon be plentiful.

A few weeks later, the party happened upon several bands of Matonabbee's countrymen, settled in for the season along a chain of frozen lakes. They had established corrals into which they drove game, easing their hunting, and allowing them to collect tall piles of pelts. Even in the depth of winter, they were healthy and robust, a far cry from the Home Guard on the bay, and Hearne realized that of the Indians "those who have the least intercourse with the Factories, are by far the happiest."

Matonabbee secured dried provisions and supplies to make canoes. He also wished to take more wives, because they "pitch our tents, make and mend our clothing, keep us warm at night; and, in fact, there is no such thing as traveling any considerable distance, or for any length of time, in this country, without their assistance," he said.

Matonabbee purchased another wife, giving him eight, and he prided himself on their height and strength; Hearne told him that they could make "good grenadiers" in the British army. All of his wives were named for the marten, the weasel of such fine fur: White Marten, Summer Marten, Marten's Heart. In this way, they shared a kinship with Jumping Marten, who, according to the elders' stories, once used her owl medicine to escape a group of men who kidnapped her. Jumping Marten gained power over them by sleeping with them, and then made them crazy and sent them into the winter with vacant eyes where they stood in the cold until they died.

No man could know if his new wife was full of such medicine power.

The party assembled, Matonabbee wanted to press north, even though one of his wives had just given birth and was miserable with pain. Still, she threw her babe on her back and trudged on. Would she not stay behind? Hearne asked. Matonabbee didn't see why. "Women, though they do everything, are maintained at a trifling expense," he said, "for as they always stand cook, the very licking of their fingers in scarce times is sufficient for their subsistence."

———

Spring came on, the ice began to break, and when they arrived at a place called Clowey Lake, they found an even larger encampment of Chipewyan. Again among the main band of his people, Matonabbee had work to do to guarantee the success of their journey to the copper mines. He gave tobacco and gunpowder to every chief he met in exchange for the promise of safe passage, and in doing so established his prominence in the eyes of all that he was leading a band of warriors and women north and that Hearne was under his protection.

One day, the former husband of one of Matonabbee's wives arrived at the winter quarters, newly back from the hunt. Matonabbee had acquired some of his wives from their fathers, and some he had won in wrestling matches, pinning their husbands and thus earning the women's hands. Matonabbee was a jealous defender of these wives, and so, upon seeing a former husband, he felt compelled to act. Matonabbee went to this wife's possessions, removed her own long box-handled knife, calmly went to the man's tent, and without a word grabbed him by the throat and stabbed him. The blade entered the man's back but was turned aside by the bone of the shoulder blade. The man screamed and fell on his face, but Matonabbee raised the knife and stabbed him twice more. Then Matonabbee left, returned to his own tent, asked his wives for water to wash the knife, and smoked his pipe in peace.

"I have done right, have I not?" Matonabbee asked Hearne.

But his wife thought not and left Matonabbee for her bloody first husband. Hearne tried to console Matonabbee and said that perhaps she would rather be a sole wife than have "the seventh or eighth share of the affection of the greatest man in the country." But even more distressing to Matonabbee, a second man demanded his wife back, or else a ransom of ammunition and iron kettles. This man was stronger than Matonabbee and would have pinned him in a fight, so the Chipewyan chief was forced to let a second wife go as well. This troubled him greatly; the first woman was comely, the second peerless in leatherwork. Matonabbee sat down and told Hearne the expedition was over and he would go no farther. But Hearne begged him to continue and spoke of the esteem that his descendants would always have from the Hudson's Bay Company in appreciation of his service, and after much cajoling eventually Matonabbee assented.

They continued north that very afternoon, Matonabbee intent on putting as much distance between himself and his former wives as possible.

———

Everywhere Matonabbee went, warriors flocked to him. They joined him at the winter camps, at Clowey Lake, at Peshew Lake, and on farther north. When sixty more fighters joined their ranks, Matonabbee ordered a camp be built for his wives with young babies. His two childless wives stripped their loads to carry the minimum required food and powder, Awgeenah and the other men began to fashion shields from thin boards, and finally Hearne spoke up and asked what was going on.

Matonabbee was forthright about his plans. He told Hearne that from then on the purpose of their journey was in fact twofold. Yes, they were traveling to the Far Off Metal River, but they were doing so to make war on the Esquimaux.

Hearne begged them not to do it, but Awgeenah and the other warriors told him he was a coward. "You are afraid of the Esquimaux?" asked Matonabbee.

Why shouldn't he be? The fearsomeness of that race was well known to Indian and Englishman alike. How the Esquimaux hunted animals as big as houses and then ate the meat raw. How they made spears and harpoons out of the horn of the unicorn; the same royal substance that Queen Elizabeth had fashioned into a scepter, each common warrior carried into battle. They stole the wives of all peoples, survived winter without fire, and paddled boats that swam underwater faster than any Indian's canoe.

"I despise them more than fear them," Hearne said, nervously, as he looked over the scores of warriors gathered, he the only white man. "I do not care if you render the name and race of Esquimaux extinct." And then Awgeenah and Matonabbee cheered for Hearne, for they felt the same way.

———

It was the height of summer, and warm, creeks and trails like slush, rain on frozen lakes and fog rising from the cold water. There were few women to carry the loads, and only three canoes for the whole party, so progress was slow, and they took turns using the boats to cross rivers.

As they traveled, they killed large numbers of deer and fish and fur-bearing animals of every type. Some game, they ate the whole beast, and some they ate only the tongue and sucked the marrow, and some they simply tossed on the ground. The white man asked why, and Matonabbee and Awgeenah and the warriors explained that they had full dominion over all other living things. They told him that when the world was new, a giant walked the earth, his head reaching even the clouds. And with his walking stick he leveled the land and set all the rivers and streams. And then he took a dog and ripped it into pieces and threw the flesh about, so that it became fish and birds and beaver. And he told the Chipewyan people that they should kill and eat all of these animals and never spare them.

Hearne then asked about their god, and if they worshipped this man, but Matonabbee, who understood the questions, because he had been taught about the Christian god as a child, said no, that all "should pass through this world with as much ease and contentment as possible, without any hope of reward, or painful fear of punishment in the next."

Soon they came upon a band of Copper Indians, who understood their designs to attack the Esquimaux. So they gave them more canoes and threw the war party a feast and, in recognition of Matonabbee's leadership and standing, gave him all the choicest cuts. The Copper Indians had never seen a white man before, and they mocked Hearne, saying that his hair was like a buffalo's tail, his eyes the color of a gull's, and his skin "resembled meat which had been sodden in water till all the blood was extracted."

The weather had grown sultry, and no one could sleep from the clouds of mosquitoes, when they finally found the Coppermine River. It was narrow, shallow, and full of rocks, and the white man appeared frustrated; he said the river was navigable only by canoe and not ship. Matonabbee did not care about the size of the river, and sent out scouts to look for Esquimaux. They were quickly rewarded. There was a camp nearby, downriver, at a waterfall. Matonabbee led them across the river to prepare the ambush and ignored Hearne when the man bellyached that his survey was incomplete.

Awgeenah and the other warriors restrung their bows, cleaned their rifles, gathered powder for their pouches, affixed spears. They painted their wooden shields with symbols and animals and the spirits of their totems: the sun, the moon, earth, sea, sky, the trickery of raven, the speed of wolverine, the endurance of caribou. Then they chopped their hair, tied it back, stripped their clothes, and painted their bodies red and black, and though mosquitoes covered their skin, they paid no notice.

The Esquimaux camp was small, and Matonabbee had gathered a large war band; everyone knew a slaughter was upon them. Hearne wondered aloud if "Providence should work a miracle in their deliverance," as he could see no other means of their escape.

Awgeenah and the warriors instructed Hearne to stay behind, but the white man said he thought he was in more danger that way, as the Esquimaux would flee right toward his hiding spot. So they handed Hearne a spear and a bayonet, and told him to stay close.

In the early hours, just after midnight but with the sun still burning bright, Matonabbee and Awgeenah and the other warriors fell upon the sleeping camp. The Esquimaux ran from their tents naked and weaponless. One young girl was hit by a spear and fell at Hearne's feet, grasping his legs as she screamed. The Chipewyan warriors returned to the white man and stuck her twice more, and she squirmed about the poles fastening her to the dirt. The warriors asked Hearne if he wished to take her for a wife? Hearne begged the men to relieve her of her agonies, but instead the warriors berated him for his softness and sympathies. Finally, Hearne said that he would do it, that he would kill her if they would not, and his vehemence moved them. One warrior withdrew his spear from her body and then reaffixed it in her heart. Then the two men left the Englishman in contempt, but Hearne sat with the girl for a long time, as long as it took her to die.

The Chipewyan killed every Esquimaux without quarter. They plundered the tents of the copper wares, and made piles of the dead women, and remarked how ill-formed and ugly they were. Then a call went up, that a scout saw more Esquimaux in another camp on the other side of the river. They called *tima tima* to the Esquimaux, indicating their friendliness, and then shot at them with their rifles. The bullets landed short, though, embedded in the far shore. The Esquimaux came out, curious to examine the metal balls, until one man was struck in the leg, and then they fled in a fervor, paddling away in their kayaks. All except one grandfather, who was still packing his belongings when Awgeenah and the other warriors finally reached the camp. By the time they were done with him, Hearne said the man resembled "a cullender."

Through it all, the Esquimaux dogs never stopped barking, but the Chipewyan abandoned them there, still leashed to their kennels.

Away from the camps, one old Esquimaux woman sat alone by a shoal in the stream, spearing salmon for her dinner. Her eyes were cloudy, her hearing dim, and she seemed to have no awareness of what was happening to her people in their tents as she blindly poked at the water. When Awgeenah and the warriors found her, she was quiet and still, surrounded by piles of fish and squinting at them with bloodshot eyes.

She tried to run. But they seized her and transfixed her on the end of a spear. Then they held her down and plucked out her eyes and stabbed her, slowly, again and again, in the few meaty places of her body, not her organs or vitals. By the time they were done, they had penetrated her with a dozen spears, so as to stake her to the ground.

When they were finished killing Esquimaux, Matonabbee and Awgeenah and the men sat and ate, as they were hungry from their work and had not eaten in some time. They picked up the blind woman's pronged stick and caught salmon and ate them raw. On his map, the white man called the place Bloody Fall. Then they led Hearne the last few miles of the river's course to the sea. There was sealskin and whalebone everywhere. The white man said they had reached the Arctic Ocean. He tasted the water and declared it fresh, then raised his glass to his eye and looked out on it. Matonabbee led Hearne to the place where they gathered copper, but the area was small and mean, and they found only one four-pound lump. Awgeenah and the warriors said the chunk looked like a hare. Hearne said it was a waste of a trip. Then they turned around and returned south.

The journey back to the bay was grueling. The white man's feet wore raw; every step left a red footprint in the snow. Winter returned, so hard and deep that when they came upon the great lake of the Slave, they walked across its frozen surface. They finally arrived back at Prince of Wales Fort at the opening of summer. Hearne expressed his thanks to Matonabbee and said that though his trip had failed, he could take satisfaction in the fact that he had done his duty to his master and finally put to rest any speculation that there might be a northwest passage through the heart of the continent.

That last assertion proved wildly untrue.

———

Hearne would soon command Prince of Wales Fort, and Matonabbee continued to cross the Barren Lands to bring him furs, and the two grew even closer in friendship. Once, Matonabbee was troubled by a rival and asked Hearne to kill the man, who was then many hundreds of miles away. Hearne agreed and on a piece of paper drew a picture of the two men wrestling, Matonabbee holding a bayonet against the heart of his foe. Across from the figures, Hearne drew a tall pine tree. It was topped with an all-seeing eye, and a human hand reached from its branches. Hearne told his friend Matonabbee to show the paper to anyone who would look, and within the year the man withered and died, as all expected who knew the power of such medicine.

But in the winter of 1776, when Matonabbee arrived at the bay on his regular migration, he found that Hearne had changed. Matonabbee led a cohort of three hundred Chipewyan, bearing five thousand beaver furs and seven thousand pounds of musk ox flesh for the Englishmen to eat. At first, Hearne greeted him warmly and dressed Matonabbee in a captain's jacket of the Royal Navy. And then Hearne dressed Matonabbee's wives, and repaired the rifles of his hunters, and gave them powder, ball, and tobacco. But when Matonabbee requested seven jackets for his seven lieutenants, loyal men such as Awgeenah, Hearne wavered. He thought Matonabbee ungrateful and did not want to provide the gifts.

"I do not expect to be denied such a trifle," said Matonabbee.

Hearne scoffed and asked where else he would take his furs.

"To the Canadian traders," said Matonabbee. And though Hearne then grudgingly relinquished the goods, there was ever the threat implicit, and from then on Awgeenah and Matonabbee and the other Chipewyan would also seek out the peddlers from Montreal.

By their good fortune, one of those traders, Peter Pond, crossed into their watershed the next year. Matonabbee himself delivered the *castor gras* beaver furs that would make Pond famous among his business partners in 1779, when young Alexander Mackenzie first clerked in his countinghouse in Montreal.

———

Hearne was the last governor of Prince of Wales Fort. One day in 1782, as the American Revolution dragged on, warships flying British flags appeared on the horizon. The garrison cheered, assuming relief. Hearne saw otherwise. It was a ruse.

"You may cease rejoicing. These are French warships come to wreak havoc," Hearne told the men. Outnumbered and hopeless, Hearne surrendered. The French took him prisoner, razed the fort to the ground, and scattered the Home Guard.

The news traveled quickly. Matonabbee was on the land when he heard that his childhood home had burned. His livelihood, his stature, his future, fell with it. In response, Matonabbee, this leading Chipewyan, who held no belief in a future state, hanged himself from a tree. The white men said they had never seen an Indian do such a thing. Stripped of their provider, Matonabbee's wives and children starved to death that winter.

But Awgeenah would not go hungry or follow Matonabbee to the noose. Instead, he took his mentor's place as the trading chief of his nation.

Awgeenah wore both the red coat of Peter Pond and the tattoos of his people, black stripes across his cheeks set in with awl and cinders. So skillfully did he play the Hudson's Bay Company against the North West Company, and the reverse as well, that he earned the name English Chief. Trading made him rich, riches made him generous, generosity made him powerful among the Chipewyan. He traveled as far as Matonabbee had, collecting debts even from the Copper Indians who lived along Tucho, the massive lake of the Slave Indians. And everywhere he went, the English Chief was a man of stature, and power, and respect.

————

On April 21, 1786, Awgeenah delivered his own fantastic pile of furs to Peter Pond at his post, the Old Establishment, near the Lake of the Hills. He led a party of dozens of hunters, and his haul was so great that the English Chief single-handedly made the trading year a success. John Ross, Mackenzie's partner in the New Concern, could only envy Pond's clerks as they delivered the furs at the summer *rendezvous* in Grand Portage. The North West Company was winning the trade war, and the New Concern was faltering badly.

There was nothing to do but keep up the business. Mackenzie and his partners were outmanned and outgunned: fewer trade goods, fewer canoes, fewer voyageurs, inferior guides and interpreters. But each returned to his previous post—Mackenzie to Île-à-la-Crosse, Pangman to Fort des Prairies, Ross back to Athabasca to compete with Peter Pond—for the next winter.

Though still a clerk, Roderic Mackenzie was given his own post to run at Lac des Serpents, where he lived "within a gunshot" of the rival North West Company fort. As winter set in, a supportive Alexander sent his cousin letters full of tips and encouragement. How to give gifts, extend credit, and hold back liquor from those partners who grew troublesome with drink. How to shut his mouth, when it came to speaking to other traders. "Keep every thing as secret as you can from your men," he wrote, "otherwise these old voyageurs will fish all they know out of your Green Hands." And how to avoid getting stuck in the snow. "I have not a single one in my fort that can make Rackets. I do not know what to do without these articles. See what it is to have no wives," he wrote, noting that women always made the snowshoes. "Try and get Rackets—there is no stirring without them."

But Alexander also shared a fear with Roderic as the season pressed on in early 1787. It had been months since he heard any word from Athabasca, their most important department. "I am anxious not having any news of Mr. Ross," he told his cousin.

It was Roderic who got the word first. In the spring he traveled to Île-à-la-Crosse, finding Alexander already gone to Grand Portage and Ross's brigade late returning south. When the voyageurs from Athabasca did finally arrive, he discovered the cause of their delay.

John Ross was dead. "Shot in a scuffle with Mr. Pond's men."

Roderic immediately sped to the *rendezvous* to deliver the news. "I embarked with five men who volunteered and depending on my foremen as a guide." Though the man was inexperienced and was unsure of the route, the thousand-mile trip only took "a month of hard labor."

"The cause of our appearance so unexpectedly was soon known throughout the place," said Roderic, upon arrival. The New Concern and the North West Company partners held an emergency joint meeting. They would merge, effective immediately, cease the competition "for their common welfare," before anyone else died.

John Gregory, Mackenzie's original patron, would return to Montreal with his former rivals to provide credit and oversee all affairs. The collected roster of *bourgeois* and clerks was divided among the existing posts. Roderic Mackenzie was given Alexander's old assignment, at Île-à-la-Crosse. Pond had stayed at his post, had not traveled to Grand Portage, so despite the accusations against him—the Yankee of dubious morals was "under a cloud," according to Roderic—Pond would have to remain in the north for one final winter. But not alone. Alexander Mackenzie was sent to Athabasca to work with him.

It was an uncomfortable assignment. As everyone knew, Ross's murder was not the first of which Pond was accused.

MURDER AT THE OLD ESTABLISHMENT, 1787

wwww

Peter Pond came from Puritan stock, but he didn't have much use for religious rituals and never received the education biblical study required. He was born in 1740 in Milford, Connecticut, a town of ships and farms. His father was a shoemaker, his brothers ne'er-do-wells. Throughout his life, Pond maintained only a functional literacy, phonetically writing his journal in the same nasal New England accent with which he spoke: he found Indians "waryers" who were easily disturbed by an "eevel sperit," and he worked with "voigers" who were always "fiteing" and "dansing."

Frequenting local taverns in his youth, Pond grew up listening to stories from veterans just back from the French and Indian War raging on the frontier. "Thay Charmed me," he wrote, so much "Marth & Gollatrey," and in the summer of 1756, at age sixteen, with "a Strong Desire to be a Solge," he enlisted in the Seventh Company of the First Connecticut Regiment. Soon he was on a ship up the Hudson River, bound for the front, delighted to be "in the Sarvis."

His regiment camped near Lake George, a long tail of water reaching north toward Lake Champlain and Montreal. Most of his fellow soldiers got dysentery, and though Pond stayed healthy, that winter he did little but shiver and pass the time. His enlistment was only one year, but he signed on with the regiment again in 1758 and returned to the same ground, this time to attack the French fort on the far side of the water. Pond was in the lead column, and lost in thick forest the British and French forces stumbled into each other. The Connecticut militia accidentally made first contact, and General Howe "being at the Head of the British troops with a Small side arm in his Hand . . . Ordered the Troopes to forme thare front to ye Left to attack the French." Howe was immediately cut down, and though Pond's fellow soldiers killed and scattered the ambushers, the fight descended into bedlam, every man for himself. Pond and "twelve Men of my aquantans" spent the night hiding from the French, within half a mile of their line. In the morning, the British reorganized and attempted a full open assault. It was a disaster. "Three forths ware Kild in the attempt," Pond wrote, his fellow soldiers felled in waves that piled up before the French fort. The defenses held; Pond's regiment retreated. "Thus Ended the Most Ridicklas Campane Eaver Hard of."

But Pond had developed a taste for the soldiering life. The next summer he crossed Long Island Sound to enlist in the New York militia, because he was sure it would see action. Based on his experience, Pond was promoted to sergeant, and he marched west with the painted Sir William Johnson and his Iroquois allies. He was there at the walls of Fort Niagara, wounded while laying siege, digging trench lines, moving an eight-gun battery to within 150 yards of the castle. The French surrendered twenty-five days later. The next summer, his fourth year of service, Pond was at Montreal and saw the end of the war.

His wanderlust was only stoked. Twenty years old, Pond joined the crew of a merchant ship out of Milford and sailed to the West Indies. Upon return, he discovered his mother was dead and his father had left for Detroit. Pond ran the cobbler business until his father's return and then moved to Detroit himself. He acquired beaver, otter, and raccoon pelts and shipped them to Albany, and as he became a man of means he made enemies. In 1772, one fellow Detroit trader challenged him to a duel. "We met the Next Morning Eairley and Discharged Pistels in which the Pore fellow was unfortennt," Pond wrote. Having shot the man dead, Pond quietly left Detroit and returned to the West Indies.

Sailing did not last; Pond had a desire to go west. In 1773 he traveled to Montreal, loaded up on trade goods, and made for Fort Michilimackinac. There he hired clerks and voyageurs and twelve canoes and set off farther into the hinterlands, beyond Lake Michigan. They portaged into the Mississippi watershed and paddled north to trade with the tribes on the plains. The Sioux were unlike any Indians he had met. They used dogs to haul sleds, and sliced the nostrils of their horses to help them breathe on long journeys to run down bison. Pond was on his own and, forced to improvise, learned small habits of the business: to carouse with his men and Sioux traders; that if you left small items on the counter for them to take, the Indians were more likely to come back. The next season, armed with belts of wampum, Pond helped broker a peace between the Ojibwa and the Dakota. And yet war was beginning at home. By then, Pond had thrown in his lot with the merchants in Montreal, not New York. Powder and blankets were hard to come by in New England, diverted as they were to the revolution. So as fighting in the thirteen colonies grew, Pond went north, with his new business associates, to Grand Portage, Lake Winnipeg, and beyond.

Pond hardly left the northwest for the next decade, traveling only as far south and east as Fort Michilimackinac. Every year, he worked his way farther west, farther in, first to the Saskatchwine, then to the English River. He spent his winters trading, his summers paddling the headwaters of every tributary, drawing detailed maps that noted Indian tribes, landmarks, and even veins of silver in the Rocky Mountains.

In 1778, Peter Pangman and several other American and Scottish traders found themselves working the same territory. With an excess of goods on the Saskatchwine, they pooled their supplies and sent Pond north of Île-à-la-Crosse, farther up the English River than they had yet traveled. He took five canoes, crewed by voyageurs and their wives, with Indian guides to show them the route to Athabasca, a Cree word meaning "where there are reeds."

A great portage lay between the English River and Athabasca. The Cree named it Methye, after the half catfish, half eel that swam the waters of the lake at the path's southern end. It took Pond's crew eight days to complete the twelve-mile carry, longer even than the Grand Portage. The land was thickly forested, a single uphill ramp until the last few steps, when a valley fell away beneath them in a most wondrous sight: a wide clear river flowing to the west. Pond named it the Pelican River, as so many of the shorebirds were flying overhead.

The river soon joined a larger waterway flowing north, black bitumen tar oozing from the sandy banks; the voyageurs used the sticky gum to seal their canoes. The water was sluggish and shallow, and after several days of paddling, they stopped to build a home for the long winter. Pond named it the Old Establishment. This is where Matonabbee and Awgeenah found him and traded so many furs. They told Pond of rivers and lakes even farther north and said that they had led Samuel Hearne to the river of the copper mines, even as they traded with Pond to spite the Hudson's Bay Company men. Those luxurious Chipewyan beaver furs made Pond a hero of Montreal, and yet it was this geography lesson from Matonabbee and Awgeenah that most fired his curiosity.

In 1779, Pond was late returning to Grand Portage, the distance too far from Athabasca. He discovered that in his absence he had been included in a new partnership of fur traders, organized by the Frobisher brothers and Simon McTavish. Peter Pangman and his new partner, John Ross, were members as well. So was a Swiss man named Jean-Étienne Waden, who, for mysterious reasons, was also called the Dutchman. Waden had come to New France as a soldier, fought opposite Pond at Fort Niagara, then deserted the regular army and became wealthy as an independent fur trader.

In the winter of 1781, Pond and Waden were assigned to the same post on Lac la Ronge, a shattered half-granite, half-mud lake just south of the English River. Smallpox ravaged the place, and the trade was bad. Pond and Waden were nominally in the same business concern, but the two did not get along. They set up houses side by side, and the two quarreled constantly. Pond was an originator, an explorer of new territories, and worked best when in charge alone. It was not an ideal assignment.

One March evening in 1782, just before supper, Pond and Waden were arguing again. They retired to their respective quarters, but a few hours later two shots were fired. The report echoed across the compound, arousing a voyageur who ran to Waden's house. There he found Pond and a *canadien* clerk named Toussaint Lesieur standing in the doorway. Inside, the Dutchman lay on the wooden floor, his left leg shattered and bleeding freely. "*Ah, mon ami,* I am dead," Waden said to his voyageur. Two guns lay nearby, one fired, one broken. Pond picked up the second and walked away. There were powder burns all about Waden's knee, bones splintered, two bullets embedded in the floor among pools of bright red blood. The voyageur asked what happened, and Waden said, "I will tell you," and then he died.

The next year, Waden's widow in Montreal petitioned the government to make a formal inquiry into the matter. Pond was never charged with a crime. Neither was Lesieur, who headed to Athabasca soon after Waden's death. He took the pox with him, the first time it ever entered that country.

Pond returned to the Old Establishment. He traded with Awgeenah and the Chipewyan and pulled piles of furs out of Athabasca, but at the summer *rendezvous* of 1784 he rejected an offer to join the newly reorganized North West Company. Pond was offered one share and thought he deserved two, so he left for Montreal, which he had not visited in a dozen seasons, and no one heard from him for a year.

Pond did not reappear in Athabasca until late in the autumn of 1785, just as snow and ice descended. There, he discovered a familiar but unwelcome situation: competition. John Ross of the New Concern had moved into his post and was trading in a department that, since Pond had first arrived in 1778, the Yankee considered his proprietary territory.

All winter, Pond's clerks fanned out about the Athabasca country. His trusted agent was a clerk named Cuthbert Grant, and Pond sent him north to Slave Lake to intercept the Chipewyan and Red Knife Indians before they could reach Ross or the Hudson's Bay Company. Ross tried to keep up but was overmatched. Pond outmaneuvered and outmuscled him. Alcohol flowed, and one night, when a man tried to steal a robe, Pond "cutt the Beaver Indian on the head with his Poignard" to enforce his authority. Ross was gone when the English Chief arrived with the yearly bales of furs. That summer of 1786, Grant took the furs to Grand Portage, Ross went with him to report to the New Concern, but Pond stayed at the Old Establishment.

The next season, competition grew even more aggressive. One winter day, several Chipewyan headed to Ross's house to trade. But Pond's men grabbed them, steering them back toward the North West Company shack. Ross saw what was happening, called several of his voyageurs, and confronted Pond's crew. The fight was quick. Three voyageurs went for Ross. François Peche, Pond's own *devant,* pulled a gun. Ross fell, and Peche fled into the wilderness.

When the ice broke the following spring, the furs were shipped as normal to Grand Portage. But still Pond did not return. He paddled north from the Old Establishment, mapped the shores of Slave Lake— unconcerned over who his next New Concern *bourgeois* competition might be—and continued to formulate plans that had consumed his thoughts for a decade.

———

Alexander Mackenzie had forgotten his shirt. It was in a cassette, with his other necessary sundries, left behind at the *rendezvous*. Mackenzie didn't realize the mistake until well into the journey, and after sending his trusted *canadien* guide, François Barrieau, back along the route to retrieve the heavy locked trunk, he was frustrated to learn that it had been lost overboard. The mischievous Mamaygwessey, or other blue men, making trouble. Every few days he wrote another letter to Roderic, first complaining of the lost time, then of the lost gear. "I have not now a Single Shirt," Alexander wrote, "it will be the cause of all our misfortunes during the voyage."

The whole season was already fraught with delays. The emergency meeting, to negotiate the merger of the New Concern and the North West Company, had slowed his departure from Grand Portage, and Mackenzie's letters were all anxiety. "You know that I am always in haste," Alexander admitted. The HBC men were surly, the Cree were quarreling, and—Alexander didn't have to put this in writing to his cousin—he was headed north, without his equipment, to spend the winter with a suspected triple murderer.

At the summer *rendezvous,* some said Pond gave the order to kill Ross. And why not? Pond's reputation preceded him. The fur trade was violent, but *bourgeois* were off-limits. Roderic thought that "being accused, at different times, of having been instrumental toward the deaths of two gentlemen who were in opposition to his interests, he was now on his way out of the country." But first, Pond had to teach his replacement.

Rumors buzzed about Pond like mosquitoes. Everyone said that he had shot Waden through the knee and left him for dead. Toussaint Lesieur himself had told Alexander about the incident while the two were at Île-à-la-Crosse in 1785. That winter, Mackenzie's first in the north, Lesieur was a North West Company clerk, part of the competition, but his story was well-known; Mackenzie called him "the famous Lesieur." Though Pond was never officially charged, Alexander thought his "innocence was not so apparent as to extinguish the original suspicion."

Mackenzie regrouped with all his men, guides, and canoes at Île-à-la-Crosse, before pushing north in search of the Athabasca country for the first time. Knowing that Roderic was following him to this last post, he left behind all of his cousin's books, except "the History of England," which he kept for himself. "You will pass the winter in the best manner you can." Alexander promised to write often and said, "Remember me to all the men."

The chained lakes of the English River were over; a single wide arm of water stretched to the northwest, and Mackenzie followed, portaging to a prairie pond that "commands an open horizon." Crossing quickly, Barrieau led the carry to Lac du Boeuf, "which is contracted near the middle, by a projecting sandy point," Mackenzie wrote. But winter was coming on early. Ice on the banks, snow, short days, and Alexander was still thirty leagues from the Old Establishment. They made the lake's far northwestern corner and found a small river, thin and rocky bottomed, a "considerable danger" for his birch-bark canoes. The cold struck hard, the stream froze in a snap, and Mackenzie and his men found themselves marooned. Five days they waited onshore, but the weather only grew worse. Mackenzie needed to move quickly, or he'd be cut off from his winter quarters. So, to lighten the loads, Mackenzie sent back two canoes and sixty *pièces*. Then he ordered the men to ready their axes in order to make way, and though "frequently obliged to break the ice we advanced slowly," foot by foot, against the current. "I have scarcely any hopes of reaching Athabasca with the Canoes," he wrote to Roderic.

That winding, shallow, frozen river was twenty-four miles long, Alexander figured. It took his men two days to chop their way up, but once free from it, they had little opportunity to rest. They crossed the small Lac La Loche and at the far rocky shore stared down the thirteen-mile carry of the Methye Portage, the sole entrance to the realm of Athabasca.

"The weather at this time was so severe that I lost all hopes of getting further," Alexander wrote to his partners of the North West Company, "and our provisions were almost exhausted." So he decided to ditch several canoes full of goods and make a run for it. He knew at least one brigade had gotten through earlier in the year. He and Pond would have some small amount of rum and powder to trade over the winter. Now his priority must be survival.

In the driving snow, Mackenzie and his men decided to portage only three canoes. "The land is low and stony," Mackenzie wrote, "and clothed in wood," though the path itself was "an entire sand" of unsure footing. Partway through the trek lay a small pond, where they could float the boats for less than a mile; "a trifling respite of the labor of carrying." And then, at the end, the *coup de grâce,* a "succession of eight hills, some of which are almost perpendicular." Somehow, his men had to haul the three-hundred-pound canoes down the sheer face of the ice-clad bluff.

And yet, from that thousand-foot precipice, Mackenzie also beheld "a most extensive, romantic, and ravishing prospect." The Pelican River, wide and rushing and—this is the romance—flowing in their direction of travel, to the west. For the first time since the Winnipeg River, a thousand miles of hard labor behind them, they were headed downstream.

Fully loaded with *pièces*, the voyageurs could spend over a week portaging the Methye. Mackenzie and his men made the run in three days. The cold gripped tighter, and even the fast-moving Pelican River started to freeze, "the ice driving so thick further on that there was no possibility of poling a canoe into it." Mackenzie had no Cree or Chipewyan hunters with him and was desperately running out of pemmican, so he decided to split up the brigade. He hid the canoes and merchandise, to keep animals out, and then sent many of his men south, back down the portage, to establish their own winter quarters at the fishery on Lac La Loche. Mackenzie waited with Barrieau and a few other men for three days, until the ice cleared, and then paddled a single light canoe as quickly as they could to Pond's fort. It still took over a week, though hunger drove them on.

The Old Establishment was worn and frayed, a burly stockade, flooded in spring, snow drifted in winter. Peter Pond was there, waiting for Mackenzie. The two men had never met. Pond was almost forty-eight years old, with two decades of hard life in the *pays d'en haut*. Alexander Mackenzie was half his age. The Yankee son of a cobbler and the Scottish scion to a tacksman resembled each other only in geographic ambitions.

On December 2, 1787, Alexander wrote to Roderic, guardedly. "This far my neighbor and I have agreed very well, and I believe we shall continue on the same footing for the Season."

———

Fierce winter never relented. Mackenzie and Pond consolidated their men, ordered back every clerk and voyageur who had established a far-flung shack among the Chipewyan, including Cuthbert Grant and Laurent Leroux from Slave Lake. Leroux had worked as a clerk for Peter Pangman, and then for Ross in the New Concern, coming north to Athabasca in 1785 to compete against Grant for two seasons. But with such bad weather, so few trade goods, Mackenzie saw no reason to leave them stranded. In fact, he wondered how the Chipewyan would even work in such conditions. "By the ice we cannot expect a good hunt from these posts," he wrote to his business partners.

Trapped in that small outpost, with few goods to trade, few hunters about, and few visitors to interrupt, Pond and Mackenzie had many long days to talk. Pond liked to talk. He told everyone his plans, everyone who would listen.

As November turned, and the drudgery of thin wintering life set in, Mackenzie and Pond huddled around a small table in their wooden shack in the blizzard north, and the old man shared his secrets. He told Mackenzie where he had gone the year he left the north country, the only year he had left the land.

In the fall of 1784, Pond had gone to New York City. He had a map to present to the U.S. Congress. He showed it to Mackenzie as well, a broad sheet crisscrossed with every river and lake of the upper continent, every post labeled, the lands of the Chipewyan and Esquimaux. Even a grand river flowing to a sea he called the Mer du Nord West.

That river. It was the key, the focus of his life's work, the culmination of years of exploration. Pond told Mackenzie he had found the long-sought water route to the Pacific. That the next year, he would paddle the length of the river, cross Kamchatka, trade with Canton, and then push to Moscow. That he had drawn a map of the whole territory, to present to Catherine the Great herself.

That he, Peter Pond of Connecticut, was the man who had finally solved the riddle of the Northwest Passage.

To the Northwest Passage, 1788

~~~~~

In 1775, after nearly three hundred years of European nautical failure, the British Parliament authorized the award of twenty thousand pounds to whoever could discover the Northwest Passage. Such prizes had already proven successful; a similar challenge to solve the problem of measuring longitude had induced John Harrison to develop a series of chronometers between 1730 and 1773.

Captain James Cook, hero of the Admiralty, accepted the challenge, setting sail on his third great voyage in 1776. His first two journeys, to the South Pacific in 1768 and 1772, had given him a reputation for "negative discoveries," proving speculative geographers wrong. In further pursuit of the balanced-earth theory, he had searched for land below Australia and never found it. "If I have failed in discovering a Continent it is because it does not exist . . . and not for want of looking," Cook said. If Cook couldn't find a northwest passage, the thinking went, then it wasn't there to find.

Cook's plan was to turn the search on its head and scout the west coast of North America for the passage's outlet; perhaps it would be easier to start from the end and work back toward the beginning. On his way north along the California coast, Cook was beset by fog and rain. Storms pushed him out to sea for a time. Eventually, he sheltered his ship among mountain peaks that fell into the ocean, and local Indian tribes sought to trade him beaver, seal, and otter furs.

In the late spring of 1778, Captain Cook surveyed a vast inlet at 60 degrees latitude, because it might lead to "a very extensive inland communication." The water grew fresher as they worked in, and the mouth of the river was choked with timber, huge trees that had floated down from the snowy mountains. Tide and current pushed against them, and they were blocked from continuing any farther. "A fine spacious river, but a cursed unfortunate one to us," he wrote, frustrated. The inlet would be named for Cook.

By late summer, Cook and his crew had sailed up through the Bering Strait that separated Alaska from Asia. But here, above 70 degrees latitude, he encountered ten-foot-tall pack ice. Sailors of the day generally did not believe such ice could form in open salt water, that only fresh or shallow water could freeze near shore, and so the hulls of Cook's ships were not reinforced to brave such obstacles. What he saw unnerved him, and Cook retreated.

The lord of the negative discovery had done it again: there was no ice-free northwest passage, no navigable sea of the Arctic. Cook thought he was on a fool's errand and wrote a letter to the Admiralty that he entrusted with Russian sailors off Kamchatka. "I must confess I have little hopes of succeeding," he reported. There were no routes through the continent, and "the Polar part is far from being an open Sea." The whole affair was "disappointing."

In time, the letter would arrive in London. Cook did not. He was dead only a few months later, beaten to death on a Hawaiian beach and then, in a ritual reserved for royalty, cooked and deboned by the island's holy men.

Legend of Cook's travels spread, but not the gloomy qualifiers or his sense of failure. In 1783, John Ledyard, one of Cook's crew, published his *Journal of Captain Cook's Last Voyage*. Where Cook was reticent about a northwest passage in his personal writing, Ledyard was exuberant in his own volume, especially praising the potential fur-trading opportunities. The book was the talk of New York in 1784, when Peter Pond was showing off a map of potential river routes across the continent. It was missing only one key feature: an outlet on the Pacific. Pond found it in the reports of Cook's voyage.

————

Awgeenah delivered to Peter Pond more than furs. The English Chief also brought news, accounts of the land, cartographic insights from his travels to trade with the Red Knife tribes. For Pond, these tidbits of geography were even more valuable than the beaver pelts. He added each detail to a map that he meticulously drew and redrew and redrew over the long winters. Every new version revealed more of his scheme.

And Awgeenah's most important detail, first reported on Matonab-bee's deerskin map, was this: an enormous river, fed by Slave Lake, that drove relentlessly west.

During their winter together in 1787, Pond told Mackenzie of his trav-els three years before. He was searching for sponsorship and funding to mount an expedition and prove an interior northwest passage. His map showed a northern end to the Rocky Mountains and a chain of lakes and rivers stretching to the Mer du Nord West—not the Arctic Sea of the pole, not the Pacific Ocean, but rather the sea of the Northwest Passage. To boast its accuracy, Pond wrote that his chart was based upon inter-views with forty Red Knife Indians.

Pond first took his map to New York, the capital of the United States, to petition the Congress. But newly organized under the Articles of Con-federation, few members were present, and the map he showed about aroused little interest.

So Pond returned to Montreal to make the circuit of coffeehouses, business concerns, and government officials. He discovered that Cook's journey and a new map of his travels were hotly discussed among gentle-men of standing. Pond revised his chart to reflect Cook's survey, adding the coastal features of the Pacific, and secured a meeting with the British lieutenant governor of Quebec, Henry Hamilton. The two men had last seen each other in Detroit, when Pond was a new fur trader, and Ham-ilton was the "Hair-Buyer General" of the fort. In the decade since, their paths had diverged, Hamilton to urban wealth and privilege, Pond to wicked toil in the northern backcountry.

In the stately Château Ramezay, decorated by a wall-sized tapestry of peacocks and pagodas of the Orient, Pond talked of his map and his plan to access the trade with China. Alaska was all sketched out, his winter-ing quarters in Athabasca temptingly close, an easy three-day journey to Jesuits Harbor on the Pacific, he claimed. Pond was not the only trader petitioning the British government. Threatened by the New Concern, the North West Company—with which Pond was not affiliated at the time, having turned down the single share offered in the partnership that year—was also officially lobbying for a trade monopoly in the lands it explored at its own expense, "between the latitudes of 55 and 65, all that tract of country extending west of the Hudson's Bay to the North Pacific Ocean." The Russians were already trading in sea otter pelts on the coast.

The Americans would wake up and realize the opportunity at any time. They needed to go now, to the Pacific, while they still could.

Legally, much of this land was claimed by the Hudson's Bay Company. The royal monopoly of Prince Rupert's Land extended to a space ten times the size of the Holy Roman Empire, the largest piece of property ever owned by a private company. But these borders had never been surveyed, delineated, or even superficially explored and established by the HBC. Its men only ventured into a tiny percentage of that land, sleeping the winter away on the bay with such disdain that in 1749 the British Parliament chastised them for their laziness and failure to properly search for a northwest passage. If such a waterway was to be found, Pond felt, other men of industry and imagination would have to take up that cause.

Pond was relentless in pressing his case. Hamilton was convinced and wrote back to London that Pond had "a passion for making discoveries" and should be supported. But the Crown disagreed. Alexander Dalrymple, the hydrographer for the East India Company and consultant to the British Admiralty, said that the Hudson's Bay Company should be engaged in the Northwest Passage expedition instead, as the Montreal traders "seem to be scarcely less savage than the most savage of the Indians."

That letter took many months to cross the Atlantic, though, and Pond had not waited for a reply. He returned to Athabasca in the summer of 1785, to plan the expedition himself. He had heard all he needed in Montreal.

Back at the Old Establishment, Pond considered what Awgeenah had told him of a river flowing west from Slave Lake. He studied the map of Cook's travels. He had discussed the geography with the most learned minds of New York, New England, and Montreal. The solution to the problem of the Northwest Passage lay in Cook's Inlet. He was sure of it.

Cook was surveying this vast river mouth in 1778, just as Peter Pond had crossed the Methye Portage for the first time. Cook reported large amounts of timber in the water, which matched the wood-blown Slave, brought down from the mountains. Cook also noted that the water of the inlet was merely brackish, almost fresh, so a great river must flow into it. In 1787, Pond met two Indians who said they had traveled up a large river from the Pacific Ocean; they bore English blankets from Captain Cook as proof. It was the final piece of evidence Pond needed.

Pond sketched one last map. It showed the river of Matonabbee and Awgeenah as the direct connection between Slave Lake and Cook's Inlet. A broad thoroughfare, no longer than the Pelican River, driving due west, skirting the northern edge of an exhausted Rocky Mountains, and emptying in a massive fork into the Pacific Ocean. He also drew a great waterfall, many miles wider and taller than Niagara, the largest in the world even. So the Chipewyan and Dogrib had reported. But if they had made the portage, Pond figured, there must be an established path that was not too arduous.

This map, incorporating all of Pond's synthesized knowledge of personal explorations and reported geography, was published in the *Gentleman's Magazine*, London's leading monthly periodical. It was a prestigious achievement appropriate for a *bourgeois* who had spent so much time in cartographic pursuits. On one end of the river, near Slave Lake, a note: "So far Pond." On the other, at the Alaskan inlet: "So far Cook." The two were so close. Pond's Old Establishment was nearly there; as he had so often said, a three-day journey to the sea.

———

Alexander Mackenzie had just become an Athabasca man, the most revered of *hommes du nord,* and yet, in early December 1787, as soon as the rivers were shut tight, he traveled three hundred miles south, all the way to Île-à-la-Crosse, to see his cousin.

He walked on snowshoes and slept outside on pine boughs, his feet as close to the fire as he could stand, all night long. In his years in the north, Alexander had seen trees with stumps cut clean fifteen or twenty feet above the portage trail. And the old northmen voyageurs told him that the Indians of this land were thirty or forty feet tall, and that is why the trees were felled at such an unusual height. But now he saw for himself that the snow in this country mounded so high that these towering stumps were at his knees. Still, his Chipewyan robes, stuffed with moose and caribou hair, kept a man warm all night. Alexander had seen a hunter dressed as such "lay himself down on the ice in the middle of a lake, and repose in comfort; though he will sometimes find a difficulty in the morning to disencumber himself from the snow drifted on him during the night."

Alexander had made the journey because he was concerned for Roderic. "Write me the first opportunity what you mean to do—whether you mean to remain in the country or not," he told his cousin. Roderic was shaken by Ross's death, wondering what kind of business he had taken up. "After the experience you must have had of the direful effect the late opposition has had upon those that engaged in it," Alexander commiserated, "I do not know what advice to offer you." For his own part, Alexander was having second thoughts as well. "Could I in four years of hard labour and anxiety pay the debt I owe our concern in consequence I should feel satisfied," he said.

But in truth, Alexander had a second reason to trudge all the way to Île-à-la-Crosse: Pond's grandiosity. Alexander told Roderic and Patrick Small, the North West Company partner, of Pond's "incomprehensively extravagant" plans, that he had seen a map "to lay before the Empress of Russia." Small agreed that he was "quite surprised at the wild ideas Mr. Pond has of matters," and Roderic said that Pond "thought himself a philosopher, and was odd in his manners." And yet Alexander had to admit, privately, that the idea appealed to his own aspirations. Perhaps there was some merit in Pond's plan. If he stayed with the North West Company, imagine if he were the one to take the voyage instead?

On this, his "distant intentions," as he called them, he swore Roderic to silence. "I beg you will not reveal them to any person, as it might be prejudicial to me, though I may never have it in my power to put them in execution."

In time, Pond grew suspicious of Alexander's absence and wrote to Patrick Small, his trusted colleague, to ask what the young Scot was up to. Small wrote back but was cryptic in his reassurance, advising Pond that Mackenzie was doing nothing "contrary to the mutual interest of all concerned." Everyone knew Pond was on the outs and Mackenzie the up-and-comer.

Alexander stayed at Île-à-la-Crosse through mid-February. Both Alexander and Small "did all in their power to induce me to continue in the service," Roderic wrote, but he was adamant about quitting. After Alexander returned to Athabasca, Barrieau, his *devant*, served as a trusted courier, shepherding letters back and forth between the Mackenzies. "I will not pretend to condemn or approve," Alexander told Roderic, still bothered by his cousin's insistence on leaving. If Roderic left the trade, what would he do instead, Alexander wondered, warning, "It is far more easy for a man to get into troubles than to get out of them." Roderic wrote back saddened that Alexander was displeased, but said that clerking was akin to bondage. Alexander, who unlike Roderic had spent time among chained Africans in New York and Detroit, had little sympathy for this complaint. "As for your idea of Slavery I cannot approve of," he wrote. "It shows that you never was acquainted with that abject condition."

The cousins' disagreement remained affectionate, though; Alexander still referred to him as "Dear Rory," and his last letter, before their reunion that summer, contained the postscript "I won't forget your Books."

Mackenzie and Pond finished their season together in peace. No mysterious gunshots or unexplained scuffles. They even had a successful winter of trading, despite Mackenzie's initial concerns; the Beaver Indians in particular repaid their debts from previous seasons. All told, their clerk, Cuthbert Grant, took four hundred *pièces*, eighteen tons of beaver fur, to Grand Portage.

Pond left the Old Establishment on May 15, 1788, in his own canoe with eight paddlers. When he arrived at the *rendezvous*, his partners informed him that his services were no longer needed. Pond never again returned to the north.

———

Alexander was "quite out of conceit with the North West," he told his cousin. "If I continue in my present opinion I shall certainly endeavor to get clear of it." In fact, he had a plan to do so: find the Northwest Passage to China, earn his fortune, retire. And he couldn't let Roderic quit, because Alexander needed his cousin's help to pull it off.

Alexander's experience the previous fall—rivers frozen early and hard, snowbound canoes—convinced him that the main voyageur brigades had inadequate time to make it all the way to the *rendezvous* and back, not while carrying *pièces* on the portages. Instead, to cut a month off their transit, goods bound for Athabasca would be staged at a new warehouse at Rainy Lake. On July 7, 1788, Alexander fretted impatiently, supervising the cross load and inventory of canvas-wrapped bundles. The next day he would set off in a light, unburdened canoe for Grand Portage, to quickly meet with the partners and discuss his expedition. "I wish you were here now," he wrote to his cousin from the depot.

Roderic's spring journey from Île-à-la-Crosse was considerably shorter, and he had been waiting for Alexander at the *rendezvous* for some time. It was to be his last season, Roderic decided. He was done with the fur-trading business, he was sure of it. At their reunion at Grand Portage, Roderic found his cousin "extremely anxious and uncertain." Alexander "insisted upon my accompanying him once more to the interior, which, notwithstanding my high regard for him, I declined," Roderic said. But Alexander needed Roderic in Athabasca, while he made the exploration of Pond's river the next summer. He could not undertake the quest without him.

Alexander begged and revealed every bit of his "voyage of discovery" plans to Roderic "in confidence." If Roderic "could not return and take charge of his department in his absence," Alexander said, "he must abandon his intentions." The guilt worked. "Considering his regret at my refusal," Roderic "yielded to his wishes."

At the *rendezvous,* Alexander requested the top assignment: to take over Athabasca, the company's most important and productive department, and, while Roderic ran the business in his absence, to find a path through the continent. His fellow *bourgeois* signed off. Alexander was on his way to find the Northwest Passage.

———

The expedition was a year away, but time was already running out to get it properly organized. Any European provisions he wished to carry, or men he wished to take on this voyage in 1789, he would have to put in place that summer of 1788. Alexander and Roderic moved quickly back to Athabasca, only fifty-two days of travel from Rainy Lake. But their haste was not without cost: just below Île-à-la-Crosse, a canoe was damaged and floundered. "I lost two men and eleven pieces of goods," Alexander reported to his partners, with a detachment that reflected the tragedy's commonness.

The frenetic pace continued upon arrival at the Old Establishment, where there was significant work to do. Every spring, when the ice broke and the Peace River swelled with runoff from the mountains, Pond's creaking old fort flooded, water rising through the floorboards and up to the windowsills. Plus, the Cree had become unreliable traders; many were off to war. So to entice more Chipewyan to trade, Alexander ordered a new post built, to be named for their people, and he sent Roderic forty miles north, to the Lake of the Hills, to oversee construction.

Roderic chose a "conspicuous projection" on the south shore, "which appeared in the shape of a person with her arms extended, the palms forming as if it were a point." He established a fishery, which Alexander found a "very cold branch of business," sending a pair of mittens to Roderic in sympathy. But his cousin wouldn't use them. Roderic "visited six nets three times a day from under the ice," but "no mittens can be used during that serious operation," because he had to disentangle the fish from the nets while they were still underwater, or else everything froze stiff.

Under Roderic's care, the new Fort Chipewyan became a place of comfort and civility. They dug furrows for turnips and parsnips and rutabagas; Pond had the best kitchen garden in the backcountry, everyone said, and so the vegetables were easily transferred. They put glass in the windows and stored maple syrup to flavor the white fish, and Roderic gathered dozens of books to create the largest library in a thousand miles. *Tristram Shandy*, the *Perpetual Almanack* to count the days, Greek classics—the fort became known as "the Athens of the North."

At Christmastime, Alexander trudged the forty miles through the snow for a glass of wine and dinner with Roderic. It was company, a break from the loneliness, a chance to speak one's native tongue, *bourgeois* always at a distance from the voyageurs and even one's *à la façon du pays* wife. They toasted the new endeavor, and Alexander shared one final bit of good news, essential for his expedition.

That fall, Awgeenah and seven of his warriors stopped at the Old Establishment. He and the Scot had come to a mutual understanding of the benefit of their partnership. The two men had grown as close as eighteenth-century manners allowed; alone among traders, Alexander called him Nestabeck. The Chipewyan was in a good mood, said he was heading to Slave Lake to collect debts and furs from the Red Knives. They had parted with promises to meet for trade soon.

And more. Awgeenah agreed to bring several wives and hunters to Fort Chipewyan in the spring, to accompany Alexander through the Northwest Passage. Just as Awgeenah had seen Matonabbee escort Hearne to the Far Off Metal River almost two decades before, the English Chief would serve as Mackenzie's guide, his protector, his translator, his partner.

There was only one difference, and an important one.

Matonabbee knew the way to the copper mines, but Awgeenah had never yet traveled the great river to the sun.

12

All It Takes Is Time, 2016

〜〜〜

I began serious planning for my own journey six months out. I found a book online, *The Mackenzie River Guide,* written by Michelle Swallow. It was self-published, and about a decade old, but its mere existence meant I wasn't crazy to attempt this trip. Some sections seemed a massive construction site, other stretches country even wilder and less populated than in 1789. Michelle wrote that the villages were safe and the people friendly, and the book was filled with photographs and maps and telephone numbers for grocery stores. It displayed confidence on every page.

It also provided a mileage chart and timeline, the rough number of days from town to town. I counted: only nine settlements total along the route. Some sounded welcoming, like Fort Good Hope, and some were unpronounceable, like Tsiigehtchic. As a daily planning factor—knowing with sun and strong current I could do more, but during storms and wind I'd be stuck—I made a goal of thirty miles. A six-week trip. Taking into consideration daylight, bugs, temperature, and the dry summer, June 22 seemed the best day to start, just after the solstice. I'd be at 61 degrees latitude, or, as the sun sees it because of the 23-degree tilt of the earth, 84 degrees up the globe, almost to the top. Hard to get more light, and I'd only be climbing higher from there.

I told family and friends about the trip, but they didn't share my irrational fear of falling from a great height. They wanted to talk about bears, and all asked the same two questions: Are you going alone, and are you taking a gun?

The answer to both was no. Every kind of bear would be up there—black, brown, grizzly, even a chance of polar at the end—but the best defense is avoidance. Never take food in the tent; don't sleep where you cook: I planned to always paddle for an hour after dinner each night, to a clean campsite. If a bear did get too curious, we'd use bear spray, a kind of concentrated mace, or a bear banger, a pen flare that shoots a blank shotgun shell. Taking a gun would change the tenor of the trip. I wanted to meet people without a sidearm and not worry about a rifle left in the canoe.

Far more challenging than leaving a gun at home was finding someone to go with me. Practical concerns abounded. Safety, foremost, in case of sickness, injury, catastrophe. Plus I'd need a canoe to carry so much gear, rather than a solo kayak, and they are much easier to navigate with a second paddler. There were psychological reasons too; I wanted to paddle the whole river, not experiment on myself to see if I could spend two months alone.

But as I asked friends to join me, I quickly discovered that people with real jobs have much less flexibility to take so much time off. No one had a whole summer to devote, so I came up with a plan to divide the trip into quarters, ask four friends to each join me on a leg; they would be like runners in a relay race and pass me as the baton.

Four men signed on. David Chrisinger, a bearded writer from Wisconsin. Jeremy Howard Beck, the composer of the opera adaptation of my first book. Landon Phillips, an old military buddy from Iraq; while I led a bomb squad in Kirkuk, he did the same in Baghdad. And Anthony Sennhenn, another fellow bomb tech, whom everyone calls Senny. Only Senny had thoughts on bears, as he'd do the last leg with me above the Arctic Circle.

"If I get my throat slashed by a motherfucking polar bear, promise me you'll put that on my grave," he said. "Just like that. 'Here lies Senny. He had his throat ripped out by a motherfucking polar bear, bitches.' That would be badass."

We decided the logistics would go like this: I'd drive up through Canada and rent a canoe in Hay River, a small town on the south shore of Great Slave Lake. David would fly in and paddle the first leg to Fort Simpson, where he'd fly out and Jeremy would fly in. The pattern would repeat for Landon and Senny, switching at Tulita and Fort Good Hope, respectively. Senny would fly out of Inuvik, the last town on the river, where I'd pick up my truck; there is a barge that delivers freight from Hay River to Inuvik twice a summer. Then I could drop my canoe on the barge for shipment back to the rental shop and drive home unencumbered.

This plan was suggested to me by a man named Doug Swallow, who happens to be Michelle's father. Doug runs a small company that ships medical and survival supplies through the northwest Arctic, and he agreed to rent me the canoe. I asked for the longest one he had, for the sake of cargo space, steadiness, and speed; a boat's maximum possible velocity is governed by the length of the hull.

I had a timeline, teammates, and a canoe. Now I needed gear. For inspiration, I checked a favorite battered paperback on my shelf, Nicholas Crane's *Clear Waters Rising*. Crane walked from Cape Finisterre, on the northwestern Spanish coast, to Istanbul, always keeping to the mountains. The Cantabrians, Pyrenees, Cévennes, Alps, Carpathians, Balkans. One portion of the book stuck with me in particular: Crane's indulgence in taking four socks. His friends proposed that three would be sufficient; two to wear, one sock to wash and dry each day. But Crane insists on four, so he can use the spare set as mittens if required.

I intended no such monasticism. I was renting a giant canoe so I could take almost any gear I wanted. And I would use an old military planning rule of thumb: two is one and one is none. Everything critical would have a spare.

As I reread Crane before my trip, however, the rest of his choices seemed either overly British—he considered an umbrella essential—or downright irresponsible. The first night of his trek, he unrolls his cotton sleeping bag and discovers it "perforated with no fewer than twenty-four holes." He hadn't bothered to check it before leaving. In contrast, Crane takes much more care choosing a hat, a Herbert Johnson trilby, à la Indiana Jones. But, I thought, didn't Harrison Ford have to staple that fedora to his head to keep it from flying off? I was much more practical and chose a Tilley hat. Polyester, not felt. Breathable. Keeps the sun and rain off, a strap to secure it on one's head. I tried it on at the store and looked in the mirror, and I realized I had reached an age when wearing such a hat was no longer ironic. I was not playing dress up, impersonating my father. I am a father, a middle-aged man in a brimmed hat.

I trusted the Internet, rather than Crane, for my other gear recommendations. New inflatable sleeping pads and bedrolls. A gravity-powered water filtration system. A curved Hudson Bay–style Snow & Nealley ax, handmade in Maine. Three-panel solar array and battery pack. Old-school paper topographic maps of the entire route. A squat Hilleberg tent, shaped like a bunker and rated for the hurricane winds of the Himalaya; before the trip, my youngest son and I tested the tent in the backyard, so he could imagine where I was during our long time apart. Another military friend lent me his DeLorme inReach: a GPS and mapping device that also sends texts and drops virtual bread crumbs, so friends and family could follow my progress online at home. I didn't know what cooking fuel would be available for purchase in the towns we would pass through, so I brought two stoves, one that ran on white gas, and another that professed to run on anything, including diesel. Dr. Bronner's biodegradable soap to take the occasional bath in the river and wash clothes. A kayak paddle that breaks in half, as an emergency backup. A rechargeable headlamp. DEET and sunscreen. An old pair of fireman's boots as improvised waders. Head net and bug shirt. Second pop-up tent, for emergencies. A throw bag of rope for rescues, also usable as a clothes-line. Rain gear and parka, for extreme cold. "It will snow on one of you," I told my paddle mates, "I just don't know which one." A collapsible sail, from WindPaddle in Hood River, Oregon, a very breezy place along the Columbia River. In a nod to Crane, who kept all of his papers in a plastic bag he called the Office, I brought a waterproof case for my computer and electronics and gave it the same name. I also had a small dry bag we called the Wallet, for passports and money, and a larger bag for the cook-ing gear that Senny eventually named the Kitchen.

For meals, I packed simply, for minimal preparation. Oatmeal and tea is my old camping standby for breakfast, and bagels and peanut butter, plus fruit, for lunch. To add extra calories, I also packed honey and choc-olate and bars of pemmican. It was sold by a Sioux company from Pine Ridge in South Dakota and still contained bison meat and cranberries, though presumably less hair and shit than the traditional blend.

Variety would come at dinner; I wanted something besides the stan-dard dehydrated meals I bought in sporting goods stores. I discovered a company called Happy Yak, in Quebec, that sold French cooking in small packets. I bought a few and fed them to my children for lunch one weekend. Mushroom Risotto, Pad Thai, Vegetarian Chili, Seafood Delight. They were excellent, and I bought ninety, enough for forty-five days of camping. It seemed appropriate, following the voyageurs, to be a pork eater and get my food from Quebec.

But as June approached, and the practical considerations were largely set, a very specific fear began to intrude.

I had resolved to make it to the Arctic Ocean, cup my hands in the water, and drink the salt. And since I had first looked at a topo map, one section of the trip had given me pause. The last two hundred miles, navigating the delta and then the open-water crossing all the way to Garry Island, the last of the barrier islands. Out into the Arctic Ocean, in a canoe.

The rest of the twelve-hundred-mile trip was daunting, but this last section had the potential for disaster. Lost in the labyrinth of the delta, or capsized in ocean swells, or both.

I needed a rescue plan, so I spoke on the phone with Kylik Kisoun, an Inuvialuit guide in Inuvik. He and his uncle owned a small charter boat company, and Doug Swallow said no one knew the delta like the Kisouns. For a hefty fee—the cost of gasoline in Inuvik is obscene, over eight dollars a gallon—they agreed to retrieve Senny and me, once we reached our destination.

But I still felt uneasy, thinking I could not have clearly communicated where I intended to go, if Kylik had willingly signed up for the job.

"I want to make it all the way to Garry Island," I said again. "Is that crazy?"

"No, you can do it," he said. "All it takes is time, right? You can get anywhere if you have the time."

"And you're sure your boat will make it out there?" I said. "And it can fit my canoe and all my gear and . . ."

"Listen, I get it, I get it," Kylik said, laughing. "But don't worry, we run the delta all the time." And then he paused a moment, before making this promise.

"If you can make it out there, we'll come get you."

————

When the appointed day finally arrived, I got in my truck, alone with a load of expedition supplies, and drove across the Niagara River, up along the east and north rim of Lake Huron, around Lake Superior, past the Grand Portage, and into the boreal forest.

In mere hours and days, I logged weeks of voyageur travel. Over Grand Portage's height of land, separating the Atlantic watershed from the Arctic, northern plant species start to creep in. Less grass or soft moss, more sickly green lichen, the color of a child about to vomit. It was the start of the muskeg, the nefarious northern swamp. The ground was neither rock nor dirt nor plant nor dead, but rather a combination of all those, too wet to walk on and too dry to paddle through, impossible to traverse in summer.

On the drive across central Manitoba and Saskatchewan, up through northern Alberta, I avoided the main Trans-Canada Highway and stayed on the small two-lane roads, well maintained but lonesome. Canada is drunk on its northern mystique. On billboards as I entered towns: "The Spirit of the North," "North Woods," "Northern Frontier," "True North," "Last North," "Ultimate North," "Crown of the North." The award for truth in advertising went to "Gateway to the North," another way of saying "we know you're just passing through."

I found white resource towns, like Flin Flon, a copper mine perched on a bronzed granite cap, and neglected indigenous towns, like Grand Rapids, home of unemployed men and dirt paths and cages on every window. Between outposts, an abstract painter's tableau: against the uniform canvas of spruce—short or tall, swampy or burned out, always spruce—the roads seemed just a painted accent streak, the color of the local crushed stone. Salt white near The Pas, purple in Cranberry Portage.

In Manitoba, I pulled over on the side of the road at a random spot to take a piss, no towns for hours. The paved road was built on a raised man-made gravel berm, and I walked down the ramp to the tree line. The ditch was full of soda cans and Tostitos bags, and the trash continued well into the forest, as far as I could see. Mosquitoes rose from small pools of standing water and attacked me as I pissed, so I quickly returned to the truck. I found it engulfed in giant flies, undeterred by the wind, banging themselves into the glass and door panels. I snuck into the driver's seat, slammed the door, chased down four flies that followed me in, and smeared them against the windows. They were as big as the main digit of my thumb, and when I pushed on them to kill them, their bodies cracked and the meat split under my fingers, as if I had smeared a fat green grape across the kitchen table.

Except to pump gas, I saw almost no one for days. My windshield was a murder wall, the stuff of nightmares for giant flies. I was driving 140 kilometers an hour but felt hemmed in. No view, no perspective, all day an identical sight: only the slightest ripple in the flat spruce monoculture, days upon days unchanging.

How did they build these roads, have the heart to work in such a vast land? Early America, full of colonists, was comparatively compact, and the forest fell away as they traveled inland. Americans could tame their wilderness because they could see it. Man is the master of all he surveys. Americans surveyed open plains from horseback. The peddlers from Montreal surveyed impenetrable forest from their canoes.

No wonder Canadians seem to be natural socialists and praise collective effort, I thought. Their land is too big, they too few. On the drive through rural towns, I saw statues of voyageurs, lumberjacks, miners, hockey players. All nameless, faces a composite. I thought of something a Canadian historian named Douglas Hunter told me as I researched my trip.

"Down south, you guys grab guns and play Cowboys and Indians," he said. "But up here, we play Cowboys *with* Indians." If they didn't work together, they'd die.

At the Alberta border, oil derricks and hammer-headed pumps and huge yellow hazard signs shaped like moose, big enough to walk into the road themselves. Lloydminster, boomtown of the booming sands, hosts every corporate chain restaurant and retail big box on a single highway through town. In one parking lot, black ten-thousand-gallon water tanks were lined up like soup cans on a grocery store shelf, a banner draped in front. "In Stock!" it said helpfully.

I took on the last of my perishable supplies at a Walmart outside Edmonton. Tortillas, bagels, peanut butter, honey, mandarin oranges, apples, pears, peaches, oatmeal, Snickers bars.

My first stop would be Fort Smith, a little town in the Northwest Territories. It lies on the bank of the Slave River, flowing out of Lake Athabasca, the body of water Mackenzie knew as Lake of the Hills. After dropping in on this first leg of Mackenzie and Awgeenah's journey, I would drive to Hay River to get my canoe, pick up David, and start the main expedition.

North and west of Edmonton, I shed all accidental and accessory drivers. In Valleyview, American RV-clad tourists made a left turn for Alaska. The oil workers turned off outside Peace River, the loggers hours later. The road north was so monotonous that the few double-length tractor trailers drove in pairs—four loads, two drivers—presumably for safety, to keep each other awake, or assist in an emergency; no cell-phone call out was possible.

On the road out of Edmonton, I finally crossed the height of land into the Mackenzie watershed. For the first time, over the lip of the bowl, the view opened. Expansive, a wide and rolling green country, and as I drove my truck, wave after wave of land crested on my way into the valley and down.

That was it. North no longer felt up. As I crossed this last ridge, it became a down feeling. As if I were flowing into a drain, emptying into the sea. A mammoth force calling me, drawing me in with a magnetic pull, a subconscious voice, vibrating on a frequency only to be felt, too low to hear.

Into the basin, the river said, and down, down, down.

13

Embarkation, June 1789

〰〰〰

Mackenzie's expedition to the Pacific consisted of ten men and four women in three birch-bark canoes, all smaller than the freight canoes typically used in the fur trade but large enough to carry a few months' worth of pemmican. The men would paddle and hunt and repair boats. The women would paddle and cook and make camp. It was a party built for speed, endurance, and, most important, self-sufficiency.

Two smaller canoes carried the Chipewyan, one for Awgeenah, the other for the two young men—one of whom was Awgeenah's brother—who served as the party's hunters. The travel would be nothing to Awgeenah and his people, who told Mackenzie that "in ancient times their ancestors lived till their feet were worn out with walking."

The largest canoe, by far, was Mackenzie's; over twenty feet long, it bore eight souls and was crewed by four hired voyageurs. This was a coveted assignment. Among the voyageurs, prowess was measured by geography, and anyone who found the Northwest Passage and lived to tell about it would be held in the highest esteem at the next *rendezvous*.

Mackenzie hand selected the men the season before. François Barrieau, trusted courier and experienced northman, was his *devant*, the guide in the front of his canoe. His two *milieux*, the human paddling engine at the center of the boat, were Pierre de Lorme and Charles Ducette. His *gouvernail*, the steersman in the back, was Joseph Landry. Barrieau and de Lorme were former New Concern men. Landry and Ducette were longtime North West Company voyageurs, *engagés* hired by Peter Pond and Cuthbert Grant. They were also cousins from Acadia, the isolated French colony on the Atlantic coast. After the French and Indian War, many Acadians scattered under British rule. Some went to Louisiana and became known as Cajuns; some went inland and joined the fur trade. Landry and Ducette were inseparable.

The last employed member of Mackenzie's crew was Johann Stein-bruck, a Protestant German and former Hessian mercenary who fought for the British during the American Revolution. A few years older than Mackenzie, Steinbruck was born in Thuringia, a long day's walk from Leipzig. He enlisted at age eighteen and landed in Quebec in September 1778, after the decisive battles of the war. As a grenadier, he was one of the biggest men in his battalion, but he saw mostly garrison duty in northern New York and the St. Lawrence valley, the same barren posts where Alexander's father served. It was a cold drudgery that prepared him well for his future employment. He deserted the army in the summer of 1783, the war all but over, and, having learned French and a bit of writing, made his way to Quebec to work in the fur trade. Steinbruck was too educated to be a voyageur, too German to be a *bourgeois,* too poor to start his own trade. So he became a clerk with the North West Company, the same position Roderic considered bondage.

The final two seats in Mackenzie's canoe were occupied by the voyageurs' *à la façon du pays* wives. Landry, in particular, was a devoted husband; soon after he signed on with Peter Pond for a three-year stint in Athabasca, he used his new salary to buy beads and a dozen rings for his wife when passing through Île-à-la-Crosse on the way to that summer's *rendezvous.* Awgeenah also brought two of his wives, the three of them in his own smaller canoe. This was the lesson of Matonabbee, that the women performed such valuable services no expedition could succeed without them.

Mackenzie was the least experienced white man on the trip. Awgeenah was a decade older, worldly, and well traveled. But both were businessmen, ambitious, physically courageous; their partnership was one of convenience, but no less shrewd for it.

———

On the first leg of the journey, to the far side of Slave Lake, Mackenzie's party would be accompanied by Laurent Leroux, the clerk. Leroux had just snowshoed back from the lake on March 22, with promises from the Red Knives to meet him and Mackenzie that summer. Leroux was well liked by the Red Knives. Several years before, he had persuaded the English Chief to spread the word that he and the North West Company were fair and they should all come to his fort to trade, instead of crossing the barrens to the Hudson's Bay Company posts. Leroux had laid the groundwork so Mackenzie could perhaps entice a guide to show him the river that flowed from the western shore of Slave Lake, or at least stock up on provisions.

Food occupied the front of Mackenzie's thoughts, and he restricted their equipment to the basics: pemmican; clothing; crooked knives and a few fathoms of birch bark, about twelve feet total, for canoe repairs; "a proper assortment of the articles of merchandise as present, to ensure a friendly reception among the Indians"; and if that failed, "ammunition and arms requisite for our defense." Mackenzie knew his own canoe couldn't carry enough supplies, so he stocked some in Leroux's; by the time they parted company, they'd have eaten through enough stores in his own boat to make room.

They could never carry enough, though, so the hunters were essential to Mackenzie's plans. The Chipewyan men carried powder horns and sawed-off rifles, to move easily through the bush, and when pursuing game, they held the half-inch ball ammo in their mouths, to spit down the barrel to reload quick. All in the party wore moose-skin moccasins, with no socks, for ease of drying, and Awgeenah's wives were dressed in deerskins and necklaces of the umbilical cords of their children, decorated with beads and porcupine quills. Ducette, de Lorme, the women, and the hunters all used short paddles, no taller than their bellies, with thin blades that reduced drag and allowed for a full day's labor. Barrieau's paddle was a bit longer, to steer the nose of the canoe around rocks. Landry's *gouvernail* stick was nine feet of black ash.

Despite his mockery of Pond's outlandish plans, Mackenzie did pack a map for Catherine the Great and a few Russian rubles as well. Also a pocket watch and a quadrant, to make observations of latitude using the sun's height above the horizon at noon, and a compass, with which he could estimate longitude, using his speed and direction of travel. He and Steinbruck would keep detailed notes in a log, measuring each bend in the river.

"I do not posses the science of the naturalist," Mackenzie wrote, and he had no intention to pretend otherwise. Collecting plant specimens and identifying new animal species were not his objectives. This was a journey of cartography and opportunity; his only spare thoughts would be "anxiously employed in making provision for the day."

On May 22, 1789, Alexander wrote a letter to the North West Company partners for Roderic to carry to the *rendezvous*. It hedged, said almost nothing about his plans. "Should I not be back in time . . . ," he insinuated. And later, "I intend to pass that way on my voyage." All vague, no detail, in case the letters were intercepted. His secrecy was complete, and he needed no final words of encouragement or approval. Twelve days after he wrote his final letter, on Wednesday, June 3, 1789, Mackenzie's little flotilla of four canoes "at 9 oClock embarked Fort Chipewyan."

They were hungry even as the trip began, winter's deprivation still lingering: fresh vegetables and tubers long ago chopped into soup, flour stores bare, eating nothing but fish "without even the quickening flavor of salt." And so, only hours into the trip, the hunters were sent into the bush to bring back dinner. Their first day of travel was abbreviated, only thirty-six miles by Mackenzie's reckoning, across the western end of the Lake of the Hills and north on a channel that led to the Slave River. They stopped at seven o'clock to make camp, and while Barrieau and the voyageurs applied gum to seal leaks on their canoes, the Chipewyan men shot a goose and two ducks. Mackenzie was delighted, because wildfowl proved "a very gratifying food after such a long privation of flesh-meat."

The next morning, an early dawn, Barrieau called "*Star Levé*" to wake the men and get on the river. It was bitter cold, a veneer of ice on every pool of standing water, clouds of hoary breath among the men as they prepared the boats. Although it was early June, the rivers had just broken their winter crusts and were only newly free to navigate. They were in low country, a swampy maze of channels with low banks and thick woods of birch, poplar, willow. This was familiar territory for Awgeenah and the women, Leroux and the voyageurs had crossed it several times themselves, but Mackenzie diligently noted each bend and compass change for his North West Company partners who would never travel so far from the *rendezvous*.

Soon, the Peace River joined up from the west. In the spring, distant mountains flood the channel with debris torn from the banks of the headwaters. Taking on such a flow as the Peace, the current rose, water accelerating to the north, and in the distance a sound, a great torrent of barrier rapids that defined the Slave River. Mackenzie stopped the party short of the first cataract. Nearly eighty miles they had made, and all day the view had swelled, until Mackenzie thought "the River is near 2 leagues wide here." A short rest, a hard day's labor to come.

Over the next sixteen miles lay four major rapids: Cassette, Pelican, Mountain, and then Sault de Noyés, the Rapids of the Drowned. They are the largest and most extensive rapids in the *pays d'en haut*, not individual cataracts, but systems of whitewater, like nothing Mackenzie had ever encountered. The river was braided, channels between granite islands, passages of froth hidden until the last moment. And on either side of the river, tall hills of sand, dunes formed over thousands of years of floods.

They launched the canoes at three o'clock in the morning, the twilight of dawn on the horizon, and followed a sheltered channel on the eastern shore. In only a few minutes, they were on the portage. Leroux and Awgeenah knew the route, as did Landry and Ducette, who had come this way with Cuthbert Grant in 1786. The Cassette rapids were named for Grant's lockbox, lost overboard just as Mackenzie's had been on his way to Athabasca to meet Peter Pond for the first time, only two years before. Back then, Mackenzie's primary worry was a missing shirt.

The path around the first rapid was frozen, forcing them to haul the canoes over slick rock sheathed in ice: 380 paces. The next carry the men called *le portage d'Embarras*, for it was "occasioned by Drift wood filling the small channel," and they hauled the boats over spruce trees tossed like matchsticks, a tangle of ice-encrusted timber: 1,020 paces. Then 350 paces. The canoes barely had time to touch the water before they were out again, carried to another pond or small ancillary stream, anything to avoid the tumble in the meat of the main river. "All dangerous Rapids," Mackenzie wrote.

Flocks of white pelicans, up to a dozen at a time, skimmed the tops of the black spruce: 335 paces along the portage that bore the bird's name. A seabird, a sign that the ocean was close? Too much to hope, for the men knew the way and how far they were from the river on Pond's map.

The next portage was along a steep landing, 820 paces on a narrow ledge wet with spray, so close the path was to the water. "All Hands were for some time handing the loading and Canoe up the Hill," Mackenzie wrote, "Men and Indians much fatigued." Awgeenah and his wives lugged their boat, the way slick, half-frozen, water tumbling down the granite in a fall, when, suddenly, a slip, and in only a moment their canoe pinwheeled.

Awgeenah's wife jumped clear as the boat fell past her. The canoe was dashed on a rock, the birch bark split and cedar frame snapped, her supplies and provisions scattering into the rushing current. The boat was lost, and no time or materials to craft a new one; Awgeenah and his wives and the hunters would have to consolidate.

And then, after a full day of portaging, they were at the last cataract. The Rapids of the Drowned. The voyageurs sang a lament for the lost, for Landry and Ducette were there when the rapids were named, and it was their brethren who succumbed to the rushing water.

Three years before, in 1786, Cuthbert Grant led a party of white men through the rapids for the first time. They survived the Cassette, Pelican, and Mountain Rapids—with only a small loss of equipment—naming each in the process. At the last rapid, the party split. Grant took the most experienced guide, plus Ducette as a *milieu* and Landry as the *gouvernail*, and decided to run the rapid. Before they left, they told the other, less practiced men that if they found the way easy, they would stop on the bank and fire a rifle shot, as indication that it was safe to pass. If they heard silence, though, the second set of boats should portage onshore.

Grant and the men pushed off and into the cascade, and they found themselves in a storm of water. The way was tortuous, rooster-tail curls requiring every bit of Landry's skill. In desperation, the voyageurs had a song for such a moment:

Quand tu seras dans ces rapids,
Très dangereux,
Prends la Vierge pour ton bon guide
Fais-lui des voeux!
Et tu verras couler cette onde,
Avec vitesse.

When you are in the worst rapids
let the Virgin be your guide.
Make your vow to her,
and you will see the waves recede.

The whitewater engulfed them and then, miraculously, spit Grant's boat out into an eddy at the bottom of the cataract. Providence alone saw the men through. There was no way the second set of canoes could hope to make it, so Grant and the voyageurs sat onshore in silence and waited. Until one of the men did the most careless thing imaginable. He was hungry and shot at a duck with his rifle. Grant, Landry, Ducette, the guide, all ran up the riverbank, shouting, *Arrêtez! Ne venez pas!* Do not follow! They arrived in time to see the canoes push off the bank and become entangled in the churning hydraulic. The boats floundered, overturned, the water closed over the men's heads, and every one of them perished.

Two canoes, five voyageurs, and an unknown number of *pièces* never came out of the river. Brisbois. Derry. Landrieffe. Ledoux. Scavoyard. Poor and unlucky second sons, dead in the water, a thousand leagues from home.

"The Portage is very bad and 535 Paces long," Mackenzie wrote, as they tried to skirt the Sault de Noyés. Across the river lay the unmarkable graves. They had to launch the canoes. Barrieau called the line, and Landry leaned on that rudder of black ash, the lever bending with the strain of his exertion. And though his comrades had died in those waters only a few seasons before, on this day Landry again guided the boat true.

14

The Rapids of the Slave, June 2016

﹏﹏﹏

The water towered all around me, and the Virgin was nowhere in sight. The standing waves were thatched and stacked up tight, each white-topped ridge squared to the next as in a log cabin quilt pattern. *This is a slalom*, I thought, but too late. My kayak broke through the first wave, I clumsily jerked ninety degrees, pinballed back, knocked into the next wave, and tried to turn, but my edge was hopelessly off, and when I hit the third, the water grabbed my low chine and I tumbled from my boat.

It was cold and dark and I was upside down and everything was loud in my ears. I pushed off, twisted, kicked, hit my head. As if I were a clapper in a bell, the ring of my helmet on my boat in the center of my brain. My hip hit a rock, hard, and then I pulled my feet up, so they couldn't get trapped on the bottom, and I tried to swim. I was still moving with the current at speed, and I pulled the water and pushed my boat away and I broke the surface and took a breath. My paddle was still in my hand.

"Swim over here," John called to me, calm as could be.

I did, and reached out for the handle dangling from the tail of his kayak. My vest would keep me safe, I knew, so I consciously tried not to pull too hard on his boat, like a drowning victim dunking a rescuing lifeguard.

"Do you want to ride this one out?" he asked me, only occasionally dipping his paddle in the water to maneuver us around rocks.

"I think that would be best," I managed. A wave broke over my head, and I took a big long drink of the river.

Once on the granite shore, I cinched down the straps on my vest, tight as a tick, and remounted my kayak.

"Are you cold?" John asked. The sun blazed, but my arms were shaking from the shoulders down.

"No, I think it's adrenaline," I said.

"That was Sambuca," he said, naming the rapid that owned me. "Wanna try Flipper?"

"The next rapid is called Flipper?"

I followed John's line through a calm pool and to the head of the next whitewater plume. It rose before me in layers, and I felt small beneath it. I got through the first crest, the second, the third. I was through the wave train; I had made it. But then I hit the recirculating water at the bottom of the rapid, eddies on each side meeting as a boil. One eddy fence grabbed my nose, the other my tail, I felt my kayak spinning, and then I was in the cauldron again.

———

I asked Leif Anderson and John Blyth, members of the Fort Smith Paddling Club, to take me out on the river, so I had no one to blame but myself.

As a lover of whitewater, I knew the Slave's reputation—incredible volume, world-class rapids—and the chance to kayak even a section would be like getting to play catch in Yankee Stadium. So I found Leif on Facebook, and he said that if I made it up to Fort Smith, he and John would show me around.

There was no cell service on the way to Fort Smith. On my phone's useless green blur of a map, the dirt road looked like a paper cut on a whale. Google Maps' coverage of the Northwest Territories—an area the size of California, Texas, and Montana combined—is primarily low-def, feeding the impression most southerners have of this rocky socket of Arctic wilderness: it's big and it's empty.

Big, yes. But empty, not quite. Fort Smith proved to be a densely built town of tidy houses and government offices, home to twenty-five hundred people, roughly half indigenous. I arrived on the eve of Aboriginal Day. Smoke rose from the cookout at the fire circle, and volunteers set up white tents and teepees for the men to play Hand Games, a popular traditional Dene guessing game. I stopped at a convenience store to buy beer, the housewarming gift for many a paddle club, but I discovered only overpriced soda for sale. I had heard that some villages in the north were dry, so I asked the clerk at the counter.

"This might sound like an ignorant question," I said, "but do you guys not sell alcohol?"

"Not this time of night," he said. "We can only sell beer a few hours in the afternoon. Now, this may sound a little strange to you, from outside, but there are bootleggers if you really need it."

"How much?" I asked, mostly curious.

He shrugged. "Hundred bucks a case?"

I did not really need it, so I bought iced tea instead.

Driving around town, I found a public park on a bluff above the river and walked down to the water.

The Slave River is immense, as wide as five normal rivers, and criss-crossed with pour-overs and channels. It reminded me of the rapids above Niagara Falls, but many times wider. The Slave drains northern British Columbia, half of Alberta, and upper Saskatchewan, and the rapids at Fort Smith are formed where a northern quadrant of the Canadian Shield meets the tar sands. Flocks of white pelicans, the northernmost breeding colony on the continent, perched on rocks or floated in eddies, serene among the boil.

Sand and granite, gulf coast seabirds amid black spruce, it was all juxtaposed and spectacular. My mind reeled at the view.

Leif had warned me that he and John would be out on the river with a visiting film crew all day, recording their extreme-sport flips and tricks in the waves, so I hiked back up the ridge and decided to find a place to sleep for the night. The municipal campground was on the edge of town, and at the park office the same massive flies I had seen in Manitoba swarmed the windows and door frame, looking for a way in.

"Aren't the bulldogs awful," said the middle-aged woman who opened the door for me and then quickly shut it.

"Bulldogs?" I asked.

"The flies. Oh, they're bad!" she said, as she crushed one that had crawled between the screen and the windowpane. The bulldog popped, and the guts dripped down the glass.

She told me her name was Toni Heron and then offered me a cup of coffee. She and her husband, Peanuts, run the campground in the summer but return to the land in winter to hunt caribou, she said. Toni spoke with an indigenous lilt, lightening the end of each sentence. She asked what I was doing in Fort Smith, and I said I was going out on the river with Leif the next day.

"Oh, Leif. Everyone knows Leif," she said. "He lives in the yellow house. It looks like his hair. And he organizes the rafting festival every summer."

"Actually, I'm just here the night," I said. "After the Slave, I'm going to paddle the entire Mackenzie River." I caught myself. "Or, I'm sorry, do you prefer to call it the Deh Cho?"

"Some elders, they say Deh Cho. Everyone else says Mackenzie. Me, I'd never do the river," she said, noting that she was Chipewyan. She pronounced it "CHIP-you-on," revealing I had been saying it wrong in my head for months, reading my musty history books about Awgeenah. This gave me an opening to ask a question that had been on my mind.

"Is there a respectful way to ask someone I meet on the river what band or tribe they belong to?" I asked. "I don't want to be rude, but I'm curious."

Toni made a little face, but answered kindly.

"Well, I wouldn't ask like that," she said. "I'd ask them what language they speak. And if they say they speak Slavey, then you know, well, they're Slavey."

"You can always tell the Eskimo," volunteered Peanuts, from the other side of the room. He had a round belly and a thin mustache. "Indians and Eskimos hate each other. They formed their own territory a few years ago. It's like the Berlin Wall."

"And now the Slavey don't want to be called Slavey, I just read, because they aren't Slaves," Toni said. "I can't keep up."

Many First Nations are seeking to regain their identity this way, because the common names for many peoples are not their own name but rather the name given by the interpreter working for the European fur trader upon first encounter. It was the Cree who named the Slavey, and "Chipewyan" is a Cree word as well, for "pointed skins," the tail of the shirt worn by those people hundreds of years before.

Peanuts wanted to know more about my Mackenzie trip and made sure I had a whistle, to let any bears know I'm nearby. He said that because it's been so warm in the winters lately—"it used to be minus forty-five, but now it's only minus twenty-five"—the bears come out of hibernation sooner, which makes them grumpy.

"They don't sleep as long," Peanuts said. "They wake up fat, instead of skinny. We can't trust them anymore. You can't trust a fat black bear when he hasn't slept."

"Not to scare you," Toni said, "but a bear got a guy and they didn't find his remains for years. Bear dragged him away."

When I left, Toni made sure I took her bannock recipe, to cook the traditional biscuits on my journey, and then she and Peanuts wished me luck.

In the morning, I met up with Leif and John. Toni gave me directions to the house: on the main road, just east of Paddle Street and Portage Avenue. Right away, I could tell I was in the right place. The yard was full of racks of kayaks, sheds stacked with paddles and vests. It let off a pitch-perfect vibe, bright yellow siding and purple paint along the door frames, like Disneyland for paddlers.

Leif does match the house, as Toni said. He is a giant blond Viking with a raging mullet haircut. He's also a member of the U.S. Freestyle Kayak team and travels all the way from Idaho every summer to train. John, in contrast, is small and dark, with good looks that I'd call all-American if he weren't Canadian, born and bred in the north. In the videos I found of him online, John has long dreadlocks, but he had recently lopped them off; Leif picked on him for looking respectable. Like a ski-bum kid who doesn't know his good fortune to grow up in Vail or Snowbird, John learned to kayak on the Slave and has no need to travel like Leif.

Inside the yellow house I found tropical plants, open bags of potato chips on the counter, fresh dark coffee, but only a few beers in the fridge. There was a hole, with a decorative iron grate, through the ceiling of the ground level to let heat pass from the wooden stove. People came and went, barefoot on the wooden floors. A few were in town for the annual Summer Solstice Paddle, planning to kayak in the bright midnight. They all told me stories about rivers, rivers to run and rivers that have been run. This is how you run the Ottawa at full flood. This is how you descend the Yukon. This is how you skip the floatplane ride and portage to the Nahanni, the Grand Canyon of the Arctic.

One stout German man, his fingers the thick sausages of a construction worker, had become a Canadian citizen just for the canoeing. He was back from a trip with his wife on the William River, a remote winding waterway that cuts through the sand dunes of northern Saskatchewan and deltas into Lake Athabasca.

"We had portaged the first four rapids, all Class IV," he said, "but my wife, she wanted to run the last rapid, near the end of the trip. We entered on a good line but then got too high on the wave. We were sideways and I was looking down at the water and I knew we were going to go over." As he talked, he laid out the geography of the wave with his hands.

"My wife is in the nose," he continued. "I knew we were done. And I said to her, 'This is the end!' But then she reached out with her paddle. One huge draw stroke and she pulled our nose down and we made it through."

He paused.

"That's love," he said, and smiled.

"You're going to dig the Mackenzie," John said to me.

"I did it," said the German man.

"Lots of people do it, just take a few months and go," John said.

"Really, lots?" I asked.

"A few dozen people a year, I bet."

"That's a lot of people?"

"Well, this is the Northwest Territories," John said.

This place, I thought, *it's defined by the absence of humans.* So much space, but only forty thousand residents total.

"There are so many amazing people up here," another paddler said, "you're not even going to write about the Mackenzie River in your book. You're just going to write about all the people you meet."

"I went to Alaska once," John said, "and I thought it would be like the N.W.T., but it's not. In Alaska, you have hippies and rednecks and Indians, and everyone fights. Hippies have money, it causes problems. Here, we just have rednecks and Indians. We have a bush code. Be generous, don't steal. It's more harmonious."

———

After I officially joined the paddle club—for insurance reasons, to hold them harmless in case I died—Leif and John discussed which of the four main rapids to do for my orientation tour. Even today, the final cataract is still known as the Rapids of the Drowned.

"They actually aren't that bad," said Leif. "Just a small feature in a channel on river right. We figure that's where they got caught. You could get in trouble, if you don't know it's coming. Cassette is actually the worst rapid."

The best choice for me, John and Leif agreed, was the Mountain Rapid. I borrowed a sit-on-top self-bailing plastic kayak from the club, grabbed my gear, and we loaded into John's beat-up truck for the short drive to water. We parked on a sandy dune overlooking the river and stripped to our skivvies to put on dry suits. We had to work fast, the bulldogs and mosquitoes swarming as cotton balls and pollen clouded the air. An orgy of life in summer. Every tree was mating with every other tree, and every bug mounting every other bug, in the brief time they had.

Once dressed, we threw our boats over our shoulders for the hike down to the water. Give us boards instead of kayaks, and we could have been getting ready to surf at the beach.

The small cove at the bottom of the hill was piled with driftwood, enough for Pond's or Cook's reports. Leif hopped from log to log, toting his fiberglass kayak. He shuffled out each progressively skinnier trunk as if he were on a balance beam, surprisingly agile for such a big man, and after reaching the farthest log, he sat down and put on his kayak as he would a pair of pants.

I followed, with less grace. Out in the water, the river was full of wood, blown out of the Embarras Portage upstream, record rains on the Peace River. The water was brown with mud, and deadheads hung heavy, just below the surface, and bumped against the underside of my kayak as I paddled, as if the drowned or the blue men of the Minch were knocking on the door, asking to be let back in.

"I'm sorry, but to get to the rapid, we have a very boring flat-water paddle ahead of us," Leif warned. It took almost an hour to cross the river, to reach the whitewater line that Leif thought I could handle. The current was so strong we had to angle our kayak noses upstream, a technique called ferrying. On our way, we passed rust-colored granite islands, and while I could hear the roar of the river, I could see nothing downstream, so precarious the drop that the whitewater was hidden below the horizon line.

"Think of the Slave as a ski resort," Leif said, explaining why we were bypassing so many rapids to find a specific one to run. "We're at the top of the chairlift now, each line is named. We can pick the black diamond run, the double black."

"What are we running?" I asked.

"Sambuca is a solid blue."

We floated to the back of an island with a single hardy tree, and the roar ahead of us grew louder and louder. As we portaged our kayaks across the tumbling rock face, suddenly the water fell away on our left. It was a massive flume, a two-story hill of water that swept away whole tree trunks with ease.

"That's Sambuca?" I asked.

"No, that one's called Molly's Nipple," John said. "They used to run this river commercially, with big rafts, and one of the guides named it. Said it looked like his girlfriend's nipple."

Whether it matched Molly, I couldn't say, but the entrance to the hydraulic was the right basic shape, the squared-off tip of the chute ending in a frothy churn. There was a hole down there on the river bottom. Nothing that entered could escape.

Leif and John wanted to surf and practice tricks a while, and I played amateur photographer. In whitewater kayaking, "surfing" means to enter a rapid, point the nose of the boat upstream, and paddle forward just enough to stay stationary. The effect is Zen-like, peace found in the tumult due to the focus required, the water pouring in and over and past as you float. Freestyle experts, like Leif and John, skip the meditation and add acrobatics instead, always landing on the same crest of wave.

As I watched, each man took turns in the thick of it. Leif surfed heavy, nose up, stern plowing the water, as if he were planted on a throne in the midst of the rapid. John surfed light, seemed to skip along the waves like a flat stone. Through it all, the wood kept coming, sometimes whole trees.

"It's a bit of a shooting gallery in there," John said afterward.

We left Molly's Nipple to take on Sambuca, named for the producer of that same river guide's worst hangover. I was nervous after watching Leif and John take on such big water, but I paddled hard all the way into the top of the rapid. Intention, I had learned in my first basic class, is most important in whitewater kayaking. Intention. Hesitancy flips boats. If you want to enter the current, if you want to run the rapid, if you want to eddy out, then do it; not for nothing do kayakers have a reputation for sounding like a pack of Yodas.

But my book knowledge and enthusiasm far outstrip my actual ability. I'm still in that intermediate phase, where my mind knows what to do but my body reacts half a second too slow, because I am relying on conscious decisions and not instinctual muscle memory.

In Sambuca, the slalom course came in a blur, and I was swimming upside down in seconds.

At Flipper—named for its tendency to toss even large twelve-person rafts—I lost my edge after the main wave train and went under once more.

On my way to the surface, I hit my head again, this time on John's boat. This knocked him upside down, though he rolled himself back up with ease. I popped like a cork, caromed painfully off a rock, felt myself swept away. A maelstrom crashed on either side. I drank the river. The current bludgeoned me with volume, pulled on every bit of me, opened the waist of my dry pants and filled the legs with heavy sinking water. I was overcome in a deluge, caught in a prairie gale while tornadoes tore up farms all about me.

The river stripped me. Paddle gone, kayak floating downstream. My helmet was off the back of my head, and the strap choked me around the neck. I couldn't see, and I put my hand to my face and discovered my prescription sunglasses were gone. They had survived two tours in Iraq but not an afternoon on the Slave.

Leif chased and retrieved my boat, while John again helped get me to shore.

"That was a yard sale," I said, using the jargon for a particularly ugly swim that scatters gear. I was embarrassed; better I admit the humiliation before John and Leif said so.

"We're all in between swims," John assured me, also a common kayaker saying, and while true it rarely makes the swimmer feel much better.

Onshore, I emptied my pants of water and tightened the straps on my helmet and vest. I squinted in the sun, and all four limbs shook. I felt as if I had swallowed half the Slave, but my mouth was so dry. More effects of the adrenaline.

Leif was quiet, and I sensed frustration that he was spending more time rescuing me than running rapids. John offered to guide me back to shore, because even if I was done attempting named rapids, I still had to paddle an hour back across the breadth of the swirling Slave.

"You've got to put on your Slave goggles," John called out ahead of me. His head was shrouded by a cloud of bulldogs.

"What do you mean?" I said.

"Slave goggles. Like beer goggles. Make some really bad decisions. Ignore how big the river is, and just go anyway," he said, and I followed him across the spinning current.

I had never experienced a river like this. The boils and eddy fences were so powerful, driven by such volume, that seemingly innocuous flat water proved dangerous. My kayak was constantly tugged in one direction or the other; I jittered keeping my balance. I felt as if the basic laws of hydraulics, in their magnified state on the Slave, were being undone, and I didn't trust myself with even the most rudimentary moves.

"Eddies within eddies," John said, and he laughed.

When we finally approached the shore, John made a turn upstream. "We need to end on a good note," he said, and I followed him among the pelicans until we got to the top of a small rapid named Playground.

"We put our newbies in here; you'll be fine," he said, and took off. I felt skittish, self-consciously raised a knee, to gently wobble into the current after him. From upriver, Playground looked like an idealized wave train, a series of perfect crests. Three strokes forward, and I topped the first, pushed my nose through, then a second, and more. I rode up and down like on a merry-go-round, and the water was so soft, big downy pillows off the bed of a fancy hotel.

John was right. I felt a little better, but not much.

Once through Playground, I headed for the takeout. There was an obvious saddle in the ridgeline. *No wonder the traditional portage route starts here,* I thought. With a plastic kayak on my shoulder, I followed the same trail as the voyageurs, carrying a heavy boat up the soft sand.

The Slave had humbled me. I had overestimated my skills and learned my lesson. The next day I would start my run on the Mackenzie River, where I wouldn't have John and Leif to rescue me and capsizing would end my trip.

15

SHOOT THE MESSENGER, JUNE 1789

〰〰〰

"Had a Head wind for most of the Day," Mackenzie wrote, "so cold that Indians made use of their mittens." It seemed more than a simple chill or a late-season snap. The freeze that descended on them was violent, always in their faces as they pushed north from the Rapids of the Drowned.

The next morning a hard rain hit. "We were obliged to land and unload to prevent our Goods getting wet." The squall passed, they launched the boats again, but then the soaking returned, and misery too. Mackenzie tried to push forward, but the wind forced them to shore, and it rained all night. The hunters set out a net. No fish.

On the third morning they did not launch at all. "It blew exceeding hard with rain all last Night and this Day," Mackenzie wrote. "The Wind continued which prevented us from moving this Day." The Chipewyan hunters had stayed active in the damp chill, managing to shoot a dozen geese and ducks to fill their cooking pots, and then they disappeared back into the bush.

The voyageurs and women huddled under their canoes, smoking pipes to pass the day, pursued by mosquitoes and gnats. "People not finding this Place agreeable," Mackenzie said.

But overnight, the rain and wind slackened, so Barrieau awoke the party early, and at half past two they pushed out into a calm and foggy river. Leroux and Awgeenah knew that Slave Lake must be close, less than a day of paddling away. The water was brown in flood, and over and over again the river wound back on itself as a looped and coiled rope. Little progress as the raven flies. The riverbanks were tallow-colored clay and sand, but atop lay huge piles of mud runoff, rich black soil that "rests upon drift wood, so as to be eight or ten feet deep." They made a wrong turn, into a channel that dead-ended in a lake, and turned back, and the hunters caught up with them, delivering four beaver and ten geese.

Then, at nine o'clock by Mackenzie's reckoning, they broke free from the river, attained the lake of the Slaves. It was not a moment for celebration. Now they saw why the wind had been such "excessive Cold." The gale blew fierce over fields of snow.

"The Lake is covered all over with Ice and does not seem to have yet moved," Mackenzie wrote. "We unloaded our Canoe, and pitched our Tents, for from what we could see we would be obligated to remain here for some time."

––––––

For six days, the ice anchored them to the shore of Slave Lake. It was the largest body of water Mackenzie had seen since Lake Superior. Awgeenah knew none larger, other than the Arctic Ocean with Mattonabbe and Hearne, and it was the center of his navigation since he had walked across it, frozen in the winter, on that journey to the Far Off Metal River almost twenty years before.

Awgeenah's people told a story of a flood, that long ago there had been a terrible winter, cold that never ended, and the animals discovered seven bags of weather. Mouse opened the warmth, but the snow melted too quickly, and the world was covered with water. All of the animals got on a raft, and each animal took turns looking for land, but it was muskrat that dove down and returned with mud. Now Mackenzie needed mouse's warmth again, to cross the lake and reach the Red Knife Indian encampments on the north shore. Awgeenah and Leroux knew the traditional path among the scattered granite islands on the lake's eastern side. But the way was ice clogged, crammed and piled against the stony archipelago, and there was nothing to do but wait.

They bedded down on a sandy bank covered in willow bushes and trees in full bloom. The voyageurs slept under the overturned canoe. Steinbruck set up the tent for himself and Mackenzie and scouted for evergreen boughs as a rough mattress on the frozen ground. Their camp lay just opposite the trading posts that Cuthbert Grant and Laurent Leroux had built three seasons before. Landry and Ducette had felled the poplar and spruce, squared the logs, set the frame, but in only a short time their handiwork was already decayed, affected by the weight of snow and rot, and the party didn't use the cabins for shelter.

Mackenzie was again thinking about his stomach, and Awgeenah told him that to either side of the river were plenty of moose, and caribou, and vast herds of buffalo, if only their hunters could reach them. They would have to settle for fowl instead. "We killed 2 swans, 10 Geese, 1 Beaver this morning without losing an hour's time, so that if we were for the purpose of hunting we might soon fill our Canoe."

The water was open right at the lake's shore, so Mackenzie "ordered the Men to set Nets immediately as we could not touch our Provision during our stay at this place." The Chipewyan hunters said not to stretch two nets, for each would grow jealous of the other, and neither would catch fish. Mackenzie ignored them and for a time suffered no ill effects. "Caught plenty of Fish for our Supper. Say Personenconu, White Fish, Trout, Carp." They had lost some supplies with the wrecked canoe at the rapids, but at least here they would eat fresh stocks.

It rained all the next day, and Mackenzie thought the ice began to weaken. The next day the winds shifted, the clouds broke, and the wives went to gather cranberries still stuck to the trees from the winter before. Mackenzie and several of his voyageurs gathered swan, goose, and duck eggs, and killed a brace worth of the birds.

But tempers were already running short. "Our old Companions (the Muskettoes) visit us in greater Numbers than we would wish as they are very troublesome Guests," Mackenzie wrote. Everyone's long hair kept only the worst of the pests away. Steinbruck stuffed moss around the bottom of the tent to keep the mosquitoes out, and the men filled the fires with rotten wood to make smoke. Nothing helped. When Mackenzie returned from collecting eggs, he found Leroux and his *devant* in a shouting match. *C'est un maudit, chrisse, osti, calisse de tabernac!* Christ, Communion, and even the tabernacle damned and named profane. Mackenzie left them alone to work it out themselves. Everyone simply sat and watched the lake, and finally Mackenzie hiked up a hill for a better view. "The Ice moved a little to the Eastward."

Nothing to do but wait, pray for warmth, toss tobacco in the water to beg off the weather. They waited so long that a family that had left Fort Chipewyan on foot, at the same time as Mackenzie's canoes, caught up with them and asked for food, because "they marched so hard, that they could not kill enough of Provision for their Families." Mackenzie was annoyed they did not bring him food either, as his hunters had suffered a streak of poor luck—no large game, just a few swans and gray cranes make a meager meal—and the wind had blown the ice over the nets of his fishery. When there was no fresh meat, the voyageurs ate the limited pemmican, but the Indian hunters would not. They ate pemmican in the winter, rarely in summer, because they knew so much fat would make them weak.

Finally, at sunset on the fifth day, a violent thunderstorm rolled in from the south. "The Sky in that Quarter of a sudden became the blackest dark blue Color and lightened much." The gusting front passed quickly, but then a soaking rain fell, and Mackenzie knew that their forsaken time was ending.

At noon on the sixth day, the wind shifted once more, blew the ice sheets off their fishery nets, and opened a thawed channel to the first set of islands. Immediately, Mackenzie called the men to break camp and set out. They pulled up the nets and found them in tatters, cut by the ice; the Chipewyan hunters knew why. They launched the canoes, a *grande traverse*, eight miles of open water to cross to the first island. The voyageurs mumbled an extra decade of rosary and the Ave Maria and then dug in and pulled, Ducette and de Lorme leaning out over the water with their paddles, maximum technique, for this was a race, to attain land before the free channel was shut by ice.

———

It was nearly midnight when they stopped at the first small island to make camp; in the twilight, Mackenzie was amazed the horizon glowed "as clear as to see to write this." Mackenzie was used to long summer days—Fort Chipewyan was the same rough latitude as his birthplace of Stornoway—but the phenomenon was increasing rapidly, as the voyageurs regummed the canoes after the long crossing.

In the rest of the *pays d'en haut,* the trees required to make and fix the birch-bark canoes were found all along the rivers. If one wished to invent ideal natural materials for boat construction—light and strong framing, water-resistant and pliable fastening binders, flexible sheeting—it would be hard to best cedar planks, *watape* spruce root, and birch bark. And unique in North America, they all grow, together, in the one place they are needed most, as if nature first carved the system of rivers and streams to breach the continent and then grew the perfect boats to traverse it. This was true to the south, but now, for the first time, as they hopped from gravel speck to gravel speck, if they broke a canoe hard, they would have to repair it with the supplies they carried or make do without. And they were already short one canoe, lost in the rapids of the Slave.

The next day the north wind roared, the ice clumping in the channels and stranding them. The voyageurs and Indians caught a few trout with a hook and line, and when the wind died later in the day, they set out again. Their canoes leaked, and the chop threw water over the gunnels, and the boats were full of slosh by the time they limped ashore again. Several days passed this same way, hopping island to island: thunderstorms would blow a passage through the ice, they sprinted to landfall, then huddled under the canoes to avoid the lightning lashing their exposed granite spit.

And still they were "pestered by Muskettoes, tho' we are in a manner surrounded by ice."

On each traverse, Mackenzie would drop a lead weight, to sound for the depth of the lake, and then call the readings to Steinbruck, who recorded them in their journal. Six fathoms, then twenty-one fathoms, then forty-four, sixty, seventy-five fathoms. Four hundred and fifty feet deep, between flecks of rock.

On June 21, the longest day of the year, Mackenzie sat up to count the few hours the sun disappeared below the horizon. Four hours and twenty-two minutes. They were at a place the voyageurs called Isle de Carribo, as the Chipewyan hunters had slaughtered seven of the large beasts, "the poor Creatures having no Place to run for Shelter." Their hot carcasses steamed on the ice-sheathed islands, and the women built a fire and roasted dripping haunches, withers, back straps, ribs, liver: full-bellied relief after meager rations. Mackenzie feasted and took his compass readings, and when the liminal darkness descended with the sinking of the sun, the water "froze so hard during his absence that the Lake crusted half a quarter of an Inch thick."

Finally, on the seventh day of their island-to-island crossing of Slave Lake, the party reached what they thought might be the far shore. It was very different from the one they left. "One continued View of Mountains & islands & Solid Rock covered here & there with Moss," rather than the rich earth and sandy soils dumped by the Slave River. In fact, the shore was so checkered with granite and standing water that "we did not know whether it be the opposite side of the Lake or Islands," Mackenzie wrote. Leroux decided to leave two bags of pemmican on one rock, food for his return journey in the fall, and he named the place Is la Cach. They threaded westerly, among ice and pocked stone, and, after seventeen hours of paddling, finally camped on one larger shelf. Mackenzie had left the hunters behind, he was so desperate to push on. "The Muskettoes are so numerous tho' the Weather is so far from being warm we cannot rest for them." The Chipewyan men paddled all night to catch up.

In the morning the whole brigade launched and began to cross a very large bay. The wind shifted, to the south and west, and Mackenzie ordered the sails put out. The men hammered a wooden foot into the cedar frame among the *pièces* in the bottom of the canoe, and a mast was raised from the brace, and a piece of canvas tied off as sailcloth, and the voyageurs sang for the wind to carry them to safety. "*Souffle, souffle, la vieille*," the voyageurs sang, "blow, blow, old woman."

Finally, a few moments of fair weather arrived, and *la vieille* blew them twenty-five miles to the far end of the bay, where there stood three lodges, domes covered in caribou hides, and Laurent Leroux found a happy reunion with the Red Knife Indians he had left a few months before.

———

They slept two nights among the Red Knives, who were also known as the Copper Indians as they lived near a hill made of the stuff. That ridge was called Sat in the Same Place, because there a woman sank into the earth.

She was a Chipewyan woman, and the Esquimaux stole her, the elders said. They took her to an island, an island made of nothing but copper, and she wore a copper dress and carried a copper knife, and she had two babies by the Esquimaux. She tried to escape, and she followed a wolf that walked through the shallows of the sea, and the caribou followed her, and when she reached the shore, she killed thousands of the animals with her copper knife. She skinned them and lined a cave with their hides and then cooked the meat and placed it in the cave, and then she left her babies behind in the cave with the food so she could move quickly to find her people. But after many nights a group of hunters found her and raped her, every one of them taking a turn, and there she sank into the ground in her copper dress. And her children in the cave lived with the Esquimaux and taught them to speak, and that is why those people only say short baby words, *tuk tuk tuk,* and no long ones.

The Red Knives were happy to trade with Leroux and Mackenzie.

Among those Indians, the *bourgeois* and voyageurs had come to be called Pale Men. The Pale Men were known to live in beaver houses—low, chinked with mud, covered in sod—but inside those mounds of dirt were piles of goods made of a metal stronger than the copper they dug from Sat in the Same Place. Two leaders among the Indians near Slave Lake were a pair of mixed-blood brothers, François and Jacques Beaulieu. Their father was a Frenchman, their mother a Cree, and they took Chipewyan wives, and they spoke all the languages of their people. François had a teenage son, also named François, and the three acted as interpreters between the North West Company and the tribes.

In previous seasons, Leroux had told the Beaulieus that everyone should bring beaver pelts to the Pale Men who lived in the beaver homes, and they would trade. As a sign of his friendship, Leroux had given the Indians tobacco, but it smelled so bad they were afraid it would scare the fish away, so they hid it in the snow. But the other goods were useful, especially the ice chisels. Theirs were made of bone, but the metal ones from the Pale Men cut the ice like rotten wood.

Now the Pale Men had reappeared. The Red Knife leaders said they had many friends nearby, Slave and Beaver Indians, as well as their own kin, who "will be here by the time that the Swans cast their Feathers." Leroux had extended credit to these tribes and now collected the past winter's furs as payment, eight packs of beaver and marten. Awgeenah had many years' worth of credit to collect as well, for he had often shuffled goods and furs between these tribes and Peter Pond at the Old Establishment. The English Chief collected a hundred skins, immediately handed forty over to Leroux for debts from 1786, and then used the remainder to buy rum from Mackenzie for his hunters. Awgeenah knew his stature as the trading chief of the Chipewyan was always tenuous, and dependent on his generosity with his followers. Mackenzie understood this as well. He gave the hunters "some more," which "made them get Drunk," and in so doing secured their loyalty for several more weeks of the expedition.

But Mackenzie really cared about the great river that flowed from Slave Lake, and on this point he was frustrated by the Red Knives. "They know nothing even of the River but the Entry," he wrote. This would get them started, though, so for the price of a pair of drawers and one knife, Mackenzie purchased the guide services of a young man, plus a canoe to go with him, to replace the one lost at the rapids on the Slave River. Then Mackenzie gathered the tribe around him and, with Awgeenah acting as interpreter, told the Red Knives that he was leaving in the morning, but that they should all trade with Laurent Leroux, who was staying with them for the summer season.

The Red Knife Indians said they understood, that "it would be great encouragement for them to have Frenchmen upon the Land, that they would work hard to kill Beaver, when they were sure of getting Value for their Skins." Mackenzie was satisfied, and wrote a note for Roderic and Normand MacLeod and gave it to Leroux to deliver, outlining his progress so far and announcing that he was pressing on to the west.

———

At three o'clock the next morning, Mackenzie and Awgeenah pushed on in their three canoes. Leroux and the Indians fired a rifle volley in salute, and Mackenzie's voyageurs did the same in return, and Mackenzie's canoe was very heavily laden, for it was full of *pièces* from Leroux's boat, to trade with any Indians he found along the river and, eventually, the Chinese and Russians.

The drifting ice hampered their progress, and "with some difficulty" they beached on an island covered in rotting stumps, cleared as if it had been an Indian encampment at one time and was now abandoned; the Cree often chased off the Slaves. Mackenzie thought they couldn't stay in such an inhospitable place, so they pushed out into the ice floes, "thro' some Broken Ice tho' at the Risk of damaging our Canoe." They pushed on, hard, made another twenty-one miles along the shore, and everywhere they looked were "old deserted lodges" of tribes that had been exterminated.

The next day the swells were heavy on the lake as they skirted bay to bay with a tailwind. They spotted caribou on one island, and put in to let their hunters run them down. Mackenzie grew frustrated waiting—"we lost 3 Hours aft Wind going for them"—but the rich meat was essential. Bloody, heavy big game, to sustain them as fish and geese could not. They needed to stock up while they could; though the white man was anxious, the Chipewyan hunters knew they still had to carefully bleed the animals and contain all that was spilled, as anything else was taboo.

The wind-driven ice eventually forced them to ground, and they set up camp early on yet another island. Mackenzie saw that the shore of the mainland was low and covered in moose tracks but also "very flat and dangerous there being no safe place of landing in case of bad weather." It was a most unsettled feeling, looking for a secure place to pass the night. At the fort, at the *rendezvous,* in Montreal, even along the established voyageur routes where campsites were known and marked, there was never a question of where to sleep. For the first time, Mackenzie was learning the anxiety of searching out safe harbors but also the great satisfaction and relief of such a discovery, the peace when it's a "good spot."

That night, they had not found one. They all slept poorly. Mackenzie complained of "a very restless night being tormented by Musquittoes." Landry had it worse, arguing with his wife to the point of such frustration that he "arranged for her to remain at the Campmt." His Acadian cousin intervened. Ducette and Landry's wife had an understanding: Mackenzie's called Ducette "her *furreaux,*" her fur dealer, though insinuating more. Ducette calmed the dispute—Mackenzie noted "the Husband said nothing to the contrary"—and then they all loaded back in their canoes as per usual.

But their frustration bled over to the water. Fog obscured the view. Their Red Knife guide admitted it had been "8 Winters since he has last been here," and every bay was looking like the mouth of the river. They picked their way among islands, lost in a cloud, until finally Mackenzie called a halt in the darkness and they made camp.

Another early morning, probing bays in the fog. After forty miles of paddling, Barrieau guided them into "a deep Bay" to the west, "having no land in *Sight* a head in hopes to a Passage which the Indian informed us was to be met with." Perhaps they had at last discovered the mouth to Peter Pond's river? But then a storm rose, "a strong aft wind," and in the rising surf the canoe brigade became separated. Mackenzie ordered the sail cut, and Ducette and de Lorme started bailing water with a large kettle. "We lost sight of the Indians, nor could we put ashore to wait for them without running the Risk of wrecking our Canoe," Mackenzie said. The wind drove them to the far western shore at the back of the bay, and they beached in a pile of willow bushes; "we found there was no Passage here." Barrieau ordered the men to build a fire, and they waited two hours, then three, until finally the Red Knife's canoe appeared. It did not land. They stopped in the shallows, dumped water from their boat, which appeared nearly full to the brim, and turned back out. Mackenzie followed until sunset, when they made camp, and then Awgeenah flew into a murderous rage.

For incompetence, for untrustworthiness, for foolhardiness, the English Chief wanted to shoot the Red Knife dead. Nowhere to camp, nowhere to eat, nowhere to hunt, plagues of mosquitoes and gnats and storms upon the lake. "For having undertaken to guide us in a Road he did not know, indeed, none of us are well pleased with him," Mackenzie admitted. "But we don't think with the English Chief that he merits such severe punishment." Their Red Knife guide assured them they were getting close, and Mackenzie soothed Awgeenah, and they tried to sleep, grateful for having "narrowly escaped" capsizing.

They found the current at half past five the next morning. The water was shallow, and the channel not very wide, but there was a hint of movement beneath the canoes, fish visible just under the surface, and "the Place was almost covered with wild Fowl, Swan, Geese & several kinds of Ducks." Eventually, they realized they were tracking along a large island. The southern shore collapsed to a point, and the main river came in from the left, a waterway "upwards of 10 Miles across." An enormous river, just as Pond had drawn on his map. Since Montreal, Mackenzie had trudged up and down the watery ladder, but now, at last, they had come to their final descent to the sea.

The current grew and grew and grew. The river narrowed, banks of yellow clay and rock rose on each side, and the wood that covered the land seemed burned over by fire. "Have a stiff breeze from the Eastward wch drove us on at a great Rate under Sail," Mackenzie wrote, as they wound westward among tall forested islands.

The water turned a shocking emerald green, the same green as the Niagara below the falls, and the rate of the current accelerated still further. It bubbled and boiled, like the cooking pot of *Macbeth*'s witches, and quickened still further, pushing them past high mud banks, until, all at once, the current and wind fled and their momentum faded.

"Here the River widens," Mackenzie wrote. They drifted into a lake, the voyageurs and wives began to paddle. But to where? Their guide knew that they were in a basin formed long ago by the tail slap of a giant beaver, when the animals could speak and wrecked the world. But of this lake's nature, the consistency of its shore, its outlets and destinations, he could say nothing to Mackenzie and Awgeenah.

"We cou'd see no opening in any Direction so that we are at a loss what course to take," Mackenzie said. "Our Red Knife Indian has never been further than this."

THUNDERSTORMS AND RAIDS, JUNE 2016

∿∿∿

Hay River is a small industrial town on the south shore of Great Slave Lake, about thirty miles east of the mouth of the Mackenzie River. For a hundred years, Hay River has been the place where Canada's freight railroads and asphalt highways and Arctic shipping lanes all meet. A port town, a logistical hub, the home of semitrailers and boxcars and tugs and barges and sporadic fishing vessels.

I stayed only one night, at a dingy motel that catered to transient construction workers. In the parking lot I met an out-of-place white man named George. He was walking a dog, a small furry thing bred for laps, and his white T-shirt bore a silk-screened photo of two of the dogs with ribbons in their hair. He was late middle-aged, with a gentle bearded face and the sad look of a man who wore a T-shirt with two dogs but only walked one.

George's station wagon had Ontario license plates and a canoe strapped to the roof, so I stopped to speak to him. He said he was on a self-appointed quest to reach the far corners of Canada. He had already paddled to the southern point in Lake Erie, and along the Arctic Ocean to the Alaskan border in the west. Now he was working on the east, toward Nunavut and then on to Labrador. In the morning, a floatplane would fly him and his canoe and all their provisions to the shattered eastern coast of Great Slave Lake, where he would paddle up the Lockhart River, six hundred hard, lonely miles to Hudson's Bay.

"There are undiscovered places," he said. "Gems that only you will find." I wished him well; there were no Chipewyan or Inuit settlements along his route through Awgeenah's barrens, and George and his dog wouldn't see another human for months.

In the morning, I picked up David Chrisinger, my first paddling companion, at the tiny one-gate airport. After Wick Walker's warning about the fragility of my team, my biggest headache, I feared, would be getting my shipmates in and out on time, but David was punctual. His musk followed him into the truck; he smelled like he had already been camping a week.

David Chrisinger is a big man, a former college football defensive tackle with a soft polite voice and a dense red beard. We were not long fast friends—our week in a boat would be the most time we had ever spent together—but we had similar writing interests and experience camping and canoeing. "I've always wanted to do a trip like this, ever since I read *Canoeing with the Cree* as a kid," David told me. He grew up deer hunting with his grandfather, a game warden in central Wisconsin, a place I used to think of as prohibitively northern. I laughed at such thoughts now.

Before our trip could begin, David and I had one final piece of business: purchasing tobacco. "You have to give something to the river. It's an indigenous belief," I explained. "Loose tobacco is the traditional gift. If you don't freely give something, the river will take it. I didn't make an offering to the Slave River, and it took my sunglasses. I can't afford to give the Mackenzie my only spare."

We stopped at a local grocery store, and a young Korean girl at the customer service counter didn't understand what we wanted. Swisher Sweets cigars? Marlboro cigarettes?

"No, no, loose chewing tobacco," I said. But then I saw the right package and groaned. "Um, how about the Red Man?"

"Which one?" she asked.

I was embarrassed to speak louder. "The . . . Red Man."

"Which?"

"By your knee," David said, trying to help.

She eventually found the small white and green pack; in the logo, the eponymous chief wears a large feathered headdress. The pouch was smaller than my hand and cost forty-five dollars.

"Is the river going to think we're racist if we give it Red Man chew?" asked David.

———

Doug Swallow runs his medical supply and canoe-outfitting business from a sheet-metal warehouse on the other side of the railroad tracks.

He had bandages all over his rough fingers and moved quickly about the small store, gathering us bailing buckets and bear bangers and large food barrels and other survival equipment.

Doug made me promise, for safety's sake, that I'd send him a text every day, from my inReach GPS, to say all was well. He could track my location on the device's linked web page, but that wasn't enough. "If you don't move for a day, I need to know you're not hurt, that you're just wind-bound on Mills Lake."

"I read that in Michelle's guide. That wind is a big problem there," I said.

"The lake is so shallow, the wind picks up just a little and you get big whitecaps. You could get stuck three days, easy," he said, and I thought again about Wick's admonition, that the team logistics were the weak spot in my plan. We had eight days to get to Fort Simpson; that's where David and my next paddler, Jeremy, would swap. The thirty-miles-a-day plan was tight but doable. Even if wind did slow us, with so much sunlight we could paddle all night if we had to.

Doug had other pieces of advice: Great Slave Lake is too shallow to paddle near the shore, Point Roche was a good place to camp tonight, there was a "wicked strong eddy line" where the Liard River meets the Mackenzie, and the campgrounds at Fort Providence and Fort Simpson were good places to stay. Towns offered shelter, showers, food. "Can we just leave our canoe?" I asked. "I don't want to be the suspicious New Yorker."

"People respect your gear. You need your equipment for survival," he said, echoing what I had heard from John in Fort Smith the day before. "As long as you don't leave that GPS hanging from your paddle and walk away, you'll be fine. None of our customers have ever had a problem."

Out in the gravel yard, Doug introduced us to the third member of our team. The Sea Clipper canoe was lipstick red, eighteen and a half feet of unblemished fiberglass and Kevlar. A few feet shorter than Mackenzie's, but still long by modern standards.

"I just drove it back from B.C. the other day," Doug said.

"I don't know if you can trust us with a new canoe," I said. I knew that that candy-coated shell would be scratched beyond recognition by the end of our trip.

Doug drove the canoe to the boat launch while I dropped off my truck at the barge company next door. They said my truck was guaranteed to arrive in Inuvik in about four weeks; I handed over my keys and walked—vehicle-less, an odd feeling after driving four thousand miles from Buffalo—to where David was loading our boat. The gear was all new to him, and having finally seen the canoe and barrels, I had no better idea than he on how to best pack. We had no routine or habits yet, and it all felt clumsy, not knowing the one best way to puzzle in all the gear. We stood the barrels up to save space, tucked in the maps along the sides, David stuffed extra food in the black nylon bags. It was motley and inefficient.

A fisherman motored past in a serious-looking commercial rig. "I wouldn't do the Mackenzie in a canoe. Maybe in this thing," he said, but in a way to indicate there was little chance of that either. We took a final picture, Doug waved, David dropped a little tobacco in the water, and then—about noon, with the skies starting to gray—we left.

The first step in a new pair of shoes always feels a little odd.

The water was dark, and the riverbank industrialized, held up by rusting metal bulkheads. To get to the Mackenzie River, we had to paddle the few miles out of the commercial docks and canals of the Hay, then skirt left along the coast of Great Slave Lake. As we passed shipyards and warehouses, men onshore sandblasted and welded hulks that appeared long past serviceable life. Once at the lake, we headed out as Doug instructed, to avoid the shallows, but our top-heavy canoe wobbled as breeze-blown rollers came in off the open water. David and I had never paddled together, and we would never be heavier, I realized. So much food, plus David, the largest of my companions. But the weight didn't add stability; the canoe felt slow and unresponsive and yet still tippy in the swells.

We had paddled two hours—but only six miles, according to the GPS I was just learning to use—when the sky in the west turned the color of slate. Over the lake, feathers of rain hung from the underside of dark clouds.

"Should we stop already?" I asked David.

"Let's ask them," David said. "Maybe they have a weather report." He pointed to a beach campground full of pop-up trailers and RVs. With a sinking feeling, I realized we had not yet even made it all the way out of town.

We grounded the canoe in the sand, and David approached a small group drinking beer at a picnic table. They didn't have advice on the weather, but looked skeptically at our boat and gear.

"Got a quad? And a gun?" one man asked David.

He told them no.

"That's a mistake," the camper said.

We remounted, but only a mile later lightning lit up the sky, forcing us to shore again. We set up the tent on the edge of a sandy beach, where green bushes and grass met piles of driftwood. The Hilleberg is actually two tents, a ruby-red outer shell and a bright yellow inner core suspended inside, a substantial air gap between the two layers. This keeps rain from reaching the sleeping chamber, but it also stretches the skin tight as a trampoline. We barely had the shelter up when the storm hit; rain beating against the tent, it sounded like we were hunkered down in a popcorn popper. Several mosquitoes had followed us inside, and when David squished them, they sprayed our blood all over the fresh ripstop nylon.

All afternoon, we lay on top of our sleeping bags, listening to the driving rain. David wrote in his journal and then took a nap. The weather forecasting app on the inReach said there was a 10 percent chance of light drizzle in our area. Outside, we heard a pickup truck driving up and down the beach, splashing through the water like a dog.

"Well, this is a fuck of a way to start," I said.

————

We got to Point Roche about ten o'clock. The sun was an orange ball four fingers above the horizon, but the warm golden hours did nothing to improve the view at the point. Bulbous rocks, fishing flotsam—ripped nets, a rusty fillet knife, empty oil jugs, half a particleboard cabin with a rotting mattress—and standing at the highest point, a metal-framed marine marker that looked like half a Christmas tree. Despite what Doug said, we didn't see anywhere to put up a tent.

We reluctantly pushed on, into a sun that refused to set. All had calmed after the storm, loons sat on liquid glass, and the lake was the color of the sky. In contrast to Mackenzie's experience, no fog and ice floes blocked our view. Just before midnight we found a gravel beach, adjacent to a bog built by beaver dams, and set up camp in the twilight. Much of our gear—maps, books, spare clothes—had gotten soaked in the storm, but at least our sleeping bags were dry.

The tent was full of mosquitoes in the morning, and David and I were covered in bites. One of us had failed to double-check the two doors, and they snuck in through a small gap in the zipper, attracted by the bright fabric and carbon dioxide of our exhales. The interior of our tent was already polka-dotted, brown on yellow, every surface covered with mosquito body parts and our own blood.

All morning, the lakeshore to our left barely changed, nothing but muck and low trees, and a crosswind lapped small whitecaps against our gunnel. David and I decided to switch places. I had started the trip in the back, my traditional place as a guide, but we wanted to see if the canoe handled better with his greater weight in the rear; we wobbled less in the breakers, but our speed didn't improve. Sandbars and shallow flats, hundreds of yards from shore, would betray themselves by producing riffles in the olive-green water. We ate a lunch of bagels and peanut butter on a tern rookery, a gravel mound two inches above lake level.

We didn't reach the mouth of the Mackenzie River until afternoon. Stuck in shallow water between barrier islands, I pushed off the bottom with my paddle and noticed streamers trailing off the high grass poking out of the water. Ahead, all the submerged reeds were lying down in the same direction.

Current. We had finally found it. Our moods improved dramatically, and as if on cue the sun broke free.

The storm and rain of the previous day were forgotten. A breeze stirred from the east, and I unfolded our small round sail and lashed it to the front of the canoe. Sun, wind, sail, current, we surged ahead of the waves with each gust, our prow cutting the water. No more struggling to make three miles per hour, now we charged ahead at eight.

A feeling had been building in me, since I crossed the 60th parallel into the long summer sun of the Northwest Territories, and in that moment it coalesced. I felt solar powered. I didn't want to eat or sleep. The continuous daylight was a manic party drug, and I felt as if I could go all day and night.

We got cocky, pushed past normal dinnertime, and stopped late on one small island, no bigger than a suburban ranch-style house. A few trees on one end hid a tent, but when David and I checked, no one was there. I was cooking spaghetti on the white gas stove when we saw a motorboat approach, our first encounter with anyone out on the land.

The old woman in front was bundled in a winter coat, and a man in back ran the outboard motor. They pulled up right to us, staying just off the bank.

"This one's for fishing," the old man said, pointing to the island.

David and I gave each other a look. Did we hear him right?

"We're just having dinner," I called back.

"This one's for fishing," the man said again. "You go out here. I'll show you."

And he turned his boat around and jetted away to the shore, pointing at trees in the distance.

"I think he wants us to leave," David said. Our noodles were almost done cooking.

"Let's eat quick and go," I said.

When the couple returned, they drove the boat up onto the bank near their tent. There was a lot of frantic movement in the trees, and I eventually figured out they were taking down their shelter.

"They really don't want us here," David said. I had to agree. We cleaned up our supplies and pushed off.

Michelle's guidebook said there was a good camping spot at the Kakisa River, a major tributary coming in from the south. Reaching it would require several more hours of paddling, but energized by the sun, we felt we could make it. Plus, history was now on our side; we were about to finally link up with Mackenzie, whose route thus far had tracked the northernmost channel. At the point our travels merged, Mackenzie had found clear sailing for the first time, as did David and I. On the calendar, we were even a few days ahead of him; it was June 23, but Mackenzie didn't make it through the fog of Great Slave Lake until June 29. The swampy shore provided few immediate options, so we pushed hard, knowing that stopping short a second night wouldn't get us to Fort Simpson on time.

Once at the Kakisa, though, no campsite appeared. Only the same marsh, grass, and occasional twisted bushes, no earth above the waterline. It appeared that full trees rose farther inland, so we fought upstream on the Kakisa, but we saw nothing dry enough to call a campsite. After exhausting ourselves paddling against the current, we gave up and drifted out.

"If the English Chief was here, he'd have thrown Michelle in the river for that," said David.

According to the guidebook, the next good spot for camping was at Burnt Point, four hard hours away. It was almost ten o'clock—according to my watch, not the sky that just blazed away—and suddenly I wasn't sure solar power would see us through. We paddled to the next small point, hoping for something rocky—like Point Roche, which we had so haughtily abandoned the night before—but saw only waterlogged reeds along the shore.

We were in the heart of Beaver Lake now; the far bank was over five miles away, a ninety-minute open-water paddle. We pressed on, sun slowly sinking lower. My back hurt, legs cramped. Ironically, large hidden rocks rose from the river bottom, scraping the canoe. According to our map, there was one more major point ahead and then a wide bay. Hope rested on that peninsula.

On our arrival, we chased off seagulls from a bare patch of wet mud and bird shit and soft sticky fledgling feathers. The very tip of the marshy point was just large enough for our tent. David and I looked at each other, and I was so tired I considered it. White goo soaking up through the floor.

"I'm sorry, David, we can't," I said.

"Oh, thank God," he said. "If you had said to stop, I would have."

Eleven o'clock. We had been paddling for sixteen hours and were four thousand miles from home and had no idea where to stop for the night. Gulls squawked at us, and I got out of the canoe, stood in the two-foot-deep water, stretched my back, and then rolled out the paper topo map. David got out too, held the canoe with one hand.

"My knees and hips are screaming at me," he said, and they made popping sounds as he bent over.

On the topo map, every bit of shore between us and the camping at Burnt Point was labeled "swamp." But how could we trust the book about Burnt Point anyway? According to her notes, it had been twelve years since she had paddled this way, and the river and water levels had clearly changed. The book was proving as reliable as Mackenzie's Red Knife guide.

David started to shake, from head to toe.

"Are you cold?" I asked.

"I don't know," he said, but his face looked worried. After the sweat of the afternoon, standing in the cool water, hypothermia was a possibility.

"Let's keep paddling and warm you up," I said, as the dad and trained wilderness guide in me kicked in.

"You know, we might not find anywhere," David said, and his teeth chattered. "What do we do then?"

"We keep going," I said. He was a former college football player; I had gone to war. "We're tired, but we've both been through worse. At least it won't get dark."

We crossed a small inlet. The shore was a continuous thin green line. Waterlogged horsetails. Demoralized, we paddled into a furious midnight sun.

My thoughts mirrored David's. There was no reason there *had* to be somewhere to camp nearby. We weren't in a designated park; no human had worked to make this piece of wilderness more accessible. It could well be—in fact, it was becoming probable—that there was simply nowhere to stop. We would just have to be lucky.

And then we were. It was David who spotted it.

"Could that be something?" he said, and pointed, tentative. Through the green soda-straw reeds and masses of dead seaweed, beneath a line of bushes: grass growing from dirt. I didn't trust my eyes until we made it to shore, a real shore, small pebbles that crunched under my feet. When I knocked down high brush to make room for the tent, I could smell mint in the broken stems.

"I just want to close my eyes," David said when we got in the tent, and he was asleep in a moment. I don't think I moved in my bag all night.

Forty-five miles that day.

———

In the morning, my body registered its objections: sore muscles, sunburned skin, calcified sweat. The trip was only two days old, but already felt way too big. How to keep doing this for another six weeks?

David was more cheerful. "I usually like the smell of my crotch," he said. "It's got a Frosted Flakes vibe." He rubbed two fingers between his legs and then lifted them to his nose. "But today it's rotten vegetables."

Our goal for the day was Fort Providence, and after only two days I imagined a restaurant meal and maybe a shower at a campground. My paddle felt heavier in my hand, but we made good time. Bald and golden eagles hunted the river for fish, and when we passed Burnt Point, we saw no campsite. We ate a lunch of pemmican and bruised peaches outside a small decrepit fishing shack. No one was home—a padlock kept bears and squatters out—and in the water dead freshwater shrimp floated in clumps.

And then civilization reappeared. Tall nautical markers, as big as billboards, to indicate the shipping channels. Then on our left, a wide gravel road—the ice road, I figured—drove straight into the water. Then a monstrous bridge, two hundred yards high and over a mile long, held up by a series of massive rusting Ys. The current grabbed us and swept us under as we tried to ferry across. The green water was roiled, and we saw fishermen along the bank trolling the Providence Rapids. This name had worried me when I saw it on the map, but it proved only a strong current that tugged at the nose of the canoe. The fishermen called to us, "Where are you going?" and I replied, with pride, "We're doing the whole river, but we're staying in Fort Providence tonight."

A white steeple appeared first, then other small structures high up on the riverbanks, cut away by the fast-moving water. Providence Island, across from the town, looked like a cupcake, black spruce icing and dirt cliffs for the wrapper.

After our struggles the night before, we didn't want to worry about finding a campsite, so we decided to stay in a designated spot in town. We stopped the canoe at the public boat launch and on the bluff above found empty flat grass; such luxury, I was overwhelmed. Two Slavey men sat there, drinking beer and watching the river.

They introduced themselves as Gilly and Mark. Both had sparse mustaches and baseball caps and held cans of warm beer that came out of a cardboard box at their feet. They fished the river, they said, but only this small section, between Beaver Lake and Browning Point farther on.

"The water on the Mackenzie is high this year," Mark said. "I remember in 1964, the river went dry, and the whole town had a picnic on the river bottom. But then the water started to rise all of a sudden, and one fat nun, she had to pull up her skirt and run." He laughed at the memory.

"You call it the Mackenzie?" I asked.

"We say 'Mackenzie,'" Gilly said. "The elders say 'Deh Cho.' Deh Cho means Long River, eh? The elders say, 'He only paddled it once, why did they name it after him?'"

I wanted to talk to Mark and Gilly more, but my stomach was rumbling. Our guidebook said you could get a hot meal at the Snowshoe Inn.

"David and I are going into town to get dinner. Are you going to the bar later?" I asked, but Mark laughed.

"Only white people go to the bar. It's too expensive," he said. "Indians buy a case a day and go home."

"But you guys gotta be careful," Gilly said. "Here, you're okay, because we're watching your canoe. We'll keep an eye on it for you, but downriver they'll steal your stuff."

"Especially in Wrigley," Mark said. "They're terrible in Wrigley. Thieves. But here in Fort Prov, you're fine."

Our walk into town was very short. Ravens had taken over the belfry of the church, and the scattered homes consisted of single- and double-wide trailers, some well maintained, some not. A few had teepees, for drying fish, skinned with plastic tarps to keep the smoke in. For curiosity's sake, I tried to spot the house of the richest man in town, a habit I continued the rest of the trip, but didn't spot an obvious Old Man Potter in Bedford Falls.

A few indigenous locals stood in a group outside the Snowshoe Inn, and when we passed, they asked us to buy them beer inside. One woman, Edna, had the small wide-spaced eyes indicative of fetal alcohol syndrome. She was already intoxicated and asked what the two new white guys in town were doing.

"We're paddling the whole Mackenzie River," I said.

An old man in a plaid shirt shook his head. "You're crazy," he said.

"We used to have a Mackenzie festival here," Edna said. "Then a girl went into the bushes and came out pregnant. They stopped it after that."

The interior of the Snowshoe Inn recalled my 1980s childhood: dark wood paneling, jukebox, low half-moon cushioned chairs, billiard tables with padded pleather legs. We ordered breaded chicken wings, bison burgers, and French fries with gravy, all frozen food tossed in a fryer.

After dinner, two white men, obvious outsiders like us, asked if we wanted another round of beers. Steve and Jim were wildfire researchers. Steve was quiet, chose his words with care. Jim was a gregarious engineer, glasses and stubbly beard, a smiling but intense look. The Northwest Territories provided them plenty of space to set forest fires—the biggest, nastiest, hottest fires possible—to test new heat-resistant materials, such as emergency foil shelters for firefighters using the skin off NASA's reentry vehicles.

Steve and Jim seemed eager for conversation with newcomers, and David and I too, but the longer we talked and drank in that dim tavern, the more I sensed an odd fur-trading fort vibe from our surroundings. It was clear we were drinking far slower than the rest of the clientele. Teenage indigenous women sat with the few older white men. Loud youngsters shouted about their drunkenness while playing pool. When an older gentleman woke up and tried to order another beer, the bartender said she couldn't legally serve him and told him he had to go. The sign behind the bar read, "If You're Asked to Leave and Refuse, You'll Be Bared Entry for 1 Month."

Jim and Steve wanted to get another round of Kokanees, but I begged off, and David agreed. We walked back to our boat, checked to ensure our canoe was tied up, and then went to sleep in the sunshine.

Groggy, I roused to the sound of pickup trucks and quads barreling past us, honking the horn. It was bright in the yellow tent. I checked my watch. Three in the morning. Still in a stupor, I grumbled about kids playing pranks to keep us up and then rolled over and went back to sleep.

I awoke to the sun in my eyes. Eight o'clock. It was quiet. David offered to walk down to the canoe to get our cooking supplies and oatmeal for breakfast. I dressed slowly and was just emerging from the tent when I saw David's head poke up above the bluff. His face was blank.

"Our canoe's been ransacked," he said.

I ran down the bluff. The boat was still right where we had left it, but every bag and container was open and tossed and all the contents were scattered on the ground and in the water. The food barrels and shrink-wrapped cube of toilet paper were floating in the river eddy. Seagulls were eating dehydrated peas from dinner pouches that had been opened and poured out. Every pocket of my parka was emptied. The bottom of the canoe was full of dumped medicine bottles and unwrapped granola bars.

Something righteous and bigoted boiled up in me from the lizard stem of my brain. *Drunk thieving fucks.* I was angry at Doug and Michelle and all the paddlers in Fort Smith for persuading me to let go of my suspicions, and I was angry at myself for prioritizing open-mindedness over security and safety. I wasn't naive. I had been around the world and made a deliberate choice to trust that I could sleep fifty yards away from my boat without incident. But now that choice looked more enlightened fool than careful pragmatist. Why would the poor and desperate in the Arctic really behave differently than anywhere else?

David and I did an inventory. We had the Wallet and the Office—our passports, money, maps, computer, inReach—in the tent with us, but much of our survival gear was stripped out. They had taken a haphazard combination of supplies: the ax, small food barrel, multipurpose stove that would burn any fuel, the gas canisters for the stove they left behind, one stockpile of pemmican, and all of our energy bars. Much of the rest was soaked or scattered or ruined.

Mosquitoes drank from my neck and arms. My empty stomach rumbled. I had to take a shit, but there was no such thing as a public toilet in Fort Providence.

David was cleaning up the food that was strewn about the boat launch, scaring away seagulls as he went. "You're so Wisconsin polite," I said. "Someone rat-fucks your canoe and you pick up the litter?"

"What else would you do?" he asked, and continued his work.

Then I took a breath, and the sober and well-trained military problem solver in me regained control.

We could buy more food and could make do without the ax, but we needed a stove to cook breakfast and dinner. So I called Doug—"our first trouble in twenty years," he responded, extremely apologetic—and asked for help. "Can you drive up a new stove, so I can buy it from you?" I asked. Fort Providence was three days from Hay River by canoe, but only ninety minutes by car. Doug offered a brand-new kind, a BioLite that burned wood and grass, so we didn't have to worry about buying fuel. I wasn't in a position to bargain, so despite my misgivings about being at the mercy of the weather to start a fire every night, I just said thank you, and Doug said he was on his way.

David pulled out his toothpaste, and I gave him a curious look. "No matter what happens, you always feel better after you brush your teeth," he said. I joined him, and he was right.

About noon the town woke up, people drove by in their pickup trucks and quads. I felt like all of Fort Providence was watching. Not just curious stares, but knowing ones. So much for the bush code, I thought.

Then my phone rang, with a blocked number. Curious, I answered.

"This is Corporal Shoeman with the RCMP in Fort Providence," a woman's voice said. "I hear you guys had some trouble last night."

Royal Canadian Mounted Police. Doug must have contacted them.

"We did. We had some things stolen from our canoe," I said.

"Balls!" she said, with surprising vehemence.

"Yeah, we're not too happy this morning. We're canoeing the whole river; they took some essential gear."

"Oh, that sucks so bad!" she said, and I could hear her sigh on the phone. "It was a late night for me," she eventually went on. "Give me a bit to shower and I'll be down to see you."

Corporal Shoeman arrived in a white pickup truck, the crown and maple leaf crest of the RCMP on the side, and was fully kitted out: vest, Taser, boots, turtleneck, heavy coat. She was young, vaguely Italian, cute under different circumstances. I gave her an inventory of what we lost, and she was professional, until I showed her the sopping-wet toilet paper.

"Dicks! Am I right?" she said, again with commiseration.

"I feel dumb, like I did something wrong," I told her. "Like I'm a tourist who just got mugged in the subway because I didn't know to put my wallet in my front pocket."

"You didn't do anything wrong," she said. "A bunch of drunk Indians stole your shit. They steal from each other. Some around here, they don't have anywhere to live, they just scavenge. This is my fourth call from last night."

That the people who stole our gear needed it more than we did would eventually provide some consolation, but not right away. In a similar situation, Mackenzie himself concluded, "I suppose they think provision should be common Property among all People."

"Should we worry about further on, down the river?" I asked, thinking of the advice from Gilly and Mark last night.

"You need to be careful. Towns with no roads are sometimes better," she said. "Except Wrigley. It's really bad in Wrigley."

————

It grew hot. Great Slave Lake had been cool and damp, Beaver Lake sunny but breezy, and in town there was air-conditioning at the Snowshoe Inn. But after Fort Providence, the wind died and the sun never truly set.

Just above Mills Lake, that pond slapped by a giant beaver tail, David and I stopped on an island, sandy where the point broke the current like an arrowhead. It was our first chance to take a bath in the clean cold water, and I wanted a fresh start after the theft at Fort Providence. But while washing my clothes in the current, one of my convertible pant legs, unzipped from the shorts, floated away. I only noticed it was missing when I got dressed, and discovered one leg, not two.

"We didn't give the river a tobacco offering today, did we?" I said.

"No, I forgot, with everything else going on," David said.

"I guess the Deh Cho took its share anyway," I said. *If I keep losing things at this rate*, I thought, *I'll be naked in a canoe by the end.*

We had been warned that Mills Lake was dangerous—easy to get wind-bound, unsafe in a storm, stay to the south no matter what—and because the weather was hot but calm, David and I decided to paddle late once more, to cross the lake in one day. We snaked through islands, and then the river widened again, into a gargantuan view.

Before us, no horizon, only a single steel-blue vista as water and sky merged, cotton-ball clouds perfectly mirrored in the lake surface. "Such sights as this are reserved for those who will suffer to behold them," wrote Eric Sevareid in David's favorite *Canoeing with the Cree*. The sun was so bright and continuous that every exposed bit of skin burned. Then the breeze came up slightly, and the light reflected off the ripples like a strobe.

No wonder Mackenzie had no idea which way to go, and his guide had never ventured farther. How to know where to find the exit of such an expanse?

The south shore was swampy. After we paddled for several hours, the north bank reappeared. The land was rising there, looking firmer for a tent, so once Mills Lake tapered back into a river, we dared to cross. It took forty-five minutes of open-water paddling. The wind was down, there was no obvious danger, but still David and I talked the whole time to keep our minds off the agoraphobia until we closed in on the far bank.

"Oh yeah, that's good camping right there, eh?" David said in an exaggerated northern Wisconsin accent that came off as vaguely Canadian. It had become a game, since the lack of options at the Kakisa River: all day long we called out good camping spots not mentioned in the guidebook. This time, David found us a beach full of seashells, an open flat piece of country, like an alpine meadow, purple wildflowers and wild strawberries with runners that looked like red wires crisscrossing the ground. We hoped to catch a bit of breeze on such open land, but our camp remained triple buggy: mosquitoes, horseflies, bulldogs. David and I sat on a log and watched two thunderstorms roll away into the distance.

"This river is so big it's like the size of Lake Winnebago," I said, using a reference from his home.

"This water is different than any water I've ever been on," he replied. "The scale is really daunting, when I think too much about it. I've never been anywhere that made me feel so small and insignificant."

———

In the morning there was no dew, because it didn't get cool or dark at night.

The Mackenzie kept narrowing and finally began to resemble a river from back home. So far, David and I had paddled three lakes, and we were sick of them. But once past them, suddenly we had a cushion of a day or two to arrive at Fort Simpson, and I realized how stressed I had been to make time at the start of the trip.

There were two sounds: the headwind and David's constant chatter. The current was still sluggish and the going slow. On either side, banks of pale dirt were followed by walls of black spruce, so tight to the water that no wider view was available, only the impression of unending flatness and forest beyond. The sun was unrelenting, no shade on the water, so we gave ourselves a break after so many stressful days and stopped early, at only half past eight, at a flat spot just short of White Man's Point.

But there was no shade onshore either, crumbling driftwood and wolf prints dried into the mud. Resigned to pitching the tent in the sun, David and I unrolled it and dozens of bulldogs, trapped in the seams of the tent since we broke camp that morning, roused to life and swarmed. It was too hot and sweaty to rest inside the tent anyway, and I wondered how I might ever get out of the sun again. Mackenzie made his trip in the Little Ice Age, when summer crops regularly failed. How different this June.

I stood in the river to cool my feet and avoid the bugs, made notes in my journal, and used the inReach to text Jeremy, Landon, and Senny, my future paddling companions, that the most important piece of gear was a floppy hat to keep the sun off. My left wrist—a strip exposed between my long-sleeved shirt and my paddling gloves—was blistering from sunburn; I covered it with gauze and surgical tape. Eagles floated on the thermals. A swan honked and it echoed down the valley.

It was quiet. I heard a dripping and babbling, and I followed the sound and discovered a tiny brook emptying its brown tannins into the green of the Mackenzie. It was a short stream, spilling down the bank. I could see and understand its entire length. The stream emerged from a dense thicket, so dense I could only see a few feet in. There was no way to pierce the tree line. The Mackenzie River was too big to comprehend, and yet beyond it was somehow a wilderness many times larger still.

The breeze came up. The air said a storm was coming. "The cottonwoods are gonna be all worn out," David said, as puffballs filled the air.

I looked in the sky and saw three enormous flying saucers descending on us from the west. The clouds were layered, like plates or shelves, the sky behind nothing but black. The temperature dropped twenty degrees, and David and I took shelter.

None too soon. The front hit like a concussion, a wall of thickened menacing air. The tent recoiled as if struck, the outer shell suddenly pummeled by wind and fat drops of rain. The whole shelter was vibrating.

"They're here . . . ," David said, imitating the little girl from the movie *Poltergeist*.

Then both stakes on the tent's front sloped vestibule, the side facing the storm, suddenly tore out.

David turned back to me, this time with a bit of fear on his face. "It's not going to blow away with us in it," he started to assure me, when all at once the rear stakes ripped, the back vestibule popped, and half the tent collapsed on us.

David crawled out and started to reset the stakes, but too late, the remaining half of the tent fell with me inside. I scrambled and saw David retrieving boulders to weigh down the tent anchors. The river had turned as dark as the sky, and whitecaps stood like bared teeth.

We had to get the tent sheltered and out of the wind or it would rip to pieces.

"Is it calmer up there?" I called to David, and pointed at the woods. I had to yell to be heard over the wind.

"I'll check," he replied, and ran up the bank and plunged into the trees. I gathered the corners of the tent, our sleeping bags and other kit still inside, and started to drag it up the slope, as if it was a giant hobo handkerchief. At the wood line, I saw David making a space to put the tent; the clearing was chocked with primrose, and he was tearing out huge hunks by hand. But he quickly tired.

"There's no way to pull it all out," he said, and then showed me his palms. They were bloody and already swollen, pocked with thorns.

"Then we put the tent back where it was," I said. "The wind will be better once the front passes."

"How long will that be?"

"I don't know!"

"What do we do until then? Just stand outside and hold it?"

"If we have to," I said. We were both soaked in the driving rain and only half-dressed, boxers and no shirts, as we had been ready for sleep.

I pulled the tent back to the original spot on the beach. The wind was merely howling now, and grommet by grommet David and I set the tent up again, using additional emergency stakes from the spare shelter and then piling rocks on each corner. When it looked like the tent was out of danger, David single-handedly dragged the half-loaded canoe up the beach until it was level with the shelter. With much of our gear, not to mention all our food, still inside, it weighed at least five hundred pounds.

"Is it high enough?" I asked.

"If it gets water, we get water," he said.

That night, I stayed awake long after David fell asleep, exhausted, watching and listening to the rain and thunder.

———

The next day we arrived at the hamlet of Jean Marie River.

The level of activity along the river grew and grew as we approached the town. A thousand trickling brooks fell off the steep banks, and a beaver slid on its belly down the mud and then swam with us for miles. Three long barges were anchored along shore, loaded with dump trucks and backhoes returning from the Arctic winter construction season. David pointed to a dead spruce in which a golden eagle perched. It spread its wide wings—the feathers curved in anticipation of flight, majestic as a silver dollar—and then let loose a giant shit that splattered down the tree trunk.

Even the current built as we approached the Head-of-the-Line, named by boat captains to indicate where the Mackenzie starts to drop and accelerate. At the channel markers, the water sounded like a jet engine as it rushed past, a massive hydraulic pillow on the buoy's leading edge. The river tightened into a narrow channel. The mountains were coming soon, and in the distance we saw a long low mound of a hill, the first change in elevation we'd seen.

At Jean Marie River, we beached the canoe on a grassy bank next to a few Lund aluminum fishing boats, and I walked into town while David stayed to nap next to our gear. Jean Marie River barely qualifies as a settlement: seventy-odd residents, no stores of any kind, a cluster of log homes and prefab trailers and a volunteer fire station. A bicycle lay abandoned on a dry ice rink. The First Nations band office has solar panels, but a power plant drones away near the gravel airstrip; mail is delivered on Thursdays.

The song of the north is not a loon's call or a wolf's howl, as many famous outdoor writers contend, but rather the hum of the diesel engine. Three massive diesel generators per power plant: one to run, one in maintenance, one emergency backup. Harmonizing with this perpetual rumble is a symphony of extended quad-cab pickup trucks, four-wheelers, dirt bikes, powerboats, personal home generators, and heavy construction equipment. Fuel is expensive, and yet motors run all day and night.

I wanted to stop in Jean Marie River because I had heard that it was hosting the annual Deh Cho First Nations assembly, drawing Slavey members from Hay River, Fort Providence, Fort Simpson, and Wrigley. I didn't know what to expect and found something like a county fair paired with congressional testimony.

Inside the round ceremonial hall were plenty of traditional elements— fire at the center, fresh-cut willow branches blocking the sun—but the tone was official and high-tech, interpreters in soundproof boxes translating English to Slavey and back in real time. The theme of the conference was nominally "Adapting and Thriving with Climate Change in Denendeh," referencing the lands of the Dene people in the upper Mackenzie River valley, and appropriate to the subject matter it was wickedly hot.

Outside the hall, though, was a carnival. Children playing tag, vendors selling survival gear, a free cafeteria line for First Nations members. I was far from the only outsider. A few RCMP cops stood idly, a white woman passed out flyers about solar panels, and I spotted a lone black man who turned out to be the government-assigned economist.

Tacked to the outside wall of the meeting space were a series of notices.

One declared the assembly an alcohol-free zone. Others depicted a time-line of the Dene and Slavey land claims process. According to the history cards, it began in the late nineteenth century, when "Southerners find minerals, oil, and gas." After brusquely noting the illegitimacy of the first federal treaties of the early twentieth century, the story quickly jumps forward to an almost month-by-month rehash of every legal maneuver, sidebar working group, threat to walk away from talks, and judge's ruling. To the layman, the timelines were nearly incomprehensible, filled with jargon and acronyms.

"They never should have hired the lawyers," said a thin older man sitting nearby, passing the heat of the day in the shade thrown by the ceremonial hall. He introduced himself as Allan, a Dene elder.

"This is just like the Indian Brotherhood days, back in the '60s and '70s. Remember that?" Allan said, elbowing another elder next to him. "They start with the lawyers, and that confuses everyone and gets them off track, and then they talk about treaty claims and not climate change."

"Thirty years from now, all these kids"—here Allan gestured to the children running around, raiding the communal cafeteria food line in the adjacent tent—"will still be sitting here, having the same talk."

"Fishing isn't like it used to be anyway," the other man said. "It's too warm. The fish are slow. And too many otters. You put out a net, they take the fish before you get there."

Allan asked what I was doing in Jean Marie River, and I told him my plans to paddle the entire river.

"No one paddles anymore," he replied. "Everyone has a motorboat. Are you going to stop at Pandaville in Fort Simpson?"

"What's Pandaville?"

"It's a Chinese restaurant. Have you ever had Chinese food? And you have to stop and see Jonas. He lives at the Willow River. Look, he's right over there."

Allan pointed to another elder eating at the cafeteria. I walked over and introduced myself. Jonas had thick glasses and wore a long-sleeved purple shirt left over from an American 5K run. He made me promise to stop when I paddled past, which I told him would be in a few days, though honestly I had not looked far enough ahead on the maps to have any idea how far away the Willow River was. One day at a time; I only wanted to get David to Fort Simpson.

We camped for the night just below Jean Marie River, at an open spot on a point where, according to Michelle's guidebook, there once stood a sawmill. We could find no trace of it, only the charred stumps of trees from a large wildfire. The land was covered in flowers full of blimp-like honeybees, and it seemed perfect bear country, Winnie-the-Pooh's favorite haunt. I kept the bear spray and flares next to my pillow.

That night, as part of the annual gathering, there was a talent show. We could hear the oompah oompah of polka music echo as we tried to sleep in the brilliant hot sunshine.

―――――

I developed a morning ritual that grew in importance as the trip progressed. The sun said we lived in a continuous now, but my body, after only a week of travel, was already showing wear. So I'd wake up and, while still in bag, do a status check from head to toe. I might be day to day on the map, but physically I couldn't lose track of the long term. Not the next thirty miles, but the next thousand. Be extra cautious and not strip my gears. That morning, I had a growing sunburn-induced blister on my left wrist and four more converting to calluses on my hands. My legs and arms were covered with bulldog bites—they don't sting or suck blood but rather take huge bites of flesh, especially on the shins and ankles and forearms—and my lower lip was still numb from my sole application of DEET. I'd never use bug spray again. Only physical barriers, like head nets, kept the mosquitoes away anyway.

But I had no major injuries, no pulled tendons or ligaments from incorrect paddling technique. My shoulders and triceps ached, and my ankles and knees were sore from being crammed in the boat all day, but I was holding up.

I was grateful, and so that morning, when we loaded the canoe and pushed off, I paid extra attention to David's tobacco rite.

"Dear Mackenzie, please bless us on this day," he said.

"Are you making the offering to the river or to Mackenzie?" I asked.

"Mackenzie," David answered. "I think he's watching over us, saying, 'Look at what those two idiots are doing.'"

"I think you're supposed to thank the Deh Cho, make the offering to the river."

"Okay," he said, and pulled out more tobacco. "Dear river, old man river, please don't fuck with us today."

We made good time. An aft wind sprang up, and we could deploy the sail again, attaining ten miles per hour for a stretch. Through a section called the Green Island Rapids we found swift water, but nothing danger-ous, and could easily steer around the few standing waves. We stopped to eat bagels and peanut butter and honey and mandarin oranges on a beach full of skipping stones, and when a powerboat sped by, the driver yelled, "See you at Willow River!" and I figured it was Jonas.

To avoid camping in Fort Simpson—and thus make ourselves vul-nerable again to the poor and desperate—we stopped an hour upriver, at a small stream where beaver and jackfish jumped. There was a trail to a clearing on the ridge above the Mackenzie, an area of high grass and unskinned two-by-four cabin frames. A laminated sign tacked to one read, "Dene Youth Camp. Connect to the Land. Many Elders Will Be Here, Ask Them Why." The mosquitoes were unendurable, so David and I returned to the big river.

We fell into our camping routine, as we did each time we stopped. David would set up the tent, unroll our bags and pillows, and purify water, wearing the bladder of the gravity-fed filter from his forehead like a tumpline. "Camping is just a series of chores," he said. "That's why I like it." Cooking was my job, and after a few days of struggles—marked by cold oatmeal and crunchy pasta—I figured out how to start and main-tain a roaring fire in the finicky BioLite stove. Fortunately, the banks of the Mackenzie always had plenty of driftwood and dried grass, and I could cook our chili or beef stew right in the main kettle, no extra dishes required. I always served David his dinner first.

The next day, Jeremy would fly in, and I'd drop David in Fort Simp-son. *I'll really miss him,* I thought. David's a good traveling companion. He liked to talk, to fill in the quiet spaces, but I eventually grew to wel-come the distraction. Always good company, not picky, did his share of the work without complaint.

After our dinner, a boat pulled up to our campsite, a white family from Fort Simpson. After a week alone or in indigenous towns, it was jarring to see this polo-shirted group out on a jaunt, as if they were just taking a drive to get ice cream, as if this wilderness was not wilderness but tamed for precocious five-year-olds with flip-flops and toy fishing rods.

It was clear that David and I were out of place, maybe even in the way, as though we had pitched a tent in a town park. So I asked, "Where do people usually camp along this stream?" and the father answered, "They don't. You're only twenty minutes from town."

Twenty minutes from his home, weeks away from mine.

———

For the first two hundred miles, from Great Slave Lake to Fort Simpson, the Mackenzie is green, and when the wind ripples the water, it looks like alligator skin.

But then the Liard River comes in from the west, flush with silt from the melting glaciers of British Columbia, and where the two great rivers meet, Doug had warned us of an eddy line large enough to dump our canoe. I had no desire to tumble as I did at the Slave, as the consequences would be far worse.

I took this seriously—checked that our gear was tied to the canoe's thwarts and then checked again, squared our line through the eddy wall—but when David and I did cross to Fort Simpson, we saw no swirling boils or dangerous rip currents. Only a color change, from green to mud, chocolate smoothie in the blender. The meeting of the rivers was a bit of a disappointment, as had been Mills Lake before, though we counted ourselves fortunate to catch the Mackenzie on a tame day.

At the public boat launch at Fort Simpson, the shore was flat and inviting, but when we ran aground, our canoe did not grind to a halt as it would on gravel or sand. It squished. I got out and my feet sank into the dark Jell-O, almost up to my knees. Fort Simpson sits on an island of silt ten thousand years old, the slough formed when the clear main channel meets the laden mountain river. Mound and scrape, mound and scrape, the Mackenzie and Liard work like a painter preparing drywall.

David stayed with the canoe while I walked into town to look for coffee. Morning tea had so far kept away my caffeine-addict headaches, but so close to civilization my desire for black coffee went all the way to my groin. While searching for the convenience store, I was approached by a white guy with a long goatee. He said his name was Dean, and he offered to show me around town.

"Welcome to the last stop of civilization," he said as we drove in his big-wheeled pickup truck. Fort Simpson is no metropolis—a gas station, hotel, liquor store, tourism office, grocery store—but it is the final commercial stop on the highway. From here, the dirt road trickles only a little farther to Wrigley, which Dean said "doesn't count," because it's so small. Otherwise, for the next seven hundred miles to the north, the tiny local communities are accessible only by boat, plane, and winter ice roads. Dean said he used to live in a village like that. Originally from Alberta, he had worked as an educator in the far north for decades. His last assignment was in Nunavut, and he took the Fort Simpson job "to move south." He was wearing a purple T-shirt with a spell-casting wizard on it because he was on his way to work; he was using medieval-themed board games to teach adults to read, making the shirt a sort of uniform.

"You have Dene in America, you know," he continued. "You just call them Navajo. That *Windtalkers* movie, it's all Slavey words."

This is true. The Dene tell a story of wandering, that thousands of years ago there was a cataclysm in the north—the geologic record confirms a volcano eruption in the right place and time—and the whole of their people fled south, along the front range of the Rocky Mountains. Some kept walking, and settled in the desert, and now call themselves the Navajo. But some turned around and returned to the north. Both groups, though, the Dene and the Navajo, remember that story and can each understand large portions of the other's language.

At a gas station, Dean and I picked up coffee, so hot I couldn't drink it, and delivered it to David, who was struggling to move the canoe in the suctioning silt. "We call this our beach!" Dean said, and then, "It's almost lunchtime, we should go to Pandaville."

"We've been told we have to go," I said, but then I explained our experience in Fort Providence and how we were reluctant to leave the canoe unattended. Dean was sympathetic.

"We have problems with alcohol and poverty up here," he said. "But our drunks don't come out until after three. And just because you had your stuff stolen in Fort Prov doesn't mean it will happen here."

Dean helped us drag the gear and canoe into the bushes, camouflaged in the willows and invisible from the road, and then we returned to town.

Pandaville was furnished with folding chairs and stainless steel food warmers and served a "smorgasbord" for lunch: double-fried chicken wings, double-fried dumplings, rice, egg rolls, noodles, wonton soup out of a can. It was hot and salty and I ate four plates.

Two men joined us during our meal. Sean, the former mayor, had a long gray beard and sunken cheeks that made him look like he had stepped out of Yukon gold-panning central casting, but his eyes were sharp and he asked smart questions about American politics. The other man was Reg, fat and happy and crude. "I've never paddled the river," he said, "but I've paddled a couple young girls in my life." He owned the Mackenzie Rest Inn, the best in town, where David would stay the night.

After lunch, David and I quickly returned to our canoe and found everything intact. Jeremy was not scheduled to arrive until evening, so we took turns walking into town to stretch our legs. I stopped at the grocery-and-hardware chain known as the Northern store—founded in 1987 and named for the North West Company—and stocked up on oatmeal, trail mix, apples, and pears still covered in frost from shipment. Dean's prediction proved true; after three o'clock the streets were packed with intoxicated panhandlers, the largest crowd loitering outside the liquor store. David wanted to check into the Mackenzie Rest Inn and take a shower and I didn't blame him, so I killed time alone on the edge of town, guarding our belongings.

I felt like a tramp, and looked like one too: unwashed, ripped shirt, soiled pants rolled up to mid-calf, all my possessions lashed to a boat. I matched the children's book illustrations of Huck Finn. Not Tom Sawyer, mind you, but Huck. Tom was always welcome back in town after his short doses of romantic pirate life. Huck was the one actually stolen from. No one had run me out of town exactly, but I did feel confined to the outskirts, ducking in quick to grab some food before pushing off down the river.

Jeremy's plane landed in Fort Simpson on time, and then he hitched a ride from the airport to the boat launch. The van pulled up and I gave David a hug good-bye and then Jeremy got out. He was sparkling clean, with a long beard and bright white sandaled feet. His face looked nervous.

Blue-black clouds were building quickly in the south. We had an hour to get out of town and find somewhere to camp.

"Let's go, man," I said. "We've got a thunderstorm to outrun."

INTO THE MOUNTAINS, JULY 1789

ﾊﾊﾊﾊﾊ

The water held as "a fine Calm," and Mackenzie found equal harmony in the geography and the land, as everything lay before him exactly as he expected.

The day before—lost in the lake of the slapped beaver tail, their Red Knife guide as ignorant of the land as they—Mackenzie chose to follow the north shore. Soon it had grown shallow, though, and dangerously so. The lake bed rose ever so slowly, imperceptibly, until it became a bog; they were trapped on an inch of water in every direction. They pushed back, turned west, discovered deeper water along the southern rim. The sun was setting when they finally made camp on the marshy banks and ate a supper of days-old caribou, their hunters returning with meager fare despite the throngs of waterfowl breeding in the reeds.

But in the morning, there was reason for optimism and expectation. The narrowing river pushed south and west, just as Mackenzie hoped. His latitude readings thus far put them in line with the large inlet discovered by Captain Cook. Pond's map had proved correct to this point: the Slave River deposited them on the south shore of Slave Lake, they found the river to the west, and it was wide and strong. They launched the canoes at four o'clock, and soon the river bent, "our Courses S W b S 36 Miles." Perfect, veering southwesterly, right on target for the inlets of Alaska. At this rate, they'd make the Pacific as planned, if Mackenzie could keep the flotilla on schedule.

They had attained the edge of Peter Pond's personal knowledge. "So far Pond," the map had read. White men had never gone farther than this. Only two more landmarks remained before they reached "So far Cook." The hobbled Rocky Mountains to the south, and then, soon after, the great waterfall, the largest ever seen.

———

There appeared before them the barest hint of elevation. "Upon the South side of the River is a Ridge of low Mountains running East & west by Compass." It was a worn massif, indicative of an exhausted range that would succumb to the riverine thoroughfare he transited. A hopeful sign that Pond's reports were accurate.

To the north also lay a wide low plateau covered in thick forest. His Red Knife guide called it Horn Mountain, the land of the Beaver Indians. Those Indians traveled to Fort Chipewyan and the Old Establishment to trade, and while Mackenzie saw no sign of them on the shore, his hunters did find a white goose "which appeared to have been Shot with a Bow & Arrow & quite Fresh."

They paddled another fifteen miles, by Mackenzie's reckoning, and then, in the early sultry evening, an "appearance of bad weather." They made for shore but not in time. "Before we could pitch our Tents it came on a violent Tempest, of Thunder, Lightening, wind & Rain." The voyageurs couldn't even take shelter under the canoes before getting "a compleat soaking." To Mackenzie's surprise everyone was in high spirits, though, he later discovered, for a troubling reason. "The Men and Indians are not so much displeased with it being the Means of their camping a couple of Hours earlier than they would otherwise have done & the latter are very much fatigued having ran much after wild Fowl, which have cast their Feathers." Mackenzie was setting a grueling pace, especially for the Chipewyan hunters, who were tracking game all day and then paddling hard to catch up after killing the party's supper. Despite the early camp, they made fifty-five miles that day.

They embarked a full ten hours later, their longest rest since sleeping and trading with the Red Knife Indians on Slave Lake. It was July 1, four solid weeks on the move. Soon the river tightened as it never had, down to only half a mile wide. The current increased still further, and the walls of the channel closed in, "the land high on both sides." There was a great sense of expectation in the air. Perhaps the waterfall was coming.

Mackenzie started taking more measurements, sounding the river depth in the heart of the current and then calling the readings to Steinbruck; the Scot spoke in English to a German writing in phonetic French, his spelling as consistent as Peter Pond's. Nine fathoms in the narrowest stretch, twelve fathoms where a small river flowed in from the south. But then Mackenzie's lead bob snagged and the line started to play out, the weight held "fast at the Bottom," and Mackenzie ordered the canoe back. Barrieau called the reverse, and the *milieux* dug in but still they drifted on. "The Current is too strong to steer'd." Normally, Steinbruck and Mackenzie did not paddle with the men; their gentlemanly class rarely allowed such an infraction. But now, against the heart of the current, everyone took up the labor, to work back upstream. Barrieau, Ducette, de Lorme, Landry, their two wives, the two gentlemen. They failed. "With 8 paddles, as a Man, could not break it," Mackenzie said. The lead weight still tangled at the bottom of the river, eventually Mackenzie was forced to snap the plumb line, and they floated on at the mercy of the current.

————

That afternoon the storms came again. "Thunder, Lightening, Wind, and Rain, which ceased in about 1/2 an Hour and left us wet to the Skin as we did not land." The heat of the day was forming fast-moving thunderheads, and yet in these far northern latitudes the detritus of winter followed them. "Great Quantities of Ice along the Banks of the River," Mackenzie wrote, as they wound among islands of tall mud banks topped with hedgehogs of spruce. They landed on one and found the wooden poles for four lodges, much broken and rotted, "which we concluded to have been Crees, upon their War Excursions." Judging by their condition, Mackenzie thought the camps six or seven years old.

A little farther on, they stuck to the northern shore, seeing the land on the other bank rise to a rocky cap and then yawn open, where "the River of the mountain falls in." The water was still moving at great speed, but now it was swollen with the flow of two rivers. They covered the next thirty miles in only a few hours, and then a daunting view. "The Mountains of the Southerd in sight." A blue ridge of far-off peaks, stretching across the horizon.

The current was still roaring, the great waterfall surely just ahead, and Mackenzie began to imagine portaging his cargo through and over such an expanse. "As our Canoe is very deep laden and that we are in daily Expectations of coming to the Rapids, which we have been made to dread, we hid 2 Bags of pemmican in the opposite Island."

It was a considered, though risky, plan. It would reduce their weight in heavy swells, and lessen their burden for the long journey ahead. If they lost boats, rifles, provisions in the upcoming rapids, at least there would be a backup stockpile of food available. And on a return journey, back to Fort Chipewyan, they'd be glad for the stores, if hunting proved elusive. "I expect [the stock] may be of service in time to come," Mackenzie wrote.

Awgeenah and the hunters felt otherwise; get too hungry too far down the river, and they'd starve before they could make it back. "Our Indians are of a difft. Opinion, they having no Expectations of coming back here this Season, [in which case] of course it will be lost." When the Chipewyan traveled such long distances, they followed the herds; when Awgeenah and Matonabbee took Hearne to the Far Off Metal River, their journey lasted many seasons, and they did not return the way they had come.

On this, Mackenzie kept his own counsel, and the party landed on an island, to cache the pemmican and set up their tents for the night. They found two encampments that appeared fresh, maybe only a year old. The lodges looked familiar, like many other Indian settlements Mackenzie had seen, except for one key detail.

"By their way of Cutting the Wood they must have had no Iron Works," Mackenzie wrote. He had reached a place where not even the tools of white men had yet penetrated.

———

Early morning sun warmed the mountain air rolling over river chill; they awoke to fog. They launched the canoes anyway, and when the fog cleared several hours later, they discovered the water was no longer pale green. It was muddy and rich, the silt of mountain runoff, and Mackenzie thought he knew the source: "the Fog prevented our seeing" more streams joining this grand river, tumbling down from "very high Mountains ahead."

They were the largest mountains any of them had ever seen. Taller than the cliffs around Lake Superior, taller than anything in Awgeenah's Barren Lands or along the Coppermine. "The Tops of them hid in the Clouds, ran as far as our view could carry," Mackenzie wrote. They were a horrid barrier to his progress, "Barren and Rocky," inhospitable to life and monstrous in their impenetrability. Nothing grew on their slopes except at the base—a green forested wedge, flat and tilting into the river—and then to the north, even more knobby mountains, great irregular lumpy crests.

At noon another storm hit, more rain and lightning, and when it passed, Mackenzie saw the mountains glow. "There appears a No. of White Stones upon them which glistens when the Rays of the sun shines upon them. The Indians say they are *Maneloe Aseniah,* or spirit stones."

Cliff edges, canyons, summits in the clouds. The whole party was set on edge; how big was this waterfall, to be formed by such peaks? "We went on very cautiously here expecting every moment that we would come to some great Rapid or Fall. We were so full of this that every person in his turn thought he heard a Noise & the falling of water, which only subsided in our Imaginations." The river turned—Mackenzie noted the change as west by north to north by west, for twenty-one miles—before heat and exhaustion forced them to camp on the rocky ramp along the river's edge. The Chipewyan hunters returned late, worn out, carrying only a beaver and a swan. Mackenzie dismissed their weariness. "The Indians complain much of our hard marching, that they are not accustomed to such hard fatigue."

The morning rain hung heavy on them. They were among the mountains, rising on either side, and trapped in a funnel of wind that blew hard in their faces. They paddled for only three hours before Mackenzie called a halt to wait out the rain. He had Steinbruck add up the mileage from the logbook: 217 miles west, 44 miles north, since Mackenzie's last celestial observation on Slave Lake five days before. While stranded on that lake's south shore, waiting for the ice to clear, Mackenzie had calibrated his compass, by using his quadrant to determine when it was noon, precisely. That is, to measure when the sun reached its peak, relative to the horizon. At that moment, the sun aligned with true north, and by comparing that reading with the direction in which his compass pointed, he could determine its declension, how far it skewed. At the time, at Slave Lake, he figured the magnetic gauge pulled 20 degrees east of true north. But now, in the mountains, storms blocked the sun at noon, and he could not use his quadrant. His measurements were disrupted; he could only make estimates. But still, they seemed on track.

The rain abated that afternoon, and they launched into swirling waters, the mountains rising in layers into the far distance. "The Current became strong and rapid amongst Rocky Islands, the first that we saw in this River, and which we thought a sure indication of soon meeting with Falls and Rapids." The peaks retreated on the left bank but climbed ever higher on the right, the river splitting the ranges. The eastern arm was tall and stood pink in the afternoon sun. Ahead, four distinct mountain ridges rose in succession, each a progressively paler blue, cobalt down to a shade nearly indistinguishable from the sky.

One string of mountains crossed the river, and the water cut right through them, "the North Shore part of it perpendicular with the River," the sloping rock face a thousand-foot mound. Mackenzie ordered camp at the base of the hill, and then he and Awgeenah and two voyageurs and the hunters trudged up its flank, to see what waterfall or ocean awaited them. All of Captain Cook's reports of Alaska described their scene: snowy mountains, thick forests, piles of driftwood, a wide river with unbreakable current. Surely the sea was around the next bend.

The way was difficult, gravel that fell away beneath their feet, and a cold wind blew. When they finally reached the top, "I was very much surprised to find a Campment on top of it," Mackenzie wrote. But Awgeenah was not surprised, for he saw it for what it was: sanctuary and refuge. He said that "it was the custom of all the People who have no Arms to make choice Places of this Kind for their residence, as they could easily make them inaccessible to their Enemies." All lived in dread of the Cree, who made constant war upon them. In any case, the camp was abandoned, a lonely shrine to past defeats.

Mackenzie was discouraged. Mountains lay all about, so "our view was not so extensive as we had expected." They saw hills clothed in thin forest, small lakes filled with swans, and, of course, the river in an unbroken valley dominating the scene. All day, the current had been so strong it "makes such a hissing and Ebbillion as a kettle moderately Boiling." But there was no sea, no falls, no end to the river. It just stretched on and on, to a point far out of sight.

Only a few minutes later, they retreated down the hill in disappointment. "We were obliged to shorten our Stay here on account of the Swarms of Muskettoes that attacked us and were the only Inhabitants of the Place."

THE PLAGUES OF THE DEH CHO, JULY 2016

~~~~~

The air was electric. Too late I realized how badly I had misjudged the thunderstorm. It was towering, and fast, far too fast, and it chased Jeremy and me north; we got under way and then it was nearly on top of us. With David's bulk out of the boat, I had retaken my position as guide in the back of the canoe, and almost immediately, upon leaving Fort Simpson, I began looking for somewhere to take shelter.

I had never seen so much silt. The banks were the color and consistency of dark chocolate mousse, and though the thunderstorm loomed behind us, there was nowhere to stop. Silt bars rose from the riverbed like hands grasping at the underside of our canoe, and the low deep banks were squishy and eroded sloughs slumping into the water.

"We have to look for good camping," I said. "You can't trust the guidebook."

"What guidebook?" asked Jeremy.

"Michelle's guidebook," I said. "We have to find good camping on our own."

"What does good camping mean?" Jeremy shook his head. "And who's Michelle?" But I didn't answer, because I was distracted by the search and the crash of thunder behind us.

I wanted to camp in the tree line, so as not to attract lightning as the highest point on the beach, but our options seemed either cliff or boggy floodplain. Finally, the lightning all around us, I simply picked the firmest bank available, even though the nearest cover was a field of bushes hundreds of feet in. I tried to drive the nose of the canoe hard into shore, but we stuck fast in muck. I waded through, ran up the silt, and found a spot for the tent, flat but overgrown with willow that rose to my shoulders. I yanked at a root ball but it was surprisingly sturdy, so I started snapping branches, flattening stems, carving out a bed. I was so intent on my work and the ink-sky above that it took me a few moments to realize that Jeremy had not followed me. He was waiting at the canoe.

"Bring the tent!" I called through the wind.

"Which one's the tent?"

"It's red. Plus, the sleeping bags—they're in stuff sacks!"

"What are those?"

I ran back to the canoe, loaded Jeremy with gear, and then we waddled up the beach together. Mosquitoes rose from the malarial plain and surrounded us like a biting fog, the thickest swarms I had yet seen. They crawled up inside my head net, found my ankles, covered my exposed hands. Swat, crush, pound a tent stake, smear, swat, pound again. My hands were covered in my blood.

The rain came while Jeremy was still toting gear from the canoe. Hard and cold and wild blown, splashing silt. I had never done such a poor job setting up the tent, and by the time I was done, Jeremy and our gear were soaked and broken willow stems poked at the floor and sides of the shelter. I dumped everything—Jeremy and equipment—inside the tent anyway and then returned to the emptied canoe, to pull it farther up the beach.

The rain struck in waves, and lightning and wind lashed the hillside.

I finally crawled into our shelter and saw Jeremy had set up the sleeping bags all wrong. His shirt was off, and every bit of revealed skin was covered in hives.

"The mosquitoes?" I asked. "Are you allergic?"

"I don't think so," he said, shaking, and I realized it could be stress and fear, a reaction to physical danger. Who knows what unfamiliar hormone cocktail was loose in his veins?

The lightning strikes were approaching, growing closer and more regular, and the thunder rolled down the valley like a tidal wave.

"We're not high enough into the trees. We need to get into the lightning position," I said to Jeremy, and then crouched so that only my feet touched the floor of the tent, arms around my knees.

"What does that do?" he asked.

"Minimal height and surface area on the ground. I studied before I came." I got the information from the website of the National Outdoor Leadership School. "Don't worry," I said. "No one has ever died in the lightning position."

The storm raged for hours, finally letting up in the early morning twilight. Two miles behind us, David was snug in bed, in a civilized cocoon.

———

Jeremy Howard Beck is a compact man, with a shaved head, heavy brow, and long crinkly beard, so Jewish as to look Amish when he wore a wide-brimmed hat. Clean and a bit fussy, he had a special waterproof case for his iPhone and brand-new hiking boots tied to the outside of his bag. He brought beard oil and citronella for his skin and washed his hands in the river with soap.

I learned later that Jeremy had never before spent more than one night in a tent, had barely camped in any capacity at all, and had never, not even once, shit in the woods.

"I googled it," he said. "I watched a video. It said to make a little hole and then cover it. Like a cat."

We both knew that Jeremy's primary qualification for coming on the trip was his availability. Several other friends of mine, military buddies and outdoor enthusiasts, signed up and then had to cancel. A month away from leaving, I was desperate. So I called Jeremy because he's an opera composer and makes his own schedule. I hoped he could drop everything for two weeks, and I was right.

"I was on the rowing team in high school," he said, and though he initially held his paddle wrong, with two hands on the shaft, that sounded enough like canoeing experience to me.

After ten days with David, everything was packed just so. No more awkward ungainliness; every bag had a place and every bag in its place. But Jeremy knew none of that. Not how to pack the canoe, not how to unload it, set up and break camp, gather wood for the BioLite stove, filter water.

I thought of Amos Burg, who, in June 1929, traveled much of the Mackenzie River basin for *National Geographic*. Journeying by rowboat, and occasionally towed by motorized craft, Burg explored the valley with an unlikely companion, Professor George Rebec, the sixty-six-year-old head of the philosophy department at the University of Oregon. Burg encountered dirty blocks of ice as far south as Lake Athabasca and torturous pests. "Each bite of bacon is punished by six bites from the mosquitos," he wrote; eventually, he ran up and down the shore as he ate. But Rebec couldn't similarly adjust to the rigors of river travel. He didn't paddle, exhausting Burg, and, with no wilderness experience, quickly became sick. A few days past Fort Simpson, Burg put Rebec on a steamship home.

I needed Jeremy to learn quicker than Rebec. My next paddling companion was due to fly into Tulita, hundreds of miles and ten days away.

The next morning, Jeremy tried to load up the canoe. "This is like walking on cake," he said, bowing the silt as he carried gear. The sun came out, and I showed Jeremy how to filter water as David did, with the bag hanging from his head. "Teach a man to fish," I recited to myself as a mantra.

After the Liard's mountain flow fell in at Fort Simpson, the Mackenzie became bipolar: clean on the right, dirty on the left. Not toxic, not contaminated, not diseased, but dirty. Full of dirt. Stick your hand in the river up to the wrist and you lose sight of your fingers. The water filter clogged on chunks of espresso, and when I dipped in my paddle, it came out grimy, like it needed to be washed. Cold green Great Slave Lake water on the right, the loam of British Columbia on the left. As soon as we could, we paddled across to the other shore; I wanted my old river back.

All day, the current steadily increased; we made forty miles with ease. On either shore, we saw big blowdowns caused by the storm, mighty spruce crashed into likely camping spots, and suddenly our exposed field of willow bushes didn't look so bad. The banks were high, no more marshes, and no more waterfowl or the bald and golden eagles they attract.

That evening, we camped on the north shore, just past a few islands at Trail Creek. It was July 1, and on the same night in 1789, Mackenzie persuaded Awgeenah to cache pemmican on those Trail Creek islands and then make camp. For the first and only time, Mackenzie and I were sleeping on exactly the same rock on exactly the same day, united by both calendar and geography, precisely 227 years apart.

And then the next day he woke at two o'clock in the morning and paddled on, farther and faster than we could ever hope to match.

———

The mountains. By midday they rose in the distance—hazy, broken-toothed, relentless—and our spirits, of their own volition, did the same.

First a big blue, with three sisters to the south. Then a lone peak, bare topped and gray. It was easy to paddle into such a view, and I felt the coming of the Camsell Bend with great expectation.

The Camsell Bend is the great turn of the river, like the Big Bend of the Rio Grande but on a far larger scale. The flow hits the Rockies and makes a hard right, to become a fundamentally north-flowing river, rather than western. The mountains would never be closer, the landscape never more sublime, than in this pocket of crags.

This is a new notion, sublimity via elevation. As the British mountaineer Robert Macfarlane has written, "Three centuries ago, risking one's life to climb a mountain would have been considered tantamount to lunacy." To Mackenzie and the pre-Romantics, mountains were a wasteland full of terrifying beasts, nowhere to farm, nowhere to build. Ideal beauty was to be found in the pastoral, agricultural plenty. Only in the early nineteenth century, when Europeans began to creep out on alpine glaciers for a thrill, did perceptions and art change.

Consider, for example, Edgar Allan Poe's incomplete 1840 novel, *The Journal of Julius Rodman*, about a fictitious first man to cross the Rockies. Even macabre Poe stirs the mountains with romance and redemption in solitude. Nature is full of "majestic novelties," and Rodman's account, full of "affectionateness" for "the severest hardships and dangers," is meant to stir "envy" in the reader. In contrast to Mackenzie, Rodman was not searching for something as crudely commercial as the Northwest Passage, but rather had an "ulterior hope," to get "beyond the extreme bounds of civilization—to gaze, if I could, upon those gigantic mountains." He was "urged solely by a desire to seek, in the bosom of the wilderness, that peace."

It is worth noting that in Poe's book, Rodman never does cross the Rockies. The novel is cut short, because Poe wasn't paid on time by his magazine patron, and he stopped writing. The story ends mid-chapter, in a heroic fight to the death with a grizzly bear.

As for myself, I admit that after several weeks on the river, bug bit and thunder shook, my eyes had calibrated to the pre-Romantic notions of Mackenzie and Awgeenah. I felt more vulnerable than peaceful.

In the far distance, the mountains appeared mighty, grew and grew, and then all of a sudden we had arrived, we were at their bases, before and behind us and all around. Their height had been an optical illusion;

once we were among them, the mountains proved more modest than they appeared from miles away. Nahanni Mountain, at 4,038 feet, was the closest, standing nearly by itself. The Camsell Range ran to the north, each lump only rising to three or four thousand feet. Tall for Mackenzie, but midgets compared with the Rockies of the south and farther west. These peaks obscured more majesty than they showed.

We camped directly at the bend, a 270-degree swing of peaks as our view, and the scenery was so welcome after the low marshes off Great Slave Lake we took our time cooking and doing laundry, drying our clothes on a rope in the inexhaustible sunshine. The rocks on the beach were laid out like cobblestones, flat on the surface, rounded on the edge, gravel and mud fitted in between as mortar. Perfectly level, like a patio, or a Roman road. I found it hard to believe that natural processes had crafted such unity, but could find no explanation other than the scouring force of high rushing water.

To mark the occasion, I cooked Vegetarian Chili, a particularly good dinner I had been saving. Jeremy pulled out a titanium spork he had purchased for the trip. "I thought, I'm a titanium atom. I was forged billions of years ago in a far-off star. I came to earth and was lodged in the crust for millions of years. Now I'm in your spork."

I added tinder to the coals in the BioLite stove and Jeremy asked, "Do you want me to blow on the fire?" Was this a gay joke that I was missing? Jeremy correctly guessed my thoughts and said, "I also play the trombone, remember?"

I laughed.

"How does it feel to be the first gay Jewish opera composer to do a major descent of the Mackenzie River?" I asked him.

"Pretty good," he said, and smiled.

From shore, I could see no navigation aids or signs, no buoys, no channel markers, no fishing shacks, no boats, not even a contrail in the sky. This had surely been true previously, somewhere on the trip, but I never consciously noticed. Maybe the Romantic mountains spurred a closer observation.

"Do you know how this valley looked five thousand years ago?" I said to Jeremy. "Exactly like this."

"I feel like a little smudge," he said.

In the morning, I awoke eager to push my head out of the tent and see the front-lit mountain faces in the eastern sun. The whole Camsell Range was pink and gray, streaked with landslides of sloped sedimentary rock, but verdant behind, green with summer.

The birds, whether compelled by instinct or joy, sang all night into the rosy sky, in perpetual anticipation of a dawn that never ended.

———

"These mountains were a storm center," Amos Burg wrote in *National Geographic*, "for below the North Nahanni River their summits seemed to spout clouds that spread across the heavens and resulted in a gale that blew for two days."

After the Camsell Bend, unbroken heat produced nothing but gales. The towering mountains of the valley were made not of stone but of cloud; some looked like tightly packed bags of coiled rope, and others were frayed and blown out when hit by the upper jet stream. They formed to our east and west, and the only section of sky free from thunderheads was above the cool water, as if the river had thrown up some magical shield.

All morning, storms grew in the thermals thrown off by the mountains, the radiant warmth rising from bare rock. Then, in the afternoons, when sufficiently tall and menacing, they would swoop in from every direction, chasing us off the water with lightning and rain. While Jeremy took a siesta in the tent, I stayed up and watched the clouds scatter, some dissipating, others stacking to turn the horizon black. They moved in all directions, seemingly at random.

I enjoyed writing outside the tent while the storms rolled. You could see the entire rain cycle, tight and crisp thunderheads reduced to fuzzy remains as they lost their moisture. The breeze was strong and cool, and even the bulldogs were kept at bay. But there was also a sense of giddy dread in the face of such a powerful force. For a combat veteran, it was a familiar and unwelcome sensation, this particular combination of helplessness and trepidation. Crouching exposed inside a lightning storm felt a little too much like taking cover in Iraq, and I was relieved to see the storms move away.

The mountains formed a single ridgeline to the west, like the jagged crest of a dinosaur, and looked a bit like Utah, stripes of gray and brown tinted blue by the bright sun. *How could Mackenzie not notice he had turned north?* I wondered. Storms hampered his ability to use his quadrant, so he trusted his compass, maybe more than his senses, and it betrayed him. On the morning paddle, the sun baked my right elbow, rather than my back, and in the late evening the sun clearly lowered on my left. How did he ignore this? Up here, the sun was piercing, headache inducing, unavoidable.

The magnetic north pole moves, and when Mackenzie made his journey, it was located at modern-day Victoria Island, just above the Canadian mainland. Mackenzie knew about the magnetic variation from true north, correctly noted in his journal that on Lake Superior the two roughly aligned, and calibrated his compass when he could. But as he moved farther north, the error increased quickly; the magnetic north pole actually lay more to his east than north. This positive declination skewed every measurement he made. When he stood on the riverbank and looked in the direction that his compass claimed was north, in reality he was looking northeast. When he thought he was paddling northwest, he was really paddling due north. And the farther north he went, the more incorrect every measurement proved.

From the moment he made the turn at the Camsell Bend, Mackenzie was headed in the wrong direction, and staring at his bewitched compass, he had no idea.

———

Two days past the bend, I made good on my promise to visit Jonas Antoine at the Willow River, as I had pledged to him at the Deh Cho First Nations Annual Assembly in Jean Marie.

We could see Jonas's camp from miles away, a homely house against the wilderness. He met us at the dock at the base of the bluff and helped us tie off our boat next to his flat-hulled Lund. "You made it!" he said with warmth and then, looking at our laden canoe, added, "You've got everything in there, even a satellite dish, eh?"

Jonas's home sat in a compound at the exposed point where the Mackenzie and Willow Rivers meet. It was open and grassy, a few log cabins crumbling into memory near the cliff edge, three overturned canoes—red, yellow, and green—the first I had seen since we rented ours in Hay River. Jonas was wearing a Ducks Unlimited hat, stained sweatpants, bifocals, and galoshes with no socks. His modern home had an open-air porch, where he invited us to sit and swat bulldogs as he lit a Player's cigarette that he pulled from a small tobacco pouch.

Jonas offered us coffee, which I gratefully accepted and then he forgot to provide. I had read that it was always polite to bring a gift, so Jeremy gave him a bag of loose tea from the Edmonton airport, but Jonas only glanced at it once and then ignored it the rest of our conversation. Maybe we had messed up the ritual somehow? I didn't want to offend him, but I also really wanted the coffee.

Then Jonas's brother-in-law, Tony, stepped out, and I stood and shook his hand. Back in Jean Marie, Jonas had warned me that Tony only speaks Slavey, but I said hello anyway. Tony smiled and nodded his head up and down to the rhythm of our handshake.

"I worry about him, to take care of himself, but he won't leave the land," Jonas said, explaining why, though his wife works as a health-care aide in Fort Simpson, he lived with Tony.

"And I'm a dog person," Jonas said, "but he forgets about them." Jonas had half a dozen dogs, bruisers with matted calico coats and rough haunches and thick strong jaws. They were chained up outside, and at one point, when a stray dog or wolf came through the wood line, they leaped and barked, flinging mucus from their bared teeth and lips. Jonas was on his feet in an instant, and his brother-in-law too. "They'll fight if they break loose!" Jonas yelled to me as he ran up to the head bitch and whispered in her ear to calm her. Tony yanked another's choke chain and dragged the gurgling dog back to a kennel.

Jonas said he is seventy-five years old, old enough to have been stripped from his family and forced to attend residential school in Ontario. "The only thing I learned is church and English and Shakespeare," he said. "'True courage rises as occasion.' That's *King John.*"

When he was a young man, Jonas moved to America to play in a traveling rock-and-roll band. He saw the country and then eventually settled in Sheboygan, Wisconsin, got married, became a Packers fan, worked as stage crew at a television station and then in a factory that made plastic trays for Burger King. His children stayed in the United States when he moved back north.

"I told people in Sheboygan about where I'm from, and they don't believe me. And I tell people here about Sheboygan, and they don't believe me either." I mentioned that I went to college in Wisconsin, at

Marquette in Milwaukee, and he immediately mentioned Al McGuire and the 1977 NCAA National Championship in basketball. "The whole state felt a part of that," he said.

This connection, this is why I think he chose to share his vision with me.

We were making small talk when out of the blue he said, "I saw skyscrapers rise out of the ground. In Wrigley, looking out over the Deh Cho valley, during a drum session. With the elders. We're drumming, drumming"—here he closed his eyes tight and made the motions with his hands—"and I saw them. In the distance, rising out of our beautiful mountains. And I thought, 'This can't happen here.' I knew I had to stop it."

"Was it a medicine dream?" I asked. It was an inappropriate and rude question; I didn't really know what I was saying. Later, I learned from anthropologists that the residents of Wrigley are known for their medicine power, but also that those with medicine don't talk about it.

Jonas ignored me as he should have. Instead, he told me about the Mackenzie Gas Project that threatens to put hydro-fracking wells throughout his valley, and the pipeline that leaked several thousand gallons into the muskeg a few years ago, and the caribou that are frightened to mate near gas-turbine-powered pumps. His niece was in the new *Revenant* film, he said, so he wanted to contact Leonardo DiCaprio to talk about climate change.

"Our culture is the land," he said. "Take that away, we go away. I realized, everyone has their business. And for me, and our nation, our business is taking care of our people."

Eventually, Jonas wanted to talk about our trip as well. He hadn't seen a canoe like ours in some time. "People stopped paddling. Now you can google everything," he said, adding that he had paddled the entire river once, a six-man canoe race to Inuvik in 1989. "Some bicentennial thing for Sir Alex. I heard that when Mackenzie did the Deh Cho, he broke down and cried."

As we left, Jonas gave us tips, where to stop, whom to see, including Chief Frank Andrews in Tulita, to ask for permission to cross his nation's land. He also told us to stop at Northern to buy a fishing pole, and showed us what wild mint looked like. "Does it keep off the mosquitoes?" I asked. "My old grandpappy said it did," he replied.

Stay on the right side, Jonas said, the clean side, and drink from the small streams that come in to join the Deh Cho. "I've spent forty years of my life protecting that plateau," he said, gesturing to Horn Mountain behind him. "I know the water is good to drink."

I said I would, and then asked for advice for the hazard that had nagged us thus far.

"Is there a trick to knowing when a thunderstorm will come your way?" I asked.

"Just look at the clouds, eh?" he responded.

———

After we left Jonas, we spent more than a week looking at the clouds and fighting the unrelenting north wind.

Once, seeking shelter, we stopped at Old Fort Island, a slab of gray stone rising out of the river. We were nearly swept past it, as the current veered to either side of the island's rocky prow. We got caught in the rapid, were pulled around, and then fought through a huge eddy line on the leeward side of an outcropping. There was still water in a cove, and we grounded the canoe and climbed the rock face. We discovered a grotto full of stinking mud and bright orange algae, and a little shelf with a rapid at the center of the island.

"I feel like I'm on the moon," Jeremy said as we walked across the cracked and fragmented surface of the rock.

It was like another world, an oasis of geology and plant life separate from the spruce valley that surrounded it. A porcupine shuffled toward us and made a noise, something between a chirp and a whinny, and then turned its back and entered the tall grass. We gave him plenty of space. I grabbed the bear spray and screwed in the banger to the pen flare for the first time.

We waited out the storms that scattered around us and paddled until late at night, camping along a cliff in the golden night.

All the next day, headwind. Filthy, sore, wet, exhausted, we found ourselves stuck on a sandy beach next to a small creek when the rain hit. The mass of clouds to our east did not move; it simply grew like a black fungus that cast darkness over us, half a true night. The deluge washed away the sand beneath us so that a stream ran through the tent vestibules; we had unknowingly sought shelter in the drainage. I left the tent and saw the creek was widening, our boat parked in its delta. I dragged the canoe up higher just in time; fifteen minutes later, the beach was under water. As soon as the rain turned to drizzle, though, the bulldogs returned, joined by energized mosquitoes.

I built a cooking fire, and as had become his custom, Jeremy stayed in the tent. We had begun to call it the Fortress of Solitude. The bugs tormented Jeremy, and he sequestered himself behind layers of gear— head nets, jackets with hoods, boots—and retreated to the tent at the first opportunity, where he hunted the bugs that pursued him. My style was to pick at the blood-filled mosquitoes, gently popping them one by one between my thumb and forefinger. But Jeremy was vicious, clapped like a maestro chastising a musician, a sharp crack that startled me every time.

Jeremy did not participate in dinner, because, as I had feared, he had become sick, light-headed, and was living on Imodium. Poor guy had never shit in the woods, and now he had the runs. Even when healthy, Jeremy had plenty of ailments and ointments and treatments, flavors and scents and tonics and rituals. Now he was gutting out a stomach virus that could dehydrate him, just as the weather was turning and I needed his help.

Paddling with Jeremy was wearing on my body. I did everything twice as much: two tent stakes driven for every one of his, two paddle strokes, two bags carried. At this pace, like a voyageur, I was due for a hernia. My left shoulder and left elbow had begun to ache badly. I told myself that I was sleeping odd, as my left arm was numb each morning, but that explanation felt insufficient. More likely, it was a repetitive use injury, five hundred miles of paddling thus far.

That evening, lying in my bag, I did my regular body checkup. I was starting to lose weight, and my hair and beard were getting long. I stretched my back and hips, tight but okay. My sunburn blisters had scarred, and a cut on my right ankle was healing. Good news, since the bulldogs liked to eat from open sores, and I was afraid this one, after standing so often in river water, had gotten infected. A fever out here could be dangerous.

Physically, Jeremy relied on me, and with professional rescue help so far away, I felt alone and on my own.

———

The next morning, I stood on the shore and made my daily offering to the river, asking for an easy day of travel. The Deh Cho threw the tobacco back at me, driving waves against the rock.

"That's a bad sign," said Jeremy.

We reached Wrigley in the early afternoon. We had enough food and were healthy and safe, so we didn't even stop. I didn't want the hassle, after all the words of warning we had received from the residents of Fort Providence, Dean, even the mounted police. So we just turned on our cell phones, downloaded our e-mails and texts and correspondence—"Thanks for the signal, Wrigley," Jeremy said—and then floated on by.

Jeremy took many paddling breaks, but he always kept his face up, to watch the sky and try to predict the storm tracks. So that afternoon, he suggested a new strategy, to preemptively siesta, so we weren't caught exposed. We chose Rock Island, north of Wrigley, to wait out the thunderstorms and then paddle afterward. Pillars of clouds, the size and shape of mountain ranges, hung above us to the east and west. So we planned to bunker down early, gather wood to cook dinner, wait out the north wind and heat of the day.

After Old Fort Island, we thought we were ready for a rough approach, but the current still managed to surprise us. The strength of it, so strong that the island's nose tossed off whirlpools that stacked up in a traffic jam. The water couldn't get out of its own way fast enough, and boils imploded with a mix of suction and noisy spray. The impromptu rapids were unpredictable and loud, popping high with a boom on one side of the canoe while opening deep vortices on the other. I guided us away from the island, drifted along its flank, and then we landed on the far side.

When, in mid-afternoon, you find a spot—that Goldilocks spot near the trees but not too near—when the tent is up and all of the gear is safely under cover, there is a sense of relief. That I have made myself safe. A cabin is never cozier than in a rainstorm, and our tent had not yet leaked. To pass time on such an occasion, Jeremy had brought along two books—*Tainaron*, by the Finnish author Leena Krohn, about a woman who sails to a land of giant bugs, and *The Once and Future World*, by J. B. MacKinnon, about the return of wilderness—and it seemed both applied to our current situation.

MacKinnon argues that our conception of nature is actually a denuded shadow, and we find peace and serenity there only because we have, over millennium, slaughtered everything trying to eat us. When we go for a quick hike in the woods, we are not returning to nature but rather strolling through a Potemkin park of our own creation. We have forgotten that we humans made nature safe.

In contrast, I was reading *The Lonely Land,* the naturalist Sigurd Olson's 1961 paddling travelogue through central Saskatchewan. He is a follower of Thoreau, who wrote, "We need the tonic of wildness." And so Olson too has a dreamy-eyed adventure: "phantom brigades" of voyageurs paddle his river, "singing can still be heard on quiet nights," after a long day "an expedition means the most; for a moment life had been seasoned with excitement," and out of doors he found a "zest for living and joy on the trail." Life was simpler on a canoe trip; one could "iron out the wrinkles in my soul."

But to me, in our present circumstances, Olson seemed all romantic bullshit. Out here, life was not easier, or simpler. It was tedious and exhausting to do simple things: eating, sleeping, shitting. Jeremy found out that having the runs is not easier in the wilderness. Nor washing dishes with sand, collecting wood to cook, counting rations, being exposed to the weather. Microwaves and beds and toilets are easier. We had descended several rungs on Maslow's hierarchy of needs; food and shelter trumped all, and it seemed to me that Olson, writing safely at home in front of a fire, had confused his memory of the trip with the real thing.

And anyway, Walden Pond is only a mile outside Concord, and Thoreau sent his laundry out to a maid.

We passed the afternoon with our books, Jeremy slept, but our preparations were for naught, because the storm never came. The clouds stayed motionless and only expanded. We ate dinner, bathed unsuccessfully—in the silty water, we came out with a film, and the riverbed sucked at our legs like quicksand—and then I grew impatient, so we packed and pressed on, so as not to lose a day of progress.

The paddle started easy. We passed the hill Mackenzie and Awgeenah climbed to get a better view; it was obviously overgrown and impossible for us to hike. But then a huge north wind descended on us, and the Deh Cho erupted in whitecaps. We fled the chop, finding calmer water on the dirty side of the river. My paddle felt gritty in my hands again. Lightning moved in from the southwest, the storm traveling in the opposite direction of the wind, and we were forced to beach on the left, the silty floodplain we had been avoiding since Fort Simpson. We grabbed the secondary emergency shelter and ran across the soggy cake, looking for higher ground. The rain pounded us, and three hundred yards in we finally put up the triangular tarp in more willow bushes. We huddled back in the lightning position, under the tiny pop-up tent, and eventually the thunder moved on.

"It's just rain," I said, of the lashing against the tarp. "We can paddle in the rain. We have to."

Back on the water, we immediately looked for somewhere to put up the main tent. The western floodplain was an unsafe choice, but ahead a high ridge was coming in on the left, to match the one on the right. The valley was tightening at the moment we needed a loose beach. No good camping anywhere.

According to the map, a few miles farther on several smaller rivers joined in from the east. Our best chance for flat land lay at those intersections, so we decided to cross the river. Half an hour in open water, in the midst of the storm.

We started our ferry, and as encouragement the rain slackened to a drizzle. But then behind us, the left bank started exploding with lightning, no gap between the flash of the strike and the wrenching crack of the thunder. My heart rate doubled, and we dug in and pulled as hard as we could. The river had narrowed, and we ground up on the right bank and took cover against a cliff face. When the wave of lightning rumbled past a second time, we ran back to the canoe and pushed off and paddled down the eastern shore.

Then I heard a sound behind me like a waterfall. I turned over my shoulder and saw a curtain of rain moving north, chasing us, gaining on us. There was nowhere to put a tent, nothing to be done, and when the opened heavens arrived, we got soaked straight to the skin. A deluge from a bucket poured by God himself. The surface of the river looked as if every second it was being hit with a million gunshots simultaneously.

The banks were steep, and at the waterline the beaches consisted of nothing but rocks the size and shape of watermelons, multicolored, every kind of rock in the world. The weather struck in fronts, and the sky was roiling, like a squirming mass of monstrous gray snakes. Nowhere to put a tent, no flat space free from the boulders, we pressed on.

The delta of the Ochre River, where it joined the Deh Cho, was clogged with gravel bars and flotsam and stumps of spruce trees, floated down from the upper reaches of Horn Mountain. Every bit of flat ground was silty and scummy, under a thin layer of water, and full of fresh moose tracks. We continued in the rain. Our canoe kept getting stuck, and on the north side of the delta we found more boulders and small patches of silt covered in bear and wolf tracks. I told Jeremy to get out the tarp, to keep our gear from soaking any further, and he tried to attach the covering to the canoe using a few of his new mini-carabiners, each the size of a paper clip.

While Jeremy held on to the canoe against the surf, I ran around the north shore of the beach, searching for any patch of sand bigger than a dinner plate. I ran a hundred yards across the plain to the bluff, along an impenetrable hedgerow, down the shore, and eventually found it, half a mile away: a sandy triangle in the center of a pile of driftwood trunks, just large enough for the tent. Fresh wolf and bear tracks were everywhere, but we decided to brave it, because our tent's profile would duck below the woodpiles and thus be somewhat sheltered from the lightning. After five hours of struggling in the rain and wind and thunder, we camped at the watering hole of the region's big game.

After midnight, another round of close lightning came through, shocks that lit the air. We squatted in the lightning position until almost two o'clock, and though I saw Jeremy shivering in the damp chill, he kept drinking from his water bottle.

"My mouth is so dry," he said, and I thought of my adrenaline on the Slave.

Early the next morning, the rain unremitting, I texted my children using the inReach, looking for some small comfort in the normalcy of their lives at home. I also texted David, guilting him into sending us hourly Doppler radar checks. I no longer trusted the inReach's forecast, a vague percentage chance that it might rain or thunderstorm. For several days, the forecast had been the same: rain today, but sunny tomorrow. Perpetually optimistic, and yet always wrong.

I wanted to understand the prevailing paths of the storms, and David confirmed that according to the radar they grew all day, drifted east, and then turned northwest. My perception was correct: yes, they really were chasing us. Were they following the cold river? I didn't know enough meteorology to say.

Jeremy and I got a late start, sleeping until the rain let up. The sun broke through and the clouds shriveled, revealing brilliant golds and reds overhead.

"It's like it never happened," Jeremy said.

"That's the funny thing about the sky," I replied. "It's always wiped clean."

We loaded the canoe, and when I made my daily offering to the river, this time I didn't ask for anything. As I dropped in the tobacco, I simply said, "You're in charge, Deh Cho. Please be cool to us."

"I love how your morning ritual has changed," Jeremy said. "You used to ask for good camping, like you were sitting on Santa's lap. Now you tell the river that it's all powerful and you accept your fate."

"I can imagine it was hard to be a missionary up here," I said. "Imagine the response: 'What do you mean all the old stories aren't true? And some old guy thousands of miles away from here is really god? Um, I can see the river right here.'"

"If I lived here, I'd believe in the river," Jeremy said.

I felt it then, how "Mackenzie River" is just a geographic label, a reference from a white man's book. But on the water, when the skies darken and the water turns a putrid green and the whitecaps spring to life, then the river reveals itself.

It is truly the ancient and mighty Deh Cho, and we humbly beg its mercy.

———

Brought low by a powerful god, and paired up in a boat with a Jew, it is no surprise that Jeremy and I started counting the plagues of the Deh Cho.

Lightning for sure. Rain and wind and sun, never-ending sun. Plus the bugs, mosquitoes and bulldogs. That was five, though I was sure, without too much trouble, we'd soon find a perfectly biblical seven. Not all the plagues hit at once—the wind often blew away the bugs—but you could never hope to be really free from them all.

For a time, though, we were free from thunderstorms. As if the sky had exhausted itself and couldn't muster the energy for rain. Instead, the heat grew rapidly, and the wind, shifting to the south, never ceased. Caught in a hair dryer, and no shade on the river, my skin turned dark, darker than

I had ever been, even in Iraq, where I was covered in armor from head to toe. Every scar on my arms and legs showed as bright white, but I didn't feel tan as much as dried out, like a fish left to hang on a line.

The silt of the Liard had finally, and thoroughly, mixed with the original Mackenzie, and there was no more escaping to a clean side. When we washed our pots and bowls, a film of dust was left upon drying. For drinking water, we started searching out tiny side streams; the main Deh Cho packed our filter with grit. At Birch Creek, the water was clean and clear, tinged the blue of a Bombay Sapphire gin bottle, and icy cold, like draining permafrost.

The current accelerated further, and the land seemed to slope away from the river in all directions, like the inner surface of a bowl, and the mountains beyond appeared to be at eye level, so the effect created, with so much tailwind and current, was not traveling along the river but sinking into a depression, swept forward and falling. It was a re-creation of the feeling I had driving my truck over the ridge into the Mackenzie watershed, down and down, but magnified and accelerated so close to the Deh Cho's heart.

Then the land opened. Mountains dwindled, sporadic peaks above the flattening plain, including one lonely cone that looked like a volcano. "It looks like the Long Island pine barrens," said Jeremy, of the scraggly beach with stunted pines. Unlike his childhood home, though, here there were moose prints everywhere and massive logs chewed by beaver in barber pole patterns. The banks were a mixture of ash, silt, sand, and mud, bleached white in the sun. There were still very few places to pitch a tent, though, because the shore looked as if it had been torn up by construction equipment, a function of the power of floodwaters to shape mud and gravel, the swirling currents petrified on the beach.

The terrain became so flat my paddle hit bottom even when I thought I was in the main channel: two feet of water below us, two miles to shore on each side. And yet the current was still fast, no correlation between the river's width and speed. Gradient is king, and we were losing so much elevation so far inland I began to dread how much sluggish water and wind there was to come at the exhausted end of the journey.

The river braided among mud islands, twisting, high dirt banks alternating on the outside edge of each curve. It was clear, though, that we were headed straight north, and I still didn't know how Mackenzie could have thought otherwise. "Wind, water, and denial are three very powerful forces," Jeremy said.

All day, we paddled. To the point, the intersection of water and land at the horizon, the shortest distance on the winding river. Then, to the next point. Then the next. And the next. I measured distances not in miles but in hours and minutes, how long to reach each new landmark, indistinguishable from the one behind it.

It is important to say this again: all day we sat in a boat and did nothing but swing a two-pound weight, first on one side of the canoe, and then the other, and then back again. My paddle drank every stroke. The rhythm and form perfected—a downward thrust with the top hand, sweep the shaft along the gunwale—I made great guzzling sounds every time I pulled, whirlpools and vortices in my wake. Sometimes I put my blade in a boil and pulled, and there was no resistance. I used to fear the boils, back on the Slave and the upper Deh Cho, but now I looked for them, because within their uneven surface the water moved just a hair faster downstream.

The river was a funnel of mud cliff and black spruce and nothing else. For a week, the view never changed. The emptiness smothered comprehension, like a heavy blanket draped over my head. Jeremy always volunteered to set up the tent, lay our bags, and blow up the pads, and I didn't blame him for wanting to retreat to the tent, where at least the objects were of human scale.

"Things out here change so slow you're hyperaware of every current, every bug, every cloud. That's actually the point of minimalism," Jeremy said, referencing the artistic movement. "When you constrain everything else, the one thing you change really pops."

But I wasn't thinking about art. I thought of Kylik, the owner of the charter boat outfit in Inuvik, and his promise to retrieve us if we made it to Garry Island. I had come to understand—by paddling point to point to point—why he also measured distance in time. "You can get anywhere if you have the time," he had said. That was right. If you live in a city with traffic, sometimes it takes ten minutes to cut across town, and sometimes it takes an hour. You can affect the time—avoid rush hour, go an alternate route, drive faster—if not the distance. But it worked different up here. There are no shortcuts. If it takes twelve hours to paddle somewhere, it takes twelve hours. All it takes is time.

In camp, all I thought of was time. The days felt so long, doing the same monotonous repetitive task, in this timeless land.

At the poles, conventional timekeeping loses meaning as the time zones collapse; your feet could stand twelve hours apart at the apex. That fungibility trickles down the side of the globe. Even a thousand miles south of the pole, I was caught in an endless day. The sun didn't rise and set so much as rotate. And in the winter, in endless night, the sky is a permanent mask of stars, reflecting the universe not as it is, but as it has been through all time, as the light from each sun and galaxy and nebula takes millions and billions of years to reach earth.

Endless day, endless night, endless now. I felt caught in the northern recirculation. Every day was the same. But on the river, at least there was current and a wind from the south; if the tunnel of the Deh Cho was infinite, we were nonetheless moving through it at speed.

————

Three o'clock, and the sun shone brightly outside the tent when the noise pulled me from sleep. A huge sound, a storm barreling down the valley toward us. The air was vibrating, and I stuck my head out of the tent, expecting the worst.

But instead of dark clouds and trees blown sideways, I saw a massive ship motoring down the river, hugging the red and green buoys to find the deep channel. Nine hundred feet long, tall white tugs pushing flat decks, each laden with construction equipment and shipping containers full of toilet paper and cans of soda and diesel fuel hidden in the double-hulled holds. I looked for my truck but didn't see it. The barge displaced so much water that the wake crashed to shore like an incoming ocean tide.

It took a moment for me to understand. It was the barge that woke me, not a storm. I was afraid it was a storm. I realized, I was afraid all the time.

Paddling the Deh Cho felt like walking a tightrope. Don't look down, don't look around, don't think too much about what you are doing, don't think about being small and exposed, just put one foot in front of the other, paddle to the next point. That's it. If you pick your head up, look around, you'll realize how far from help you are, and the enormity of the task.

I had a dream that night, that I could punch the ground and make it submit to me. That I went to dinner with an overweight friend, and we ate three hamburgers, made of beef patties and chicken breasts, and then we had chocolate-covered strawberries for dessert.

I told Jeremy that I was having food dreams and fantasies of hitting the earth.

"Feeling pretty powerless, huh?" he said.

Even our gear was starting to wear out. Our stove was a blackened husk. There was a small hole in our tent. The leather on the palms of my paddling gloves was rotting, and smelled like the elephant house at the zoo. People say, "I love my camping gear; it's lasted for years." But how often have they actually used it? One or two weekends a year? Most popular brands, I was learning, are simply not durable in continuous use.

To his credit, though, Jeremy was listening to instruction, had proved a quick study, and was small and fit easily in the tent, which, with David gone, had seemingly grown to twice its size. We had learned to work together and function as a team, and Jeremy had gotten good at setting up camp, keeping everything as clean as possible.

And he taught me an obvious trick that I should have figured out long before. I had been losing things, including a spare cord to charge the GPS, and it was bothering me, like my head was somehow not in the game.

"I've figured out the problem," I said to Jeremy. "We all drop stuff all the time. The sock falls out of the hamper on the way to wash clothes. But it falls in your living room, so you can find it. Out here, the living room is the last campsite, way upriver."

"So put everything in your pockets," he said. "Make that the living room." And it worked. My pockets filled with lids and cords and socks, but they were safe in the living room, and I never lost anything on the river again.

———

That day, with a strong tailwind, we put out the sail and made our best time yet. The water was green and disorganized, choppy, yanking at the canoe and pushing us around, but Jeremy was unfazed. His high school rowing team practiced in Long Island Sound, and one summer he worked the docks, ferrying boat captains out to their anchored ships. "This feels like home," he said, over and over, and it made him fearless. In his narrow view off the front of the canoe, he wasn't walking the tightrope in a foreign land; he was back at a crew meet.

But then the south wind, at first a blessing from the Deh Cho, became another plague. Battling a headwind is tiring work, but too strong a tail-wind is dangerous. We went fast, too fast. The water was serrated. A gust twisted the boat and then nearly ripped the sail. I stopped paddling and it was all I could do to hold the rudder, slowing us to keep control while Jeremy struggled to take down the sail.

"We're surfing" said Jeremy, and he was right. The waves were break-ing all around us, under us, to the side, above our gunnels, above my shoulders, pushing us at cross-purposes. One came from behind and lifted us high and then as we dipped in the trough the canoe wallowed like a fat sow settling in the mud, our nose swinging one way and the tail the other, sinking into the soft water between breaking crests.

"This is fun," Jeremy called back to me.

"That's only 'cause you aren't responsible for steering. You're too trusting," I said.

"You know, the third movement of Debussy's *La mer* is called 'The Discussion of Wind and Water,'" Jeremy replied, but I ignored him.

The river turned, and in the crosswinds the waves became confused, slosh in God's bathtub. We cut to an island, to get in the leeward shadow, but the chop grew worse. "Is this a mistake?" I asked, nervous at how the canoe was twisting, the nose riding up and smacking down. "No, we're good; I haven't felt weightless yet," said Jeremy.

Eventually, the river forced us sideways, and I just ferried back and forth, dodging islands while the current and wind on the boat's broad-side pushed us along. On one crossing, to make it around a shoal, I turned our nose upstream to gain time. "Paddle hard!" I yelled, like I was in my whitewater raft guide job back home, and we dug in, but the current beat against our chine and threatened to pull under the upstream side. "I can't hold it," I said to Jeremy, and we had to turn the nose downstream to regain control.

We had learned that the Deh Cho was a series of localized wind tun-nels. The windy places stay windy, the calm places calm, according to their geography, and there is no waiting it out. To make it safe to launch the boat, you have to stop in a calm place. But no way to apply that les-son now. To keep from foundering, we just needed to get off the water as soon as possible.

I pointed the canoe straight downriver at a bank of dried mud, and the gale drove us up on shore. We made camp there, on a floodplain, placing our tent in a tiny cleft out of the wind, and added a new plague to the list: dust. The hot south wind kicked up clouds, choking brown funnels and devils. All of our gear was impregnated with the talcum powder. We could do nothing but hope it would be cooler and calmer the next morning and were stuck waiting out the day, confined to the sweatbox of a tent.

Above, a jetliner flew overhead. A silver speck, and two perfect white contrails against a blue sky, while our feet were stuck in a dusty past, the future far out of reach.

In the morning, the winds were low enough to launch, and eventually we approached Tulita. I had paddled 557 miles since Hay River, three weeks before. Jeremy and I had not spoken to another person in ten days, since we stopped to see Jonas. Michelle's guidebook said there was a campground and showers at a public swimming pool, and we looked forward to both.

"I think I'm admirably grimy," Jeremy said. And he was. What a difference from the man who jumped in my canoe at Fort Simpson.

THE DOGRIB, JULY 1789

〜〜〜〜

Heavy gray columns rose on the distant shore, and Mackenzie's spirits with them. Those were cooking fires surely, fed with wet wood. Mackenzie checked his pocket watch: three-quarters past seven o'clock in the morning. It was July 5, and they had not seen another human being in ten days. But there ahead was a most welcome sight, signs of life. "We perceived several Smokes, which we made for with all speed."

They had traveled seventy miles the day before, through embankments of orange shale and grim mud walls rimed with ice, inhospitable to waterfowl, and the Chipewyan hunters had secured very little fresh meat. Barrieau and the voyageurs spotted one beaver and killed it themselves, but in its throes the rodent filled with water and went to the bottom before they could retrieve it. They ate pemmican again that night. Mackenzie sat awake to count the hours of darkness, in truth mere twilight, as the sun only dipped below the horizon for four hours.

They pushed off soon after two o'clock. The river wound but then made a dramatic turn west. The current slackened, snowy mountains lay ahead, plus those black plumes off the cooking fires. They sped up, for momentum's sake, the voyageurs leaped from the canoes in the knee-deep water, and the boat drifted in, so as not to drive the delicate birch bark on the exposed rock shore. But in the face of such an invasion, the encamped Indian families scattered. "Soon saw the Natives run about in great Confusion, some making for the Woods and others for their Canoes," Mackenzie wrote. Awgeenah ordered his hunters to chase down the fleeing men and women. His followers spoke Chipewyan, and the new Indians acted as if they didn't understand and made motions with their hands to stay away. Mackenzie and his voyageurs did so, though they also unloaded their canoe and pitched tents, while "the English Chief and his young Men were very busy reconciling them to our Arrival."

Mackenzie took a keen interest in these new Indians, making copious notes on their unfamiliar appearance. He found their hair disheveled, two black and blue stripes tattooed across their cheeks like the Chipewyan, but with goose quills stuck through their nostrils. They wore bands of leather around their heads, decorated with horn and bone and the claws of bears, and some of the old men grew long beards and the women wore mittens even in summer, held by a cord around their necks. Their long robes of moose hide were big enough to sleep in, but strangely, the men wore almost no covering over their circumcised penises. "Their want of Modesty & their having no Sense of their Nakedness," thought Mackenzie, "would make a Person think that they were descended from Adam." But how did they deal with the cold? he wanted to know. Should not the frigid air compel them to wear more clothes? Surely if Adam had "been created at the Arctic Circles he would not have had occasion for Eve, the Serpent, nor the Tree of Knowledge to have given him a Sense of his Nakedness," so harsh was the climate, Mackenzie thought.

This is where the English Chief proved his worth, coaxing a frightened people out of hiding. Awgeenah eventually identified five families living in that place, as many as thirty people, from two tribes: a few Slavey, and the numerous Dogrib. The Slavey had been named by the Cree, as good for nothing but bondage and servitude. The Dogrib, though, were known by all as brave warriors with powerful medicine. Their first mother took a husband that was a man by day and a great black dog at night. She gave birth to a litter of puppies that could shift their skins back and forth, as both men and dogs, and from these few all Dogrib claimed kinship.

The Dogrib were wary, and for good reason. They knew the pale strangers could be the *nakan*, the men who come only in summer to make trouble, start fires in the forest, and steal women and children. The *nakan* were known to carry rifles, leave hard-soled tracks in the mud, hunt without dogs; the voyageurs matched the description well. And Awgeenah's hunters were no more welcome, recognizable in their distinctive shirts with pointed tails. The Chipewyan brought the pox and made war.

The story of the fight goes like this: Near Slave Lake, Chipewyan warriors had crept into a Dogrib camp and slashed holes in every one of their canoes. Then the Chipewyan attacked, to rape the women and steal the children, as everyone knew this was the best revenge, because children were most beloved by every tribe. With the advantage of surprise they slaughtered the Dogrib, and the few who fled drowned when their death-trap boats filled with water and sank in the dark lake. The Chipewyan were far more powerful, so the Dogrib leader, Edzo, made a plan that used powerful medicine. Edzo put all of the Chipewyan minds into a beaver hide, so that he could control them as long as he sat on the hide. Whatever he thought, his enemies would think as well. So Edzo thought only of peace. But those days were long before.

Facing the *nakan* and Chipewyan, the Dogrib should have fought or fled. But Awgeenah did his job well. When "they saw we intended them no hurt, it was found that some of the Men understood our Indians very well," Mackenzie said. Awgeenah "partly removed their Terror" and persuaded them to call back their relatives, despite their "evident Signs of Fear."

Awgeenah offered them a pipe, but the Dogrib looked at it strangely; Mackenzie realized "they did not know the use of Tobacco." So he opened a cask of rum instead. "We likewise gave them some grog to drink, but I believe they accepted those Civilities more through Fear than Inclination." Mackenzie judged them practical, so he dug through the trade goods packed in the *pièces* from Laurent Leroux. The Dogrib pots at the cooking fires were merely woven *watape,* the same stripped spruce root the voyageurs used to fasten together the cedar frames of their canoes. They couldn't put the pots over a fire, of course, so the Dogrib dropped red-hot rocks into the kettles instead, to heat the water. Mackenzie could see how valuable his iron pots would be, so he started handing them out, along with "Knives, Beads, Awls, Rings, Gartering, Fire Steels, Flints and a couple of Axes." These metal tools proved immediately popular, and everyone became much at ease, so much so that Barrieau had to put the men on guard duty. "They became more familiar than we expected," Mackenzie wrote, "for we could not keep them out of our Tents, tho' I did not observe that they tryed to steal anything from us."

Mackenzie wasn't there to trade, though. The gifts were simply a diplomatic tactic to get what he really wanted: knowledge about the river, as his Red Knife guide had been useless for a week. Awgeenah translated for Mackenzie, but what he heard seemed hardly possible.

"The Information they gave us respecting the River, seems to me so very *fabulous* that I will not be particular in inserting it," Mackenzie wrote in his journal. "Suffice it to say that they would wish to make us believe that we would be several Winters getting to the Sea, and that we all should be old Men by the time we would return."

———

Long ago, Yamoria and his brother, Yamoga, were foundlings, pulled from a muddy hole among the roots of a bush. They were not born of woman, they simply appeared there, and a girl found them when she heard crying from beneath the earth. She wrapped the babies in a hide and took them home, where her father and mother fed the babies broth made from the brains of rabbits.

Yamoria and Yamoga grew strong with medicine. In this time, the world was full of giant animals that made trouble for everyone. And the brothers were great men and decided to fix the animals so it was safe for people to live. Yamoria walked the length of the Deh Cho, and fixed all of the problems he found there, but Yamoga went west, over the mountains, and fell out of the stories.

Yamoria went everywhere to set the animals right, and was an old man who leaned on a stick by the time he reached the sea. Sometimes he walked, and sometimes he stepped out of time and simply appeared in a place, from nowhere. He went to the moose and told him to eat willow instead of people. And he went to the eagle and told him to eat fish instead of people. Three giant beavers swam up and down the Deh Cho, slapping their tails and wrecking the land. So Yamoria chased them to a tall rock that lay at the river's edge, and he beat the three beavers to death, and skinned them, and stretched their gory hides and pinned them on the great rock to dry. And then he cooked the beaver, and the grease dripped down and smoldered, and some people, when lucky, see that smoke even today.

Down the river, just past the Dogrib encampment, rose that same tall bloodied rock, three monstrous stains of red upon the slab. Mackenzie saw no smoke.

———

The Dogrib told Awgeenah many things. They said that in their travels down the river they "would have to encounter many Monsters." That much farther on "there are 2 impracticable Falls or Rapids in the River, the first 30 Days March from us." And finally, and most ominously, "there were very few Animals below this, and the farther we went the fewer there would be." The Dogrib said that they "should Starve, even if no other accident befell" their party.

Mackenzie thought all this "can only exist in their own Imaginations" and "put no faith in those Stories." But Awgeenah was dismayed, and the two men began arguing "with much ado." Awgeenah said they must turn back, "should absolutely return" the way they had come. The river was not at all as Peter Pond had described, and the lack of food should be the deciding factor. Awgeenah said his hunters were "already very tired of their Voyage" and would be exhausted trying to keep the party fed if game grew any more scarce.

Mackenzie would have none of it. He cajoled Awgeenah until the trading chief relented and agreed to continue. But both men agreed they needed a new guide and would ask the Dogrib to provide one.

By now a full musical performance was under way, welcoming Mackenzie's company. The Dogrib swung bone daggers above their heads and sang atonal songs, howling like wolves to prove their stamina. Mackenzie was frustrated, tired, impatient to move, and thoroughly unimpressed. He thought their dancing full of "Antic Shapes" and "very clumsy." What's more, he was repulsed by the lot of them, their "Dirty way of living," their legs "full of Scabs" from smallpox, the "Dust & Grease" that caked on "their whole Body." He decided they were an "ugly meagre ill made People," and he wanted to be rid of them as soon as he could.

Though Mackenzie had declared his aversion to playacting naturalist or anthropologist, he nonetheless felt an obligation to report any potential commercial prospects to his North West Company partners, so he diligently wrote down in his journal every mean facet of Dogrib life, especially their weapons and methods of hunting. Bows and arrows, clubs, daggers of stone and copper. Spears taller than a man, with a long barbed hook of bone. The size of their fishing nets and composition, the sinews of their snares, every decoration on their garters and shoes. And he tried to discern where they had already acquired their few small bits of iron that they used as needles and razors. He decided they must have traded with the Red Knife Indians and Chipewyan.

By the time the talk and music were done, it was three o'clock in the afternoon, and Mackenzie was impatient after seven hours onshore. "They promised to remain upon the Banks of the River till the fall in case we should come back," Mackenzie said, but at the pace things were going, he was afraid he'd never leave. Barrieau ordered the canoe repacked, and when they were finally ready to launch, Mackenzie called over his "new Recruit." A Dogrib man had agreed to guide them for the price of an iron kettle, ax, hoe, and knife, but now he had second thoughts. He dithered for an hour, first in a show of collecting his belongings among their conical lodges of branches and bark, then in trying to persuade another to take his place. No one would, and Mackenzie pressed him; the voyageurs "in a manner compelled him to embark." But not before he performed a departure ceremony.

The Dogrib man cut off a lock of his hair, and blew on it, and spoke words over it, and divided it into three, and tied it to the hair of his wife and two children, as if he would never return that way again.

The western sky was black with storm clouds, and the Dogrib elders said, "Father comes."

————

They got under way at four o'clock. The party was up to fifteen now, still in three canoes. Mackenzie, Steinbruck, the four voyageurs, their two wives, Awgeenah, his two wives, the two hunters, the new Dogrib guide, and the poor Red Knife Indian stuck with nowhere else to go.

Almost immediately, alongside the rock upon which Yamoria hung his sopping red beaver pelts, a large river joined in. The Dogrib said its source was the "great Bear Lake," and Mackenzie thought its water "quite clear, of the colour of Salt Water Sea." Then the heavy thunderstorm, which had threatened all afternoon, finally arrived, and a "heavy Gust of Wind" blew hard in their faces with driving rain, and they made camp at the base of the ridge. Mackenzie's reluctant Dogrib guide was miserable in their first camp. "Our new Conductor told us that it blew every day in the Year on the Top of this Hill." Only a few miles from the guide's home, Mackenzie grew suspicious and thought he was "pretending sickness, that we might let him return to his relations." Mackenzie felt "obliged to watch him all Night," in case he ran away.

They were shivering when they awoke to overcast, windy, "raw Weather this Morning," Mackenzie said. He pushed them to the water at three o'clock anyway, enough sun to see, intent on maintaining a hectic pace. In obvious contradiction to the Dogrib's tales, Mackenzie could see for himself that the river was approaching the Pacific. Around them was a "Ridge of Snowy Mountains always in Sight," as Captain Cook had described his inlet. For a hundred miles, the river had braided among islands, but now it had reunited in a single channel, wide and strong. They had finally pierced the Rocky Mountains and were heading in the right direction, west-southwest according to his compass. The current was still powerful, but slowing a bit, as one would expect when a waterway of this kind reached the sea.

True, they had not yet crossed a waterfall of any kind, much less the largest in the world. But Mackenzie only knew of that feature from Pond's reports, which had already proven inadequate, in the river's length if nothing else. The Dogrib said that a large cataract lay a month ahead, which also seemed impossible. If Mackenzie would trust anything, it would be his eyes, and the land around him, the direction of the river. At that moment, it all matched Cook's reports of the river's exit into the Pacific.

Mackenzie set a grueling pace that day, over one hundred miles in sixteen hours of paddling. Dictating to Steinbruck, Mackenzie measured every last quarter mile. Not so his paddlers. The voyageurs noted progress by counting pipes, that is, how long it took to smoke one. In other words, they measured distance in time.

The river narrowed again, entered a canyon with gray rock walls that appeared scraped, as if by the claws of a giant wolverine; the voyageurs called the beast a *carcajou*. Awgeenah knew that the wolverine could fold the earth in half, like a piece of paper, so that it only took a few steps to travel very far. This is why wolverines never tire. But their paddlers were flagging in the cold and wind, always in their faces.

Soon the hills closed in ever tighter. To Mackenzie's right, a headland thrust toward the river, and to the left its shorter counterpart, and the river turned north and poured over the bar in the bed that joined them. Mackenzie ordered the canoes to shore, and they camped at the base of the high hill on the northern shore, and while the voyageurs sat and smoked and regummed the canoes, Mackenzie was determined to summit the ridge.

"Our Stranger," the Dogrib guide, "informed us that there are a great Number of Bears and White Buffaloes in the Mountains," Mackenzie said, so he took one of the Chipewyan hunters to investigate. Perhaps they could see the ocean, or at least kill a bear to eat. Normally, the Chipewyan preferred hunting bear in winter, not summer, when they could scout the den, and then thrust in a long stick to prod the bear, and shout, "Grandfather, grandfather, wake up!" Then, once they were sure the bear was awake, they'd crawl into the den and tie a rope around its neck, and then drag it out and cut it apart. But in summer, bears were dangerous and best left alone.

But they had no time to hunt anything, as they could not even make it to the top of the mountain. "We were obliged to relinquish our design half way up it being nearly suffocated by Swarms of Musquittoes." Mackenzie saw enough, though, to be discouraged. "I could see that the Mountain terminated here at least as far as we could see." The snow-covered mountains that matched Cook's reports were ending. And below them was a new hazard. "Observed a strong Rapling Current or rapid close by under the Hill which then was a Precipice."

In the morning, they quickly ferried to the other side of the river, to avoid the whitewater Mackenzie had seen the night before. But it was no matter. "This proved to be one of the least dangerous Rapids we had to pass & convinced me in my Opinion respecting the falsity of the Natives Information."

They were wrong about the size of the waterfall. They were wrong about how long it would take to reach the trifling rapids. And they would be wrong about monsters guarding the approaches to the sea.

In only a day, their prospects had shifted considerably. The end of the river was not in sight; the coastal mountains must lie farther on. But Mackenzie remained determined.

He would not be an old man when he arrived at the Pacific that summer.

RAPIDS WITHOUT RAPIDS, JULY 2016

~~~~~~

The blood-splattered peak of Yamoria, slumped on the river's shoulder like a great beast slumbering, is now known as Bear Rock. Beneath it lies the Sahtu Dene village of Tulita. Eight months a year, no road connects Tulita to the outside world. Only in deep winter, when the swampy muskeg and lakes freeze, when the snow fills ditches and divots of pocked earth, does the winter road open to the south. In endless summer, plus the slushy shoulder seasons, the small village of five hundred souls is only reachable by expensive plane ticket or a very long boat ride.

The public dock was a dirt ramp, and Jeremy and I grounded the canoe on the flotsam beach and staggered out on a sweltering afternoon. Kids splashed in the silt, and fishermen launched their workhorse Lunds. It was odd to see roads and trucks again, and Jeremy agreed to wait with our gear while I walked into town.

"What's your plan?" Jeremy asked.

"Ask the first person I meet where the campground is. And the showers," I said. Landon, my next paddle partner, was scheduled to fly into Tulita the following afternoon, and I welcomed the brief respite from the boat and the river. "Plus Jonas said to talk to Chief Andrews, remember?"

I followed a gravel path, and at the top of the hill I found four indigenous men and women sitting on an old concrete block, watching the river. Three looked a bit unsteady, but a round man in the center spoke up as I approached.

"You're new. How can I help you?" he said. His whole face smiled as he spoke.

"Hi, I'm Brian, from New York. I'm looking for Chief Frank Andrews," I said.

"Well, you've found him, Brian from New York," he said and stuck out his hand, and I marveled at my good luck.

"My friend and I are paddling the whole Deh Cho," I said. "I left Hay River a few weeks ago. Thank you for allowing us to paddle through your land." Jonas had said it was important to be respectful and ask permission.

But then Chief Andrews said, "Turn around and go back!" and I just looked at him a moment, before everyone else laughed.

"It's good water this year," the chief continued. "The Sans Sault Rapids ahead, you'll be good. There is a ledge that runs all the way across the river. One fall, I was flying back from Inuvik, and the plane was low, and it looked like a giant beaver had built a dam all the way across the river."

"I actually have a friend flying in tomorrow," I said. "We need to stay the night. The guidebook says there's a campground in town. Is it still there?"

"Well, I don't think it floated away!" he said, and a woman next to him almost fell down giggling. "But it's at the base of Bear Rock, eh, across the river." That was another hour paddle, and then returning to town, against the current, would be an even tougher chore.

"Well, what about the showers, at the public pool?"

"Oh, there are no showers, Brian from New York," Chief Andrews said. "The kids broke in and broke the pumps."

"And they threw crap in the pool," said another man.

"Yeah, pool's closed I think, eh," the chief said.

We started to attract a little crowd, and I felt like the daily village curiosity. A white man pulled up on a quad. He had a mustache and a tank top, and introduced himself as Ron.

"My wife and I run a B&B," Ron said. "We can get you a room. Or just a shower. Whatever you want." And he gave me his phone number.

I felt discouraged, so I walked the rest of the way into town, to scope it out before returning to Jeremy with the bad news. There was a ramshackle fire department, a two-story building decorated with strings of lights that read "Merry Christmas," and a small village square with a sheltered fire circle hosting a card game. The Northern store was a prefab metal warehouse on stilts, and to soften the bad news, I stopped in to buy a treat to take to Jeremy. Nine-dollar gallons of milk and four-dollar candy bars and a frozen Slurpee machine, but no cups.

"The kids steal them," the white manager said, apologizing, and then he poured me two raspberry-flavored ices.

I was walking down the hill, back to the canoe, when a man crossed the street to speak to me. He had a gray buzz cut and six hairs of a gray beard, and wore galoshes with no shoes or socks and a black T-shirt that read, "Aboriginal Day '08."

"You, what's your name?" he said. His eyes looked past me, and I had to listen hard to understand his words.

"I'm Brian," I said. "What's your name?"

"My name is Richard," he said. "I am one of the last Mountain Dene. There are only three or four of us left now. I grew up on the other side of the river, in the mountains"—and he pointed across the river to a forested ridge well inland—"and I used to make the moose-skin boats." Now he made great scooping motions with his hands to indicate their size.

Then he put his head down. "I wasn't going to say that," he said quietly, "but I just did."

He turned back to me and stuck a finger back toward the river. "See that creek, you go up that creek, all the way to the mountains, that's where we lived, until my parents died."

I didn't see the creek, just the standard black spruce blur.

"How long did it take, to get to your home?" I asked. The mountains looked far away, nearly to the horizon's edge.

"A month! The old-timers, they didn't rush. You have to hunt, fish, trap, go slow to feed yourself." He made to leave, took a step, and then abruptly stopped and turned back to me and grabbed my shoulders with both hands.

"Brian. Pass it. Pass it." And then he shuffled up the hill.

The Slurpees were half-melted by the time I got back to Jeremy. We were hot, exhausted, filthy, and hungry. Paying a little money to stay in the bed-and-breakfast with Ron was the easiest decision of my trip.

———

Ron Oe is a small-engine mechanic and runs ground control at the airstrip, and his wife, Wendy, works at the church, but to help make ends meet, they rent out the spare rooms of their modest home. In the yard are silver willow bushes and rhubarb and raspberries, stacks of wood for heat in the winter, plus a small stockpile of white birch bark, the same as I had in my canoe, to start a fire each day.

The Oes are Pentecostals from Alberta but talked of themselves as transplants rather than missionaries. A friend invited them to Tulita to help out in the church for a summer. One year turned to two, then three. They left and returned, to buy a house and minister full-time. "There is so much need up here," Wendy said. Plus, they fell into the lifestyle, the freedom of no time all the time. "We're completely ruined on nine to five," Wendy said. "Ron just told me he'd rather work seven to midnight than nine to five."

Wendy is a sturdy woman who smiled more and more as the day went on. She did our laundry and said we could take a shower, after she and Ron discussed how much water was in their basement tank and when the next delivery would arrive. Wendy did the math, then said, "You can take a five-minute shower, if we're going to do laundry too."

"It's okay, take your time," Ron said, "make sure you take a good shower."

"Yes, a good five-minute shower," she repeated.

While the Oes made water plans, a young woman sat in their kitchen, a church volunteer who came north to run the pool for the summer.

"They threw crap in it, so we had to close it," the young woman said, in a tone of disbelief. It was starting to dawn on me that the "crap" thrown in the pool might have been actual human feces.

"It's good they closed it," Wendy said. "Maybe the young people will learn that there are consequences for their actions."

I read widely in Canadian newspapers before my trip, and seemingly every day there was another story about the crisis among young indigenous men and women in the north: suicide, unemployment, alcoholism, isolation. Most of all, idleness, acknowledged in the name of an indigenous ecological movement: Idle No More.

"I know there are a lot of struggles up here," I said, hoping vagueness would sound like tact. "Lack of opportunities. It must be tough."

"Yes, but some of them are just bored," she said, and there was disapproval in her voice. "Ron told me about your trouble in Fort Providence. Doesn't surprise me. So we're going to bring your canoe up to the house, and you can lock your gear in our trailer. You have to be careful."

For dinner, Wendy made us pork chops in the frying pan with mashed potatoes, carrots and rutabagas, plus coleslaw with cabbage that she had picked fresh from the community greenhouse. Ron said grace, and other than one brief implication that global warming is continued melting from Noah's great flood, that was the end of the proselytizing. Jeremy and

I tucked in, took seconds and thirds, and I had to consciously slow myself to stay polite. Jeremy and I both eyed the last two pork chops.

"Please, eat," Wendy said. "That's why we made extra."

Later, Ron insisted on giving us a driving tour of the town. I thought this odd—a roadless town, disconnected from the rest of the country, where could we drive?—but later discovered the few streets clogged with trucks and quads. It seemed to be Tulita's primary form of entertainment; one old man, who could barely see over the steering wheel of his massive pickup, we passed seven times.

Ron started by showing us where the winter road enters town. It was barely more than a rutted cut through the boreal, a swampy overgrown track that looked impassable even for hikers. The year-round road to Wrigley was completed in the 1970s, and the Oes blame politics for it ending right there. The lack of an all-weather road turns Wendy and Ron's otherwise working-class lifestyle on its head. Once a year, when the marshes freeze and snow tamps down the brush, they drive the winter road twenty-four hours south for a weeklong shopping spree, buying all the clothing, electronics, home improvement supplies, and frozen food they'll need for the next year.

Our driving tour was exhaustive and included the airport, the lake that serves as an emergency landing strip when frozen in winter, and the town dump, where ravens and sandhill cranes pecked the rotting food and plastic. We stopped at the water pumping station and stepped into the clear and frigid Great Bear River, and Ron told us the story of how the uranium for the first atomic bombs was mined up on Great Bear Lake, then floated on a series of barges, all the way up the Mackenzie to railroads that bore it to American ordnance factories. Ron took us to a road officially named Sesame Street, for the many "characters" who live there, such as a snow-machine mechanic who is a giant grouch. Last stop was the old church, now a landmark. The floor of the old 1880 mission has heaved in the permafrost and is now curved like a bow. A gold-leaf scroll above the pulpit reads, "Till He Come," and a page of the pastor's concordance still rests on the rail. A padlock keeps the door shut, and the dovetailed log walls are caulked with mud.

It was impossible to ignore the poverty of the town, and I was reminded again that when humans live in wilderness, true wilderness far off the highways, almost by definition it must be in material want, because population density is required for the conspicuous consumption most Americans consider normal.

What work could there be up here, beyond the government jobs— schoolteacher, game warden, police officer—almost always taken by white outsiders? Because few indigenous young people take up the traditional lifestyle of living on the land, they are left with rampant inactivity, and thus hopelessness, the unintended consequence of globalization for those so marooned. They can see the culture on satellite television but cannot touch it, except to purchase the veneer on Amazon—yoga pants and smart phones and straight-brimmed New Era baseball caps with the gold foil sticker.

None of this is new. In 1931, for *National Geographic,* Amos Burg noted "a certain moral and physical decline" among the indigenous population, and that "the death rate exceeds the birth rate among the tribes." Burg was a product of his patronizing time, and attributed it to a new sedentary lifestyle, the Dene clustered in towns rather than following herds and living off the land. I read a similar story in *Ultimate North* by Robert Douglas Mead, who paddled much of the Mackenzie River in 1974. Most of his stories are of alcohol and pickpocketing kids prowling around his canoe, trying to swipe his gear.

I thought it was all dated racism, and myself suitably awakened, until Fort Providence. "A bunch of drunk Indians stole your shit," the cop had said. The drunks come out at three in Fort Simpson. We skipped Wrigley entirely. Now Tulita. My aspirational empathy and daily reality were in conflict.

On the way back to his home, Ron stopped to talk to a young man walking on the side of the road. "Roy, what's going on?" Ron asked. Roy mumbled something I didn't understand and swayed slightly, and Ron opened the back door of the truck to give him a ride. We drove a few more streets and passed a group of young men with brown bags, and Roy banged on the truck door to indicate he wanted to get out.

"Roy knows he has problems with the drink," Ron said, when we pulled away. "But he's such a good person. He cares for the elders. He takes tea every day to his grandmother. He has a good heart."

"You're a good man, Ron," I said. "You can see past the alcohol. Not everyone can." But then Ron was quiet.

That evening, Ron and Wendy and Jeremy and I talked long into the sunlit night. We talked about everything you shouldn't, guns and politics and religion and the environment, and were still friendly and laughing by the end. Wendy brought out bowls of vanilla ice cream and glasses of cold water. Jeremy was the chosen favorite, and both Oes dropped Torah quotations. We played Ron's guitar, and told stories of our travels, and I mentioned that earlier that day I had met Richard, one of the last Mountain Dene. "Ricky, you mean?" Ron said. "He is a great boat maker." And then Ron pulled up a video on the Internet of a moose-hide boat landing on the shore at Tulita, only three years before. "Ricky has struggled lately," Ron acknowledged. In the video, Richard stands at the tiller, tall and strong.

Past midnight, the sky nothing but red, a pair of foxes approached the window of the Oes' living room, looking for peanut butter. By then, my eyes were closing of their own bidding. I begged off, and lay down in a bed for the first time in weeks. I was asleep in seconds.

———

Landon Phillips was my third paddle mate, and he flew in, right on time, the next afternoon. By then I had cleaned and dried all of the gear, restocked our stores at the Northern, and taken a shower. I felt awkward in the shower, more wistful than satisfied, and when I stepped out, warm and wet, I mostly felt regret, that it would be so long until my next one.

Landon was flying from Italy, where he had just finished a tour as the commander of the engineering squadron at Aviano Air Base. He was still a lieutenant colonel in the active-duty military, and coming off a workaholic assignment, he had agreed to spend nine days of leave with me instead of his wife and three sons because I promised to take him through the two biggest landmarks on the trip, the Sans Sault Rapids and the cliffs of the Ramparts.

Some people wonder how their lives might have been, had they taken a different fork in the road. I never have to, because my doppelgänger is Landon, and if I had stayed in the military, I'd be living his life. We met as brand-new second lieutenants, attended initial training together, and then met up every year, hitting the same career milestones. When I ran a bomb squad in Kirkuk, Landon did the same in Baghdad. Then our paths diverged, but not our friendship, so that by the time he got off a plane in Tulita, we had known each other almost half our lives.

I met Landon at the airport. Any passenger on his flight could tell he was the military guy: trimmed hair, stocky, broad shoulders. His call sign is Short Round.

"Your hired voyageur has arrived," he said in a Tennessee twang. "I've been looking forward to this for months. Let's do it." After his stressful job in Italy, he smiled like a man just let out of jail.

We hit the water right away. As I packed the canoe, Jeremy gave Landon pointers, on how to set up the tent and filter water. I hugged Jeremy and thanked him. With a shower and cell-phone signal, he was a happy man, off the next day to meet up with his boyfriend in Colorado. There was little ceremony, and Landon and I left quickly; if we stayed much longer, I would have wanted another shower myself.

It was four miles to the campsite at the base of Bear Rock. We crossed the Great Bear River, crystal clear and icy, and I stopped and gulped two bottles before filling all of our water bladders; too soon this beautiful water would be lost in the dirty Deh Cho. The campsite itself was marked with a sign—"This is what it's like every night, right?" Landon asked, sarcastically—and downright posh, with a grill and an outhouse and a picnic table. There was little room to pitch the tent, though, so we put it directly on the trail. "That's like hot dog in a hallway," he said of the setup.

Landon was jet-lagged from four days of flights, but we woke early anyway, to follow the trail to the top of Bear Rock, twelve hundred feet above the river. I had been in the wilderness almost a month, but had barely walked, and I wanted to stretch my legs. I was winded almost immediately; what a strange activity paddling is. The view was a carpet of flat green, occasional ridges of rock poking up in isolated mountain ranges. I felt as if I could see the curvature of the earth, but no sea was in sight.

After only thirty minutes, the trail petered out. We scrambled up a ledge, surprised a fox, and then thought we found a very faint path, heading into a copse of trees. We followed, but the trail ended immediately in a massive pile of bear scat.

"We found their shit spot," Landon said, and we turned around.

The day stayed fair, and we made good time. The current was definitely slowing, but Landon's fresh arms pulled massive strokes. Landon describes himself as "short but very dense," and he muscled us forward, kicking the paddle at the end of each draw so that we rocked, chine to chine, to reduce drag. I had become accustomed to compensating for Jeremy, and now I laid back and rested in amazement.

By evening, we had fought our way to the outskirts of the oil town of Norman Wells. Along the way we passed a wildfire. From the river it looked relatively small and manageable—a few smoking pockets in the black spruce that hazed the sky a sickly brown—but it was fought with the ferocity of a major blaze. At least three orange airplanes dropped retardant in a continuous circuit, and helicopters toted huge buckets of water via steel cables attached to their undersides. The aim was to keep the blaze away from the refineries, I realized, or the town. I wondered, briefly, if I should add fire to the plagues of the Deh Cho.

We stopped that night at McKinnon Territorial Park, the first spot that felt like a domesticated campground from back home. The beach was full of oversized Easter eggs, multicolored rock, but the bluff above hosted gravel pads for tents, picnic tables, water reservoirs, freshly chopped wood for a fire. It was almost too perfect, completely empty, and we couldn't believe our luck.

"Two for two!" Landon said. "This trip is a breeze with me around."

The park was an easy drive from Norman Wells, and eventually a few families drove up, the kids fishing and swimming. They stayed a distance away, but then a young boy and his older sister appeared at our tent with tea bags and two dinners wrapped in tinfoil: steamed salmon in one, zucchini and peppers and celery in another. "Thank you," I said. "We have some granola bars. We'll give you some, but go ask your parents if it's okay first." But the children never returned.

We tried to enjoy the site, stay awake, and play cards, but it didn't last, and we crashed in the tent. "Okay, I'm going to switch-off mode," Landon said, and two minutes later his whole body jerked violently, and he slept without moving for six hours.

In the morning, the sky was bloodred, and the tent was covered in a layer of ash. Landon was awake before me, made a fire and breakfast, and brought me a mug of tea with honey. For two weeks, I had done all the cooking and had to poke Jeremy with a stick to get him to wake up and eat breakfast. I was overwhelmed.

Norman Wells was only an hour away, and though we had just left Tulita, I craved a greasy breakfast and coffee. The guidebook said it was the last restaurant until Inuvik, five hundred miles away.

"Let's go get some fried moose nose and whatnot," Landon said.

In northern Saskatchewan and Manitoba I had found poor indigenous towns and white resource towns, and under that taxonomy Norman Wells is the second.

Canadian geologists struck oil in the 1930s, but large-scale production didn't kick in until the Japanese invaded the Aleutian Islands in World War II. To fuel the fight in the Pacific, Canada and America teamed up on the Canol project, six hundred miles of pumps and pipeline from Norman Wells directly west over the mountains to the coast. Across the north, they laid airfields to bring in men and equipment, and built the now-famous Alaska Highway through the Canadian Rockies.

The Canol pipeline pumped four thousand barrels a day between 1943 and 1945, and then it was abandoned; the roads, the pumps, the pipeline, were all simply left to rot in place. They say you can still find rusting jeeps out there in the boreal forest.

The river at Norman Wells is extremely wide, and today man-made islands—platforms for drills, pumps, bobbing oil derricks, and generator stations—dot the harbor offshore of the town. Landon and I stopped at a busy dock choked with barges and commercial vessels and tugs and tenders, and above, on the bluff, hunched oil tanks and the bright refinery flame.

We agreed to eat in shifts so someone could stay with the gear, and I walked into town alone on a gravel road sprayed with grease to keep the dust down. Everywhere I looked, there were pipes, culverts, shipping containers, radio towers, front-end loaders, trailers on stilts. The diner was named the Yamouri Inn, but it felt like stepping into a greasy spoon in Omaha, except for the prices, twenty-dollar omelets and thirty-dollar steak and eggs. The two waitresses wore push-up bras and see-through tank tops and skintight yoga pants, surely useful in collecting tips from the roustabouts. I tried not to stare, but seeing a woman dressed so triggered hormones I had not needed in quite a while; I felt like I was in middle school and had just discovered an older brother's stash of *Playboy*s. The two women ignored me, except to bring me my food, as they complained to each other that last night they had held the restaurant open late for forty firefighters but they never came in.

I felt fat and spoiled: bed and shower two nights ago, two campgrounds, a breakfast of eggs and potatoes—the Colossal Scrambler, they called it—so big I had to force myself to finish it. But I took it where I could; I was fattening up for harder times to come.

Landon took his turn at breakfast, and I sat at the harbor. Jet aircraft came in and out of the busy airport. A family loaded plywood in their Lund boat to take out to build or repair a fishing camp. "Someone's been sleeping in here," the boat driver said, tossing flattened cardboard and a pink blanket into the dirt. He couldn't properly dispose of the trash because the nearby bear-proof garbage can was so stuffed with empty cans of beer as to be overflowing.

———

Landon remained a lucky charm. He was optimistic, the energetic shot in the arm that I needed. Torrential rains upstream raised the water level, picking up driftwood from shore and clogging the channels, but when we found beaches flooded, and thus few places to camp, he remained undaunted. "Throw some more tobacco in the water, I bet we find something," he said.

Near the Carcajou River, everything was low and swampy, terrible for camping, and the sun was unrelenting. Landon wanted to check the island across from the Carcajou's mouth, a silty brown lump with drunken spruce tumbling down, mounds of muck along the water. I was unconvinced, having spent weeks scouting riverbanks for flat spots, and I thought I knew all the tricks. But behind a large mound—"everyone knows to look behind the mound; it's always flat," Landon said—there was a little shelf, an oasis of grass and sand and mosquitoes.

"The streak is alive!" he said with relish. "Greatest shelf ever."

To get out of the sun, we hid beneath some bushes, among piles of goose shit. I was thirsty and filtered brown goose-shit water; in the silty river bottom, right below the surface, were fields of baby goose prints waiting to become fossilized museum curios in millions of years.

In the morning, Landon again rose first, and I asked what he did while I slept in.

"I got up, piddled about, washed my such and such and whatnot," he said.

I did not wash my such and such. The night before, squatting in the mud to relieve myself, mosquitoes attacked every inch of bare flesh, and my balls and inner thighs were covered in bites. I was reminded again of

Sigurd Olson, and how simple and idyllic everything in nature was to him, and briefly considered using his book as toilet paper. We had left the bulldogs behind, but the mosquitoes were growing thicker as we went north, and I resisted DEET or putting on my head net too early, as I knew the delta would be many times worse and I needed to toughen up.

That day we were due to face the Sans Sault Rapids, two and a half miles wide, the largest on the river. Michelle's guidebook claimed they were easy to run on the left, because the main rapid was to the right, though on Google Earth that portion of the river was covered by blurry cloud, so I couldn't confirm. Chief Andrews, in Tulita, said we'd be fine at this water level. But back in Hay River, Doug Swallow had provided us special nautical charts that showed rapids spread across the entire river. Capsizing would mean disaster. An insurance adjuster might define the risk as low-probability/high-impact.

We pulled up short of the rapids to scout, and while they roared ominously in the distance, we could see nothing at the horizon line. The guidebook also said there was a memorial near the beach to several young men who had drowned in the rapids a few decades ago. Like a voyageur wooden cross, but sheet metal. From the water, we saw a small fishing cabin up the bank, and so Landon and I thought to start there.

We climbed the beach and entered the tree line, an overgrown path revealing itself only a few feet at a time. The mystique of the bushwhacker is found in the potential that a hidden city might be revealed by the next machete thwack, but we proved failed explorers, finding nothing but mosquitoes and more bush. The willows closed around us, and swarms attacked us in waves. In a moment, simple annoyance morphed into panic as they layered our eyes and ears and throats, and I coughed out whole clouds of the bugs. "It was a mosquito mirage! A hologram to draw us in," Landon yelled, and we gave up on the cabin and memorial and ran for the beach. The mosquitoes attached themselves and followed us to the coast, back into the boat. We had to get out on the water and kill them all one by one before they were through with us.

Landon took off his shirt to check the damage. "I look like Franken-stein, like I've been stitched together by mosquito bites and whatnot," he said.

And then there was nothing ahead but the Sans Sault Rapids. I threw extra tobacco in the river, and Landon, who developed a taste for Red

Man while working with Special Forces in Afghanistan, said, "I gave up a chew for you, Deh Cho, so be cool today, dude."

The current rose, and the swells rose, and the sound with it, a white noise building to our right. There was a sense of momentum, a volume of water in motion that I remembered from the Slave, and with that flash-back my knuckles whitened. The roar ahead of us grew, a mighty sound accented with the popping of whitewater, and suddenly I feared we were not nearly far enough left. The surface of the water started tilting in all directions, rolled like ocean waves without the breakers, and then ahead of us a sandbar appeared, studded with driftwood trunks.

There was no such island on my map. Which side of it were we sup-posed to be on?

I cut us hard to the left, nosed upstream to gain us time, and ahead of me Landon, with no Slave memory to haunt him, happily paddled away. The canoe undulated and pitched like a storm-tossed whaler, and when we reached the far western side of the river, we ran along a high buff wall. We were in the heart of a wave train now, and square to it, through one crest, two, three, but then the whitewater receded and we drifted safely in simple current.

For curiosity's sake, I grounded the canoe on the uncharted island. It was completely flat and made of gravel, obviously submerged during spring melt. Landon and I walked across the plain to view the main rapid. Mountains were all around, though half as tall as those at the Camsell Bend. In the far distance, I spied only a few whitecaps in the meat of the Sans Sault Rapids. I tried to take a photograph, but it was too distant to look like much. It turns out we could have run the river straight through the center, along the barge buoys with the tugs and freighters.

The Sans Sault Rapids lived up to their French name: the Rapids With-out Rapids. In the end, the most difficult bit was the end, sinking to my crotch in the silt while trying to walk the canoe to the island.

———

It was hot all day, and we were surrounded by it, the sun above and radi-ant heat coming up from the ground as the whole country was continu-ously barraged by never-ending daylight. I felt like I had been left under the heat lamp at Burger King, shrunken and dried.

Seeking shade, we stopped for dinner on the south bank of the Hume River, on a wide lawn covered in primordial grass, some sort of mini-horsetail with tiny branches. We hoped to eat in the shade of the hedge-row, but the mosquitoes owned that territory, so we were forced back onto the sunny green field. The grass seemed to grow as I watched it, like the lawn of Eden, fresh and new, like the first idea of a lawn. To celebrate surviving the feared Sans Sault Rapids, I made Pad Thai, the best of our dehydrated dinners, and we ate sitting on a dried mud bank full of wolf and grizzly prints. My full stomach made me sleepy, and I lay down right there, my bowl and spoon on my chest.

"You mean we're gonna fall asleep on a shitload of bear tracks among a stack of dirty dishes?" Landon asked.

"Yup," I said, and then I stretched my aching back and closed my eyes in the bug-less breeze.

We finally camped that night a few miles farther, on another shelf that Landon, the good luck charm, spotted from the river. Nearby lay a dead spruce, half the needles still attached, and piles of driftwood, and so for the first time on my journey, we made a real campfire. It looked huge, compared with the tiny twig-and-grass smokers I built in the cooking stove. "Now it's a fucking adventure!" Landon said, and I craved a little alcohol, to sit and reminisce with my old friend whom I had met so many summers before.

We were two days ahead of schedule and, if all went well, would make Fort Good Hope the next afternoon. Landon didn't care about thieves and wasn't leery about spending too much time in towns. "You con-tracted me to get you from Tulita to Fort Good Hope. Whether that takes five days or eight days, I don't give a shit," he said. My voyageur wanted to get moving.

In the morning, we approached the Ramparts, a set of limestone cliffs that temporarily squeeze the Deh Cho into a tight gorge. But the river digs so deep no cataract is formed, and though Doug had provided a spe-cial marine chart, we saw no great hazard after a close study. We hoped only for scenery, a break in the monotony of the black spruce funnel.

As we paddled the western shore, the cliffs a thin yellow line on the horizon, I had a sense of déjà vu to the day before. A driftwood-clogged island on our left, where there should be none, a familiar white noise ahead. Suddenly it became very shallow, a rock garden of boulders rising from the water, so we ferried out to the center of the river, still over two miles wide ahead of the Ramparts.

But the current had caught us. I could see now whole formations of standing waves, blocks of whitewater with calmer channels between. We had waited too long to cross, and though I angled the nose of the canoe upstream, the far shore receded even as we dug in. Our exertions bought us a little time to work around one cluster of rapids, but no matter how we paddled, it was clear we'd never stay upriver of them all. It was all too big. The river was too wide, the current too strong, the lines of rapids too thick, the cliffs of the Ramparts rising from all shores.

"I can't hold the nose," I called up. The water beat on our starboard side, shearing waves that relentlessly knocked our bow downstream.

"Then let's do this!" Landon yelled.

So I ruddered the boat around, and the rapids were so close the brown water raised like teeth in a saw, and when Landon reached out and pulled his next stroke I could feel the boat lurch forward. We sped up, face to the rapids, right on the line, and for a moment I was in disbelief that I was attempting a whitewater raft maneuver in a canoe, alone but for Landon, laden with expedition supplies, thousands of miles from home, days from safe rescue.

We cleaved the first wave, and it fell away from our prow. Then the second, and the third. Our boat was so long, and so heavy, and moving so fast that we pushed the waves aside. In seconds, it was done, we had cut through them all and were floating in a pool of still water.

Before us, the Ramparts stood like the pale walls of a fortress, stretching to the horizon in each direction, and us through the gate, the Arctic Circle on the other side.

And yet, as our tiny canoe floated to the base of those bulwarks, the Ramparts seemed to diminish in strength, overwhelmed by the width and depth of the Deh Cho. Nothing compared with the scale of the river or withstood its scrutiny. Every mountain bowed to foothills, adjoining streams but trickles, and at times even the sky seemed to shrink. Each lost its sublimity, cowed to submission. And us, just bits of yeast, alone, insignificant motes upon the water, subservient in all ways to the current. If even the Ramparts were so reduced, then what were we? The vast river swallowed all.

Of all the plagues of the Deh Cho, the worst is emptiness.

You Can Starve on Rabbits, July 1789

The old man stood alone on the beach. He was pathetic, deserted by his people, standing among empty cooking fires. The camp smelled like fish entrails and wet wood smoke, and in the distance rose a front of limestone cliffs.

When Mackenzie's canoes approached this camp, several families fled up the steep gravel banks and disappeared into a wall of spruce trees, as had the Dogrib two days before. Awgeenah and their commandeered guide disembarked and spoke to the old man, who then proved not quite solitary; behind him, an old woman poked her head out of a lodge.

The elder said he was "pitifully worn out with old age" and that he had not run away, like his family, because "for the time he had to live it was not worth while." Then he started yanking on the hairs on his head so they fell out in clumps, and he passed them to Landry and Barrieau and the other voyageurs, "begging that we should have Mercy on him & his relations."

Awgeenah eventually calmed the man and convinced him to call back his family. A dozen or two Dogrib returned down the hillside, and Mackenzie immediately dug through the stores in the bottom of his canoe and began handing out gifts, metal knives and sewing needles and decorative beads. This improved everyone's mood, and they offered Mackenzie's men fish to eat, just boiled in their wooden pots. The Chipewyan hunters had not killed fresh game in several days, and Mackenzie had allowed no time to set out nets, so there had been nothing to eat but pemmican and rotting crane and scraps of caribou. Mackenzie accepted and thought the fish "very well boiled." And the Dogrib proved so overjoyed by the new friendship with the Pale Men that they wished to accompany Mackenzie downstream to keep him safe, as there were large whitewater waves ahead. Mackenzie had grown suspicious of every Indian's "many discouraging stories," but he accepted the assistance. The villagers said they had other families living farther down on the bank, so four of the men agreed to be their guides in their own canoes, to "shew us where to take the Road to go down the Rapid."

When it was time to push off, Mackenzie's new Dogrib guide tried to escape and refused to board the canoes. He said he had no use for more rapids and "wanted absolutely to return" to his family, under the shadow of the great rock two days upstream. But Mackenzie bodily dragged him into the boat, and the brigade of seven canoes launched.

Ahead, the cliffs formed a wall, only one small gap to pierce. "The River appeared quite shut up with high perpendicular White Rocks, this did not at all please us," Mackenzie wrote. No experienced voyageur would ever enter a canyon blindly. There was no way to prepare for the hazards, nowhere to swim in case the boat was upset, no way to know how long or narrow the gorge might be. The Dogrib were insistent that the rapid was severe and "made a great Noise about it," so they landed the canoes above the rocky mouth to try to scout the rapid and see the best line to avoid the whitewater, but nothing ahead was visible.

Awgeenah and Mackenzie conferred and decided that if their four guides could make it, so could they. The Dogrib boats were pointed at either end, encased completely in bark, and no bigger than a casket, space enough for only one person. If those small solo boats could breach the rapid, then surely Mackenzie's party could pass in their much larger canoes, loaded with freight and passengers and skilled paddlers.

So they let the Dogrib lead. This whole country, the Dogrib knew, had been formed long ago by a giant: boulders thrown at a huge beaver, an island formed by the giant's overturned canoe. Mackenzie sped past those landmarks unaware of their origin and "came between the steep Rock," the river narrowing into a funnel. Somehow, though, the current never accelerated. Mackenzie was confused. Awgeenah and their guide called over to the Dogrib to ask when the rapid was coming, and "they told us there was no other but what we saw," Mackenzie wrote. He dropped a plumb line to sound the depth of the river and called fifty fathoms to Steinbruck. Over three hundred feet of water was below them.

Sheer to the river, the cliff walls pressed tight, the narrowest chute that had compressed the waterway thus far. The crumbling rock was the color of rendered animal grease and layered; when each horizontal stratum was compared with the water level, it looked as if the river was tipped, the whole channel sloped downward in a flume.

The canyon turned a corner, and off one ledge wall a thin waterfall tinkled into a hidden basin. It was here, the Dogrib knew, that the giant had to piss.

———

The stone walls shrank, as if they were sinking into the earth. The formations fell away, green forest returned to the banks, and suddenly there were Indian encampments everywhere. Over the next three days, Mackenzie lingered at a succession of villages up and down the river, but none of them told him the news of the Pacific that he wished to hear.

Mackenzie stopped to speak to a few families fishing at a small creek. There were nearly three dozen of the Indians, and they made presents of many green and white fish that Mackenzie had never seen before. He thought them excellent, and everyone in his party was appreciative again for fresh food. Mackenzie gave them metal tools in trade, but when he launched to push farther on the river, all the men in the village followed, each in his own small canoe. Fifteen new boats, plus the four Dogrib canoes from the tribes above the cliffs, plus the craft of his own hunters. A veritable armada made its way down the river, as if on parade.

Only a few miles later they encountered another cluster of fires and families, and then another, and another, and another. These peoples wore the skins of hares as clothing and happily shared their boiled rabbit and fish. Mackenzie handed out more presents of metal tools, at times throwing the gifts out of the canoe without even stopping. Many of the women and children ran away when they did land, except in one village, where a woman had "an Abscess in the Belly and is reduced to a mere Skeleton," and the old women of the village sang over her and made the howls of wolves, but "whether these noises were to operate as a charm for her cure, or merely to amuse and console her, I do not pretend to determine." Mackenzie had a small kit of tinctures and liniments and poultices and Turlington's balsam, but he did not offer to attempt to heal the woman.

Most of the Indians said they had nothing to offer in return for the gifts of hatchets and sewing awls. One said they kept all their pelts at a lake many days' walk to the east. Another offered caribou meat, but it "was so rotten and stunk so abominably that we did not accept it." A third said they must avoid an island ahead, for it was the home of a "Manitoe," a spirit that "swallowed every person that approached him." When a village offered to wait on the bank for Mackenzie's return, he assured them he would return soon, "in 2 Mos. at farthest."

Their Dogrib guide said these were the Hareskin Indians, very meek and mild, with nothing else to hunt but their small namesake. For their generosity masked a shortcoming. Game was growing scarce, as the Dogrib had predicted and was evident in the rancid caribou offering. The Cree and their rifles had forced the Dogrib, Slavey, and Hare too far north and west, and now they were starving. Awgeenah's hunters had fared no better, killing only a single goose in the last week. Awgeenah knew of the Hareskin people, that they had long been at the mercy of more warlike nations, because many seasons ago they came to his Barren Lands to kill the caribou, so empty was their own home. The Chipewyan attacked the Hareskin to drive them back, but then a Hareskin elder made great medicine to scare away all of the game, and the Chipewyan starved. And so a long war began between the two peoples.

The valley was growing barren, but there was no reason to believe that more food stock was to be had off the river shores, either. Their guides said that the Mountain people lived to the west and south, many days' march up the creeks and creases of the land. Those people were dependent on hunting, because they lived in a place with no fish. But once a powerful medicine man made snowy winter come hard and drove away all the animals, so that starvation set in among the Mountain people. And they fled their homes for the safety of the Deh Cho, and the people scattered, so that one mother found herself alone with her son and they had no food. She took a needle and cut open a vein on her wrist, and the two drank her blood until they reached the river. There they found rabbits to eat, and the people on the shore gave them food and shelter, but they were the only two to survive.

There was a lesson to learn in the land. Fish were in the river, rabbits on the banks, but little more, and Mackenzie had no time for nets and snares. "You can starve on rabbits," the Indians all said. So much work for so little fat and meat. The ocean awaited, and so their pemmican stocks must dwindle.

And ever was the persistent chill. Fog. Overcast. Bouts of rain. Mackenzie had not been able to take a measurement with his quadrant for over a week, not since they had entered the mountains. But surely the river would meet the Pacific soon.

Mackenzie was beginning to think, though, that he must do it without "my Conductor," their Dogrib guide. He had grown more and more frustrated with the man, who "was become very troublesome, obliged to watch him Night and Day except when upon the Water." First the man said that they should leave him behind, because he knew nothing of the river anyway. Then he said there were more Dogrib ahead, and Mackenzie should use one of them as guide instead. "But we could not believe him as he told us 10 Minutes before that we should see no more of their Tribe." After such back-and-forth, in exasperation Mackenzie nearly left him onshore, though eventually, out of desperation, he forced the Dogrib guide back in the canoe and they embarked once more.

Mackenzie was through with the man. Awgeenah took a different tack and asked what was wrong. Were they not treating him fairly? Were they not feeding him, providing sustenance and comfort?

Their guide was obsequious. No, he was being very well treated, he said. That wasn't the problem. This Dogrib man, who had cut off his hair and given it to his wife and children before he left, wanted to leave Mackenzie's party because he was afraid, because he knew where they were headed.

Very soon they would come to the land of the Esquimaux. "They are very wicked," he said, "and will kill us all."

- **22** -

FORT GOOD HOPE TO TSIIGEHTCHIC, JULY 2016

〰〰〰

When I met Wilfred Jackson, an elder of the Sahtu Dene First Nation, he was just back from a moose hunt. Wilfred has dark skin and an avian nose and an admirable shock of gray hair that sticks straight up. His shoulders are hunched, and though he walks with a limp, he shuffles so fast you barely notice it. Most of the year Wilfred now lives in Fort Good Hope, in the side room of a hostel he runs with his daughter Rayuka, but when she and I met, this is the first thing she said: "My father, he's an old bushman. You should ask him some stories."

So I did, and Wilfred told me about the time he came face-to-face with a smoldering bear.

It was winter, and Wilfred was out on the land tending his traplines. In the perpetual dark, Wilfred used a flashlight to check each spring-loaded snare, laid out to catch martens puffed with their seasonal fur. But trap after trap, he found only a foot and fresh blood in the snow. Something was eating his catch.

Wilfred remounted his Ski-Doo and returned to his camp. There he found the culprit: a grizzly, a big one, ransacking his food and gear. It had rolled in the coals of his fire for warmth and was blocking his only route of escape.

"I tell all my children," Wilfred said to me, "don't be scared. The bears know if you are scared. The bears are good. Black, brown, grizz. All of them. Just don't be scared when you see them."

Wilfred wasn't scared, but he was trapped. To each side, the bush was an impenetrable wall. He was towing a toboggan, a sleigh to carry his tools and marten catch; he could never get the rig turned around on the narrow path. And he had not brought a gun, because it would never fire anyway, frozen tight in the extreme cold.

So he cranked the engine and drove straight at the bear. And right before he hit it, the grizzly did something completely unexpected. It jumped.

"My head was down. I could feel it pass over me. I could feel it hit the sled," Wilfred said.

The toboggan shook when the bear landed on it, but Wilfred never looked back. He just kept going, faster and faster, dragging the overturned sled all the way to the frozen Deh Cho.

To this day, Wilfred still has never had to shoot a bear in self-defense, in all his years on the land. Not that he has many left, he reminded me.

"Almost all the old-timers are dead," Wilfred said repeatedly during our time together. Sometimes he said it to make a point, and sometimes he said it simply out of the blue, breaking the silence as we sat in his truck.

———

Landon and I arrived in Fort Good Hope two days early, and we spent those days with Wilfred Jackson and his family, in their modest clapboard heap heaving in the permafrost. Wilfred calls it a Bed & Breakfast, but it's more like a Mattress & Help Yourself The Kitchen Is Over There. The communal space is painted red and purple and contains a woodstove, a small library with 1980s Reader's Digest novels, a record player, and a brand-new wide-screen television hooked to a satellite dish. Outside, Wilfred kept two pickup trucks, two all-terrain vehicles they all call quads, a snowmobile they all call a Ski-Doo, a boat with a spare outboard motor—"You have to hook them up to a computer now to fix them," Wilfred lamented—and a freezer chest stocked with musk ox quarters and fillets of inconnu, a white fish he called coney. His porch is covered in bird shit; his eaves are full of barn swallow nests. When Wilfred drives around town on his quad, he wears overlarge tortoiseshell women's sunglasses to keep the bugs from flying in his eyes.

Fort Good Hope consists of about five dozen shacks in various states of disrepair, a few newer double-wides, an airstrip, a health clinic, an old church, and a new school set on piers. Like Tulita, barely five hundred people live there, nearly all indigenous. There are no street numbers on homes, only family names, and padlocks on the outside of doors. Wilfred said the Pentecostal missionaries and young drinkers live on the north side, which is why he lives on the quiet southern end.

He didn't always. Wilfred still keeps a network of camps stretching over hundreds of miles of territory, a time and place for everything: geese in the spring, fish in the summer, caribou in the fall. He spoke of the land with less affection than respect. Bounty is hard won, and by his good fortune motorboats and Ski-Doos long ago replaced canoes and snowshoes.

Wilfred showed me a photograph on his wall, him sitting in camp surrounded by marten pelts. Last winter, he snared 108 and sold them for a hundred dollars each, to coat makers in Russia and China. It was good money for a month's work, but seasonal and short-lived. The cash was a windfall, and Wilfred knew it and treated it as such, and was back to subsistence hunting and fishing soon after.

"When you get rich, you get sick," he said to me. "You worry, when every dollar goes down. I have money, but I just pay bills. I never keep it, it all goes away. I shoot a ptarmigan"—here he made the motion of pulling a trigger—"I shoot a rabbit. It's fresh, fresh. That's what I want. Fresh."

So did I, after weeks of freeze-dried dinners. "My father got a young bull," Rayuka said and then showed me her family's smokehouse. She called it a teepee, but to me it looked more like a plywood shed, a small fire in the center and a grate over the roof. Inside the smoke was pleasant, just enough to keep the bugs away and cure the meat. Heavy loins and shanks of moose hung draped over a grill, and deep red back straps, thin as prosciutto, were stretched out like a spiderweb to dry.

"I like to cut it thin," she said, showing me the bloodstained table where she works. Rayuka is a heavyset woman just on the edge of middle age, with long dark hair and a wry disarming smile. Her name means Northern Lights in North Slavey. "I add just a little salt. Nothing else."

She handed me several pieces of dry meat, dark brown with thin white streaks of fat. I expected the sour gaminess of venison or the extreme brine of supermarket beef jerky, but the flavor was surprisingly mild, and it dissolved in my mouth.

"This is so good," I said, and Rayuka flashed a set of gapped teeth that would make most self-conscious.

I ate slowly, and still had a pile in my hand when Lucy, Wilfred's wife and Rayuka's mother, stopped at the smokehouse. Lucy is short and deeply wrinkled. She stood quiet a moment and squinted at me, lacking the eyeglasses common among older Americans.

"Are you going to eat that or hold it?" she finally said. She wore an unamused look.

"I want to savor it," I said. "You can't get moose dry meat back in New York."

She seemed to think about this a moment.

"Do your indigenous nations own their land?" she asked.

"No, most don't," I said. She didn't reply or move a muscle on her face, so I felt compelled to continue. "They're out of sight. Most Americans don't even think about them anymore. It's a sad history."

"It's more than sad," she said, and she shook her head. "It's terrible what your country has done." And she walked up the stairs of her front porch, went inside her home, and closed the door.

———

Landon and I settled easily into a comfortable life at the B&B. I was tired, like I hadn't felt since the war, from a combination of stress and exertion. Bone-heavy, weighted weariness. I didn't want to leave. I didn't want to move. And I knew the worst of the trip, the hardest sections, were still ahead.

I walked to the Northern store and bought eggs and bacon and moldy rye bread. I cooked the bacon in a pan on the electric stove and then scrambled the eggs in the leftover grease. We scraped blue off the bread and toasted it and made bacon and egg sandwiches, and the liquefied fat ran off my fingers.

I was getting soft. Every time I washed my hands, my calluses melted a little more. My sunburned arms and legs peeled. My mosquito bites itched again. My belly grew a bit; Landon and I split a half gallon of ice cream, then I went looking for more. I took a shower, and then another, and then another, until my fingernails and ears were clean. I got nervous about getting back on the water. I knew that in three days I would be wet and filthy again, hungry, in pain, eating expired food. I was homesick, and I just wanted to be done, but the Deh Cho was so big, and I still had hundreds of miles to go.

Landon rediscovered television—"I've been in Italy for two years, haven't seen anything," he said—and he just lay on the couch watching a marathon of *Alone*. In that reality show, people compete to see how long they can stay in the wilderness by themselves; most seem to have mental breakdowns after a week or two. The B&B had Wi-Fi, and I turned on my phone. My Facebook algorithm presented me with news articles from my old life: highbrow literary criticism, several essays on identity, the coming election. Completely separated from my current circumstances, they made no sense and I closed them uninterested. Maslow's hierarchy of needs remained alive and well.

Wilfred said we could eat some of the coney steaks in the freezer, so Landon thawed a few, rolled them in bread crumbs, and put them in a skillet. I walked back to the store and bought half-wilted lettuce and made a salad, the biggest treat of the day. I told Wilfred thank you, that it was our first fish from the river, and he was incredulous that we didn't at least have a fishing pole, as if we missed the essential purpose of the trip if we didn't catch our dinner.

In previous years, Wilfred worked as a guide, taking American business executives and former professional football and basketball players on great sportfishing adventures. He doesn't remember their names, only that it was funny that their feet stuck off the end of the bed.

"Look in there," Wilfred said, handing me an old photo album packed with three-by-fives. "You might see some people you know. They're from the States too." All of the pictures were from the late 1990s, fishermen from Minnesota.

But Wilfred hasn't had a client in almost a decade, so he gave up his expensive guide license six years ago. "Do you remember when those jets flew into those big towers?" he asked me in all sincerity, as if I might not remember 9/11. "After that, no one came anymore. I don't know why."

————

The next day was Sunday, and since the Jacksons are devout Catholics, we all went to morning Mass. Bells rang fifteen minutes before the service, to call the village. On the way, we walked past the graveyard, dominated by the small plots of children who all died within a few years of each other in the late 1970s.

The wooden church is 130 years old, and the interior is painted floor to ceiling, vestibule to sanctuary, with a continuous stream of ocher, maroon, cobalt, indigo, and mustard images: roses and cherubs, storks and lilies, bunches of pears and oranges and bananas, young Jesus in the temple, the Virgin Mary appearing in the cliffs of the Ramparts as Our Lady of the Rapids. When we paddled the river, Landon and I had seen a statue of Mary in the cliff wall, placed to memorialize the apparition. According to local legend, it is immovable and never washes away, no matter what plague the Deh Cho might visit upon it.

Before Mass, Lucy led a saying of the rosary, one decade in English, the next in North Slavey, the close of each segment always "Oh, Jesus, forgive us our sins, save us from the fires of hell, lead all souls to heaven, especially those in most need of your mercy. Amen." So many "thees" and "thous"; one woman wore a lacy head covering. This was old-time Catholicism from my childhood.

We arrived a few minutes early, and I spotted the priest immediately: Father Innocent is Nigerian, skin as dark as winter's night. He said he'd immigrated first to New York, settled in Staten Island, but after running afoul of the IRS—"Why do you have to file taxes if you don't make any money?" he asked me—he decided to move north. "There is such great need here," he said. "Only nine priests for the whole Northwest Territories." Every two weeks, Father Innocent travels from town to town by plane, performing a season's worth of baptisms, confessions, and Communion deliveries to sick elders. Another priest wouldn't arrive for a few months; Lucy sees to parish business in their absence.

Father Innocent said the Mass in English, but the readings were done twice, once in each language. There was a separate North Slavey hymnal too, and an old five-octave organ in the choir loft, made by the Thomas Organ Company of Woodstock, Ontario, though they didn't use it. During the homily, Lucy translated, sentence by sentence. Father Innocent's sermon was about Jesus and Martha, the importance of hospitality. At first, I thought he was talking about Landon and me, and I felt grateful to be included, but then, at the end of the service, he asked, "Can anybody give me a ride?"

That Nigerian accent, full of clipped consonants and long vowels, had not faded with his time away from Africa. Wilfred's accent was also tough, an indigenous lilt sprinkled with occasional Canadian "ehs." I had to strain to understand both men.

"Father's accent is very thick; do you have trouble with it?" I asked.

"We don't understand him at all," Wilfred said.

———

The Catholic missionaries are gone. The original Oblate fathers left long ago, and even the nuns packed up for good a few seasons past.

The Hudson's Bay Company trading post is gone, and the unpopular Northern store has taken its place.

The snow is gone, missing really, later each year. Wilfred said they only saw four inches last December. "I like to do all my trapping before Christmas," he said, "but I can't anymore." The lakes freeze, but with little snow, it's hard to run the Ski-Doo, and the winter road opens for an ever-shorter window.

The coney aren't gone, but the water is warm—the fish hardly chase his lures—and so full of driftwood Wilfred can't get his powerboat through without damaging it.

"Almost all the old-timers are dead," Wilfred says, and worse, few young people are learning to live on the land. Wilfred said that in Tsiig-ehtchic—a place he pronounced "SIG-a-check"—they still make dry fish, the traditional smoked trout, pickerel, char, grayling. A woman comes to Fort Good Hope to sell it, for as much as a hundred dollars a fish. "People go crazy for it," Rayuka said in amazement. I could tell this bothered Wilfred, not only that the young people of his town won't take up this lucrative business, but that they would rather buy dry fish than smoke it themselves.

Wilfred's children are mostly gone. Wilfred and Lucy have nine sons and four daughters, including Rayuka, scattered across northern Canada. They also have eight grandchildren, but they don't see them much.

"They hardly bother me for money at all," he said. "I give them a dollar to go to the store and buy candy. But they hardly come around." He paused a moment, looked at his hands. "They don't bother me at all."

———

Wilfred's wide-screen television stays on all day and night, pinned to a satellite channel that alternates between CNN and CBC.

"I never used to care about news," he said. "I was in the bush. But now I want to know what's happening in my world."

The day before he and I met, Wilfred was watching television late at night when he got a call for help. Lucy had taken several young women blueberry picking in the hills on the far side of the river, but somehow the group got separated from one another and then panicked. July is the traditional time to pick blueberries, but the ripe fruit also attracts bears. In the middle of the bright night, the town organized a search.

Not that Wilfred himself was concerned. "My wife knows the mountain. I wasn't worried. They could just follow the creeks down to the river," he said. Eventually, Wilfred went out in his boat and trolled up and down the Deh Cho until they appeared onshore, retrieving the whole group at three o'clock in the morning. "Now we tell them, better go pick your blueberries at the store!" he said, laughing.

Wilfred told me this story while watching the news, coverage of the Republican National Convention and the shooting of six police officers in Baton Rouge. Prompted by the headlines, Rayuka asked me to explain Donald Trump, and why Americans carry guns, if we live in cities and not out on the land. "It would be scary to live down south," she said.

"But I want to say to you," she continued, "it was nice to meet you. I told my friends, there is someone from New York at the B&B. They couldn't believe it. Said you must be famous. How did someone from New York make it to the B&B?"

I assured her that I was far from famous, but I did want to write about my time in Fort Good Hope. Wilfred jumped in.

"There was a white man who wanted to write a book, so he went up the Mountain River," he said, "and he spent a year up there. He built himself a crappy cabin and heated it all winter. He shot one moose and lived on it all winter. But when he paddled out, he capsized his canoe and lost everything. All his notebooks to write his book. He walked for days, maybe weeks. No matches, no gear. He couldn't build a fire. Finally, I picked him up when he made it to the Mackenzie."

I had never heard a clearer warning.

———

Anthony Sennhenn's plane was right on time. Wick Walker, my gray-beard expedition sage, had said my team was the biggest hole in my plan, relying as it did on bush planes to ferry my rotating crew. So I had spent months in useless worry about flight delays and had pushed hard to hit each airstrip on time. And in the end, all that stress was for nothing, because every trip was on time, no hiccups.

When Senny got off the prop plane, he was wild-eyed but grinning like a kid at Christmas. *Same old Senny*, I thought. The nickname had stuck because it matches his disposition: boyish, familiar, bright. I asked Senny to come on the trip because he was competent in fundamental ways. Like me, he was a bomb tech and veteran of Iraq. But far more important, he was an experienced sailor, owned his own twenty-two-foot Catalina sailboat, and, as a present to himself, had spent a post-deployment vacation as crew on a three-masted ship touring Antarctica. Senny was tough in an uncomplaining sort of way. He knew hardship, having grown up on the Bad River Indian Reservation, in far northern Wisconsin, on Lake Superior. For a time, he lived on an island accessible in winter by an ice road. I wanted someone to navigate the delta and brave the ocean with me, and when I asked Senny, he said he'd bring his sextant.

I left Landon and Wilfred and the comfort of Fort Good Hope with more than a few regrets. Ahead of me lay the longest sustained stretch of wilderness of the trip, a full two hundred miles to the next town, Tsiig-ehtchic. After that, more than a hundred miles to Inuvik, and even far-ther to Garry Island, at the far end of the delta. It was gut-check time.

Wilfred offered Senny and me the use of his hunting camp, sixty miles downriver; he looked over our map for a long time, then marked the cabin with a very careful X. "The key is by the door," he said, "in case anyone needs to get in."

It was raining the day Senny landed, a change after nearly two weeks of sunshine and occasional tailwind. The weather finally broke by evening, and I told Senny it was time to go. Wilfred volunteered to drive us a few miles farther north, to a put-in at the Hare Indian River, across from Manitou Island. But I declined, not out of stubborn pride, but because I didn't want to take advantage of the man's generosity any further, after he fed and hosted me for two days.

As Senny and I hefted the canoe, ready to portage down to the river, a marked First Nations security truck pulled up next to us. For a moment, I was nervous, as one is when approached by police in a strange place. A young man in a canvas jacket rolled down the driver's window.

"Aren't you the guy paddling the whole river?" he asked. He held up his phone, tuned to Facebook. There I read my own posts, loaded using my GPS inReach, and then shared in some unknowable string—the modern version of the "moccasin telegraph," the running joke of northern communication—until it arrived in Fort Good Hope.

"My friend says, 'Better get this guy some bannock for the trip!'" The young policeman laughed.

"Well, yes, that is me," I admitted.

"You're famous, in the N.W.T. anyway," he said, and laughed again. "Good luck on the Deh Cho."

After he drove away, Senny said, "That must happen all the time, huh?"

We launched under a sky of swirling clouds. A dark band from the north pushed off a clear patch in the south, the clouds moving in opposite directions at different layers. The rain restarted, then grew, then more. Terrible soaking rain; at Wilfred's B&B, I had spent an entire day cleaning and drying gear, and all that work was undone after an hour of paddling.

We stopped to put on our ponchos, but then the wind rose, from the north, and a crosswind too that raised the waves. "I find the waves endearing," Senny said, smiling through the misery. It felt like we had ground to a halt, no forward progress in the lax current. As a reasonable goal, I had hoped to reach the Loon River twenty miles away, but now that would be impossible. I was determined not to burn out Senny on his first night, for no purpose.

We achieved a point, and as we rounded the bend, somehow the wind grew still stronger. The water was now all big lolling combers, which I had not seen since Great Slave Lake. "They're not endearing anymore," Senny said, as we rode up and down each crest. We made for the point, saw a gravel beach—"that's good camping," I called—and ground the canoe in. The fierce winds scattered the clouds and revealed a double rainbow against a backdrop of dark gray seas.

We set up the tent quickly, in case the rain returned. Senny had just attended Marine Corps Mountain Warfare school, a course he dismissed as "advanced camping." His outdoor skills were newly sharpened, but as we crawled into our bags, his first night in the bush, he did have a question.

"So, remember before I came, I joked about that bear throat-slashing thing, to put it on my grave?" asked Senny.

"Sure."

"Um, seriously now. What is the bear plan?"

"We avoid them. Never sleep where we eat. If they get curious, we have bear bangers and bear spray. If that doesn't work, there are two of us. We stand our ground. They stole my ax, but we have knives, rocks. Keep your vest on. We fight."

"Like in *Predator*?"

I nodded.

Senny thought a moment. "I'm good with that," he said, and we went to sleep.

———

We crossed the Arctic Circle that afternoon, and my journey—thus far beholden to heat, sun, and lightning—was irrevocably altered.

All night, the wind and rain drove waves against the shore in a regular rhythm, as if we were sleeping by the ocean. The morning was ugly and cold, impervious to hot tea and oatmeal, and we shook our limbs for warmth. The clouds were very low. We ate a dirty lunch shivering on a sandbar, as seagulls dove and squawked to protect their rookery. I put away my sandals and laced up boots with wool socks for the first time. According to the inReach, the temperature was thirty-eight degrees, a drop of more than thirty from the day before.

We paddled hard in the chill. The current had slowed so far that I now actively sought out every slight advantage, boil to boil, the slight acceleration along curved cliff faces. The water was still warm, though, relative to the air, producing a shimmering mirage effect. The ridges to either side of the river appeared cantilevered out over the waterline, and islands floated in the air.

"I wonder how many flat-earthers believe it," Senny said, "and how many are just contradictory buttholes. I can watch islands appear out of the horizon."

The wind shifted to our tail, and Senny, the mariner, put out the sail. He seemed disappointed by the lack of nuance—it's little more than a big closed wind sock, a lever for the breeze to push against, no real sailing and tacking possible—but we made good time until the wind shifted again. Senny said he felt fresh and eager, and so I kept driving him on. It would be our biggest day, fifty miles in eleven hours of paddling, just fighting the cold.

All afternoon and into the evening, we searched for Wilfred's cabin.

I felt we must be close, that around every bend it would appear on the bank. "There's some wild tree parallax," Senny said, noting the optical illusion that closer spruce moved by more quickly than those farther away. But close or far, it was all spruce, and I started to wonder, maybe we'd passed the cabin because, like the memorial at the Sans Sault Rapids, it was swallowed by the thick bush.

Eventually, the headwind and bursts of rain exhausted us, and we camped on a low bluff above a stream, hard against the willow bushes, to block the worst of the gusts.

"This is the weirdest weather I've ever seen," said Senny, noting the different layers of clouds. All day, they seemed to produce different kinds of rain too, big and fat from one layer, small and stinging from another. But then, after we set up the tent, it cleared, leaving very, very high clouds, on the edge of the atmosphere, and so thin that through them the sun looked silver, as if there was moonlight on the water.

"Mare's tails and mackerel scales," Senny said, and pointed to the sky.

"What are you talking about?" I asked.

"Mare's tails are the wispy stringy clouds. Mackerel scales are the ones that look like cottage cheese. When they're in the sky at the same time, that's bad. It's from the old sailing rhyme":

Mare's tails and mackerel scales,
Something something something,
The weather's going to suck.

———

We would be stuck in the tent for the next thirteen hours. The storm blew a bitter damp cold, and I lay in my bag, shivering with stubborn wet wool socks that kept my toes numb. I had long underwear and a parka stuffed away, but avoided succumbing to them, on Senny's advice. "We have too far to go, and it will only get colder. You always need another layer available to step up to," he said. Outside, I heard trees falling, and rocks plinking the water as they tumbled from the bluff. Was the bank eroding away beneath us? Would the tent fall in the water? Had the canoe already floated away? Occasionally, I stuck my head out to check. Still there.

Our plan was to wait for the rain to pass, then paddle against the wind and cold; I could only take on so many of the plagues of the Deh Cho at once. I drifted off in the midst of writing these notes in my journal.

"I think I fell asleep," I said to Senny. "Did I snore?"

"Yup," he said. "It was adorable."

Eventually, hunger got the best of me, and I got up to make lunch in the drizzle. I discovered rotting food crushed in the bottom of our barrels. Landon had caught a few bagels turning green, but sitting in Wilfred's warm B&B, the mold had secretly and rapidly spread. Plus, a bag of nectarines had been smeared in the surf the day before, creating a sticky bug attractor. I had purchased some fresh supplies in Tulita and Fort Good Hope, but it was all past the sell-by date and already covered in blue as well. Somehow, the apples from Edmonton were in the best shape of all.

I ditched the decrepit new pears that had deteriorated straight from frozen to brown paste, molting off their skins. Then I threw two bags of bagels and all our English muffins in the water. That left twenty bagels flecked with green; I picked off each growth like a gorilla looking for ticks and carefully repacked them. All the pemmican, granola, dried fruit, peanut butter, chocolate, and honey was still good too. We'd have enough, if we were careful.

The rain dwindled, and we pushed off at noon. We rounded a point, and Senny shouted and waved. There, on the bank, above the spring flood, was Wilfred's cabin, right where he said it would be. Plywood and shingle, bent sheet-metal chimney, a pine tree trimmed to a lobstick to mark the spot in the traditional way.

Fifteen more minutes of paddling, just one more mile, we could have made it the night before.

"Do we need to stop and see what it looks like?" I called up to Senny.

"Kinda," he said.

I had no intention of stopping long—after a month of occasionally seeing such shacks from the water, I was curious to get a quick peek inside one—but when we got to shore, the west wind slammed our canoe against the gravel beach. We were soaked regaining control, dragged the canoe off the water, hiked up the bluff, and then all of a sudden we found ourselves in a different world. The wind was gone, the sun warmer, the ground soft with moss. Blueberries grew everywhere, and I picked a handful. There were two cabins in the clearing, plus several unskinned teepees to smoke fish, two Ski-Doos, an overturned boat, piles of unchopped firewood. We approached the first cabin and saw the key hanging by the padlock.

Inside, Wilfred's camp was almost as well furnished as his hostel, and that's when I knew I wanted to stay. A woodstove and kitchen stocked with canned food. Next to the door were several rain jackets and a new pair of traditional moccasins. A crucifix hung over two beds and a cot. A wooden pot holder displayed Jesus in His Glory. A sign above the kitchen table read, "Hello Welcome to the Jackson's Bush Cottage!! make yourself welcome But clean up after yourself Have respect."

We looked through a dirty window, out on the river, and saw raging whitecaps and black clouds. "Are we pussies to stay?" I asked. "Or smart?"

"Smart," Senny said.

I knew we made the right decision when I walked down to the shore to collect driftwood as kindling. The wind was so strong I had trouble walking. How would we paddle? A cold front swept the valley and fog stood up on the water, blown away in feathers moments later. I piled the driftwood by the woodstove and, opening the iron door, discovered a dead northern flicker. The large woodpecker was perfectly preserved in the dry ash, spots of red and yellow bright as life.

When the hail started, I made a fire.

I spent the day sitting at the kitchen table, solar panels spread to recharge our batteries, looking at the map, hoping we'd somehow magically transport to the end. The weather forecast on the inReach predicted twenty-knot winds until the wee hours the next morning, so Senny and I decided to pass the day in the warmth of the cabin and wake early, an alpine start, as the sun would be up anyway.

Instead of being frustrated at the delay, I knew I should be grateful for Wilfred's cabin. But I figured we had another four hundred miles to go, about a hundred hours of paddling. Ten hours a day for ten days, and I wanted to move. As Kylik—our Inuvialuit charter boat guide waiting for us at Inuvik—had said, you can get anywhere, it just takes time.

The hail let up, and I went outside to split firewood, but the head on Wilfred's ax was so loose on the shaft that I nearly sent it flying, and the wood was soaking wet anyway, so I gave up. I pissed, lay on a cot, made green tea on the woodstove. My fingers cracked and bled, as one's do in winter in a dry house. My sons texted me on the inReach to say our favorite hockey team had made a big trade, but the homesickness was too much, so I put it away.

"You know, sailors used to wait a month or two for the winds to shift around Cape Horn," Senny said.

"That's not helping, Senny," I said.

But I should have been kinder; Senny was the perfect companion for a writer. Traveling with Senny was like traveling by myself. He was so quiet there was plenty of space for my own thoughts. "I'm bad at everything that involves communicating," Senny explained. "Writing, poetry, painting, music. My wife says I'm bad at talking too."

We made dinner from the pantry shelf, meatball stew, with canned pears in heavy syrup for dessert. The cabin was warm, and I lay on top of my sleeping bag, in my underwear alone. Despite my brief gluttonous binge in Fort Good Hope, I looked thin, atrophied legs, wiry arms, reduced all over. Wasting away. Stress and exertion had taken their toll; in a flashback to boot camp, I had not had an erection in over a month. Before the trip, I thought I'd get in shape up here. "Better than P90X," a buddy had texted me, referencing the strength-training routine. But as Senny noted, that's like saying running should get you huge quads. But it doesn't. Your insides shrink, and your skin hangs.

I dozed. I knew I was asleep because I was dreaming, but I was dreaming of paddling. A rosary with an image of the Virgin hung from the nail over my bed. The fire went out, the cabin cooled. The wind howled through the eaves and played the chimney like a flute.

Over the last thirty hours, we had gone a single mile.

A little after midnight, I heard Senny packing gear. I got dressed, put my head outside, and saw the river was still. Our plan worked. We were on the water at two o'clock.

It was eerie, perfectly calm under a dank ceiling, and we paddled river center to find the current. Occasionally, the wind gusted, but the water remained flat, and, desperate for progress, we pulled hard. Ten miles, fifteen, twenty.

Then the banks of the Deh Cho rose and rose, so that we had entered a canyon many times deeper than the Ramparts, though still several miles wide. The wind came up from the northwest, and then the river turned northwest as well, and the current increased its pace, and with all the elements thus aligned, I should have known what was coming.

A fierce blow in our faces, and the river bristled like one of Jonas's fighting dogs.

"Should we pretend this isn't happening?" I called up to Senny. "Should we head in?" Was I too skittish?

"We're okay for now I think," he said, and then a moment later the water leaped upward all around us, all at once, like an ambush of waves. On instinct, I turned the nose of the boat forty-five degrees, to make toward shore, but the waves beat our port side and started pushing us sideways. I knew immediately we were in terrible trouble.

Five-foot seas, the frothing white crests high above my shoulders, far over the gunnels. I cinched my life vest tighter. Sometimes Senny paddled and hit air instead of water, and it looked like he was swatting at the waves to keep them at bay. I started to tack, plowing the nose of the canoe square into the swell and then jerking back to shore, a few paddle swipes in a direct line to safety, then turning the nose again so the surf didn't catch us broadside. The boat would tip, throw us off balance until our hips righted us, and Senny looked like he was riding a bucking bronco at the saloon. We were still over a mile away from shore.

"Maybe we should turn with the waves!" I yelled, and Senny agreed. I thought, I hoped, we could ride them in, as I had with Jeremy, turn a headwind into a tailwind. Ever so carefully, I turned us around. But paddling upstream, with the gale at our backs, we became stationary, completely motionless, suspended between the wind and the current and surfing a huge wave, like Leif and John at Molly's Nipple on the Slave, except in an open boat and all alone.

There was nothing to do but rudder back. "Hold on, I've got to turn us," I yelled. Time stopped. *We're going too slow. There is no way we make it,* I thought, over and over.

And then a swell caught us hard across the flank. We rocked to starboard, tipped the gunwale precariously close to the water, and then the pendulum swung us back hard to the left, as the swell passed beneath us. But an even larger wave rose behind it, the biggest yet, and our momentum rocked us too far. The next wave hit, and we jerked violently to the right again, and my back seized, twisting to compensate. Our port side lifted and our right gunnel dipped down, down, down and I saw it dropping into the water. If the rim of the canoe dipped below the waterline, the current would flood the boat. We'd take in the whole sea in an instant and tumble, overturned. It was a point of no return that I had known, as a whitewater guide, many times.

This is the end, I thought. No, I felt it, in my muscle memory. *We're done.*

The gunnel dropped and dropped and dropped and then just kissed the water and Senny and I kicked our hips and jerked the gunnel upward and that swell passed beneath us as well.

Senny dug in, hard, willed us to land. An eternity, and then the bank was in reach. I turned the canoe and tried to crab along the shore, but the waves drove us in. The surf slammed us against the beach, lifted us, dropped us again. I felt like I was being kicked. I stuck my paddle in the gravel to steady us, but we were heaved again and tossed sideways. I rolled out, soaked, and then the waves threw the canoe on top of me and I held it there to keep myself from being kicked again.

"Can you believe we didn't capsize?" I said.

"I was making plans to swim to shore," Senny said.

I looked out on the Deh Cho and saw a monstrous scoured trough, four miles wide, draining all the water in the world. Ever since Fort Simpson, the river had been a funnel, solid spruce on the top of the ridge, flood-stripped bare banks on the water's edge. At this bend in the river, though, the canyon and the gale perfectly aligned, and we were caught, pinned to the back wall like bugs on a board.

I checked the map. Our escape—the head of the wind tunnel, where the Deh Cho made a grand curve—lay more than twenty-five miles away.

Senny and I were jittery with adrenaline. It was eight o'clock in the morning, and we had been paddling six hours, but there was nothing to do but set up the tent and, for the third day, try to wait out the wind.

We walked the shore for an hour in either direction, looking for flat grass, but the thicket at the top of the ridge was so dense I couldn't even step into the tree line. The whole area, muddy banks and exposed gravel bars, was paraded with bear tracks, full-grown adults and cubs. One massive clawed print was four times the size of my boot sole.

"Now I have to worry about Bigfoot too?" said Senny.

The only space for the tent within two miles of the canoe was a small shelf behind one measly willow bush that did little to block the wind. It was mid-morning when we crawled into our bags, and despite the incessant howling we both immediately fell asleep.

I was awoken by the tent's fabric wall battering my head; in the comparative heat of the afternoon, the wind had somehow grown even stronger. I got up, unpacked the secondary emergency pop-up tent, and erected it upwind of our main tent. When that proved ineffective, I dragged driftwood logs from the beach up the hill and stacked them in a wall. Nothing worked.

I was glad I'd bought the pricey Himalayan tent. It never stopped shuddering, the poles bowing and pulling each seam to the point I feared it would tear to tatters. So I sat with my back against the rounded wall, barring the door against the monster trying to beat his way in.

There was nothing to do. I compulsively checked the inReach, noting the predicted gusts hour by hour, speed and direction. Always out of the north and northwest, between fifteen and twenty-five knots. It had to be higher along the water, in the Great Wind Tunnel, but how would the forecasting app know that? To launch, we'd need just a little window below fifteen knots, predicted to come early in the morning.

We had another eighteen hours to wait.

On a whim, for the first time I checked the current weather at our final destination, Garry Island at the far northern edge of the river delta. Twenty degrees, snow, twenty-five-knot winds. Do I have the gear for this? The stomach? "Today is the day I feel in the Arctic," I wrote in my journal.

There are places on earth that protect themselves, and nature still has the upper hand.

I felt stir-crazy. The tent absorbed the perpetual sunshine and grew too hot. But outside, it was too windy and cold to pass the day. I couldn't sleep. The sunlight never stopped. At first, north of 60 degrees latitude, I felt solar powered. But that had slid into mania, and now I just felt strung out.

Sitting in the wind. The tent shook; the stitches strained. Time again, too much time to think about time. A land of timelessness. A land out of time. But also a land so vast and empty and lonesome it was time-consuming to cross, time made slower by the monotony. Sit and meditate an hour and achieve immortality. Time stops.

"You can get anywhere if you have the time," Kylik said, in this land where all Wilfred's old-timers are dead.

My mind ran in circles. And then I realized, I had finalized my list of the seven plagues of the Deh Cho. Heat. Cold. Wind. Tempest. Bugs. Timelessness. Emptiness.

I just wanted to go home.

For something to do, I made dinner. To raise our spirits—avoiding the spoiling bread and fruit—I cooked Seafood Delight, dehydrated fake crab, one of our favorites. We used the canoe as a windbreak, and Senny even tried to start a tiny fire behind a wall of stones, but neither the meal nor the fire provided comfort. Any warmth was blown away.

"Hey, Senny," I said. "No bugs." He laughed. Good ole Senny.

We crawled into our bags and hoped for a better tomorrow.

———

I woke early, five o'clock, and the tent was shaking. I got up, pissed, walked down to the canoe. There were still a few whitecaps in the center of the Deh Cho and angry gray clouds that threatened rain, but conditions had improved, just a bit, and I was done with the wind, done sitting, so I woke Senny and we launched.

We hugged the river's east bank, close to land but just far enough out to avoid the pounding surf, like two medieval sailors scared of the sea. It all felt precarious, that tightrope; don't think too much about where you are and what you are doing.

We paddled continuously, uphill, without stopping, for six hours. Progress was excruciating, one or two miles an hour at most. Senny's sailboat tops out at five knots, and his example of satisfaction taught me patience. My shoulders and wrists and groin ached, and with each stroke the tendons in my hip popped over the bones.

The Deh Cho threw every kind of wave at us. Sharp ones, driven by wind. Wide rollers reminiscent of the lake. Standing waves in current. Bubblers around the lips of boils. I wondered, do the Inuit have as many words for waves as they do for snow?

We plotted a course between the sheer banks of two silty islands, hoping to rest in the wind shadow. But the gusts grew in strength in the channel, and we drifted backward as we regained our breath. Following the path of the mud, island-hopping along their shores, we had accidentally reached the center of the river again and had a choice to make.

In a few miles, the great Thunder River, cleaving through the ridgeline to reach the Deh Cho, would meet our eastern shore. Through luck, good or bad, so far I had not met a bear the entire trip, seeing only their ever-expanding tracks. But everyone had warned us—Wilfred, Michelle's guidebook, strangers at church in Fort Good Hope—that we were guaranteed to face grizzly at the Thunder River. They were thick in summer, eating fish, and so we needed to avoid that place at all costs.

We would never have a better shot to cross the river than from these mud islands. Either we made an open crossing now, a mile and a half to the western side, across whitecaps that had nearly capsized us the day before, or we stuck to the eastern shore and, if a storm came, would brave the bears when forced to land.

Senny and I talked it over. I thought of the Bigfoot grizzly print we had just found. I thought of the gunwale licking the river and how lucky we were to kick out of it.

"We should cross," Senny said, without indecision. And to my surprise, I realized I agreed. We knew how to deal with waves but had never fought off a bear. Counterintuitively, maybe, it was safer to cross.

I guided the boat away from the mud islands and into the main river. Senny was silent, intent on the far shore, and paddling hard. In the near distance downriver, breaking the solid rock wall of the Deh Cho chasm, was the deep gash of the Thunder River. To flee one danger, we faced another that had nearly wrecked us. The wind-driven waves were fierce but only occasionally broke into whitecaps, and after an hour of concentrated paddling, the trance of the work overcoming nerves, suddenly our hull ground on land.

I stepped from the canoe. There was no wind. I could see its effects on the river, hear it shake the spruce above, but where I stood, on that beach, all held still. The high western ridge shielded the worst of the northwest wind. Senny built a fire, and I broke out our best food, boiled a kettle of water, and made tea. We ate dried apricots and candy bars and drank a second mug, and steam rose from my boots as they dried before the flames. My toes were warm.

I felt energized again, and our spirits lightened as the sun finally broke through. We would get back on the water soon, but now the waves felt bouncy, less threatening, and I saw the Deh Cho with new, confident eyes; we didn't paddle any faster, but we did enjoy it more.

We still had another two days of hard paddling to Tsiigehtchic, but we had accomplished something important in this test of wills. We had broken free. The Thunder River marked the end of the Great Wind Tunnel, fifty miles long, that had harried us for three days. Tiny progress is better than no progress. That was the lesson.

I felt better than I had in a long time. I yelled into the wind.

"Hey, Deh Cho, is that all you've got? Bring it on!"

Senny responded immediately.

"He's fucking kidding! Don't listen to him!"

TOP: Alexander Mackenzie.
(*National Gallery of Canada*)

MIDDLE: Roderic Mackenzie.

BOTTOM: Hendrick, the
Mohawk Chief. (*Courtesy of
the John Carter Brown Library
at Brown University*)

TOP: *A Chipewyan Woman,*
1928, by Edward S. Curtis.
*(University of Southern
California Libraries)*

BOTTOM: *The Death of
General Wolfe,* 1771, by
Benjamin West.

TOP: Mishipeshu, the horned serpent that lives at the bottom of Lake Superior.

MIDDLE: Great Slave Lake, as drawn by Samuel Hearne.

BOTTOM: Peter Pond's Beaver Club Medal. *(Peter Pond Society)*

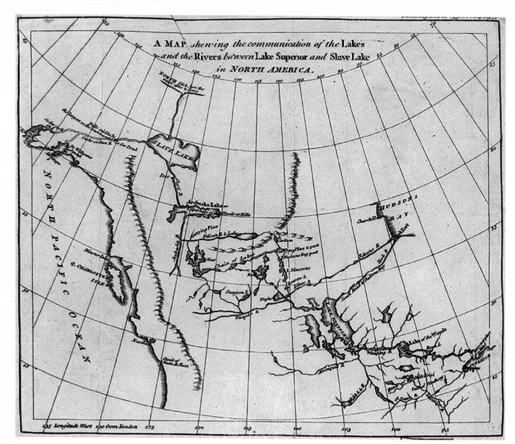

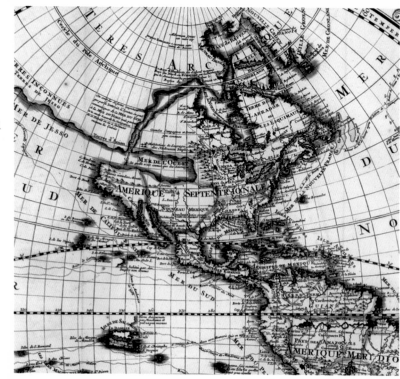

TOP: Peter Pond's map in *The Gentleman's Magazine.* *(Library of Congress)*

BOTTOM: Typical map of the day, 1780. Note the Straits of Anian and Sea of the West.

TOP: Barge traffic on the Mackenzie River today.

MIDDLE: *Shooting the Rapids*, 1879, by Frances Anne Hopkins.

BOTTOM: John and I scout the rapid at Molly's Nipple on the Slave River. *(Leif Anderson)*

TOP: David and I set out in Hay River.

MIDDLE: Jeremy hates bugs.

BOTTOM: Coming into the Camsell Bend.

TOP: Wilfred Jackson at home in Fort Good Hope.

MIDDLE: Church of Our Lady of Good Hope.

BOTTOM: "Bigfoot" grizzly track near the Thunder River.

TOP: An unexpected hut on Garry Island.

MIDDLE: Senny and I celebrate success at Garry Island.

BOTTOM: Senny, Jeremy, me, David, and Landon. The only time all of us were ever together, at a Christmas party in Atlantic City, December 2016.

SATISFY THE CURIOSITY, THO' NOT THE INTENT,

JULY 1789

~~~~~~

In the beginning, in the oldest of days, giant spirit animals walked the land, and they and the Gwichya Gwich'in people were equals. Each could speak, and could change into the form of the other, everyone and everything in balance. Raven tricked people, and Bear killed them, and Wolverine stole their food, but Caribou provided bounty for everyone, and Bluefish broke up the lake ice each spring and will until the end of the world.

Those days are called *ts'ii deii* days, and no one knows why.

The Gwich'in people had always lived in that place, and they called themselves Gwichya because they made their home in the flats of the Nagwichoonjik river valley. And the great Atachuukaii traveled up and down the river, and fixed Raven and Crow, and chased away giants, and fought three beavers and stretched their skins on a rock far to the south. One winter, Atachuukaii even survived alone on the land, without shelter or supplies, and from then on he was also known as Man Without Fire. Some Gwich'in hunters made medicine to move very quickly, and they carried bows hewn from raw skin that only the strongest men would draw. And there was a place for everything, to fish and smoke and kill caribou, and time was circular, season by season by season. The muskrat ate its tail.

In *ts'ii deii* days, there was a Gwichya Gwich'in man named Daii dhakhaii. He had a dream that he must visit a hill, and so he did. He climbed the hill until it became a cliff, and then he climbed the cliff and found a door, and he entered the door and had a vision. There were people living in the hill, and they gave him a pot made of hard gray metal. He had never seen such a pot before. And the people told him not to return the way he had come but to leave the hill by another door farther ahead. "If you continue, and go through the door ahead, your country is going to be like it is now, forever," they said, "but if you turn back and return the way you came, someday this country will change."

Daii dhakhaii didn't want anything to change, but he was also scared and didn't know where this second door led, so he turned around down the hill and returned to his family and showed them the pot made of metal.

And then, as the vision said, something different happened.

At a Gwich'in camp in a big bend of the Nagwichoonjik, chips of wood floated into the eddy and got caught in the driftwood. The Gwichya Gwich'in had never seen wood chips like this. Not splinters, or scraps. Too large for a beaver, too precise for their own bone and stone axes. The Gwich'in realized that these chips were cut with something sharp and strong, like the metal of Daii dhakhaii's pot. They must have come from *aachin*, strangers, from upriver.

That was the moment that *ts'ii deii* days were done. The time of the long now came to an end. The muskrat released its tail. Medicine started to fade, history marched forward, and from then on the Gwich'in were caught up in all of it.

They were not afraid. Four men at the camp gathered their wives and children to seek the source of the wood chips. They loaded in their canoes and turned upriver, paddling into the future.

———

"Thunder and Rain last Night, and, in the course of it, our Conductor deserted." Mackenzie was relieved to be rid of the troublesome Dogrib man and immediately sought a more competent guide to show him the way. He ordered the voyageurs to claim "one of the others against his will," and as a press gang Barrieau and the voyageurs snatched a new young Dogrib man from the closest cluster of cooking fires. He fought, but the *canadiens* outnumbered him, and had rifles besides, and though he threw a paddle in the shuffle, Mackenzie "pacified him," and they pushed off the canoes at half past three in the morning.

Soon smoke appeared on the right side of the river, and when Mackenzie ordered his boats in, their new guide became apoplectic. "Our Stranger began to Hallow to them in a very strange manner," Mackenzie wrote. This encampment, he said, was "not of his Tribe," and they would "beat us all, and pull out our Hair." Four hardy men stood onshore, the women and children having made for the spruce on the high mud bank.

They were dressed in shirts of muskrat skins, and wore mittened gauntlets stretching to the elbow, and were armed with bows made of sinew. They did not cower or run or beg for gifts or offer tokens of friendship. Instead, they commenced to "Harangue us all at the same time before we Debarked seemingly in a very violent Passion."

Mackenzie wasn't fearful, but he was confused, because the meaning of their words was far less clear than the tone of their voices. The Chipewyan hunters could understand nothing, Awgeenah only the words of a single man, though the English Chief's replies proved ineffectual. Their new guide spoke briefly, and the four men went quiet. Mackenzie put out his hand to shake, and they looked at his empty palm confused. Mackenzie took this as a signal to pass out iron gifts. At that, "the Women and Children came out of the Wood and met with a similar treatment," and the tension left the air.

Using their new bondaged guide as an interpreter, Mackenzie traded sewing needles and knives for several large moose skins. He was "surprised to see them have any as I did not think there were any of those Animals in the Country, and they tell us that they are very scarce." So were many other fur-bearing animals; "they don't know what Beaver is." Mackenzie had finally reached the point where traveling farther north and west did not yield richer pelts. A three-century-old truism of the fur industry had reached its limit.

The voyageurs' clothing was in rags, and their arms in short supply as well, so Barrieau, Landry, Ducette, and de Lorme purchased shirts, bows, two-feathered arrows, and snares as well; if there was nothing to eat in this place but rabbit, they must be caught somehow. The Indian women offered fish, which Mackenzie found "most delicious," and one of the men, of his own volition and without cajoling, agreed to accompany them down the river to introduce them to more of his people.

Mackenzie was impressed by the new tribe. This new man "spoke much in derision of the last Indians who we had seen, that they were all like old Women & great Liars, which coincides with the Opinion I had already entertained of them." To Mackenzie, they did not call themselves the Gwichya Gwich'in. Awgeenah heard their name as Diguthe Dinees, the Quarrellers. Mackenzie thought they "had a better appearance than any of those we had yet seen, being healthy and full of Flesh." Clearly the pox had not reached this far, nor trade goods either, as the men possessed only small bits of salvaged iron that they used as razor edges.

Mackenzie's crew reloaded their boats and pushed off, and in a tradition reaching all the way back to Montreal, several voyageurs "fired a Couple of Guns loaded with Powder." Their new guide was "startled, having never heard or seen any thing of the kind before." He refused to join Mackenzie's canoe, the source of the noise, and insisted on paddling his own instead, asking two of his brothers to join him in their own boats.

The rest of the day they traveled southwest, by Mackenzie's observations. The river was laced with sandbars, and battlements of rock enclosed their passage. In late afternoon, they saw more cooking fires in a bay framed with aspen, and their guide's brothers paddled their solo craft ahead to warn their families of strangers. But still, when Mackenzie landed, the Quarrellers who encamped there "made a terrible uproar speaking quite loud & running up & down like perfect Madmen," he thought. "Perceiving the disorder which our appearance occasioned among these people, we waited some time before we quitted the canoe; I have no doubt, if we had been without people to introduce us, that they would have attempted some violence against us."

There were five families there, Mackenzie figured, though he "did not see them all as they kept in their hiding places." Their hair was long and tied off at the temples and hung before their ears. He offered gifts, as was his custom, and discovered they wanted nothing but blue beads to decorate their clothing. So he bought new shirts for the Chipewyan hunters, and more arrows for his voyageurs, and dry fish to supplement their ever-shrinking pemmican stocks.

But always, Mackenzie wanted information on the Pacific. "Those Indians told me that from where I met the first of their People this Morning it was not far to go to the Sea over Land on the East Side & from where I found them it was but a short way to go to it to the Westward that the land on both Sides the River was like a Point." He was getting close, and his new Quarreller guide predicted that "we will sleep 10 Nights more before we come to the Sea." And what's more, the Esquimaux, now only "three Nights farther."

———

The Esquimaux. They had come at last to the sticking place. No longer a far-off threat to be dealt with later, the Esquimaux were now an immediate hazard.

At times the Quarrellers traded with the Esquimaux, who provided all their knives, arrows and bows, the method of their canoe construction. And yet their guide also indicated a nearby hill where his grandfather had been killed by the Esquimaux only three winters before. There had not been war since, but what did that mean?

Their Gwich'in guide knew that a raid could come at any time. A woman of his tribe, Ahts'an veh, had once been taken by the Esquimaux and held in captivity for years, long enough to give birth by her new husband. They raided the Gwich'in villages, killed her brothers and brought her the heads, and when she escaped, they hanged her new baby from a tree.

The young Quarreller knew the Esquimaux, everything about them, he wanted to assure Mackenzie and Awgeenah. His two brothers mockingly sang "in Imitation of the Esquimaux," which "amused us" and "enliven[ed] our new Guide." He danced Esquimaux dances and, in a final show of encyclopedic knowledge, "pull'd his Penis out of his Breeches, laying it on his hand & telling us the Esquimaux name of it."

Their new guide, who had joined them only hours before and "took much Pains to shew us that he knew the Esquimaux & their Customs," wished to go no farther. "He was afraid that we should not come back this way," Mackenzie said, because the Esquimaux were too dangerous. They would "perhaps kill us," take the wives of "my Men & Indians." He feared for his life.

But Awgeenah and his Chipewyan hunters said that "we were not afraid & that he need not be." Their rifles were their phallus. Perhaps they could take the Esquimaux scalps to Hudson's Bay and sell them, pass them off as some animal that lived in the water.

For Awgeenah knew the Esquimaux as well. He knew their cruelty and deceit. He had run their naked bodies through with spears and then bathed in their heart-blood. His instinct was war, but he also knew that he did not lead a party of warriors as had Matonabbee almost two decades before. He traveled with only two of his own retainers. What use would be their equivocating guides, and even the voyageurs, who endured hardship and toil and beat one another with their fists, but did not know the art of battle?

Mackenzie, for his part, remained quiet and ambivalent but undeterred. For days, he and his voyageurs were the first white men ever to meet a succession of Slavey, Dogrib, Hare, and Quarreller tribes, people whose languages were foreign even to Awgeenah. Their small party had survived thus far without bloodshed. They would press on, he decided, even to a place of frozen monsters and the Esquimaux who hunt them.

———

They slept long into the cold morning and did not launch until four o'clock. "Not far from our Campment the River narrows between high Rocks," and they followed a twisting course until, in dramatic fashion, "the Banks get low" in all directions. Far in the distance, "Snowy Mountains ahead," but all around them "the River widens & runs in many Channels amongst Islands some of which are nothing but a Bank of Land & Mud." In those walls of silt he found "a face of solid Ice intermix'd with Black Earth," drooping into the water as it melted in the hot sun. Some larger mounds hosted trees larger than he had seen in months, but they were tipped and dizzy, tumbling about. Mackenzie had entered a new kind of country: expansive, marshy, and, but for the peaks in the distance, completely unlike the descriptions of Captain Cook's inlet.

The sun was blazing, relentless, but, most important, visible. For the first time in two weeks, since they probed their way along the north shore of Slave Lake, the sky was clear at noon, and Mackenzie could use his quadrant to measure the sun's distance off the horizon. The reading could not have been more disheartening.

"I got an Observation which gave me 67 degrees 47 minutes North Lat., which is farther North than I expected, according to the course I kept." What had gone wrong? He had dutifully marked his mileage, checked his course constantly. Perhaps his error was "owing to the Variation of the Compass which is more Easterly than that I thought." There had been so many storms he had not been able to recalibrate his instruments via celestial readings, and so never considered accounting for a drastically shifting magnetic deviation. Hundreds of miles behind them, in the mountains, the river had turned northward, but he never realized it. For weeks, they had been going the wrong way.

"I am much at a loss here how to act being certain that my going further in this Direction will not answer the Purpose of which the Voyage intended, as it is evident these Waters must empty themselves into the Hyperborean Sea."

The Arctic, the Northern Ocean, the White Man's Lake known as Bill-hully Toe. There were many names for the same body of water, but Mackenzie called it the Hyperborea, a term from his Scottish school days and Roderic's books on Greek history and philosophy. Pliny and his ilk said that the warm Hyperborean Sea was home to nine-foot-tall men who lived a thousand years. Eighteenth-century geographers held a similar consensus: at the warm North Pole lay a shallow temperate ocean completely encircled by high walls of ice, as Captain Cook had encountered in the Bering Strait. The only question for Mackenzie was whether the mouth of this river was locked in ice as well. Summer navigation was a minimal requirement for any practicable northwest passage.

In either case, he was as far from the Pacific as ever. To go on "would satisfy Peoples Curiosity, tho' not their Intentions."

That night, full of discouragement, Mackenzie left his tent and stayed up "to observe at what time the Sun would set." He sat and sat, on that mushy shore, for one hour, then two, then three. Just after twelve o'clock, Mackenzie stood and walked to the canoe and shook awake Barrieau, his old Athabascan guide, trusted for so many seasons, to show the man "what he never saw before." Barrieau was groggy, confused, thought it was time to embark, and woke Landry, Ducette, and de Lorme as well, and none could "scarcely be persuaded" by what they beheld, as all the voyageurs stood with Mackenzie and looked at the midnight sky in amazement.

After weeks of nighttime storms, Mackenzie wanted to see when the sun set, but "found that he did not set at all."

Into the Earth Sponge, July 2016

〰〰〰〰

The Gwich'in village of Tsiigehtchic appeared not so much quiet as abandoned, a few tidy homes, a stately church on the hill, and every business locked up tight. I had made contact, via e-mail, with an elder who agreed to meet and talk, but she had warned me she might be out on the land, fishing, when I came through. I wanted to talk with her about the efforts to save the Gwich'in language, about the book of Gwich'in stories she had provided me, and about *ts'ii deii* days and how her people know the word contains great meaning but have lost the ability to translate it. Mackenzie's Quarrellers have stayed feisty and resilient; one council recently voted to ban hydro-fracking under its lands.

I walked the hilly gravel streets of Tsiigehtchic, looking for anyone to speak to, but found not a single soul. Only flocks of the ubiquitous ravens and the foreleg of a cloven-hooved animal lying on the roadside. Eventually, I gave up. It was a Sunday, after all. No meeting would occur, and with the Northern store closed, no supplementing of our moldering bread and fruit. We'd live on the staples we had.

The only life in town was on its edge, along the Dempster Highway, where a single industrial tug kept a regular business shuttling trucks back and forth across the river. The sun was full and the air was cool. Maybe everyone was off fishing?

Since we had broken free from the Thunder River three days before, the wind had not changed, but our attitudes had. We were weary but resolved. We would not stop. We would always attempt progress, no matter how small. The goal of reaching Garry Island, previously so far off as to be incomprehensible, was drawing near. And yet, even as we approached, I recognized more and more that the river was in control of whether we succeeded. We would keep working, and the Deh Cho would stop us or not.

Between the Thunder River and Tsiigehtchic, we solved mazes of unmapped sandbars, repeatedly crossing whitecapped water. At times, the waves were three feet high while the river was only one foot deep, and I wondered how we didn't get marooned in the middle of the channel, dropped and lifted and dropped again as one does in surf at shore. There were dust storms off bare islands, sunburns in frigid north winds, and the nights were bone-shivering cold; no amount of hot oatmeal in the morning seemed to warm us. The great river was the color of old dishwater, and just as dirty, so we stopped when we could at smaller side streams to filter for cooking and drinking. The Tree River, where it entered the muddy Deh Cho, was so deeply tannined that their junction looked like a meeting of two completely different substances. "Look, it's a peanut-butter-jelly line," Senny said of the contrast between brown and purple. The Tree River was just warm enough to consider bathing, and Senny volunteered to go first. He dove naked into the iced-tea stream and immediately leaped out with a yelp. I contented myself with a rinse of my dank and greasy hair.

At Cony Bay, where Mackenzie met the Gwich'in, we saw our first massive chunk of dirty ice onshore, a railroad car covered in grime. The bay itself was wide and empty and thick with white birch as we had not seen in weeks. I replenished our supply of bark—I hoarded a stash in a dry corner of the canoe, to start cooking fires—in case it would be hard to find in the swampy delta.

It was bright and clear, and while Senny lay in the sunshine, I studied the sky. Mare's tails and mackerel scales, horizon to horizon.

"Oh shit," Senny said, when I pointed.

The final leg to Tsiigehtchic passes the Lower Ramparts, an enormous horseshoe of shale that created a circular wind tunnel, blowing always in our face all the way around the dial. Progress was excruciating.

"Senny, I think we've stopped," I called.

"No, we're moving," he said, and pointed ahead. "Look, cliff parallax."

And he was right. With the speed of a glacier cutting or a continent thrusting, the shale cliffs opened and shifted as we dug our paddles around the horn.

But this great curve of the river would prove the last gasp of descension. The valley was over. We were done dropping, and though still 150 miles inland, a mere dozen feet above sea level. All the downward movement, since driving that ridge near Edmonton, had led here, to the delta, and Tsiigehtchic served as its head.

As a sign that the funnel was spent and the swamp had returned, just outside Tsiigehtchic a loon floated on the water, diving and fishing. I had not seen one in a month.

"It's good to see a loon," I said. "I was afraid we were too far north for loons, which I didn't think was possible. Loons *are* the north to me."

"Like koalas," said Senny. "There's no place too Australian for a koala."

At Tsiigehtchic, Senny and I were cooking dinner at the empty dock, enjoying the seats of a picnic table, when two men pulled up in a rickety powerboat packed with gas canisters. They wore heavy parkas with the hoods up, and one had a thin black goatee; I thought they were indigenous. But in fact, they were German, Matthew and his son Jan, from Basel. They were traveling down from Inuvik and needed gas. I gave them the bad news that everything was closed, so they prepared camp, right there at the dock.

Matthew said he was doing the river in stages, had already completed several upper sections, and was now working toward Norman Wells. I asked him why he traveled so far, just to boat the Deh Cho, and he said, "I saw a big river on the map, and I wondered, what is there?"

"Turns out the answer is nothing!" said Jan, with a smirk.

Senny and I pressed on that night, following my habit of not spending more time in towns than necessary. We camped on a slimy, mosquito-choked beach, and the next day faced the first navigational decision of the trip.

At Point Separation, the Deh Cho's unchanging valley forks into the delta, the three major routes each as wide as any normal river. On a map, all distributaries bear the likeness of a tree canopy, trunk and associated branches. The Mississippi's delta, from above, looks like a southern live oak, as wide as it is long. Similarly appropriate, the Deh Cho appears as a spruce, constricted but tall, 50 miles wide but over 150 miles long. This is a matter of geography and not design, of course, because the Deh Cho is trapped between two mountain ranges. The accumulated flotsam of the river can only expand outward, a cone of silt stretching ever northward, speckled with innumerable tiny ponds. When Senny looked at the map the first time, he came up with his own analogy.

"It looks crazy, like an earth sponge!" he said.

Using our chart, navigating the earth sponge, I had this new thought: *Am I going the right way?* To the left, the western channel, to the Yukon and Alaska. To the center, the main flow, where Mackenzie first glimpsed the midnight sun. To the right, the eastern channel, where the next day we hoped to reach Inuvik and Kylik. Unlike Mackenzie, I intended to seek out the Inuvialuit, the western Arctic Inuit whom he called Esquimaux. I felt a hint of regret that surprised me, as I realized that for the first time there were parts of the river I would never see.

Senny and I tracked east, with hope that smaller waterways would support less wind and thus fewer waves. But instead, gusts blew from the north, the current disappeared entirely, and the bulldogs, mercifully absent for weeks, flew out to greet us. Somehow our pace slowed further, the channel winding and looping. On the banks, the spruce leaned a kilter, tipping into the water; scientists call it drunken forest. It was a landscape composed entirely of silt, flat shelf islands, and mushy shore. And overhead, in contrast, was a snake's nest of contrails, so many jets leaving white streaks across the sky. Where were they all going? Beijing to New York? London to Vancouver?

"Maybe they're Russian Bear bombers and the world is ending. Would we even know?" Senny asked.

"Yes," I said. "We'd know immediately, because our GPS would stop working."

That night, we camped on the only gravel spit we could find. The mosquitoes were a terror, worse than ever on the trip, worse than I had ever experienced in my life. I wanted nothing but ibuprofen and sleep in the Fortress of Solitude. So we ate dinner quickly and, as a brief reward, added dessert.

"Dried mango in the Arctic," Senny said. "What a world we live in."

———

If the upper Deh Cho valley is an enormous cathedral, a sheer nave of repeating spruce and rock, then its delta houses every associated cloister and crypt and sacristy and side altar. The river had finally shrunk to reasonable human scale, and we were grateful for it.

In the morning, mist off the water, and a blazing sun above.

It took all day to reach Inuvik, but the time passed more quickly in the tighter channels. I felt as if I could get my head around the delta. I started to wonder what was around the next bend, a feeling I never had on the upper river because the view was too broad, too slow to shift, or simply unchanging. The sun warmed our backs, and we stripped down to our T-shirts, but still wore long underwear and pants and wool socks and boots below, because my toes were still numb in the shade of the canoe even as my face and ears sunburned.

There was almost nowhere to stop. The river was chocolate milk, and the banks were like a trampoline that won't spring back, so we were careful not to stand in one place too long, for fear of breaking into the quicksand. It was easier, we discovered, to take breaks on the water and avoid the mosquitoes. Sun's out, bugs out.

We approached Inuvik in the early afternoon. On the way in, random cliffs sprouted from the tree line, and a few supported extravagant vacation homes, more costly than anything I had seen since entering the Northwest Territories. There were more fishing camps as well, not rotting particleboard shacks but sturdy cabins, each with a satellite dish. There was money in Inuvik, I predicted, though only relatively. The Mackenzie delta is the size of Connecticut, but only forty-five hundred people total live there, in three human settlements.

The largest by far, Inuvik, the Place of Man, is a modern invention, barely a campground in Mackenzie's day, built by the Canadian government over the last several decades. The traditional delta home for the indigenous peoples lies a few dozen miles to the west: Aklavik, Place of the Bear. And Tuktoyaktuk, a small Inuvialuit fishing village, is on the far Arctic coast. Inuvik and Tuk, as everyone calls it, are reachable by road, on the gravel Dempster Highway. The end of the line.

We knew we had reached Inuvik when we spotted the marine debris, rusting freighters tossed onshore. On the side of the river, a long banner hung from a fence: "Welcome Home, 2008." The first sight of the town proper was the power plant, three large mufflers from the diesel generators pointing in the air, and a hum that carried across the water.

We broke from Mackenzie's path and took the brief detour to Inuvik for one reason: to see Kylik Kisoun. He could confirm the charter boat pickup on Garry Island, and I planned to ask for advice on the best route through the delta. I steered our canoe around one tug and then another. Since Hay River, I had seen only three or four barges total plying the river, but here in Inuvik whole squadrons were tied up—the tenders that served the tiny Inuit communities in Nunavut and the Queen Elizabeth Islands—lashed to various industrial docks.

I eventually found the public boat ramp, packed with trucks and clusters of men and women loudly passing bottles in brown bags. A white woman in trendy athletic gear ran past, clearly on her afternoon jog, and she gave us a quizzical look. Senny walked up the gravel boat launch and found a Porta-Potty to sit in, and I turned on my cell phone and called Kylik to let him know we had arrived.

Kylik did not match any of my preconceptions. He rode down to the dock on a bike with fat snow tires, and wore a green skateboarding helmet, a checkered shirt, and a bandanna around his neck. I figured he was in his thirties, though he looked younger; when he took off his helmet, he revealed earrings and a mop of stylish hair. Kylik ran an Arctic charter boat company, but of the two of us I looked like the river rat and he the urban sophisticate.

"You made it! It's been windy lately, but I don't need to tell you, eh?" Kylik said as a greeting, and laughed.

I asked for advice on the best route to Garry Island and handed over our topo map. He looked thoughtfully, carefully folded it into smaller squares, and started tracing tiny twisting curlicues with a borrowed pen. "I want to show you the good ones," he said, explaining his choice of the thinnest blue lines that cut through major islands, avoiding the main channels. "I think wind beats current," he said. "There isn't much current anywhere, but we take the boat through the small ones because it's sheltered."

The route he marked struck north out of Inuvik on the East Channel, then almost immediately ducked into a maze of tiny creeks. At one point, we'd take a shortcut through Richards Island, the largest in the delta, at a place called the Yaya River. Then we were back to the main channel, to Niglintgak Island, in the Kendall Island Migratory Bird Sanctuary, and finally the two open-water crossings, first to a flat unnamed mud patch, then to our destination. It was those last two legs that had made me queasy from the start of planning months ago, and my experience on the river thus far made me even more cautious.

"From here, it's about a hundred miles. When people go out to Garry Island, that's how they do it," Kylik said.

I felt a little better when he said this, as if we were doing something commonplace, and the path would be well trodden.

"Oh, a lot of people go out there?" I asked.

Kylik laughed and made a face. "No!" he said. "One every five years? I've run this business fifteen years, and I've seen three total. But power-boats. In a canoe, never."

On my entire trip, I never did see a single other canoe on the water.

We asked about the Northern store, to restock our larder, but Kylik said it was a long walk into town, so we decided to skip it. Before we left, Kylik and I exchanged cell-phone numbers and confirmed that the inReach could text him using the satellite system. He made me promise that we'd call him for rescue if we got stuck by the weather or found any trouble at all. It might take a few days, he said, but if we hunkered down, their boat could get through eventually. And he repeated the promise he had made me months before: "If you guys can get out to Garry Island, we'll come get you."

I had been saying that to myself as a mantra the whole trip.

That evening, Senny and I made camp a short distance north of Inu-vik, on a silt bar covered in green horsetail grass. With no current and the constant headwind, one hundred miles meant several long days of hard paddling.

The afternoon had been warm and sunny, and thus instilled with hope, I checked the long-term weather report off the satellite. Nothing but strong storms for the next week, sustained winds and rain turning to snow. I made the mistake of showing Senny. "That looks terrifying," he said.

But then I switched to the hour-by-hour forecast, and nestled between predictions of twenty-five-knot winds and high seas, I found a single break. Four days away, for a few hours early one morning, broken clouds and a light easterly breeze. A tailwind, for the last five miles in the Beau-fort Sea.

We had a goal. If we could cover most of the one hundred miles in three days, then we could camp at a launch point just short of the final crossing, wait out the night, and make an attempt. The Deh Cho had provided us a window, but only one.

———

Whenever I awoke that night, the tent looked like it was swaying back and forth, as if I was still in the canoe, matching the rocking of Senny's hips. It wasn't a dream. This rhythmic sensation of our paddles, I had begun to feel it whenever we got onshore. The only difference was now I felt it as I slept as well.

No wonder. I had just passed a thousand miles of paddling.

I lay in my bag and did my morning check-in. My hands were cramped, fingers split and bloody, dirt in every crack. Wrists, elbows, and back sore, tired in a way I had never felt before. During the night, when I woke up swaying, I found my arms bound up, in a palsy position, as if all my muscles and tendons had retracted. I consciously extended them, forcing my biceps out of their contracted state, and when I did, my hands had no strength. I could barely raise my arms, like a stroke victim. Eventually, I dropped them, exhausted, and went back to sleep.

I felt more wasted away than ever. Mackenzie had done this trip at age twenty-seven. I was a dozen years his senior, the age of the old-timer Peter Pond when he crossed the Methye Portage. I used the selfie camera of my phone and saw a stranger, visibly aged. Gaunt. Skin hanging, new creases on my face, eyes sunken, almost given up on hygiene. I looked like my cooking pot, covered in a layer of blackened potato. I gave no more thought to smell or dirt or clean clothes. We were just trying to make it.

And yet, after I stretched and had oatmeal and tea, both doused in honey, my spirits were high. We had a route, a plan, everything was set with Kylik, and we were in sight of the goal. Free from Inuvik, no more towns; since Fort Providence, I felt more comfortable in the wilderness in a tent, where I didn't have to worry about the security of our gear. Other than two bags of pockmarked bagels, we had eaten through all the spoiled food. What remained would be plenty, as long as we weren't wasteful and avoided disaster. We were tired but healthy enough. The river had already soaked us, baked us, blown us around. What else could it do? We had done the work, done our part, and might really make it. We'd at least get a good look at it. You can get anywhere if you have the time.

We launched the canoe and immediately took one of Kylik's secret channels, a narrow creek that split the island's muddy bank. "It's a secret garden," said Senny. "I hope there's nymphs, but not sirens. They're obnoxious."

Senny would be disappointed, because the islands, predictably, held no hidden gems, only the same willow and black spruce and soda-straw reeds. The channels were so narrow I felt as if I could reach out my paddle and touch both shores. Yes, the ways were sheltered, out of the wind, but that meant they were also infested with mosquitoes and offered no good camping, the banks as overgrown as my beard. No side channels—we were on the side channel, after all—meant no peanut-butter-jelly lines to filter water. The few trickles leaking out of the tree line were clogged with dams.

"This stream is rich with beaver," I said.

"Story of my life," Senny said.

The day extended. Initial annoyance at nowhere to stop eventually turned into frustration and then genuine concern. We were nearing the end of the marathon and too tired to paddle all night looking for a camp-site. It's not that there was nowhere good to camp—this was an anxiety I had dealt with every day on the water—but that there was nowhere to camp at all. Even tying off would be a challenge, as the shores were noth-ing but brush and deep reed beds.

Late that night, we pushed out of the small corridor and back into East Channel, miles wide, and found a familiar shelf above the waterline. We started to get out, but a flock of arctic terns attacked us, dive-bombing Senny. It was funny, then unnerving, then downright dangerous, as they snapped and pecked at Senny's head. "Fine! You win, bird," Senny yelled, and we paddled on, finding a small sandy spot on the back of an eddy, festooned with garbage-dump-sized piles of driftwood.

The next day, we passed the Caribou Hills, mounds of dirt that hem in the delta to the east. They bore the last spruce of the boreal forest, an ecosystem that I had first entered thousands of miles away in Ontario. Newfoundland to the Yukon, a giant arc across the continent, the tradi-tional home of the voyageurs, was spent.

The land was opening, and for hours at a time Senny and I paddled down channels flanked by nothing but flooded grass, home to cranes and seagulls, but not a speck of dry land to be found.

At Tununuk Point, the southern tip of the large landmass known as Richards Island, the current momentarily reappeared. We had a tailwind and crossed to the west of Tununuk, near a solitary hill rising from the deep water in the center of the East Channel. It was called Burial Island, and on its northern side was a totally flat beach, like I had not seen in a week.

"I'd camp the fuck out of that," I said to Senny, "even though it's prob-ably haunted by a thousand years of Inuit dead."

"Maybe it's just where they keep their time capsules," Senny said.

We put out the sail and were pushed all the way to the Yaya River. The Yaya was another of Kylik's secret passages, "the good ones," that avoided the wind. While the main channels wound back on themselves, the Yaya went straight north and west, cutting Richards Island in two, like a shortcut to our final destination.

This Deh Cho delta is so large, I thought, *that the islands have their own named rivers.* Rivers within rivers.

Richards Island's hills look like an Irish postcard. The Yaya River itself was green, made not of Deh Cho water but of rain and snow filtered through that gentle island. We stopped at a rocky beach and drank freshwater and made dinner, Vegetarian Chili—with only a few days left we were eating all our favorites—and I stretched my legs by walking up a slope of twisted brush.

It had been sunny for two days. I turned my face to the sky to feel the warmth, but when I did, I saw the return of the mare's tails and mackerel scales. I didn't tell Senny.

We paddled a little farther and found a narrow sandy shelf tucked into a cove, barely big enough for the tent. While I set up camp, Senny scrambled up the slope and then called to me, excited. He had discovered tundra.

Rolling mounds stretched to the horizon. Beauty in miniature, as giant honeybees buzzed like zeppelins over blueberry bushes and soft beds of moss and lupine. Senny found a king-sized section that sank like marshmallow under his feet, and he stretched out, spread eagle. I rested my aching back and stared at the sky. Senny fell sleep in the lichen. I picked at club moss that looked like tiny pine trees laden with black berries, ate one, and then thought better of experimenting with unknown foraging and stopped.

I lay down and considered the perfect blue. Clouds rolled past. The smell was intoxicating, mulched soil and pollen and cracked mint. Warm sun on one side of my face, cool breeze on the other. My head net kept the mosquitoes off, and my brimmed hat shaded the sun from my eyes, and my back, spasmed from a thousand miles of paddling, eased into the moss.

It was a place of peace, the likes of which I had not yet experienced on the river. A moment of pure solemnity.

"This might be worth the whole trip," I said.

"Pretty close," Senny said, groggy. "I feel like I lay down in the soap aisle. With mattresses."

I wanted to sleep all night there, but dark clouds were forming on the horizon, and we needed to take shelter. That night, before bed, I took off my boots and warmed my feet in the sand and I knew it would be the last time.

The storms returned before morning. All night, waves beat against our low beach, and I felt the tent rocking. But there was an odd sound as well, water breaking on the side of the boat, and finally I got up to discover the canoe, which had been up on the sandy beach when we crawled in our bags, was now in the water and tugging at its emergency line. The storm had washed away half our campsite, including the sand under the boat. I dragged the canoe higher, set it in the bushes, and then had trouble sleeping, for fear that the ground beneath us might wash away too.

In the morning, the mosquitoes were huddled in the vestibule of the tent for warmth. I checked my watch and the weather off the inReach. The window was still there. If all went according to plan, in thirty hours we'd be on Garry Island, though we might not sleep much between now and then.

———

All morning, a capricious cold rain fell from black clouds that crisscrossed erratically overhead. Richards Island fell away behind us, leaving only reeds and marsh and rude tongues of mud. All headwind, no current, we gutted it out, sweating through layers. Fortunately, I was wearing so many clothes I couldn't smell myself. We were in the Middle Channel, the river's main effort and as wide as ever; no more sheltering possible for our final push to the launch point that night.

Gray cranes squawked at us when we stopped to eat lunch on their nesting island. "They sound like a rusty swing set," said Senny. The delta was running out, and we had entered the mucky Kendall Island Migratory Bird Sanctuary, the first designated park I had encountered. The Deh Cho, for the majority of its length, doesn't need a legal designation to declare itself wilderness.

That afternoon, the clouds broke briefly and, high in the sky, again nothing but mare's tails and mackerel scales.

As we struggled to the mouth of the Deh Cho—or one of many mouths, the river like a Hydra as so many channels found the sea—the view stretched again into incomprehensibility. No more of the delta's human scale, it was as if we were back on Mills Lake at the start of the trip, the far shore a thin green line, and the horizon and sky merged into a slate nothingness.

We hugged the shore; only a few miles left to our last camp. We expended so much effort struggling against the headwind we were down to our T-shirts, steam rising from Senny's shoulders. Then the rain returned. The storm came from the south and chased us, as they had when Jeremy and I paddled the mountains. Invisible silt bars rose from the riverbed to suction at our boat. Lightning flashed in the distance, as if every plague was determined to strike one last time. Hot, then cold, then wind, tempest, alone on the vast river. Our pace was a crawl, buffeting wind in our faces, and the deluge soaked Senny and me through our gear and down to the skin.

The delta was ever widening, the gaps between islands growing, and as the view opened, as river became ocean, that's when I saw it, out in the bay, the natural summit of our river descent.

There stands Garry Island tall on the horizon. It was enormous, a black mountain rising from the sea.

THE HIGHEST PART OF THE ISLAND, JULY 1789

~~~~~~~

Alexander Mackenzie had no idea what to do. They were well above the Arctic Circle, approaching the Hyperborean Sea, not the Pacific. They were entering the land of Esquimaux with few men and minimal armament. And worst of all, they had no fresh food, and their pemmican was running out.

"It is my Opinion, as well as my Mens, that . . . we would not be able to get to the Athabasca this Season by Water," Mackenzie wrote. Not that they didn't have the time before winter set in, but rather "our want of Provision would prevent us."

Their new Quarreller guide was "quite discouraged and tired of his Situation" and, anyway, had never been as far as the sea. He only knew the route to "Esquimaux lake," an inland body of water where those people "pass the summer." When it came to managing food stocks, Steinbruck could be petty, surly, mean-spirited; even when wintering over at fur-trading posts, in typical annual deprivation, he was vocally sarcastic in his complaints about food. Without sufficient stores or a knowledgeable guide, the Chipewyan hunters grew despondent as well; Mackenzie was "confident were it in their power they would leave me, as they are quite disgusted with the Voyage."

The hunters had been unsuccessful for days. They didn't know where they were going. So continue into the unknown land of the Esquimaux, and hope to hunt supper? Or return to the meager country behind them, knowing they lacked the food to make it back to Fort Chipewyan? "Our pemmican has been mouldy this long time past, but in our Situation we must eat it & not loose a particle of it," Mackenzie said.

In the north, the voyageurs said it was the Windigo that came for desperate men. Yes, they could forage. They had all staved off hunger pangs with the root of the licorice plant, or boiled *tripe de roche*, moss scraped from rocks, to make bouillon and tea. But when even those measures failed, when their moccasins were roasted and tunic fringes chewed, the creature with a heart of ice would hunt them, and inhabit their bodies, and force them to commit unspeakable crimes.

Awgeenah and his wives knew that anyone who ate human flesh must be killed or his disease of the mind would spread. It was everyone's duty, even the women's, to use knives and hatchets to cut cannibals into small pieces, or to grind their bones to dust and burn their bodies with fire. This must be done immediately, even to one's own family. Anything less and the cannibals would return to life in a reanimated form. Once, a whole clan of these undead Windigos removed their frozen hearts from their own bodies and hid them in a hole, and the monsters could not be killed until the organs were found and dashed apart.

"I determined to go to the discharge of those Waters," Mackenzie said; they had come this far and would try to confirm what lay ahead, leave no more white space on the map of this river. Still, Mackenzie knew that ultimately their stomachs must rule the day. In a concession to the doubters in his party, Mackenzie "satisfied them a little by telling them I would go on but 7 Days more, and that if I did not come to the Sea in that time I should return." This quieted some grumbling, though Mackenzie readily admitted it was practicality, not compromise, that formed his mind. "My scarcity of Provisions will make me fulfil this promise, whether I will or not."

Awgeenah and the Indians nodded their grudging assent, but Barrieau and the voyageurs needed no encouragement and continued to lust for the journey. "They love to breathe a free air, they are early accustomed to a wandering life; it has charms for them, which make them forget past dangers and fatigues, and . . . leads them to undertake and execute what would appear impossible to others," wrote Father Pierre-François-Xavier de Charlevoix about the voyageurs of his flock in 1740. On this journey, few portages burdened Ducette and de Lorme, Landry had steered worse rapids, Barrieau had guided rockier streams. The fur trade life produced strength, endurance, and joviality. Happy warriors.

Three roads lay before them. A smaller branch to the west, the biggest waterway at center, a narrow eastern corridor. Now that it was obvious he was stuck coming along, their Quarreller guide had an opinion of where to go. "Our Conductor was for taking the Eastmost, on account as he said that the Esquimaux were close by on that Road," Mackenzie said. Their guide was scared of the Esquimaux and now wanted to seek them out? Was he trying to get them all killed? Ambushed and escape in the confusion?

Mackenzie chose otherwise. "I determined upon taking the middle as it was a large piece of Water and running N & S." If they were short on food and truly headed to the Hyperborean, they would do it on the shortest route possible.

———

They pushed north, the current still surprisingly strong in the twisting channel. The view was wider than any they had seen since the mouth at Slave Lake, the overcast sky and cold water merging in a single tableau. Ducks and cranes honked overhead and hid among the waterlogged reeds, though the hunters had no luck killing any. On a dry shelf, they found clear signs in the mud of three campments. "Our Conductor says they were Esquimaux," Mackenzie wrote.

The evidence of Esquimaux occupation grew. "We landed at a plain where we observed some of the Natives had been lately," Mackenzie said. "I counted the places of upwards of 30 Fires and some of the Men went further where they saw many more." Poles were stuck in the river to string nets for a fishery, and among the ashes lay pieces of whalebone and leather and scraps from the construction of small canoes, stone kettles and strips of bark plaited into thread. The place was marked with a lobstick, a spruce tree relieved of its branches except for the very crown, a signal visible from far away. They moved quickly on.

The trees fell away, and then even the willow bushes as well. "On several Islands we saw the print of their Feet on the Sand, running after wild Fowls, and by appearance not 3 Days ago." On another they found three huts of driftwood and dried grass that sheltered strange holes dug in the ground, covered with willow and just large enough for a man. "I suppose serves for a Bed for all the Family," Mackenzie guessed, without confidence. Nearby lay net buoys of poplar, and sledge runners for winter, and tree stumps to dry fish, and again they pressed on, before the occupants would return.

"All day we expected that we should meet with some of the Natives," Mackenzie wrote, but they never did.

Cold rain forced them to shore that afternoon, "the Weather raw and very disagreeable," which put the Chipewyan "in a very bad Humor." They made camp and, despite the chill and damp, sat up and discussed the remainder of the journey. Their Quarreller guide said that "we will see the lake tomorrow" and that "it is not a small one." His people knew nothing of that water, except that "the Esquimaux live about it, that they kill a large Fish in it which they eat." In summer, the Esquimaux traveled to the east, to a place called Kitigaaryuit. Each hunter wielded his own harpoon, marked with his own symbol. They killed the giant beasts out in the bay and then, to haul them back to camp, drove a pipe into their bodies, blew air into the carcass so it would float, and then tied it off to their boats to drag in.

From this description, Mackenzie guessed this fish must be a whale, but the Quarreller man also told stories of Esquimaux canoes so large they held five families, and of bears the color of snow, and of other monsters with tusks that defied translation by Awgeenah.

"The toil of our navigation was incessant." In only two days, they made a week's worth of Quarreller travel. They were miserable with damp cold, had yet to kill fresh game, and the next day they would attempt to reach the ocean. Mackenzie decided to try to "cheer their fainting spirits." He gave out presents, a warm moose skin to their guide, and one of his very own long hooded coats to Awgeenah.

This gift to Awgeenah was not about comfort. It was a ceremonious act that forever bonded the two men. In stature, achievement, influence, Awgeenah had now surpassed all other Chipewyan traders, even his mentor Matonabbee. For as befitted his status and station, only the English Chief wore the coats of Samuel Hearne, Peter Pond, and Alexander Mackenzie.

It rained all night, and nothing broke the cold. The blowing wind scoured the land, which was "high and covered with short Grass and many Plants, which are in Blossom." Mackenzie thought the whole country "has a beautiful appearance, tho' an odd contrast, the Hills covered with Flowers and Verdure, and the Vallies full of Ice and Snow." The skeletons of sea creatures were heaped on the banks, animals like Mackenzie had never seen, "part of two big Heads" that he determined to be "Sea Horses."

The current was "yet very strong" but branching between islands that grew ever more distant; no obvious path presented itself. "We embarked, tho' we did not know what course to steer, our Guide being as ignorant in this Country as any of ourselves." It was a frozen empty place. "The Earth is not thawed above 4 Inches from the Surface, below is a solid Body of Ice," Mackenzie wrote. The skies opened, and he took a reading with his quadrant and calculated they were past 69 degrees latitude. The waves and water felt to him as "to be the Entrance of the Lake," and they pushed farther on, with the unremitting flow of the river, making for "a high point about 8 Miles distant," and then for the next mound, and the next.

The brown water was so wide as to become the bay, and the bare mud banks dissolved to an archipelago of drowned hulks, like the prone bodies of leviathans rotting for the ages. For forty days, they had worked their way ever north and west, nearly five hundred leagues, and now beyond lay only Hyperborea.

For ahead they saw a single "high Island and the most Western land in sight distant 15 Miles." They had finally run out of river.

This was the last push. The trees had failed, and in the plain hills on the sea Mackenzie could see something of the Isle of Lewis, his childhood home. There, the grasslands. There, the moors. There, between him and the last island, the Minch.

Awgeenah once told Mackenzie the story of his people. This is what he said:

At the first, the globe was one vast and entire ocean, inhabited by no living creature, except a mighty bird, whose eyes were fire, whose glances were lightning, and the clapping of whose wings were thunder. On his descent to the ocean, and touching it, the earth instantly arose, and remained on the surface of the waters.

The great bird, having finished his world, made an arrow, which was to be preserved with great care, and to remain untouched; but that [we] were so devoid of understanding, as to carry it away; and the sacrilege so enraged the great bird, that he has never since appeared.

Immediately after [our] death, [we] pass into another world, where [we] arrive at a large river, on which [we] embark in a stone canoe, and that a gentle current bears [us] on to an extensive lake, in the centre of which is a most beautiful island.

In the view of this delightful abode, [we] receive that judgement for [our] conduct during life, which terminates [our] final state and unalterable allotment. If [our] good actions are declared to predominate, [we] are landed upon the island, where there is to be no end to [our] happiness.

But if [our] bad actions weigh down the balance, the stone canoe sinks at once, and leaves [us] up to our chins in the water, to behold and regret the rewards enjoyed by the good, and eternally struggling, but with unavailing endeavors, to reach the blissful island from which [we] are excluded for ever.

———————

Island in sight, they launched their canoes into the choppy near sea. The way was open, though beyond "we could see the Lake covered with Ice at about 2 Leagues distance and no land ahead."

The last crossing to the last island passed easily. The water grew ever more shallow, voyageurs' paddles struck bottom, and then they were out of the boats and wading ashore. Gulls circled overhead. It was five o'clock, and Mackenzie immediately ordered the hungry men to put out fishery nets to catch their supper. As Steinbruck pitched his tent, Mackenzie explored the hummocks, blown by a ceaseless wind. He found nests of ptarmigan eggs, and white owls, and the graves of an Esquimaux marked by the man's harpoon and double-bladed paddle, and his Chipewyan hunters reported caches of boiled whale blubber and the bleached bones of massive bears.

A few old Esquimaux huts crumbled away on the eastern point, but otherwise the island was abandoned, and they were the only souls upon it. Mackenzie named the place Whale Island, and despite the exotic and completely novel nature of their destination he could not help feeling discouragement. "My Men express much sorrow that they are obliged to return without seeing the Sea," he said of their desire to reach the Pacific. In this, "I believe them sincere for we marched exceeding hard coming down the River, and I never heard them grumble; but on the contrary in good Sprits, and in hopes every day that the next would bring them to the *mer d'Ouest,* and declare themselves now and at any time ready to go with me wherever I choose to lead them."

But where was that? Where had they ended up? Mackenzie called to Awgeenah, and the men began to hike.

"I went with the English Chief to the highest part of the Island from which we could see the Ice in a whole Body extending from S.W. by Compass to the Eastward as far as we could see."

This was surely the girdle of impenetrable ice that encircled the North Pole. All learned geographers agreed that the warm and open Hyperborean Sea was guarded by this pack of floes. If that ice extended even to the mouth of this river in the warmth of July, then the way was perpetually blocked. This was no highway to Russia and China. It was a taunting dead-end road, a cruel plug in the mouth of all of his commercial aspirations.

Mackenzie had failed. This northwest passage would be forever encased in ice.

"We were stopped by the Ice ahead," he concluded, "and we landed at the limit of our Travels."

And that is the story of how Alexander Mackenzie traveled the river that would bear his name, and how Awgeenah, the English Chief, his Chipewyan partner in all things, the heir to Matonabbee who became the greatest of "the great travelers of the known world," stood on the shore of the Arctic Ocean for a second time.

26

A SEA OF ICE, FROZEN NO MORE, JULY 2016

〰〰〰

Mackenzie had named it Whale Island. Modern geographers call it Garry, though for many years both islands appeared on maps; World War II–era aerial photography finally proved them one and the same. Whatever the name, it was finally in sight, though still eight miles ahead. Niglintgak Island, our planned staging point, lay immediately to our left. It looked perfect on the map, but now that we had arrived, Niglintgak was revealed to be swampy and reed choked, nowhere to stop at all. So we crossed the river, against the whitecaps, and tried the opposite shore, a flat mud shelf three feet above the river. Pitching in the surf, I held the canoe against the permafrost wall while Senny crawled up.

"It's a prairie. It looks like Mongolia!" he yelled back through the rain.

I tied the boat off, poked my head over the lip of the island, and saw Senny was right. The island was a thatch-colored grassland stretching to the horizon, not a single geographic feature to break the gusting north wind. Nearby, though, lay a hefty driftwood log, a star-shaped root ball with a burned trunk that resembled the stub of a cigar. No tree grew to such a size for hundreds of miles; I realized that it must have floated down the river all the way from a forest fire in the mountains of British Columbia. We set up camp on the leeward side of that lone trunk, tying off the tent to the splayed roots to keep us from blowing away.

Everything soaked, we were too tired to cook, and so we ate a cold dinner from the remaining sundries: soggy tortillas, bruised apples, dried apricots, trail mix, chocolate, candy peach rings, venison jerky, pemmican. Senny read that last package intently. "Oh, good, it's gluten-free," he said.

My long johns and knit hat were wet, my wool socks were wet, every wicking high-tech layer was wet; the only dry piece of gear I had was my sleeping bag. Senny was in the same situation, and with a howling and freezing wind, we crawled into bed early. Then we heard a rumbling outside.

"That's a powerboat," I said to Senny.

I stuck my head out of the tent, and there, right offshore, was an idling Lund with three Inuvialuit hunters on board. Two middle-aged men and a teenager, wearing fluorescent-yellow rain jackets and pants. All three looked curious but unconcerned, despite the pitching of their boat.

"You guys okay, eh?" the man at the helm said. Or I thought he said. Between the storm and his accent, it was hard to tell.

"Yes, thank you," I called out.

"Where you guys going?"

"Garry Island, tomorrow."

"Oh," he said, like that was the answer he expected. "We're hunting beluga tomorrow. See you there." And then he drove the boat away.

"Did he really say he'd meet us out there?" Senny asked.

"That can't possibly be right," I said, and we zipped the tent back up.

I was a bit unnerved by the visit, and sleep left me, so I wrote the day's events in my journal; checking the map, I realized the island we were camping on had no name.

"What should we call this place?" I asked. Senny was lying on his back, eyes closed. He shrugged.

"I think we should call it Senny Island," I said. He smiled at my joke.

"Do you remember that crossing at the Thunder River and the lunch that ended the War Against the Weather?" Senny asked. He said it like it was capitalized, a military campaign he had fought in, reminiscing already about a time little more than a week past. "We built a fire, had tea. It was nice. We need one of those lunches again."

"No more lunches, Senny," I said. "Tomorrow we cross."

The forecast had not changed all week: between nine o'clock and noon, thirty-eight degrees, ten-knot winds from the east. That predicted window had proved stubborn and fixed, and we had a shot at the thing, if we could ride out the night's gale.

The frigid north wind off the Beaufort Sea pelted rain against the tent. We did not sleep. We merely passed the night, prone in our bags, shivering until morning.

———

The next day looked the same as every other day. It was July 30, but the sun still never set, barely dipped to twilight. Ostensibly the days should have been growing shorter, but I had paddled north in equal measure to the earth's orbit, and so the proportion of sunlight in each of my days had remained unchanged since I got in the canoe.

Now, though, our destination lay in sight. Which is to say, I had hope that the timelessness would soon end.

You can get anywhere if you have the time.

The morning was cold and overcast but dry, and the wind had slackened just within tolerance. Rain had become sleet in the wee hours, and I got up long enough to make sure the ends of the tent were still anchored and our gear had not blown into the sea.

"It was expensive, but this has been a good tent," I said to Senny in the morning.

"So far," he said, as if there was still time for it to betray us.

I tried to make tea, but my numb fingers barely functioned, skin cracking anew between my knuckles so my hands bled. My gloves had rotted through, my palms were exposed, and they provided little warmth. Without wood to start a cooking fire, I used our emergency backup gas stove, and broke a box worth of matches trying to light it. The canoe had filled with rainwater, so we had to unload everything, dump it, and then pack again from scratch. That seemed appropriate, somehow. I brushed my teeth and felt better, as David said. Senny and I didn't speak much, bundled in layers of Gore-Tex and wool, and then we broke camp and pushed off.

The drizzle started right away. Then a wave front hit, surprising in the low wind; I figured it to be ugly disorganized chop left over from the storm the night before. Dark clouds hung all around, but the sky was lighter ahead. Senny wanted to follow a small channel to the left, which we did, staying close to shore.

Despite the slosh, I felt confident. I had been nervous about this last leg from the initial planning months ago, but now that we were here, I felt calm. There were two crossings, three miles to an unnamed island, then one and a half to Garry. I couldn't see it, but I knew Garry Island was there, hidden behind the profile of our first target. We had made crossings of similar length on the main river, and the weather was scheduled to cooperate. Plus, I was a much better canoeist now. We had survived all the plagues. Whether the Deh Cho let us cross or not, I was content.

The shore of our prairie-island ran out. "You ready, Senny?" I asked. He grunted, and I turned the nose of the canoe out into the sea and we began our *grande traverse*.

I thought of Mackenzie and Awgeenah and their flotillas of birch-bark canoes. The challenge of reaching Garry Island had not changed significantly in 230 years. True, we had a fancy GPS and life vests, but Senny and I had a much smaller boat and were all by ourselves, and in that moment I felt both vulnerabilities acutely.

Our topo map said the first section was shallow, and the forecast promised light easterly winds, so we knew this was the easy crossing and the hardest test would come on the final approach to Garry.

But as we got out into the bay, the north wind—north, not east, I thought, too late—only grew, until it was screaming in my ears. The surf never faded, the whitecaps rose, I pushed my paddle down into the water and never struck bottom, and that's when I realized that our official government map and the revered forecast were both wrong.

The whitecaps came in at forty-five degrees, threatening to snatch our gunnel, just as they had when we nearly capsized above the Thunder River. I angled the nose to cut the waves, but then the rain began to stick, frozen sleet, and my hands were still numb, though maybe from gripping the paddle. We were out in it, but it didn't smell like salt. It smelled fresh, and I understood why; though we had reached the point where the river and ocean and north wind were finally all free to collide head-on, still the Deh Cho was triumphant, dumping half a continent of freshwater into the sea, defeating a thousand miles of fetch. The waves tumbled against the gunwale, and Senny paddled like a machine. Our battered canoe twisted along all three axes. If we flipped we'd live—I knew that, I repeated it over and over—but what a swim it would be to shore. We'd activate the beacon and then sit, cold and wet, for days maybe, until Kylik could make it through the weather.

All these thoughts, the waves and the wind and the swim, spun in my head as my muscles kept the nose of the canoe true. Senny and I didn't speak a single word on the crossing, not a peep, until almost an hour later, when we approached the far shore.

"That wasn't shallow," I finally said.

"Nope," he said.

"Or calm."

"That was terrifying," he said, and we left it there, because the harder crossing was still to come.

As we curled around that unnamed mud clod, though, Garry Island reappeared, and suddenly it looked so close we could touch it. I pulled out the pouch of tobacco, and emptied it in the water. "Deh Cho, here's the rest of the Red Man," I said.

"Please don't be offended," Senny said quickly.

But the worst was behind us, and we knew it, because the eastern-most leg of Garry Island was a stone's throw away. There was no pomp or ceremony as we paddled the final fifteen minutes of the journey. As we approached our goal, as we completed the crossing I long feared, we laughed and joked. Because what did we see on the point directly ahead? A hunter's bush cabin.

I felt as if I had just found a yak pen on the top of Everest. The wood-framed hut was skinned with plastic sheeting, and next to it was a teepee frame to build a smokehouse. We had heard the hunters right the night before, I realized. Like so many "discoverers" before me, I had traveled to a place I considered one of the most remote on the planet, and what I found was another person's home.

I swung the boat through the strait and then lined it square to the gravel beach. Without consultation, Senny and I both dug in with our paddles. Finish the race strong. The bow of the canoe hit, scraped up the beach, and Senny jumped out and pulled us forward as he had for weeks. I waded to shore, sat on a driftwood log, put my head in my hands, and wept.

"I just need to sit a minute, I'm so tired," I said. "But I'll take a Snickers, if you're getting one."

———

There was no one home at the cabin. After so much time alone, it felt weird to camp next to a building—we didn't want to be rude and crowd the hunters if they came back—so a few minutes after landing, Senny and I got back in the boat and hooked around the island. We picked a spot a few hundred yards away, beaching the canoe among huge piles of driftwood, so much wood it was as if Garry had a magnet for the stuff.

I needed to walk, so Senny and I hiked up Mackenzie and Awgeenah's hill to get a better view of the ocean. To the west, the island stretched on and on in a wedge, a carpet of orange moss and pale green lichen, small bushes that dug themselves holes to escape the wind. We tromped the incline, and the land fell away as cliffs to our south, a wide bay to the north. The whole thing smelled unexpectedly rich and earthy as we balanced on unsure footing, tussock to tussock, like soft sand. Up the slope, we gained a ridge and looked out, our faces to the north wind.

We saw open water. Not a sliver of ice anywhere. The ocean was not a shocking polar blue, as you imagine from the movies. It was dull, the color of a worn-out coffee mug, all the way to the northern horizon.

Senny didn't bother to pull out his camera. "Photos never look like eyeballs, which drives me nuts," he said. So I put my camera away too, and we just took in the view together.

I knew it was likely I would see open water—since 1980, summer pack ice in the Arctic is down 80 percent, as the whole region warms twice as fast as the rest of the planet—but it was still unsettling, knowing how the ice completely shaped Mackenzie's experience. I had only seen that single dirty lump just south of Tsiigehtchic, but for Mackenzie the ice was definitive. And permanent, because the climate was fixed; the concept that it could change was more fantastical than his giant sea horses.

I checked my GPS and took a photograph of the screen. It read 69 degrees 26.5 minutes north, "the extent of our travels," as Mackenzie said. In 1915, Ernest Shackleton's famous ship, the *Endurance*, was crushed in the ice, near Antarctica, at 69 degrees 5 minutes south. In that context, it really felt like we had accomplished something.

All I had done, though, after 1,125 miles of paddling, was make it to a place that Mackenzie did not want to be. My success was his failure. There was no pot of Chinese gold waiting for him at the end of this journey. He would return empty-handed.

And yet, I had just canoed his Northwest Passage. The way is open. Mackenzie was simply two hundred years too early.

Senny and I decided to fire the bear banger for the first time, a victory volley as the voyageurs did. We screwed in the flare, pointed it in the air, pulled the trigger, and nothing happened. I pulled again. Click. Senny tried, and it finally fired on the third go.

"Good thing we never had to use it for real," he said.

I sent Kylik a message on the inReach. If you can make it out there, we'll come get you, he had said so many months ago. I texted him the good news, and I got a message back in only a moment, beamed from the satellite.

"We will be there."

————

We passed two days on that island, waiting for the charter boat, sitting by a fire on a rock beach at the end of the world.

Not a single bit of land lay between us and the pole, and the north wind never relented. Senny and I used large driftwood logs to hold down the sides of the tent. We filtered the water and drank deeply. It was fresh Deh Cho water, no salt, not a hint of brackishness. When it was raining, snowing, sleeting, we slept. When it was dry, we restoked the fire and simply sat next to it, silently. A hundred years' worth of driftwood lay around us, an island full of bones, and we built the fire generously; when it grew very hot, the wet rocks beneath boiled and exploded. I cooked valedictory Pad Thai, our favorite dinner, and Senny skipped stones in the sea.

I grabbed a few bags of tea, as a gift, and walked over to the Inuvialuit shack, but there was still no one there. It did not appear recently lived in. The shit bucket was frozen tight. Fish drying racks were empty. No blood on the rickety butcher table or two *ulus*, their traditional skinning knives.

So I returned to our fire, ate whenever I felt hungry, and when the snow returned, I slunk back in my bag and slept.

The last afternoon, I took a walk alone, along the base of the island's southern cliffs. The beach was made of sand and silt and gravel, and I saw bear tracks imprinted in the mud. I wondered what he ate, this bear, and where he slept, and I laughed to myself, that he had been born in the very place I worked so hard to get to.

Does the bear walk and wonder at his fortune to be on this island at this time? Or, like me, does it come upon him an absolute necessity to move?

No, of course not. How foolish.

I followed the bear tracks for a while, along that lonesome beach, but eventually they turned inland, attained the slope, and disappeared.

27

Many Returns

‿‿‿‿‿

Mackenzie slept four nights on Whale Island. The tide came in and soaked their baggage and they moved farther up the beach. His men spotted white whales in the distance, and Mackenzie grabbed several voyageurs to launch the canoes and pursue them, but fog came in and they nearly wrecked the boats on the ice floes and returned to camp with two men bailing for their lives. "Never was happier than when we got safe to Land."

Just hunting for dinner had proven a near catastrophe; how could trade ever transit such floes? Later polar explorers would fall in love with the ice, the echoes, the bare hues, the extreme majesty of it all. Not Mackenzie. He was a practical man. All he saw was the barrier to commerce and progress.

They were hungry, short on pemmican, short on time to return to Fort Chipewyan, and so Mackenzie "engraved the latitude of the Place, My own Name & the Number of Men with me & the time we had been here" on a wooden post and drove it into the spongy ground, and then he ordered his brigade south and they paddled back up the river.

No white man would stand on that island, or anywhere in the Deh Cho delta, for three decades. In that time, the Esquimaux called it home and thrived as they had for ten thousand years.

It would take Mackenzie and his party two full months to get home. For the first time on the journey, the river beat at the noses of their boats, and once back within its banks their Quarreller guide deserted. Progress was slow, but the Chipewyan hunters' luck finally improved. They snared a few fish and waterfowl, and then, salvation: two caribou. They gorged for the struggle ahead. For weeks, there was so much current they were forced to tow the boats while walking onshore. "We make much more way with the Line than Paddle," Mackenzie wrote. The jagged rocks were unforgiving; the men constantly wore holes in their leather moccasins, and so the four women, floating in the canoes while the men pulled, stitched them a new pair of shoes every single day. When violent summer storms raged, they "were obliged to throw ourselves flat upon the ground to escape being hurt by Stones that were hurled about by the Air like Sand."

Mackenzie would not let go of the promise of the Northwest Passage, and so he perpetually interrogated the Indians he met on where to find the true river of the west. Nothing but frustration came of it. "I made the English Chief ask them some Questions which they did not, or pretended not, to understand." Some said that a river lay on the other side of the mountains, but that it was guarded by giants who "have Wings but don't fly" and are "very wicked and kill Common Men with their Eyes." None knew more than conjecture and hearsay, and they refused to accompany Mackenzie over the mountains to search for the river that "ran towards the Midday Sun." When Mackenzie persisted with the idea anyway, they begged Awgeenah to stay, saying that "if he should go he should be killed." Mackenzie stewed at the lack of cooperation. That night, when one of the Indian dogs scavenged his provisions, he shot it dead. Awgeenah was in no better humor, saying that "it is hard to have come so far" and not return with plunder; the Dogrib "hide all their Goods and Young Women."

Their pemmican ran out, and they had to eat mashed corn, their final staple. "Yesterday the Heat was insupportable, and today we can't put clothes enough on to keep us warm," Mackenzie said. And ever, the river current hampered all progress. "All Day upon the line."

Finally, after weeks of upriver labor and recalcitrant Indians, Mackenzie could stand it no more. He was convinced that a path to the Pacific lay just over the mountains flanking their western view. So they stopped to camp early, and Mackenzie enlisted one of the Chipewyan hunters, his voyageurs "being more fatigued than curious," and hiked directly toward the closest, highest peak. The trees were so thick they had trouble forcing their way through; three hours of labor and the mountains "appear'd as far from us as when we had seen them from the River." Mackenzie pressed on anyway and fell into a marsh "up to the Arm Pits & with some difficulty extricated myself. I found it impossible to proceed." He and the hunter retreated, beaten, under a sky full of stars. Summer was spent, and darkness ruled midnight again.

The party started to fracture. Mackenzie broke up a fight between Barrieau and Landry; frustrated by the hard labor, they "wanted to land to see who was the best man." A rifle fell overboard, from careless exhaustion. One of the hunters mocked Barrieau for his method of paddling, and another became "too intimate" with one of Awgeenah's wives. Throughout their trek, Mackenzie had consciously kept the voyageurs separate from the women, lest the English Chief grow jealous and despondent, and now, just as he feared, Awgeenah fell into a stupor at the news that his wife had taken a new lover. Like his patron Matonabbee, Awgeenah lost interest in the journey.

Awgeenah told Mackenzie he was finished, was abandoning this errand to find the river of the west. Awgeenah refused to help Mackenzie coax fleeing Dogrib or interpret their words. He worried that if Mackenzie got some promising lead on the Pacific, the Scot might wish to set out that very moment, though August was wearing on. Awgeenah said he only wished to return home, collect his debts, winter along Slave Lake. At one camp, the fleeing Slavey and Dogrib had left behind their property, and rather than give chase, Awgeenah and his men began to divide the goods up for themselves. When Mackenzie intervened, "the English Chief was very much displeased that I had reproach'd him, and told me so." But Mackenzie was ready to fight. "I had waited for such an Opportunity to tell him what I thought of his Behavior to me for some time past, told him that I had more reason to be angry than he."

After all, Mackenzie was the one with so much to lose: a business and geographic achievement, the fortune that would go with it, his reputation with the North West Company. He told Awgeenah that he "had come a great way at great Expense to no Purpose."

Mackenzie continued to light into Awgeenah, accusing him of dishonesty, laziness, jealousy. Months of frustrations boiled over. But the English Chief then "got into a most violent Passion" and said he would paddle no farther. Though he had no ammunition, he would rather live with the Slavey people on that river than travel with Mackenzie one more moment. "As soon as he was done his harangue he began to cry bitterly, and his Relations help'd him," Mackenzie wrote. "I did not interrupt them in their Grief for two Hours."

That night, when both men had cooled their tempers, Mackenzie invited Awgeenah to his tent, to eat dinner and drink rum alone. "I gave him a Dram or two and we were as good friends as ever." Awgeenah said that he would not leave after all, that he would continue to act as Mackenzie's good partner and even continue to trade furs with him. But he "had shed tears," and in order "to wipe away that disgrace," he would very soon "go to War after the Crees," as was the tradition of his people, to regain his stature. "Gave him a little grog to carry to his Tent to drown his chagrin," Mackenzie said. A flippant act, and a friendly one, but also a final toast.

Awgeenah had been clear. Mackenzie had his goal, to reach the Pacific, but Awgeenah did not share it. The Chipewyan chief had his own purpose and would pursue it, and soon their paths would diverge.

There was still a month of hard travel ahead. They survived violent storms on Slave Lake, and then Awgeenah and his wives and hunters took their leave. The remainders pressed on, their provisions spent, their canoes broken and patched, their clothes "almost rotten." It snowed by the end. Mackenzie was exhausted.

The party landed at Fort Chipewyan on September 12, 1789, "102 days since we had left this place," Mackenzie wrote, to end his journal.

At the next summer's *rendezvous,* he caught up on news. George Washington had been inaugurated president, and while Mackenzie sat on Whale Island—Tuesday, July 14, 1789—the French had stormed the Bastille in revolution.

Conspicuously, though, conversation among the North West Company *bourgeois* did not surround his journey the year before.

"My Expedition is hardly spoken of, but this is what I expected," Alexander wrote to Roderic. But why should it, when it had failed so spectacularly?

For him, he wrote, it was nothing but a "voyage down the River Disappointment."

———

The Inuvialuit charter boat arrived late in the day and idled well offshore, so as not to ground itself on the sandbars surrounding Garry Island. So Senny and I got soaked one last time, filling our canoe with gear and then walking it into the shallows, to cross load each piece onto the charter's deck and strap it in place. The canoe went on last, lashed to the top of the cabin as one would use a car's roof rack.

Kylik Kisoun's promise to come get us had fortified many an hour of our trip. And yet on the day in question, he didn't even pilot the boat. Kylik was busy in Tuktoyaktuk, so his uncle, Gerry Kisoun, fetched us instead. As soon as we got on board, Gerry gave us reindeer dry meat and fresh-baked bannock from his wife; Senny and I ate every crumb. Gerry is of mixed Inuvialuit and Gwich'in heritage, a former park ranger and police officer turned guide, though still a protector of the land. "Right now, you can drink that water," he said, "you can walk that hill, you can breathe that air. We want to keep it that way."

Gerry has a round soft face and thick hands and never stopped speaking in an earnest and clear voice. He's spent most of his life in the delta, and on our way back to Inuvik told stories in an unceasing stream: how to hunt beluga in small open boats, digging into the permafrost to find solid ice to store game, and the details of their traditional Christmas feast, Anglican ham on the holiday, but muktuk, raw whale, the night before.

Gerry said that in decades past, he occasionally made the trip to Garry Island, to drop off a man he called "the ice doctor." Kisoun was talking about J. Ross Mackay, one of the greatest Arctic scientists of his generation, who had died only two years before at the age of ninety-eight. From 1954 to 2011, Mackay spent part of every year, winter and summer, in the western Arctic. He built a field cabin on Garry Island in 1964, covering the area in sensors to measure the temperature belowground. In the winter, via snowmobile, Kisoun would drop off Mackay at the cabin, retrieving him weeks later. Over the summer, Mackay's research shifted to measuring the speed of the thaw.

"He would go looking for the permafrost and have trouble finding it," Kisoun told me. "Mackay used to say, 'You can put your ear to the ground anywhere in the western Arctic, and if you wait long enough, you'll hear the earth crack.'"

Garry Island lies one hundred miles from Inuvik, and it took more than five hours for us to navigate the delta back to town. Gerry showed us the old reindeer crossings, the oil-drilling sites that were being reclaimed and cleaned, and had a thousand anecdotes on how the weather was changing. The latest happened only two weeks before. On July 15, 2016, the beach at Tuk boasted the warmest water in Canada. Gerry was so confounded that he told me three times. "Twenty-two point two degrees Celsius!" he said, having committed the exact number to memory. "Can you believe it! The warmest in Canada."

It was midnight, the deep orange sun still blazing overhead, by the time Gerry docked in Inuvik. The town is big, over three thousand people, and we got a ride to a modest hotel, a modular prefab box on stilts. I wanted so badly to sleep in a bed, but I was absolutely filthy: put a butter knife to my skin and scrape and you'd pull up a layer of grease thick enough to cook with. So I took a shower, then crawled into the lone double bed, next to Senny.

It was two or three o'clock in the morning. Outside our hotel window, a softball game raged, the players cheering every run.

The next morning, Senny and I took a taxi to the barge terminal to drop off the canoe and retrieve my truck, which I had shipped from Hay River seven weeks before. Inuvik is a construction hub, always waiting for the next industry and construction contract. The big work at the time was the laying of the all-weather road to Tuk, linking the village to the Dempster Highway. It would soon be complete, though, and what then? Natural gas and oil prices were down. Pipelines were unpopular. Only the diamond mine ground on.

In 1961, the great Canadian novelist and professor Hugh MacLennan, upon traveling the Mackenzie River on a barge, declared that "unless there has been a nuclear war," it did not require a "sense of prophecy to predict that a century from now this river valley will have a large population." His estimate, for the year 2061: "at least three million people," with hospitals and schools and "at least two universities."

Instead, the population of the valley has remained essentially unchanged since MacLennan took his boat ride and, very likely, since Mackenzie took his.

But what if the climate had been different when Mackenzie paddled the river? How would history have been different? Mackenzie paddled during the Little Ice Age, a few centuries of below-normal cold. If he had undertaken his trip during average conditions, or at our current global temperatures, he would not have been stopped by ice. If the ocean were free, would the fur trade have followed him down the river to China? Would Canada have its own Mississippi River in the summer Deh Cho? Would settlers have wagoned in, a northern Oregon Trail? How much of Mackenzie's disappointment was merely a matter of timing?

When Senny and I got to the barge terminal, bad news awaited us. A what-could-possibly-go-wrong worry, which had nagged me the whole trip, was realized: my truck was not in Inuvik.

I called the central customer service office in Alberta, and the company representative said they hoped to deliver my truck in a week. The Coast Guard had ordered a hold on their whole fleet, because a major windstorm—the same one that caught Senny and me near the Thunder River, I figured—threw an empty barge on a shoal near Lutselk'e, a community on the eastern shore of Great Slave Lake. They had to divert a tug to rescue it, and everything was delayed.

"But you guaranteed that my truck would arrive by July," I said to the poor representative; obviously, I still had an American expectation for timely delivery. He was apologetic, but there was only so much he could do. "It's not like a plane, where you know when it will land," he said. "It's complicated shipping in the Arctic."

So I walked down to the dock, where a tug sat idling, and talked to Terry, the foreman. He wanted to know what I thought of the Mackenzie River, having just paddled its length, and I asked the same of him. "It's where I work," he said with a shrug.

Terry will likely be out of a job soon. The shipping company was declaring bankruptcy, and over the years he had heard all the complaints from locals about the unreliability of the barge service. By the end of our conversation, he heard my frustration as well, that my truck wasn't waiting for me in his cargo yard. He recommended I find a new way home, that if my truck did arrive at all, it would take far more than a week. Then he became philosophical.

"Welcome to the north," he said.

I did not feel welcome. I felt done. I booked a very expensive plane ticket for the next day, to fly me back to Hay River to meet up with my truck there. And a good thing too, because I later learned that the barge that should have delivered my truck didn't arrive in Inuvik until October. I shipped half my gear through the postal service, and the other half I checked as baggage. "Rifle or paddle?" the airline clerk asked about my long package wrapped in tape.

I boarded the plane—a standard 737, but with only half the seats, the front modified into cargo space—and sat next to an older woman completing an Inuvialuit crossword puzzle. As we took off, I leaned toward the window, to try to see the broad land that we had paddled through, always hidden behind the wall of the spruce and bush. But the day was overcast, the ceiling low, and as we climbed, the forest was swallowed by cloud and disappeared from view.

———

In 1790, London got the bad news. That's how the report arrived, not as an affirmative, that Mackenzie had solved an Arctic geographic conundrum, but as a pragmatic negative, that Pond's map was incorrect and the river of the west was still undiscovered. In a later letter to the governor of Canada, Mackenzie summarized it this way: "Tho' this Expedition did not answer the intended purposes, it proved that Mr. Pond's Assertion was nothing but conjecture, and that a North West Passage is impracticable."

But Mackenzie wouldn't let the matter sit, and he planned a second voyage. Clearly, his trouble was one of determining longitude, for his measurements on the first journey had vastly overestimated his westward travel. So he decided to go to London to study cartography and to purchase the proper instruments, a sextant and chronometer and appropriate almanacs. But before he left, Alexander begged Roderic to "make all the inquiry possible" with any Indians trading at Fort Chipewyan, on the lands of "the Great River which falls into the Sea to the Westward of River Disappointment."

In order to avoid "inconvenience," but also certainly embarrassment, Mackenzie made himself "but little known during my residence in London the Winter 1791." When he returned, he was educated and equipped, his letters to Roderic full of references to the orbit of Jupiter's moons. Back at Fort Chipewyan, he recruited a new crew. Two voyageurs from his first journey, Landry and Ducette, the Acadian cousins, signed on for the second attempt. So too François Beaulieu, the young mixed-blood man from Slave Lake whom Mackenzie and Laurent Leroux knew from the 1789 descent. In the fall of 1792, they struck west from Fort Chipewyan, paddling across the Great Plains, and, after wintering over in a hasty fort, pushed on again that spring.

They ascended the Peace River in full flood, up the front face of the Rocky Mountains. Portages on sheer cliffs followed, then descents of alpine creeks studded with boulders and whirlpools. They smashed the boats and rebuilt them and then hauled them from watershed to watershed, a maze of narrow rivers. Near the coast, the peaks rose to ten thousand feet, the portage pass at six thousand. But finally, threading their way through one final steep valley, they met Bella Coola Indians who offered to take them to the ocean. "I could perceive the termination of the river," he wrote, "and its discharge into a narrow arm of the sea." Deep in a fjord, he had spotted it. The Pacific. The next day, July 20, 1793, his canoe touched salt.

He had done it, and yet in its own way, this journey was even more disappointing than the first. At least the great river to the Arctic was navigable. No one would follow this path to the Pacific. No one could, the way so grueling. He had found the Pacific but not the commercial route. The river of the west still lay out of sight.

Mackenzie passed the next winter at Fort Chipewyan. It fell hard on him. "I am full bent on going down" to Montreal, he wrote to Roderic in January 1794. "I am more anxious now than ever. For I think it unpardonable in any man to remain in this country who can afford to leave it. What a pretty Situation I am in this winter, starving and alone."

The snow and cold dragged on. He knew that spending so much time so far from civilization always "darkened the human mind." The lake was dark, the sky, the forest, his soul. Above, the northern green lights flickered; the Slavey people call them the Heart of the Devil.

Two months later, in March, he wrote to his cousin again, apologizing. He had hoped to provide Roderic his journal of his voyages, for editorial assistance. But it "will require more time than I was aware of, for it is not a quarter finished." Every day was a struggle. "Last fall I was to begin copying it, but the greatest part of my time was taken up in vain Speculations. I got in such a habit of thinking that I was often lost in thoughts nor could I ever write to the purpose."

His thoughts, his words, were circular. "What I was thinking of, would often occur to me instead of that which I ought to do. I never passed so much of my time insignificantly, nor so uneasy." It was the dreams that plagued him. "I could not close my eyes without finding myself in company with the Dead."

That summer, Alexander returned to Montreal. He would never again winter in the backcountry. After ten nearly continuous years in the *pays d'en haut*—his only break the single trip to London—he was done.

In 1795, when Aaron Arrowsmith, a leading British cartographer of the day, produced a new map of North America that included the paths of Mackenzie's two journeys, Alexander wrote an accompanying note that clearly articulated his views. Like Captain Cook, he was the negative discoverer: "It was in the Summer of 1789 that I went this Expedition in hopes of getting into Cook's River; tho I was disappointed in this it proved without a doubt that there is not a North West passage below this latitude and I believe it will generally be allowed that no passage is practicable in a Higher Latitude, the Sea being eternally covered with ice."

In Montreal, Mackenzie rose to managing partner of the North West Company, its agent at the *rendezvous*, and in this leadership role he badgered the British government to invest in transcontinental trade by forcing the Hudson's Bay Company, the staunch rival of the Montreal *bourgeois*, into a monopoly with his firm. He was an eligible bachelor about town, a drinker and carouser, and became famous for his late nights. In New York he bantered with the business titan John Jacob Astor, and he bought a merchant ship in Philadelphia; it was the farthest south he traveled in his life. In all this he clashed with his more wealthy and powerful colleagues and played poorly the game of business intrigue.

In 1799, his partnership in the North West Company was not renewed by his fellow shareholders. Contemporaries blamed Alexander's rivalry with Simon McTavish, the most wealthy and powerful trader in Montreal. Mackenzie's split was "entirely from a fit of ill-humor," one wrote, "without any fix'd plan or knowing himself what he would be at." He "went off in a pet," another said, as "there could not be two Caesars in Rome, one must remove."

Alexander had secured a share of the company for Roderic, but when the sundering occurred, Roderic chose McTavish over his cousin and took Alexander's place. After a series of angry and recriminating letters, the two Mackenzies did not speak for five years.

Mackenzie started his own fur company and named it after himself. He ran for the Legislative Assembly of Lower Canada and won, but quickly grew bored and stopped attending the sessions. He got caught up in a stock sale and land claim deal that turned on him. And always, he drank.

But still, the need to tell the story of his journeys weighed on him. Mackenzie expressed much "apprehension of presenting myself to the Public in the character of an Author," he wrote, "being much better calculated to perform the voyages, arduous as they might be, than to write an account of them."

So he found a ghostwriter, a man named William Combe, who was known to have assisted many a prominent gentleman in such circumstances. And he collected the observations of his cousin Roderic, who had counted the steps on the rivers between Montreal and Grand Portage, and called them "A General History of the Fur Trade" and included the pages as his own work. At the end of the book, he attached a treatise on the importance of continental commerce, securing the west coast, and shipping furs directly to China via a partnership with the Hudson's Bay Company, the same ideas that had earned him enmity and exclusion from the North West Company.

His publisher was Cadell and Davies, the house of Samuel Johnson and Samuel Hearne before him. He warned readers in the foreword "not to expect the charms of embellished narrative." Yes, he had "settled the dubious point of a practicable North-West passage" and put "that long agitated question at rest." But otherwise, he warned, the "dreary waste" was not "effectively transferred to the page," and anyone "enamored of romantic adventures" would be dissatisfied.

Despite those caveats, *Voyages from Montreal, on the River St. Laurence, Through the Continent of North America, to the Frozen and Pacific Oceans* became a bestseller, published in six editions in French, German, and Russian. Only two months later, Alexander was knighted by King George III.

The book changed the course of nations, but not in the way Mackenzie could have foreseen. Napoleon considered the volume a piece of military intelligence and devised plans to attack the United States and British Canada from the west, up the Mississippi valley; ultimately, he chose to invade Russia instead. And President Thomas Jefferson procured one of the very first American copies and read *Voyages* with his young secretary, Meriwether Lewis, at Monticello in 1802. The Corps of Discovery launched two years later, to seize the Pacific coast for the United States before the British followed Mackenzie's advice; Lewis took *Voyages* with him on the journey.

Sir Alex, as he now called himself, was frustrated. In 1808, he wrote to the British secretary of state for war and the colonies, complaining that the claim of the United States to the continent's western reaches was "notoriously groundless." In the first place, those lands were full of settlements "long before the United States of America existed as a Nation," and, second, the "expedition of Discovery under Captains Lewis and Clark" meant nothing "because I myself, known to have been the first, who crossed thro' it." The secretary's reply to Mackenzie, if any, is unknown.

By then, Mackenzie had moved to London and only occasionally returned to Montreal. "I am determined to make myself as comfortable as circumstances will allow. I have a large field before me," he told Roderic, after they reconciled. He enjoyed his time in the "immense City" and only rarely inserted himself into politics or business.

His interests declined in proportion to his health. Alexander stayed in Britain for good after 1810. Two years later, he married Geddes Mackenzie, a teenage cousin more than thirty years his junior, and retired to her family's estate of Avoch, on the Moray Firth, just north of Inverness. Alexander and Geddes socialized in London, played lord and lady of the manor in Scotland, produced three children, and borrowed money from his contacts in Montreal to maintain their lifestyle.

His body was crumbling, though, lungs winded on simple walks and legs drained of their vigor, exercise reduced to sitting in an open carriage. The lifestyle of a *pays d'en haut* trader—starvation and alcohol, chiefly— had taken an early toll. "Stuper" and "dead pain" plagued him, plus "a listlessness and apathy which I cannot well describe," he wrote in a final letter to Roderic. It reads like a final letter. He begs his cousin to come home to Scotland. He offers to host Roderic's son and place him in Scotland's best schools. Alexander had a young boy himself, and "if God spare him," the two cousins could be fast friends, as Roderic and Alexander had been on the Isle of Lewis. They should make the arrangements soon. "I have been overtaken with the consequences of my sufferings in the North West," he said. "Lady Mackenzie is sitting by me, and the children are playing on the floor."

One spring day, while returning from Edinburgh, where he had sought medical advice, his kidneys failed. Sir Alexander Mackenzie died on March 12, 1820, aged fifty-seven years.

Only a few months later, the Hudson's Bay Company absorbed its rival into a single monopoly, just as Mackenzie had petitioned, and the North West Company was no more.

———

In the mid-nineteenth century, at a settlement in the *pays d'en haut,* just south of Lake Winnipeg, a historian sat down with an old man who was one of the last living North West Company voyageurs. This is what the old man said:

I have now been forty-two years in this country. For twenty-four I was a light canoe-man; I required but little sleep, but sometimes got less. No portage was too long for me; all portages were alike. My end of the canoe never touched the ground till I saw the end of it. Fifty songs a day were nothing to me. I could carry, paddle, walk, and sing with any man I ever saw. During that period, I saved the lives of ten *bourgeois,* and was always the favorite, because when others stopped to carry at a bad step, and lost time, I pushed on— over rapids, over cascades, over chutes; all were the same to me. No water, no weather, ever stopped the paddle or the song.

I had twelve wives in the country. I was then like a *bourgeois,* rich and happy: no *bourgeois* had better-dressed wives than I. I beat all Indians at the race, and no white man ever passed me in the chase. I wanted for nothing; and I spent all my earnings in the enjoyment of pleasure. Five hundred pounds, twice told, have passed through my hands; although now I have not a spare shirt on my back, not a penny to buy one. Yet, were I a young man again, I should glory in commencing the same career again. I would willingly spend another half century in the same fields of enjoyment. There is no life half so happy as a voyageur's life.

————

Just before he died, Alexander Mackenzie began a correspondence with John Franklin, the British naval officer. Franklin was preparing for a car-tographic survey of the Arctic coast of North America, following Samuel Hearne's route down the Coppermine River, with the goal of mapping the shore in an interest of scouting, from land, a potential maritime northwest passage.

Franklin was destined for greatness and controversy. On that 1819 descent of the Coppermine, his troop would be caught by snow, run out of food, and be reduced to eating their leather moccasins and, perhaps, more. Franklin was racked by fever, holed up in camp, and kept alive only through the mercies of his voyageurs and Indian guides. He ate the meat that was put in front of him. Whether the Windigo inhabited his crew, no one said.

Rather than destroy his career, though, this brush with death launched it. Six years later, in 1825, Franklin led the second European expedition to successfully reach the delta of the Deh Cho; an earlier attempt, in 1799, failed when the fur trader Duncan Livingston and his party of five North West Company voyageurs were killed in an Esquimaux ambush. Franklin's canoes reached Mackenzie's Whale Island and then explored the coast east and west, as far as Point Barrow, before being turned aside by ice. When Franklin returned, he wrote a book about the journey, and of the river he said that "in justice to the memory of Mackenzie" it should be named for him.

Franklin met his famous end in the Arctic. In the summer of 1845, searching again for a northwest passage on behalf of the British Admiralty, Franklin led the HMS *Terror* and HMS *Erebus* through a barren archipelago north of Hudson's Bay. The ships were caught in the ice and spent a winter near Beechey Island, west of Greenland. When the ice broke, they made it only a few hundred miles south, becoming encased again near King William Island in 1846. This time the ships were crushed, and the crew spent two more winters trying to claw back to civilization. All died. Over the generations, the Esquimaux told stories of the white men lost at sea. Flotsam from the wrecks—combs, tinted eyeglasses, fishhooks—would wash up onshore, and the Esquimaux would pass them down as family heirlooms. The wrecked ships were lost on the seabed for more than a century and a half and not discovered until 2014 via side-scan sonar.

But all of that was still to come. When Franklin sought him out, Mackenzie was the experienced explorer who never lost a man. Franklin himself was the novice, and wished for any advice and encouragement the older mentor might provide.

Mackenzie wrote generously back to Franklin, advising him on many specifics: the required canoes and voyageurs, twist tobacco and "two or three Bales of Dry Good suitable to the Trade," powder and guns, "a quantity of spirits," the importance of befriending the Esquimaux. Mackenzie told him to travel by way of Île-à-la-Crosse and then proceed to Athabasca when the ice allowed. That Franklin's party—a clerk, two *milieux*, two steersmen, Indians and their wives—should look much like his own. Mackenzie, the *bourgeois* planning his last brigade, was "earnestly interested in the results of your exertion under such perilous circumstances," even from his sickbed in Scotland.

Mackenzie concludes the letter with one final piece of advice. Finding a local guide, someone who knew the land and the people and traveled its breadth, was essential. And he, Mackenzie, was not the one whom Franklin should talk to at all. There was another, far more valuable, who should serve as his partner.

"I wish you could fall in with my old Friend, if alive, Nestabeck," Mackenzie wrote. Though Franklin may know him by another name, for he was "commonly called the English Chief."

It was late February, and Montreal was burdened by several feet of snow. The slush stuck stubbornly in the streets, mushing about like mud rather than a liquid that might someday drain away. The small cars navigating the cobblestones were salt stained, and the skies were dark, nights heavy and long.

I was eating dinner in the *ville vieux,* at L'Auberge Saint-Gabriel, a restaurant that billed itself as the oldest in North America, tracing its roots to 1688. The dining room was wide, thick stone walls and exposed beams eighteen inches on center. I had roasted cauliflower and rabbit in a mustard sauce and two glasses of Malbec, and I took an old *New Yorker* along to read between courses.

For more than a decade following his journeys, Mackenzie's home was Montreal. I had spent my day looking for signs of him, poking my head in the very few old buildings remaining from his time. A random parking attendant opened up for me the modest house of Simon McTavish, the North West Company's leading partner. There were offices on the ground floor, lofts in a new addition up top. The attendant said he had been a mason previously, and he showed me the calcium leaking from the original mortar in walls two feet thick. The building that housed L'Auberge Saint-Gabriel looked old, but a historian had warned me not to be deceived. He said it was reclaimed stone and beams, but new construction. I checked the mortar. No calcium. But it was hard to get a good look around, because the bar was hosting a riotous business meeting, the kind of alcohol-fueled mixer that involved name tags and product displays and branded content.

After a day walking in the cold, it was good to sit near an open hearth and enjoy dinner with a glass of wine. I had returned from my northern travels six months before, and readapting to modernity was easy and quick. The calluses on my hands had long since faded. The weight I lost easily went back on, plus a little more; all I wanted to do was eat. I had stopped paying attention to weather reports and relished not caring about wind. One day I did the math, to figure out how many paddle strokes it took to canoe the 1,125 miles of the Deh Cho. Thirty or forty strokes a minute, ten hours a day, for over a month and a half. Almost a million swings of that wooden stick. Forty days on the water, same as Mackenzie's outward journey. Forty is a nice round biblical number. It felt like forty days.

Life in the wilderness is not simpler or easier. It is only a trade, like beaver furs for teakettles, but in reverse. Physical discomfort in exchange for an escape from the perpetual minor anxieties of middle-class American life: Am I wearing the right tie? Did I say something stupid with spinach in my teeth? Will my son make the hockey team, and if he does, did I remember the paperwork? Checking out and going north is at best a hard respite.

But Mackenzie never saw it this way. He was the product of an age. Societal expectations were the reward for business success. He wanted to be back in the cocktail scene. He wanted to make his fortune and go home.

And when he went home to Montreal, he met his fellow profit seekers and competitors and fur-trading colleagues at the fraternal order known as the Beaver Club, the most exclusive in town. They met on winter evenings, every two weeks, at supper clubs and restaurants and hotels, and membership was restricted to *bourgeois hommes du nord* only, a unanimous vote of current members required to gain entry. They were the city's elite, and knew it, and they wore silver medals, with their names and the years they first wintered in the far northwest and their motto, stamped bold: "Fortitude in Distress."

Washington Irving said that they were full of such a "swelling and braggart" style that everyone "must remember the round of feasting and revelry kept up among these hyperborean nabobs." And yet, when Irving himself traveled to Montreal, he gratefully accepted their invitation to be a guest at the Beaver Club.

I had come to Montreal to see one of the last artifacts of the order, kept at the archives of the McCord Museum. Item M14449, stored in a pale cardboard box: the log of the Beaver Club. That book records each meeting, the attendees and guests, the locations of members—"town," "country," "Scotland"—the rules of order, the fine for breaking them, and the required toasts before meals. All the *bourgeois* from the beginning were listed—the Frenchmen Charles Chaboillez and Étienne Campion in 1751 and 1753, James Finlay in 1766, Peter Pond in 1770—and next to each old-timer's name, his death, dutifully noted. As I opened the archivist's box, I expected to see a grand tome, as would befit the official history of such an auspicious group. Gold leaf, leather-bound, a locking clasp. I was wrong.

It was just a modest accounting ledger. Like a grammar school notebook. Paisley cardboard cover, pale lined pages. It was a clerk's log, I realized. A memory from their apprenticeships in countinghouses, when they were just boys.

I slowly paged through the log, wearing white gloves and using plastic forceps to carefully peel back each sheet. The grand statements, regulations, and membership votes were just prologue. The main body of the journal contained a detailed accounting of every meal and drop of alcohol, including a double-entry breakdown of the bill in pounds and shillings and pence. In a precise hand, despite sure drunkenness, they tallied brandy and tobacco and broken glasses as they had sewing awls and gunpowder and beaver furs in the *pays d'en haut*.

And so as I sat there at dinner at L'Auberge Saint-Gabriel, on a winter evening and at a location so similar to the Beaver Club, I thought of one particular night I had just read about that day in the log.

December 24, 1808, at the Montreal Hotel on the Place d'Armes. Christmas Eve, a time for ghost stories. Thirty-six men gathered that night, dressed in long coats and breeches, and buckles on their shoes, gloves and scarves and top hats made of the finest beaver felt. According to the ledger, by the end of the night, they had drunk forty bottles of Portuguese Madeira, twelve bottles of port, fourteen bottles of porter, eight quarts of ale, six quarts of cider, and four bottles of mulled wine, plus brandy, cigars, pipes, and tobacco.

Alexander Mackenzie was there, having been elected to the Beaver Club over a decade before. In 1808 he was newly knighted, a best-selling author, traveling regularly to London and Scotland, and Montreal was changing so quickly it was different every time he returned. Old landmarks were plowed under, the city's stone battlements coming down, all to make room for ships and commerce.

But the old guard of his life, the men who shaped him and his business, were all there that Christmas Eve, including Roderic, elected to the Beaver Club in 1797. By 1808, the rift had healed, and the two men had renewed their lifetime friendship, the ugliness of the North West Company purge behind them. Also present that night was John Gregory, for whom Alexander had apprenticed back in 1778, when he first arrived in Montreal. And Normand MacLeod, who gave him his first break and traveled to Detroit personally to give him the chance to head to his first *rendezvous*. The only man missing was Peter Pond, who had succumbed to consumption the year before. Pond had returned to his birthplace of Milford, Connecticut; Roderic said he "died poor." Even Sir John Johnson, his father's commander in the American Revolution, was an honorary member, and once presented the club with a poem "to recount the toils and perils past."

The evening started civilly enough, at four o'clock, with a passing of the calumet peace pipe and five toasts, to the Mother of All Saints, to the King, to the Fur Trade in All its Branches, to the Voyageurs and their Wives and Children left in the *pays d'en haut,* and to all their Absent Members. Glasses and tumblers were thrown in the fireplace at the end of each round and tallied in the Beaver Club logbook so they could pay for replacements. Then followed a proper French dinner in multiple courses, all the country delicacies. Venison steaks, beaver tail, quail, buffalo tongue. After dinner came brandy and more bottles of Madeira. The rules were clear: "Every Member to drink as he pleases after the club toasts have gone round and retire at his pleasure."

The stories would flow, as wine replaced roasts. Of their mixed-blood children left with their *à la façon du pays* Cree and Chipewyan wives. Of the beautiful miseries of Rivière Maligne. Of the terror and fierce barrier of the western mountains. Of the dreaded Esquimaux. Of the trade disputes settled with pistols. Of the horsehair-and-shit-and-fat pemmican they ate to survive. Of the Barren Lands. Of the men drowned in the cataracts. Of Pierre Bonga, the black West Indian voyageur who once, by himself, carried five *pièces*—450 pounds!—in a single portage. No, it was six *pièces*! No, called Mackenzie, it was seven! He was sure of it and told everyone who would listen.

And in the small hours of the morning, when Madeira ruled, came the *grand voyage,* when the tables were pushed aside to create a mock *canot de maître,* the behemoths in which they had earned their fortunes.

Stripped to his shirtsleeves, each man knew his place and swung canes and fireplace pokers like paddles, shooting the rapids, the brigade charging forward as the *gouvernail* bore the rudder and the *devant* called the line. They rode kegs of wine from table to floor, swimmers tossed about. That it was their voyageurs and Chipewyan guides who had actually done this work in the wild northwest mattered little. Alexander himself was famous for leading the war whoops, like the Iroquois on their way to battle, and they sang the bawdy hymns of the voyageur:

Ah! taisez-vous, méchante femme,
Je n'vous ai laissé qu'un enfant,
En voilà quatr' dès à présent!

Oh, wicked woman, be you still!
I left two children in your care,
I see that four are playing there!

Alexander Mackenzie was the colossus, known for the enthusiasm of his song and quantity of liquor held. One night the club members averaged twelve bottles of wine each, and Alexander held on as the last and only man standing in the early morning. Mackenzie was the proposer of toasts, the heart of the effort, the emptier of cups.

Reading the log, imagining that night, I had so many questions. Sir John Johnson was there when Corc Mackenzie died; I wondered if Alexander ever asked about his dad. I wondered if they missed their wives and children, abandoned in the north. And I wondered how the other men treated Mackenzie's disappointment. Would they have asked him about it? Alexander considered the whole endeavor a failure until the day he died. He was looking for the Northwest Passage, after all, and he didn't know he had found it. Maybe these gentlemen were too polite to bring it up?

No, with so much alcohol, someone's tongue would have been loosed. And these *bourgeois* were rivals as well as comrades, so whether out of affection or derision someone would have asked. In 1808, Meriwether Lewis was the toast of Philadelphia, and had just been named governor of Louisiana in recognition of his travels and success. It was a subject at hand.

It was Christmas Eve, just past the shortest day of the year, the darkness like a blanket in the Montreal winter. Maybe Roderic, his lifelong confidant, would have said it. During a lull in the festivities, a break from swimming the rapids of the English River or dodging the Porte de l'Enfer, with an elbow to his cousin's ribs.

"Sir Alex!" Roderic called. "Tell us all the story again of the first time you saw the midnight sun."

ACKNOWLEDGMENTS

wwww

It would be a grave injustice if I did not first acknowledge my paddle mates: David Chrisinger, Jeremy Howard Beck, Landon Phillips, and Anthony Sennhenn. I could not have taken my trip, and thus written this book, without your generosity, labor, and good humor. Thank you for spending part of your summer with me, doing something intrinsically difficult and potentially foolhardy. And doubly, thank you to Ashley, Will, Megan, and Katie, for holding down the fort at home while your man embarked on this adventure. You had the far larger job.

Similarly, thank you to Michelle Swallow, the author of the invaluable *Mackenzie River Guide* I looked at every day, and to Doug Swallow with Canoe North in Hay River, who endured near-daily texts about weather and logistics and life on the river. Doug will rent you a canoe to run the Mackenzie River as well, dear reader, and even drive out a stove if you happen to lose yours in Fort Providence. Thanks to Kylik and Gerry Kisoun of Tundra North Tours, for providing peace of mind for months and coming through in the end to get us on time. Kylik and Gerry can take you all over the delta, summer or winter, and tell many a story besides.

I am also indebted to a brigade's worth of historians and archivists who assisted in my research of the voyageur world. Thank you to Shawn Patterson at Fort William Historical Park, Carolyn Podruchny at York University, Douglas Hunter, Harry Duckworth, Wick Walker, Germaine Warkentin, Claude Ferland, Jan Peter Laurens Loovers, Jeremy Ward at the Canadian Canoe Museum in Peterborough, Heather McNabb at the McCord Museum archives in Montreal, Nicolas Bednarz at the Archives de Montréal, Monique Voyer at the archives at the University of Montreal, Paul-André Linteau and Robin Philpot at Baraka Books, Alan

Stewart with the Canadian Centre for Architecture, Heather Beattie at the Hudson's Bay Company Archives in Winnipeg, and to the staffs of the Francophone Museum, Musée de la Place Royale, and Morrin Centre in Quebec, Château Ramezay and Pointe-à-Callière in Montreal, and the Royal Ontario Museum in Toronto. More thank-yous to my first readers, Matthew Komatsu and Phil Klay and Elizabeth Burns, to Sherill Tippins, Kenneth Cobb, and Professor Edward Knoblauch, for assistance in navigating the public archives in New York City and London, to Andrew McKenzie, for sharing portions of his genealogical opus *May We Be Britons?*, to Ben Busch, for bear-wrestling advice, to Matt Cook and Jason Briner, for letting me borrow essential gear, and to Jeremiah Grisham, for literary inspiration and paddler-broker services.

Just after my journey, I wrote several climate change dispatches and features about the trip. Thank you to Brian Anderson and Kate Lunau at *Vice Motherboard* and Siddhartha Mahanta at *The Atlantic* for editing and publishing my stories, and to Tom Hundley at the Pulitzer Center on Crisis Reporting for providing travel funds to support the project. I'm grateful to the journalists Meagan Wohlberg, Eva Holland, and Karen McColl, for the connections and advice on reporting in Canada's north, and to all the people we met on the river who were so generous with their time, especially Wilfred Jackson, Jonas Antoine, and Ron and Wendy Oe.

My editors at Doubleday and McClelland & Stewart, Gerry Howard and Doug Pepper, are the best a writer could ask for. So too my agent, Bob Mecoy, who manages somehow to simultaneously fill the roles of first reader, promoter, interventionist, and friend. Thank you, gentlemen.

To my boys, Virgil, Martin, Sam, and Eli, who put up with a dad who was gone, again. You can paddle with me next time, if you want to.

And always, to my brilliant and beautiful bride: Jessie, I love you.

Notes

My narrative of Alexander Mackenzie's life was primarily drawn from his own words, the journals he kept from his voyages and the few letters that survive. The definitive portfolio, *The Journals and Letters of Sir Alexander Mackenzie*, was edited by W. Kaye Lamb and published by Cambridge University Press for the Hakluyt Society in 1970.

Unfortunately, Lamb had less than a full archive to work with, because Mackenzie's estate in Avoch burned soon after his death and the majority of his papers with it. The letters kept by Roderic were collected in the "Reminiscences," a portion of the sprawling and unorganized two-volume *Les bourgeois de la Compagnie du Nord-Ouest* published by Louis R. Masson, Roderic's grandson-in-law, in 1889–90. A few other papers remained with other organizations, such as the Hudson's Bay Company archives. But Mackenzie's record is thinner than that of other major historical figures of the period.

For the general culture of the voyageurs, Carolyn Podruchny's *Making the Voyageur World* is definitive. Harry Duckworth has done yeoman's work tracing the arc of individual mid-1780s voyageurs in *The English River Book*. I found Harold Innis's *Fur Trade in Canada* to still be the authoritative and exhaustive text. Two biographies of Peter Pond were published in the last few years, by Barry Gough and David Chapin, and I found both very useful. Samuel Hearne remains the best source of information on Matonabbee, and so too Mackenzie on Awgeenah, whom he always called Nestabeck or the English Chief. Recently, many First Nations have begun publishing the collected oral histories of their elders, and I quote them as often as possible.

In the following notes, I have tried to stay as concise as possible, for quoted text, for obscure facts, or to explain specific conclusions I drew from the historical record.

PROLOGUE

1 Deh Cho: Helm, *People of Denendeh,* 8. Helm uses "Dehcho" as an alternate spelling, but throughout the book I will use "Deh Cho."

1 Nagwichoonjik: Heine et al., *Gwichya Gwich'in Googwandak,* 400.

1 Kuukpak: Conversation with Gerry Kisoun.

2 Great Slave Lake: The Dene name for the lake is Tucho, meaning Big Lake. There is a movement among the First Nations of Canada to remove many colonial names and officially restore the original names for such places. See Curtis Mandeville, "Goodbye Great Slave Lake? Movement to Decolonize N.W.T. Maps Is Growing," CBC News, June 21, 2016, accessed June 26, 2017, www.cbc.ca.

CHAPTER 1: THE NORTH WEST COMPANY

3 tying up ships in a gam: Podruchny, *Making the Voyageur World,* 173.

3 of greatest esteem: Ibid., 25.

3 Voyageurs tended to be short: MacGregor, *Canoe Country,* 102.

4 They sang to synchronize: Podruchny, *Making the Voyageur World,* 86, 114.

4 "We are voyageurs": Nute, *Voyageur,* 45.

5 "Fence builders": Conversation with Shawn Patterson, collections manager at Fort William Historical Park.

5 the northmen had nothing to do: Newman, *Caesars of the Wilderness,* 41.

6 His partners thought him: Lamb, *Journals and Letters of Mackenzie,* 16.

9 He was the youngest partner: Innis, *Fur Trade in Canada,* 200. Using Innis's complete list of who held what shares, Nicholas Montour was only six years senior, but most were much older.

9 "a small adventure of goods": Lamb, *Journals and Letters of Mackenzie,* 78.

9 Indian mixed-blood families: Today, they are known as métis and recognized as First Nations in Canada.

9 "drinking, carousing, and quarrelling": Lamb, *Journals and Letters of Mackenzie,* 71.

10 "contemplated the practicability": Ibid., 57.

10 "Roderic Mackenzie, if he will": Ibid., 437.

10 "by Order of the N.W Company": Ibid., 163.

CHAPTER 2: INTO THE NORTH

13 one-fifth of the planet's supply: Frequently Asked Questions, Environment and Climate Change Canada, www.ec.gc.ca.

13 "Comes over one an absolute necessity": Lawrence, *Sea and Sardinia,* 7.

14 1998 attempt of Tibet's Tsangpo gorge: See Wick Walker's own travelogue, *Courting the Diamond Sow* (Washington, D.C.: Adventure Press, National Geographic, 2000), and Todd Balf's *Last River* (New York: Crown, 2000).

CHAPTER 3: SCOTLAND

17 His father was Kenneth: For Alexander's early life, I relied most heavily on Gough's *First Across the Continent* and Wade's *Mackenzie of Canada.*

17 family lore says: Lamb, *Journals and Letters of Mackenzie,* 2.

18 "It must be confessed": All Samuel Johnson references in this section are from *Journey to the Western Islands of Scotland,* in Johnson, *Works,* vol. 2.

19 speculative "futures" of every kind: The great chronicle of late eighteenth-century Scottish immigration to America is Bailyn's *Voyagers to the West.* I relied heavily on his work in this chapter, unless otherwise noted.

20 "As Captain McKenzie's Character": Irish Emigration Database, accessed June 26, 2017, www.dippam.ac.uk.

20 McKenzie dropped a load: David Dobson, *Ships from Ireland to Early America, 1623–1850* (Baltimore: Clearfield, 1999), 1:114.

20 Wyllie had recruited another ship full: National Archives of the U.K., T47/12, pp. 1–3.

21 he fired his gun into the air: Ibid.

21 only fifty-eight fellow passengers: Stornoway Historical Society, accessed June 26, 2017, www.stornowayhistoricalsociety.org.uk.

CHAPTER 4: NEW YORK

23 Eighteen languages were commonly: For the scenes of Revolutionary War–era New York City, I relied on Ketchum's *Divided Loyalties,* Schecter's *Battle for New York,* and Van Buskirk's *Generous Enemies.*

23 one in ten New Yorkers: Bailyn, *Voyagers to the West,* 575.

26 "Ready Money John": Wade, *Mackenzie of Canada,* 19.

26 replacing them with kin: Bailyn, *Voyagers to the West,* 576.

27 Johnson clothed Hendrick: Sleeper-Smith, *Rethinking the Fur Trade,* 346.

27 Johnson painted his face: Ibid., 344.

28 a 160-year-old physical embodiment: Ibid., 121.

30 apprenticed to the firm of Finlay & Gregory: Lamb, *Journals and Letters of Mackenzie,* 3.

CHAPTER 5: MONTREAL

31 Montreal attracted Loyalists: Morton, *Short History of Canada,* 32.

31 twenty feet high and almost as thick: Pointe-à-Callière Museum in Montreal, visited in Feb. 2017.

31 Along rue St.-François-Xavier: For property maps of late eighteenth-century Montreal, I am indebted to Alan Stewart at the Canadian Centre for Architecture.

31 a Scot named Mr. James Finlay: Innis, *Fur Trade in Canada,* 170.

31 Mackenzie heard that in 1768: Lamb, *Journals and Letters of Mackenzie,* 70.

31 "Most of the clerks": Irving, *Astoria,* 6.

32 The standard joke: Herman, *How the Scots Invented the Modern World,* 363.

33 Cotton Mather and the other: For an entertaining overview of the Massachusetts Bay Colony, try Vowell's *Wordy Shipmates.*

33 No more than a couple hundred: Sleeper-Smith, *Rethinking the Fur Trade,* 220.

33 "We rove about with them": Innis, *Fur Trade in Canada,* 25.

33 several thousand Iroquois: These were St. Lawrence Iroquois, a separate nation not part of the famous Iroquois confederacy to the south, though archaeology has only discovered this in the last hundred years.

33 "frightful and ill-shaped": Brody, *Other Side of Eden,* 219.

33 When Étienne Brûlé, the French youth: Innis, *Fur Trade in Canada,* 30.

34 "several acres of snow": Morton, *Short History of Canada,* 31.

34 "In truth, my brother": Innis, *Fur Trade in Canada,* 28.

34 Algonquin were forced to the north: Skinner, *Upper Country,* 49.

35 "In the canoes of the savages": Innis, *Fur Trade in Canada,* 20.

35 took along a Chinese silk damask: Gough, *Elusive Mr. Pond,* 59.

35 "The water here is so swift": Innis, *Fur Trade in Canada,* 20.

35 named Lachine, for China: Chapin, *Freshwater Passages,* 69.

35 Hemmed in by the Appalachians: Sheppe, *First Man West,* 6.

35 only 50,000 white *habitants*: Garreau, *Nine Nations of North America,* 368.

35 to New Englanders the French and Indians: Middleton, *Colonial America,* 177.

35 "People must be of the profession": *Dictionary of Canadian Biography,* s.v. "Wolfe, James," accessed June 26, 2017, www.biographi.ca.

36 dressed in the coat of an Englishman: Despite the implied authority of the painting, note that Sir William Johnson was not actually present at the battle.

36 easier to work with: Garreau, *Nine Nations of North America,* 370.

36 "A constitution and frame": Lamb, *Journals and Letters of Mackenzie,* 57.

37 "coarse woollen cloths": Ibid., 82.

37 "forty-two months after the goods": Ibid., 81.

38 Thirty-six feet long: Morse, *Fur Trade Canoe Routes of Canada,* 5.

38 It was an Algonquin design: MacGregor, *Canoe Country,* 212.

38 each voyageur's home parish: Podruchny, *Making the Voyageur World,* 30.

38 *devant,* the guide in the nose: Ibid., 121.

38 Each man was provided: Sleeper-Smith, *Rethinking the Fur Trade,* 330.

38 *Castor gras,* the French called them: Innis, *Fur Trade in Canada,* 94.

38 "Twice as many furs": Lamb, *Journals and Letters of Mackenzie,* 73.

39 "You would be amazed": Irving, *Astoria,* 3. Also note, an East Indiaman is an Englishman who worked for the East India Company, not a native of East India.

40 scurvy in his sickbed: Lamb, *Journals and Letters of Mackenzie,* 3.

40 closed the waters to commercial traffic: Vexler, *Detroit,* 82.

40 His Majesty's military vessels: Innis, *Fur Trade in Canada,* 181.

CHAPTER 6: DETROIT

41 "This trade was carried on": Lamb, *Journals and Letters of Mackenzie,* 71.

41 windlasses and farm labor: Innis, *Fur Trade in Canada,* 177.

42 boarded a new brig of war: Vexler, *Detroit,* 82.

42 Montreal to Detroit: In 1800, a canoe set a record of seven and one-quarter days for transit from Detroit to Montreal. Podruchny, *Making the Voyageur World,* 101.

42 Major William Ancrum: Vexler, *Detroit,* 3.

42 beat the man with his bare fists: History of Detroit, accessed Feb. 22, 2016, historydetroit.com.

42 a flotilla of twenty-five canoes: Lewis, *Detroit,* 3.

42 "timid deer and faun": Bragg, *Hidden History of Detroit,* 32.

43 "They are an exceedingly industrious": Skinner, *Upper Country,* 140.

43 whom he meant to pacify: Martelle, *Detroit,* 2.

43 "All the villages of our savages": Skinner, *Upper Country,* 94.

44 "Casting my eyes toward the woods": Ibid., 98.

44 diverted to government soldiers: Foxcurran, Bouchard, and Malette, *Songs upon the Rivers,* 156.

44 Rules for Ranging: Rogers's Rules for Ranging are still used by U.S. Army rangers today.

44 "moral certainty": Gough, *Elusive Mr. Pond,* 43.

44 "Christino": Chapin, *Freshwater Passages,* 76.

44 "We will soon see that half": Foxcurran, Bouchard, and Malette, *Songs upon the Rivers,* 156.

45 "a lazy, idle people": Chapin, *Freshwater Passages,* 46.

45 "It is not uncommon to see": Sleeper-Smith, *Rethinking the Fur Trade,* 543.

45 "careless and very ignorant": Bragg, *Hidden History of Detroit,* 53.

45 "Though he knew from the King's": *Ephraim Douglass and His Times,* accessed June 27, 2017, archive.org.

46 one man in ten was an African slave: Martelle, *Detroit,* 35.

46 highly regarded Brazilian twist tobacco: Sleeper-Smith, *Rethinking the Fur Trade,* 315.

46 "the Detroit trade has been very bad": Innis, *Fur Trade in Canada,* 187.

47 It was early June 1785: As published in Roderic Mackenzie's "Reminiscences" portion of Masson, *Les bourgeois de la Compagnie du Nord-Ouest,* 7.

47 750 gallons of rum: Innis, *Fur Trade in Canada,* 253.

47 "six hundred weight of biscuit": Most historians now credit Roderic with much of "A General History of the Fur Trade" that opens Alexander Mackenzie's *Voyages.* Lamb, *Journals and Letters of Mackenzie,* 33.

47 whoops of the Iroquois and Algonquin: Podruchny, *Making the Voyageur World,* 170.

48 Roderic thought he ought to as well: Masson, *Les bourgeois de la Compagnie du Nord-Ouest,* 7.

48 "over cragged, excavated rocks": Lamb, *Journals and Letters of Mackenzie,* 86.

48 Eight of the men: Newman, *Caesars of the Wilderness,* 37.

48 a *canot de maître* could make four miles an hour: Morse, *Fur Trade Canoe Routes of Canada,* 56.

49 "Quand un chrétien se détermine": Nute, *Voyageur,* 153.

50 "In less than half an hour": Masson, *Les bourgeois de la Compagnie du Nord-Ouest,* 9.

CHAPTER 7: INTO THE *PAYS D'EN HAUT*

52 People tend to save wedding dresses: Conversation with Shawn Patterson, collections manager at Fort William Historical Park.

53 "In several parts there are guts": Lamb, *Journals and Letters of Mackenzie,* 91.

54 "Everyone must believe in something": MacGregor, *Canoe Country,* 8.

CHAPTER 8: TO GRAND PORTAGE AND THE ENGLISH RIVER

57 "If I had not kept my face": Parkman, *Pioneers of France in the New World,* 402–403.

57 "the Westernmost military position": Lamb, *Journals and Letters of Mackenzie*, 92.

57 an attempt to latinize the Ojibwa name: Huck et al., *Exploring the Fur Trade Routes of North America*, 108.

58 "most beautiful that is known": Skinner, *Upper Country*, 55.

58 Marquette died on the eastern shore: Donnelly, *Jacques Marquette*, 265.

58 his grave lost: The grave was eventually rediscovered in 1877, though the Pere Marquette museum burned down in 2000. Marquette Mission Park, accessed June 27, 2017, www.museumofojibwaculture.net.

58 "should have been contented": Lamb, *Journals and Letters of Mackenzie*, 67.

58 The Americans promised only: Ibid., 92.

58 Roderic's brigade was in a hurry: Masson, *Les bourgeois de la Compagnie du Nord-Ouest*, 10.

58 "one half of the year starving": Lamb, *Journals and Letters of Mackenzie*, 93.

59 "the largest and most magnificent body": Ibid., 95. Mackenzie is right, if surface area is counted, and the Caspian is considered oceanic. In volume, though, Superior is third largest, behind Lake Baikal in Russia and Lake Tanganyika in Africa.

59 a temporary city the size of Detroit: Newman, *Caesars of the Wilderness*, 3.

59 "I often made the *comptoir*": Masson, *Les bourgeois de la Compagnie du Nord-Ouest*, 11.

60 "generally contrived to squander": Lamb, *Journals and Letters of Mackenzie*, 66.

60 two dozen or so total *bourgeois*: Davidson, *North West Company*, 14.

60 Pangman was from New Jersey: Chapin, *Freshwater Passages*, 142.

60 dozens of traders with twenty-five canoes: Innis, *Fur Trade in Canada*, 253.

61 Roderic would stay behind: Davidson, *North West Company*, 47.

61 Mackenzie paid each man: This section, on Mackenzie's journey to Île-à-la-Crosse, can be found in Lamb, *Journals and Letters of Mackenzie*, 97–126.

61 six miles an hour: Podruchny, *Making the Voyageur World*, 100.

61 Twenty-nine total portages: Morse, *Fur Trade Canoe Routes of Canada*, 77.

63 apostles had appeared: Podruchny, *Making the Voyageur World*, 81.

64 largest landholding private enterprise: Morton, *Short History of Canada*, 75.

65 eat eight pounds of meat: Podruchny, *Making the Voyageur World*, 38.

66 "a little time reconciles": Lamb, *Journals and Letters of Mackenzie*, 152.

66 Every waterway was full: Olson, *Lonely Land*, 206.

66 They were made in the distant past: Morse, *Fur Trade Canoe Routes of Canada*, 31.

67 "live hard, lie hard, sleep hard, eat dogs": Nute, *Voyageur*, 100.

67 clubbed them to death: Sleeper-Smith, *Rethinking the Fur Trade*, 19.

67 "They seem to be entirely unacquainted": Hearne, *Journey to the Northern Ocean*, 205.

68 Indian culture considered: Sleeper-Smith, *Rethinking the Fur Trade*, 84.

68 "a very excellent tendency": Lamb, *Journals and Letters of Mackenzie*, 68.

68 "a dose of laudanum": Ibid., 74.

68 The voyageurs gratefully married: Van Kirk, *Many Tender Ties*, 27.

68 On the night of the wedding: Podruchny, *Making the Voyageur World*, 217.

68 "it requires much less time": Lamb, *Journals and Letters of Mackenzie*, 65.

69 Indian elders told Mackenzie: Blondin, *Yamoria*, 20.

69 "tallow and dried cherries": Nute, *Voyageur*, 81.
69 shot guns in the air: Podruchny, *Making the Voyageur World*, 190.
69 "What conversation would an illiterate": Ibid., 9.
70 He planned to lie to them: Duckworth, *English River Book*, 14.
70 this chief was known as Mistapoose: Gough, *First Across the Continent*, 55.
70 he was called Awgeenah: The single definitive overview of Awgeenah's life is the short entry in the *Dictionary of Canadian Biography*, accessed June 27, 2017, www.biographi.ca.

CHAPTER 9: MATONABBEE AND AWGEENAH

71 The Hudson's Bay Company kept a Home Guard: Innis, *Fur Trade in Canada*, 134.
71 As he grew older: A basic overview of Matonabbee's life is available at the *Dictionary of Canadian Biography*, accessed June 27, 2017, www.biographi.ca.
71 "the great travelers of the known world": Hearne, *Journey to the Northern Ocean*, 92.
71 six feet tall, copper skin, dark hair: Ibid., 229.
72 a map made of deerskin: Helm, "Matonabbee's Map," 32.
72 "which flows from a large lake": Ibid., 41.
72 In 1713, Thanadelthur escaped: Newman, *Company of Adventurers*, 288–92.
73 No one saw him or his men: Hearne, *Journey to the Northern Ocean*, xiv.
73 He said his name was Samuel Hearne: Ibid., 48. Except where otherwise noted below, I rely on Hearne for the remainder of the chapter to tell the story of Matonabbee's journey to the Arctic Ocean.
73 Hearne's quadrant was broken: McGoogan, *Ancient Mariner*, 117.
75 Jumping Marten gained power: Blondin, *Yamoria*, 92.
75 Hearne was under his protection: Roberts, "Life and Death of Matonabbee."
77 They stole the wives of all peoples: Heine, *Gwichya Gwich'in Googwandak*, 31.
78 They painted their wooden shields: Hearne, *Journey to the Northern Ocean*, 109, 227; Blondin, *Yamoria*, 122.
80 five thousand beaver furs: Roberts, "Life and Death of Matonabbee."
81 Matonabbee himself delivered the *castor gras:* Ibid.
81 last governor of Prince of Wales Fort: After its destruction, the fort was rebuilt nearby but never regained its former importance.
81 hanged himself from a tree: Innis, *Fur Trade in Canada*, 152.
82 as they delivered the furs: Duckworth, *English River Book*, xxi.
82 "within a gunshot": Masson, *Les bourgeois de la Compagnie du Nord-Ouest*, 17.
82 "Try and get Rackets": Lamb, *Journals and Letters of Mackenzie*, 424.
83 In the spring he traveled to Île-à-la-Crosse: Masson, *Les bourgeois de la Compagnie du Nord-Ouest*, 18.

CHAPTER 10: MURDER AT THE OLD ESTABLISHMENT

84 Peter Pond came from Puritan stock: Chapin, *Freshwater Passages*, 12. Throughout this chapter, to relay the story of Peter Pond, I rely primarily on Chapin, except where noted.
84 "eevel sperit": Innis, *Fur Trade in Canada*, 50.

84 "fiteing" and "dansing": Podruchny, *Making the Voyageur World,* 166.

85 The French surrendered: Gough, *Elusive Mr. Pond,* 29.

86 diverted as they were to the revolution: Innis, *Fur Trade in Canada,* 180.

86 "where there are reeds": Gough, *Elusive Mr. Pond,* 93.

87 Waden had come to New France as a soldier: Ibid., 111.

87 "*Ah, mon ami,* I am dead": Ibid., 114.

88 the Yankee considered his proprietary territory: Duckworth, *English River Book,* xv.

88 "cutt the Beaver Indian on the head": Beaver Indians, part of the Dene First Nation, now use their traditional name of Dane-Zaa.

88 Peche fled into the wilderness: According to contemporary reports, Peche lived with the Chipewyan for three years, to avoid the gallows. Gough, *Elusive Mr. Pond,* 138. The two other voyageurs implicated in the murder would stand trial in Montreal, but they were acquitted. Chapin, *Freshwater Passages,* 270.

88 Alexander Mackenzie had forgotten his shirt: The story of Mackenzie's journey to the Old Establishment is told through his journal and letters to Roderic. Lamb, *Journals and Letters of Mackenzie,* 127–31, 425–30.

89 some said Pond gave the order: Chapin, *Freshwater Passages,* 263.

89 "the famous Lesieur": Lamb, *Journals and Letters of Mackenzie,* 423.

91 Leroux had worked as a clerk: Innis, *Fur Trade in Canada,* 199.

92 drawn a map of the whole territory: Chapin, *Freshwater Passages,* 232, 287.

CHAPTER 11: TO THE NORTHWEST PASSAGE

93 John Harrison to develop a series of chronometers: That story is told in Sobel's fascinating *Longitude.*

93 "If I have failed in discovering": Williams, *Voyages of Delusion,* 286. Note that Antarctica does, of course, exist, and Cook barely missed it, turned away by ice.

93 "a very extensive inland communication": Ibid., 362.

93 "A fine spacious river": Ibid., 318.

94 Sailors of the day generally: Sides, *In the Kingdom of Ice,* 44.

94 "I must confess I have little hopes": Horwitz, *Blue Latitudes,* 349.

94 In 1783, John Ledyard: According to Gifford in his book *Ledyard,* the man was America's "first explorer." I think we've already proven otherwise.

95 To boast its accuracy: Davidson, *North West Company,* 45.

95 decorated by a wall-sized tapestry: The tapestry still hangs in the Château Ramezay in Montreal.

95 an easy three-day journey: Chapin, *Freshwater Passages,* 241.

95 "between the latitudes of 55 and 65": Ibid., 244.

96 in 1749 the British Parliament chastised them: Gough, *Elusive Mr. Pond,* 127.

96 "seem to be scarcely less savage": Ibid., 127.

97 "So far Pond": Chapin, *Freshwater Passages,* 279.

97 in early December 1787: Gough, *First Across the Continent,* 74. Almost alone among historians, Gough believes that Alexander took a Cree *à la façon du pays* wife named "the Catt" while he was at Île-à-la-Crosse. While the paper evidence is thin and circumstantial, it does help explain why he was constantly returning to the post.

97 slept outside on pine boughs: Podruchny, *Making the Voyageur World,* 241–45.

97 old northmen voyageurs told him: Nute, *Voyageur*, 99.

97 "lay himself down on the ice": Chalmers, *Land of Peter Pond*, 46.

98 "Write me the first opportunity": All correspondence between Roderic and Alexander in this section is from Lamb, *Journals and Letters of Mackenzie*, 430–34.

98 "incomprehensively extravagant": Chapin, *Freshwater Passages*, 288.

98 "quite surprised at the wild ideas": Masson, *Les bourgeois de la Compagnie du Nord-Ouest*, 25.

98 "contrary to the mutual interest": Gough, *Elusive Mr. Pond*, 141.

99 took four hundred *pièces*: Chapin, *Freshwater Passages*, 289.

99 a new warehouse at Rainy Lake: Innis, *Fur Trade in Canada*, 230.

100 "extremely anxious and uncertain": Roderic's memories of this overall exchange are in Masson, *Les bourgeois de la Compagnie du Nord-Ouest*, 25–27.

100 "I lost two men and eleven pieces": Lamb, *Journals and Letters of Mackenzie*, 436.

101 "which appeared in the shape of a person": Masson, *Les bourgeois de la Compagnie du Nord-Ouest*, 27.

101 "no mittens can be used": Lamb, *Journals and Letters of Mackenzie*, 436.

101 glass in the windows: Conversation with Shawn Patterson, collections manager at Fort William Historical Park.

101 "the Athens of the North": Gough, *First Across the Continent*, 76.

CHAPTER 12: ALL IT TAKES IS TIME

104 "perforated with no fewer than twenty-four holes": Crane, *Clear Waters Rising*, 21.

CHAPTER 13: EMBARKATION

110 "in ancient times their ancestors": Lamb, *Journals and Letters of Mackenzie*, 150.

110 prowess was measured by geography: Podruchny, *Making the Voyageur World*, 70.

110 Barrieau and de Lorme were former New Concern men: Admittedly, this is an educated guess. Neither is listed in *The English River Book* as an employee of the North West Company in 1786. Both were experienced enough to be in Athabasca in 1789, Barrieau for several seasons before. Because most posts, after the merger of New Concern and NWC, were an amalgam of both firms, it is reasonable to say both men were unrecorded New Concern paddlers.

110 They were also cousins from Acadia: Much more of their genealogy is covered in Ferland's *Cadiens et voyageurs*.

111 He enlisted at age eighteen: Steinbruck, *Yellowknife Journal*, 5.

111 he used his new salary to buy beads: Duckworth, *English River Book*, xxviii.

111 Leroux had just snowshoed: Lamb, *Journals and Letters of Mackenzie*, 438.

111 Several years before: Davidson, *North West Company*, 50.

112 "a proper assortment of the articles": Unless otherwise noted, the narrative of Mackenzie's trip in this chapter is primarily drawn from Lamb, *Journals and Letters of Mackenzie*, 164–66.

112 half-inch ball ammo in their mouths: Newman, *Company of Adventurers*, 263.

112 dressed in deerskins: Gough, *Elusive Mr. Pond*, 99.

112 nine feet of black ash: Conversation with Shawn Patterson, collections manager at Fort William Historical Park; Morse, *Fur Trade Canoe Routes of Canada*, 21.

112 "I do not posses the science": Lamb, *Journals and Letters of Mackenzie*, 58.

113 "Should I not be back in time": Ibid., 437–38.

113 "without even the quickening flavor of salt": Ibid., 130.

113 "*Star Levé*": Newman, *Caesars of the Wilderness*, 39.

115 The voyageurs sang a lament: Podruchny, *Making of the Voyageur World*, 132.

115 "*Quand tu seras dans ces rapids*": Nute, *Voyageur*, 44–45.

116 The boats floundered: It is actually the infamous John Franklin who relates this story, after his 1820 trip down the Slave River. Chapin, *Freshwater Passages*, 251–52.

116 Brisbois. Derry. Landrieffe: Duckworth notes that this is only a guess, but a very educated one, from process of elimination. Duckworth, *English River Book*, xxxvii.

CHAPTER 14: THE RAPIDS OF THE SLAVE

118 Fort Smith Paddling Club: Fort Smith Paddling Club, accessed June 28, 2017, fskayak.webs.com.

CHAPTER 15: SHOOT THE MESSENGER

127 "Had a Head wind for most of the Day": Unless otherwise noted, the narrative of Mackenzie's trip in this chapter is primarily drawn from Lamb, *Journals and Letters of Mackenzie*, 166–77.

128 almost twenty years before: Hearne, *Journey to the Northern Ocean*, 185.

128 All of the animals got on a raft: Abel, *Drum Songs*, 8.

128 a rough mattress on the frozen ground: Nute, *Voyageur*, 51, 56.

129 The Chipewyan hunters said not to stretch two nets: Newman, *Company of Adventurers*, 339.

129 stuffed moss around the bottom of the tent: Blondin, *Yamoria*, 207.

129 "*C'est un maudit, chrisse*": Garreau, *Nine Nations of North America*, 389.

130 so much fat would make them weak: Blondin, *Yamoria*, 158.

130 The voyageurs mumbled: Nute, *Voyageur*, 61.

132 "blow, blow, old woman": Ibid., 26.

132 domes covered in caribou hides: Abel, *Drum Songs*, 33.

132 Sat in the Same Place: Helm, *People of Denendeh*, 286–89; Petitot, *Book of Dene*, 13.

133 Their father was a Frenchman: Note that in some versions of the story, it is Peter Pond who visits first, not Mackenzie or Grant. Overvold, *Portrayal of Our Metis Heritage*, 101; Petitot, *Book of Dene*, 15–16.

133 spoke all the languages of their people: Chapin, *Freshwater Passages*, 253; Abel, *Drum Songs*, 86.

133 Pale Men who lived in the beaver homes: Helm, *People of Denendeh*, 247–49.

134 anything else was taboo: Abel, *Drum Songs*, 40.

CHAPTER 16: THUNDERSTORMS AND RAIDS

151 "This is Corporal Shoeman": For the sake of her privacy, I have changed her name for publication.

151 "I suppose they think provision": Lamb, *Journals and Letters of Mackenzie,* 207.

152 "Such sights as this": Sevareid, *Canoeing with the Cree,* 145.

CHAPTER 17: INTO THE MOUNTAINS

163 "a fine Calm": Unless otherwise noted, the narrative of Mackenzie's trip in this chapter is primarily drawn from Lamb, *Journals and Letters of Mackenzie,* 178–81.

164 a German writing in phonetic French: Evidence of his innovative spellings can be found in Steinbruck's *Yellowknife Journal.*

165 "the River of the mountain": Now known as the Liard River.

CHAPTER 18: THE PLAGUES OF THE DEH CHO

171 Burg explored the valley: Welch, *Last Voyageur,* 100.

171 "Each bite of bacon": Burg, "On Mackenzie's Trail to the Polar Sea," 130.

173 "Three centuries ago": Macfarlane, *Mountains of the Mind,* 14.

173 "majestic novelties": Poe, *Journal of Julius Rodman,* 16.

173 "beyond the extreme": Ibid., 105.

173 "urged solely by a desire": Ibid., 13.

175 "These mountains were a storm center": Burg, "On Mackenzie's Trail to the Polar Sea," 143.

176 The magnetic north pole moves: NOAA provides maps that track the historical changes. NOAA, accessed June 28, 2017, ftp.ngdc.noaa.gov.

178 the residents of Wrigley are known: Abel, *Drum Songs,* xviii.

182 "We need the tonic of wildness": Olson, *Meaning of Wilderness,* 16.

182 "phantom brigades": Olson, *Lonely Land,* 11.

182 "an expedition means": Ibid., 129.

182 "zest for living": Ibid., 168.

182 "iron out the wrinkles": Ibid., 20.

CHAPTER 19: THE DOGRIB

192 "We perceived several Smokes": Unless otherwise noted, the narrative of Mackenzie's trip in this chapter is primarily drawn from Lamb, *Journals and Letters of Mackenzie,* 182–87.

193 Their first mother took a husband: Petitot, *Book of Dene,* 18.

193 shift their skins back and forth: Helm, *People of Denendeh,* 290.

193 the pale strangers could be the *nakan:* Ibid., 279.

193 The Chipewyan brought the pox: Hearne, *Journey to the Northern Ocean,* 132.

193 everyone knew this was the best revenge: Blondin, *Yamoria,* 130.

193 With the advantage of surprise: Ibid., 132.

194 put all of the Chipewyan minds into a beaver hide: Ibid., 97.

195 Yamoria and his brother, Yamoga: There are many spellings of the brothers' names, and many variations of the story, so I have picked Blondin's, from

Yamoria, though Helm records Yamonzhah and Yampa Deja as other spellings. Helm, *People of Denendeh*, 285.

195   broth made from the brains of rabbits: Blondin, *Yamoria*, 78–79.

195   fixed all of the problems: Helm, *People of Denendeh*, 283.

195   Yamoga went west: Blondin, *Yamoria*, 81.

197   "Father comes": Helm, *People of Denendeh*, 283.

198   In other words, they measured distance in time: Nute, *Voyageur*, 50.

198   gray rock walls that appeared scraped: The place is now called Carcajou Ridge.

198   wolverine could fold the earth in half: Blondin, *Yamoria*, 107.

CHAPTER 20: RAPIDS WITHOUT RAPIDS

203   Idle No More: Idle No More, accessed June 29, 2017, www.idlenomore.ca.

205   "a certain moral and physical decline": Burg, "On Mackenzie's Trail to the Polar Sea," 136.

209   Canadian geologists struck oil in the 1930s: A good overview of the Canol project can be found in Smith, *Mackenzie River*, which was fairly prescient in 1977 about the future battles over oil pipelines.

CHAPTER 21: YOU CAN STARVE ON RABBITS

215   "pitifully worn out with old age": Unless otherwise noted, the narrative of Mackenzie's trip in this chapter is primarily drawn from Lamb, *Journals and Letters of Mackenzie*, 187–91.

217   the giant had to piss: Sahtu Heritage Places and Sites, *Rakekée Gok'é Godi*.

217   Mackenzie had a small kit of tinctures: Lamb, *Journals and Letters of Mackenzie*, 233.

218   The Cree and their rifles: Yerbury, *Subarctic Indians and the Fur Trade*, 137.

218   many seasons ago they came: Blondin, *Yamoria*, 150.

218   But once a powerful medicine man: Ibid., 118.

218   "You can starve on rabbits": Helm, *People of Denendeh*, 57.

CHAPTER 22: FORT GOOD HOPE TO TSIIGEHTCHIC

232   a lobstick to mark the spot in the traditional way: Conversation with Dr. Carolyn Podruchny.

CHAPTER 23: SATISFY THE CURIOSITY, THO' NOT THE INTENT

241   Raven tricked people: Heine et al., *Gwichya Gwich'in Googwandak*, 3, 13.

241   they called themselves Gwichya: Ibid., 52.

241   the great Atachuukaii: Ibid., 18.

241   Man Without Fire: Man Without Fire (sometimes as Yamoria/Atachuukaii, sometimes not) is a figure in many Dene stories. See Helm, *People of Denendeh*, 57; Heine et al., *Gwichya Gwich'in Googwandak*, 22; Vuntut Gwitchin First Nation, *People of Lakes*, 21; and Petitot, *Book of Dene*, 37–38.

242   Medicine started to fade: Blondin, *Yamoria*, 28.

242   "Thunder and Rain last Night": Unless otherwise noted, the remainder of this

chapter is primarily drawn from Lamb, *Journals and Letters of Mackenzie,* 192–97.

243 they looked at his empty palm confused: Heine et al., *Gwichya Gwich'in Googwandak,* 180.

245 hanged her new baby from a tree: Ibid., 353–55.

245 "in Imitation of the Esquimaux": Note that Mackenzie uses the spelling "Eskmeaux," but for ease of reading, I have standardized it throughout the text. Lamb, *Journals and Letters of Mackenzie,* 194.

245 Their rifles were their phallus: Helm, *People of Denendeh,* 277.

245 pass them off as some animal: Ibid., 291.

247 Eighteenth-century geographers held: Sides, *In the Kingdom of Ice,* 44.

CHAPTER 24: INTO THE EARTH SPONGE

255 the age of the old-timer Peter Pond: Maybe I shouldn't be so hard on myself; I did far more paddling than Mackenzie, after all. But I could never measure up to Pond. At thirty-eight, I paddled the Deh Cho, and he crossed the Methye and then went on to work another decade in the *pays d'en haut.* Chapin, *Freshwater Passages,* 163.

CHAPTER 25: THE HIGHEST PART OF THE ISLAND

260 "It is my Opinion": Unless otherwise noted, the narrative of Mackenzie's trip in this chapter is primarily drawn from Lamb, *Journals and Letters of Mackenzie,* 196–201.

260 Steinbruck could be petty: This is the theme of many of Steinbruck's entries in *Yellowknife Journal.*

260 "Our pemmican has been mouldy": Lamb, *Journals and Letters of Mackenzie,* 205.

261 root of the licorice plant: Yerbury, *Subarctic Indians and the Fur Trade,* 145.

261 *tripe de roche:* Podruchny, *Making of the Voyageur World,* 119.

261 cut cannibals into small pieces: Hearne, *Journey to the Northern Ocean,* 43; Chalmers, *Land of Peter Pond,* 36.

261 grind their bones to dust: Podruchny, "Werewolves and Windigos," 690.

261 "They love to breathe a free air": Visit to Canadian Canoe Museum in Peterborough, Ontario, in Dec. 2015.

261 The fur trade life produced: Podruchny, *Making the Voyageur World,* 186.

263 Kitigaaryuit: A survey of the archaeological excavations at this site can be found in McGhee, *Beluga Hunters.*

263 "The toil of our navigation": Lamb, *Journals and Letters of Mackenzie,* 59.

264 Awgeenah once told Mackenzie: Ibid., 149–50. Mackenzie relates this story in his general description of the Chipewyan, and I attribute it to Awgeenah, as his closest partner.

CHAPTER 26: A SEA OF ICE, FROZEN NO MORE

267 World War II–era aerial photography: Bredin, "'Whale Island' and the Mackenzie Delta."

CHAPTER 27: MANY RETURNS

274 "Never was happier": Unless otherwise noted, the narrative of Mackenzie's return trip to Fort Chipewyan is primarily drawn from Lamb, *Journals and Letters of Mackenzie*, 202–33.

277 as was the tradition of his people: Helm, *People of Denendeh*, 176.

277 "My Expedition is hardly spoken of": Lamb, *Journals and Letters of Mackenzie*, 443.

277 "voyage down the River Disappointment": Ibid., 444. Per Lamb, there are four versions of this letter, but only one calls it River Disappointment, the others calling it the Grand River. But the earliest transcript uses "River Disappointment," and so it is the one used by Masson.

279 "unless there has been a nuclear war": MacLennan, *Rivers of Canada*, 63–64.

280 all the complaints from locals: Full disclosure: Northern Transportation Company Limited refunded my shipping costs and was extremely gracious and helpful.

281 "Tho' this Expedition": Lamb, *Journals and Letters of Mackenzie*, 457.

281 "make all the inquiry possible": Ibid., 445.

281 "but little known during my residence": Ibid., 20.

281 "I could perceive the termination": Ibid., 372.

282 "I am full bent on going down": Ibid., 453.

282 "darkened the human mind": Ibid., 68.

282 Heart of the Devil: Petitot, *Book of Dene*, 61.

282 "will require more time": Lamb, *Journals and Letters of Mackenzie*, 454.

282 "It was in the Summer of 1789": Ibid., 529.

283 "entirely from a fit of ill-humor": Ibid., 30.

283 Mackenzie started his own fur company: Innis, *Fur Trade in Canada*, 238.

283 "apprehension of presenting myself": Lamb, *Journals and Letters of Mackenzie*, 33.

284 the house of Samuel Johnson: Ibid., 34.

284 Napoleon considered the volume: Ibid., 35.

284 President Thomas Jefferson procured one: Ambrose, *Undaunted Courage*, 73.

284 In 1808, he wrote to the British: Lamb, *Journals and Letters of Mackenzie*, 518.

285 "I am determined to make myself": Ibid., 516.

285 "immense City": Ibid., 502.

285 final letter to Roderic: Ibid., 522.

285 aged fifty-seven years: History doesn't know what month of 1762 that Mackenzie was born, only that he was twelve years old in late 1774, when he boarded a ship for New York. So he was likely fifty-seven at the time of his death, though perhaps fifty-eight.

286 "I have now been forty-two years": Nute, *Voyageur*, 207–8.

286 Alexander Mackenzie began a correspondence: Gough, *First Across the Continent*, 213–16.

287 "in justice to the memory": Lamb, *Journals and Letters of Mackenzie*, 51.

EPILOGUE

290 "swelling and braggart": Newman, *Caesars of the Wilderness*, 8.

290 "must remember the round of feasting": Irving, *Astoria*, 7.

291 gloves and scarves and top hats: Podruchny, "Festivities, Fortitude, and Fraternalism," 40.

291 the city's stone battlements: Pointe-à-Callière Museum, Montreal.

292 "died poor": Chapin, *Freshwater Passages,* 309.

292 was an honorary member: Sleeper-Smith, *Rethinking the Fur Trade,* 596.

292 "to recount the toils": Podruchny, "Festivities, Fortitude, and Fraternalism," 49.

292 Pierre Bonga: The legendary Bonga appears fleetingly in the histories. See Newman, *Caesars of the Wilderness,* 38; Nute, *Voyageur,* 38; the history of the fur trade digital archives at McGill University, accessed June 30, 2017, digital.library .mcgill.ca; and MacGregor, *Canoe Country,* 103, where Mackenzie makes his claim of seven *pièces.*

293 "*Ah! taisez-vous, méchante femme*": Nute, *Voyageur,* 147.

293 Meriwether Lewis: Lewis committed suicide soon after, having never published his journals.

Selected Bibliography

~~~~~~

Abel, Kerry. *Drum Songs: Glimpses of Dene History*. Montreal: McGill-Queen's University Press, 1993.

Adney, Edwin Tappan, and Howard Chapelle. *Bark Canoes and Skin Boats of North America*. New York: Skyhorse, 2014.

Ambrose, Stephen E. *Undaunted Courage: Meriwether Lewis, Thomas Jefferson, and the Opening of the American West*. New York: Simon & Schuster, 1996.

Bailyn, Bernard. *Voyagers to the West: A Passage in the Peopling of America on the Eve of the Revolution*. New York: Knopf, 1986.

Beaver Club Minute Book, 1807–27. McCord Museum, M14449.

Berton, Pierre. *The Arctic Grail: The Quest for the North West Passage and the North Pole, 1818–1909*. New York: Viking, 1988.

Bliss, Michael. "Conducted Tour." *Beaver* 69, no. 2 (April–May 1989): 16–24.

Blondin, George. *Yamoria: The Lawmaker*. Edmonton: NeWest, 1997.

Bragg, Amy Elliot. *Hidden History of Detroit*. Charleston, S.C.: History Press, 2011.

Bredin, T. F. "'Whale Island' and the Mackenzie Delta: Charted Errors and Unmapped Discoveries, 1789–1850." *Arctic* 15, no. 1 (1962): 51–65.

Brody, Hugh. *The Other Side of Eden: Hunters, Farmers, and the Shaping of the World*. New York: North Point Press, 2000.

Burg, Amos. "On Mackenzie's Trail to the Polar Sea." *National Geographic*, Aug. 1931.

Chalmers, John W., ed. *The Land of Peter Pond*. Edmonton: Canadian Circumpolar Institute Press, 2002.

Chapin, David. *Freshwater Passages: The Trade and Travels of Peter Pond*. Lincoln: University of Nebraska Press, 2014.

Crane, Nicholas. *Clear Waters Rising: A Mountain Walk Across Europe*. London: Penguin Books, 1997.

Cruikshank, Julie. *Do Glaciers Listen? Local Knowledge, Colonial Encounters, and Social Imagination*. Vancouver: UBC Press, 2005.

———. *Life Lived Like a Story: Life Stories of Three Yukon Native Elders*. Lincoln: University of Nebraska Press, 1990.

Daniells, Roy. *Alexander Mackenzie and the North West*. Toronto: Oxford University Press, 1971.

Davidson, Gordon Charles. *The North West Company*. Berkeley: University of California Press, 1918.

Dolin, Eric Jay. *Fur, Fortune, and Empire: The Epic History of the Fur Trade in America*. New York: W. W. Norton, 2010.

Donnelly, Joseph P., S.J. *Jacques Marquette.* Chicago: Loyola University Press, 1968.

Duckworth, Harry W., ed. *The English River Book: A North West Company Journal and Account Book of 1786.* Montreal: McGill-Queen's University Press, 1990.

Ferland, Claude. *Cadiens et voyageurs: Un parcours singulier au Pays d'en-Haut.* Quebec: GID, 2016.

Finkelstein, Max. *Canoeing a Continent: On the Trail of Alexander Mackenzie.* Toronto: Natural Heritage Books, 2002.

Foxcurran, Robert, Michel Bouchard, and Sebastien Malette. *Songs upon the Rivers: The Buried History of the French-Speaking* Canadiens and *Métis from the Great Lakes and the Mississippi Across to the Pacific.* Montreal: Baraka Books, 2016.

Garreau, Joel. *The Nine Nations of North America.* Boston: Houghton Mifflin, 1981.

Gessen, Keith. "Polar Express: A Journey Through the Melting Arctic, with Sixty-Odd Thousand Tons of Iron Ore." *New Yorker,* Dec. 24, 2012.

Gifford, Bill. *Ledyard: In Search of the First American Explorer.* New York: Harcourt, 2007.

Gingras, Larry. *The Beaver Club Jewels.* Canadian Numismatic Research Society, 1972.

Gough, Barry. *The Elusive Mr. Pond: The Soldier, Fur Trader, and Explorer Who Opened the Northwest.* Vancouver: Douglas & McIntyre, 2014.

———. *First Across the Continent.* Norman: University of Nebraska Press, 1997.

Hayes, Derek. *First Crossing: Alexander Mackenzie, His Expedition Across North America, and the Opening of the Continent.* Seattle: Sasquatch Books, 2001.

Hearne, Samuel. *A Journey to the Northern Ocean.* Vancouver: Touchwood, 2007.

Heine, Michael, et al. *Gwichya Gwich'in Googwandak: The History and Stories of the Gwichya Gwich'in, as Told by the Elders of Tsiigehtshik.* Tsiigehtchic: Gwich'in Social and Cultural Institute, 2007.

Helm, June. "Matonabbee's Map." *Arctic Anthropology* 26, no. 2 (1989): 28–47.

———. *The People of Denendeh: Ethnohistory of the Indians of Canada's Northwest Territories.* Iowa City: University of Iowa Press, 2000.

———. *Prophecy and Power Among the Dogrib Indians.* Lincoln: University of Nebraska Press, 1994.

Herman, Arthur. *How the Scots Invented the Modern World.* New York: Crown, 2001.

Horwitz, Tony. *Blue Latitudes: Boldly Going Where Captain Cook Has Gone Before.* New York: Henry Holt, 2002.

Huck, Barbara, et al. *Exploring the Fur Trade Routes of North America.* Winnipeg: Heartland, 2012.

Innis, Harold A. *The Fur Trade in Canada.* New Haven, Conn.: Yale University Press, 1930.

Irving, Washington. *Astoria; or, Enterprise Beyond the Rocky Mountains.* Paris: Baudry's European Library, 1836.

Johnson, Samuel. *The Works of Samuel Johnson.* Vol. 2. New York: George Dearborn, 1837.

Ketchum, Richard M. *Divided Loyalties: How the American Revolution Came to New York.* New York: Henry Holt, 2002.

Krohn, Leena. *Tainaron: Mail from Another City.* Germantown, Md.: Prime Books, 2006.

Lacoursière, Jacques, and Robin Philpot. *A People's History of Quebec.* Montreal: Baraka Books, 2002.

Lamb, W. Kaye, ed. *The Journals and Letters of Sir Alexander Mackenzie.* Cambridge, U.K.: Hakluyt Society at the University Press, 1970.

Lawrence, D. H. *Sea and Sardinia.* New York: Penguin Books, 1999.

Levy, Phillip. *Fellow Travelers: Indians and Europeans Contesting the Early American Trail.* Miami: University Press of Florida, 2007.

Lewis, Ferris E. *Detroit: A Wilderness Outpost of Old France.* Detroit: Wayne University Press, 1951.

Linteau, Paul-André. *The History of Montréal: The Story of a Great North American City.* Montreal: Baraka Books, 2013.

Lopez, Barry. *Arctic Dreams.* New York: Charles Scribner and Sons, 1986.

Macfarlane, Robert. *Mountains of the Mind: Adventures in Reaching the Summit.* New York: Vintage, 2004.

MacGregor, Roy. *Canoe Country: The Making of Canada.* Toronto: Random House Canada, 2015.

Mackenzie, Alexander. *Voyages from Montreal, on the River St. Laurence, Through the Continent of North America, to the Frozen and Pacific Oceans, in the Years 1789 and 1793, with a Preliminary Account of the Rise, Progress, and Present State of the Fur Trade of That Country.* London: R. Noble, Old Bailey, 1801.

MacKinnon, J. B. *The Once and Future World: Nature as It Was, as It Is, as It Could Be.* New York: Houghton Mifflin Harcourt, 2013.

MacLennan, Hugh. *The Rivers of Canada.* New York: Charles Scribner's Sons, 1961.

Mandeville, François. *This Is What They Say.* Toronto: Douglas & McIntyre, 2009.

Martelle, Scott. *Detroit: A Biography.* Chicago: Chicago Review Press, 2012.

Masson, L. R. *Les bourgeois de la Compagnie du Nord-Ouest.* 2 vols. Quebec: Coté, 1889–90. Facsimile reprint, New York: Antiquarian Press, 1960.

McCoy, Roger. *On the Edge: Mapping North America's Coasts.* New York: Oxford University Press, 2012.

McCullough, David. *1776.* New York: Simon & Schuster, 2005.

McDonald, T. H., ed. *Exploring the Northwest Territory: Sir Alexander Mackenzie's Journal of a Voyage by Bark Canoe from Lake Athabasca to the Pacific Ocean in the Summer of 1789.* Norman: University of Oklahoma Press, 1966.

McGhee, Robert. *Beluga Hunters: An Archaeological Reconstruction of the History and Culture of the Mackenzie Delta Kittegaryumiut.* Toronto: University of Toronto Press, 1974.

McGoogan, Ken. *Ancient Mariner: The Arctic Adventures of Samuel Hearne, the Sailor Who Inspired Coleridge's Masterpiece.* New York: Carroll & Graf, 2004.

McKenzie, Andrew. *May We Be Britons? A History of the MacKenzies.* London: Andrew McKenzie (self published), 2012.

McMaster, Gerald, and Clifford E. Trafzer, eds. *Native Universe: Voices of Indian America.* Washington, D.C.: National Geographic Society, 2004.

McPhee, John. *Coming into the Country.* New York: Farrar, Straus and Giroux, 1977.

———. *The Survival of the Bark Canoe.* New York: Farrar, Straus and Giroux, 1975.

Mead, Robert Douglas. *Ultimate North: Canoeing Mackenzie's Great River.* New York: Doubleday, 1976.

Middleton, Richard. *Colonial America: A History, 1607–1760.* Cambridge, Mass.: Blackwell, 1992.

Morse, Eric W. *Fur Trade Canoe Routes of Canada: Then and Now.* Ottawa: Queen's Printer and Controller of Stationery, 1969.

Morton, Desmond. *A Short History of Canada.* 3rd rev. ed. Toronto: McClelland & Stewart, 1997.

Newman, Peter C. *Caesars of the Wilderness: The Story of the Hudson's Bay Company.* New York: Penguin Books, 1987.

———. *Company of Adventurers: The Story of the Hudson's Bay Company.* New York: Penguin Books, 1985.

Nute, Grace Lee. *The Voyageur.* New York: D. Appleton, 1931.

Olsen, Sigurd F. *The Lonely Land.* Minneapolis: University of Minnesota Press, 1997.

———. *The Meaning of Wilderness.* Minneapolis: University of Minnesota Press, 2001.

———. *Runes of the North.* Minneapolis: University of Minnesota Press, 1997.

Overvold, Joanne, ed. *A Portrayal of Our Metis Heritage.* Metis Association of the Northwest Territories, 1976.

Parkman, Francis. *Pioneers of France in the New World.* Boston: Little, Brown, and Company, 1907.

Petitot, Emile. *The Book of Dene: Containing the Traditions and Beliefs of Chipewyan, Dogrib, Slavey, and Loucheux People.* Yellowknife, N.W.T.: Programme Development Division, Department of Education, 1976.

Podruchny, Carolyn. "Festivities, Fortitude, and Fraternalism: Fur Trade Masculinity and the Beaver Club, 1785–1827." In *New Faces of the Fur Trade: Selected Papers of the Seventh North American Fur Trade Conference,* edited by William C. Wicken, Jo-Anne Fiske, and Susan Sleeper-Smith, 31–52. East Lansing: Michigan State University Press, 1998.

———. *Making the Voyageur World: Travelers and Traders in the North American Fur Trade.* Lincoln: University of Nebraska Press, 2006.

———. "Werewolves and Windigos: Narratives of Cannibal Monsters in French-Canadian Voyageur Oral Tradition." *Ethnohistory* 51, no. 4 (Fall 2004): 677–700.

Poe, Edgar Allan. *The Journal of Julius Rodman.* London: Pushkin Press, 2008.

Ray, Arthur. *Indians in the Fur Trade: Their Roles as Trappers, Hunters, and Middlemen in the Lands Southwest of Hudson Bay, 1660–1870.* Toronto: University of Toronto Press, 1974.

Ridington, Robin, and Jillian Ridington. *Where Happiness Dwells: A History of the Dane-Zaa First Nations.* Vancouver: UBC Press, 2013.

Roberts, Strother. "The Life and Death of Matonabbee." *Manitoba History,* no. 55 (June 2007).

Sahtu Heritage Places and Sites Joint Working Group. *Rakekée Gok'é Godi: Places We Take Care Of.* Jan. 2000. Accessed June 29, 2017. issuu.com.

Schecter, Barnet. *The Battle for New York: The City at the Heart of the American Revolution.* New York: Walker, 2002.

Sevareid, Eric. *Canoeing with the Cree.* Minneapolis: Borealis Books, 2004.

Sheppe, Walter, ed. *First Man West: Alexander Mackenzie's Account of His Expedition Across North America to the Pacific in 1793.* Berkeley: University of California Press, 1962.

Sides, Hampton. *In the Kingdom of Ice: The Grand and Terrible Polar Voyage of the USS Jeannette.* New York: Doubleday, 2014.

Skinner, Claiborne A. *The Upper Country: French Enterprise in the Colonial Great Lakes.* Baltimore: Johns Hopkins University Press, 2008.

Sleeper-Smith, Susan, ed. *Rethinking the Fur Trade: Cultures of Exchange in an Atlantic World.* Lincoln: University of Nebraska Press, 2009.

Smith, James K. *Alexander Mackenzie, Explorer: The Hero Who Failed.* Toronto: McGraw-Hill Ryerson, 1973.

————. *The Mackenzie River: Yesterday's Fur Frontier, Tomorrow's Energy Battleground.* Toronto: Gage, 1977.

Sobel, Dava. *Longitude.* New York: Walker, 1995.

Steinbruck, Jean. *The Yellowknife Journal.* Winnipeg: Nuage, 1999.

Swallow, Michelle N. *The Mackenzie River Guide: A Paddler's Guide to Canada's Longest River.* Yellowknife: self-published, 2011.

Treuer, Anton. *Atlas of Indian Nations.* Washington, D.C.: National Geographic Society, 2013.

Van Buskirk, Judith L. *Generous Enemies: Patriots and Loyalists in Revolutionary New York.* Philadelphia: University of Pennsylvania Press, 2002.

Van Kirk, Sylvia. *Many Tender Ties: Women in Fur-Trade Society, 1670–1870.* Norman: University of Oklahoma Press, 1980.

Vexler, Robert I., ed. *Detroit: A Chronology and Documentary History.* Dobbs Ferry, N.Y.: Oceana, 1977.

Vowell, Sarah. *The Wordy Shipmates.* New York: Riverhead, 2008.

Vuntut Gwitchin First Nation and Shirleen Smith. *People of the Lakes: Stories of Our Van Tat Gwich'in Elders.* Edmonton: University of Alberta Press, 2009.

Wade, M. S. *Mackenzie of Canada: The Life and Adventures of Alexander Mackenzie, Discoverer.* London: William Blackwood & Sons, 1927.

Welch, Vince. *The Last Voyageur: Amos Burg and the Rivers of the West.* Seattle: Mountaineers Books, 2012.

Williams, Glyn. *Voyages of Delusion: The Quest for the Northwest Passage.* New Haven, Conn.: Yale University Press, 2003.

Woollacott, Arthur P. *Mackenzie and His Voyageurs: By Canoe to the Arctic and the Pacific, 1789–93.* London: J. M. Dent & Sons, 1927.

Yerbury, J. C. *The Subarctic Indians and the Fur Trade, 1680–1860.* Vancouver: University of British Columbia Press, 1986.

INDEX

wwwww

Brian Castner is a former explosive ordnance disposal officer who received a Bronze Star for his service in the Iraq War. He is the author of two books, *The Long Walk* (2012) and *All the Ways We Kill and Die* (2016), and the coeditor of the anthology *The Road Ahead* (2017). His journalism and essays have appeared in *Esquire, Wired, Vice, The New York Times, The Washington Post, The Atlantic,* and other publications. *The Long Walk* was adapted into an opera that has been performed at prestigious venues nationwide.

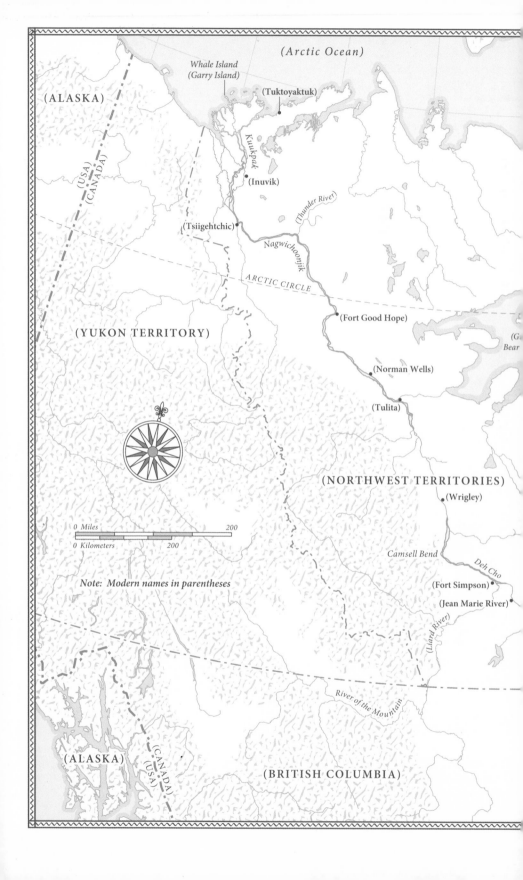

(Arctic Ocean)

Whale Island
(Garry Island)

(Tuktoyaktuk)

(ALASKA)

(USA)
(CANADA)

Kuukpak

(Inuvik)

(Thunder River)

(Tsiigehtchic)

Nagwichoonjik

ARCTIC CIRCLE

(Fort Good Hope)

(G...
Bear

(YUKON TERRITORY)

(Norman Wells)

(Tulita)

(NORTHWEST TERRITORIES)

(Wrigley)

0 Miles   200

0 Kilometers   200

Camsell Bend

Deh Cho

Note: Modern names in parentheses

(Fort Simpson)

(Jean Marie River)

(Liard River)

(ALASKA)

(CANADA)
(USA)

River of the Mountain

(BRITISH COLUMBIA)